SURPASSING THE SOVEREIGN STATE

Surpassing the Sovereign State

The Wealth, Self-Rule, and Security Advantages of Partially Independent Territories

DAVID A. REZVANI

OXFORD
UNIVERSITY PRESS

OXFORD

UNIVERSITY PRESS

Great Clarendon Street, Oxford, OX2 6DP,
United Kingdom

Oxford University Press is a department of the University of Oxford.
It furthers the University's objective of excellence in research, scholarship,
and education by publishing worldwide. Oxford is a registered trade mark of
Oxford University Press in the UK and in certain other countries

© David A. Rezvani 2014

The moral rights of the author have been asserted

First Edition Published in 2014

Impression: 1

Published in the United States of America by Oxford University Press
198 Madison Avenue, New York, NY 10016, United States of America

British Library Cataloguing in Publication Data
Data available

Library of Congress Control Number: 2013953855

ISBN 978-0-19-968849-4

Printed and bound by
CPI Group (UK) Ltd, Croydon, CR0 4YY

For Leanna

Preface

After nearly six centuries of emergence and world dominance, the sovereign state now at last has a globally widespread competitor that frequently manages to surpass its long vaunted capabilities in the areas of wealth, security, and self-determination. This book will show that in region after region throughout the world partially independent territories (including Hong Kong, the Cayman Islands, Iraqi Kurdistan, New Caledonia, and others) tend to be wealthier and more secure than their sovereign state counterparts. Often ignored because of their small size, lack of militaries, and divided powers, the partially independent territories that produce these advantages are responsible for nearly one-fifth of global capital flows, serve as solutions for some of the world's most intractable nationalistic disputes, and furnish important capabilities for sovereign states. The existence and capabilities of these polities contradict widely held assumptions of sovereign state pre-eminence and give rise to a range of puzzling issues that will be addressed by this book. Why do local nationalistically distinct populations accept partially independent unions? What guarantees do these polities have that their powers will not be usurped by internal and external adversaries? What makes core states (which divide and share powers with partially independent territories) willing to part with some of their sovereignty amidst fears that their countries will fully fragment? What are the prospects for the independence of Scotland, Catalonia, Puerto Rico, and the nearly 50 partially independent territories around the globe? This book explains how these polities emerge, maintain themselves, and sometimes come to an end.

This is really two books wrapped into one. One book (if it were a volume on its own) would be about how it is that partially independent territories (PITs) exist—according to contemporary views in the international relations discourse these political forms are not supposed to exist. According to some, it is supposedly an article of faith that no other entities besides the sovereign state possess sovereignty. Book one would therefore spell out the arguable realities surrounding PIT existence.

Book two would be about PIT causal dynamics. Namely, it would discuss how these polities often surpass the sovereign state. It would also discuss how they begin, maintain themselves, and potentially fail. According to contemporary views in the international relations discourse, the sovereign state is the world's preeminent political unit. Similar to questions of existence, other entities are not supposed to exist that surpass the performance of sovereign states. Full independence is often seen as a peerless alternative for stateless, nationalistically distinct populations, if only they could achieve such an outcome.

One can then wonder why I did not write these two separate notional books and instead combined them into the present volume—especially amidst the prevailing conditions of the academic profession in which quantity of scholarly output is highly valued. My answer is that as the project developed it became increasingly clear that it was difficult to separate questions of existence from those of causal outcome. Asserting the frequent advantages of PITs over sovereign states and elaborating upon their causal dynamics prompted a host of questions about how they can exist in the first place. Likewise, explaining their widespread existence and international significance (which is now the focus of Part II) led to demanding questions about their comparison to sovereign states as well as their origins and potentially changing nature (which is now the focus of Part III).

This division within the book makes it feasible for readers who are more interested in one topic than another to directly turn to the part of the book that interests them. For example, after reading Chapters 1 and 2, some readers may already be convinced by PIT existence and related matters, and want to turn directly to Part III, which focuses on sovereign state weakness (Chapter 7), PIT advantages and emergence (Chapter 8), and PIT evolutionary dynamics (Chapter 9). On the other hand, even if one is convinced by PIT existence, some may still be interested in the associated issues discussed in Part II, such as PIT comparisons with other political forms, divided sovereignty, and constitutional credibility (Chapter 3), the nature of unwritten constitutional entrenchment as well as constitutional controversies in the British Dominions, Northern Ireland, and Puerto Rico (Chapters 4 and 5), and the newly apparent global neo-colonialism of sham federacy (Chapter 6).

This book is the product of more than ten years of research, thought, and fieldwork. During this production period my work has greatly profited from the generous insights of many people. As a result of the inspiration, recommendations, and criticism that I have received, like a ship that is entirely reconstructed plank by plank as it makes its way from one destination to another, the original draft of the manuscript has been rebuilt over and over again. This book is particularly indebted to the encouragement and advice of the people who have read and generously provided their comments on the manuscript. I owe a profound debt of gratitude to Alex Cooley, Yusaku Horiuchi, Paul MacDonald, and Brendan O'Leary for providing especially copious comments. I am also grateful for comments from Laurence Whitehead, Alfred Stepan, Steve Tsang, the late Geoffrey Marshall, Vernon Bogdanor, Rosemary Foot, Brian Greenhill, Ben Valentino, Stanley Hoffmann, Bruno Coppieters, Robert Jackson, Robert Rotberg, Simon Chamberlin, Marie Besancon, and still others. I am thankful for the great advice of the outside reviewers of Oxford University Press. I would also like to thank the team at Oxford University Press for their diligent work on production management, proofreading, copy editing, map-creation, and still other related tasks. I am especially grateful to the senior editor, Dominic Byatt for his support. This study owes a debt of gratitude to the guidance of these individuals, while its shortcomings are the author's responsibility alone.

I am also grateful for the research assistance of Ashley Boyle, David Musil, and Steve Kovach. I would also like to thank the enormous encouragement and support from my colleagues at my various academic homes over the years including John Carey and Christiane Donahue (at Dartmouth College), Brigitte Schulz, Kevin McMahon, Andrew Flibbert, and Sonia Cardenas (at Trinity College), Steve Van Evera (at MIT), and Graeme Garrard, Steve Miller, Sean Lynn Jones, Steve Walt, Richard Rosecrance, Carol Saivetz, Robert Paarlberg, and Pippa Norris (at Harvard University).

Portions of Chapter 5 originally appeared in 2007 in the *Political Science Quarterly* (vol. 122, no. 1 published by the Academy of Political Science). I wish to thank the journal and its publishers for their approval to use this material here.

I am especially grateful to my family for their encouragement. Most importantly however I thank my wife, Leanna, for all of her love, insights, and support. I dedicate this book to her.

Contents

Contents

Part I

Theoretical Framework

1

Introduction

A certain man had several sons who were always quarreling with one another, and, try as he might, he could not get them to live together in harmony. So he determined to convince them of their folly by the following means. Bidding them fetch a bundle of sticks, he invited each in turn to break it across his knee. All tried and all failed: and then he undid the bundle, and handed them the sticks one by one, when they had no difficulty at all in breaking them. "There, my boys," said he, "united you will be more than a match for your enemies: but if you quarrel and separate, your weakness will put you at the mercy of those who attack you." Union is strength.

—Aesop (Sixth century BC)[1]

In the afternoon of November 1, 1950, sounds of automatic gunfire awoke US President Harry Truman from a nap he was taking on the second floor of Blair House in Washington DC. When the President opened the window of his room to see what was happening, approximately 30 feet away from him he could see a gun battle that was raging between security officers (who were attempting to protect him) and gunmen (who were attempting to gain access to his building to assassinate him). Before the would-be assassins were eventually subdued, one of the President's guards had been killed and several were wounded. Similarly, several years later in 1954, gunmen from the same group positioned in the viewing chamber of the US House of Representatives opened fire on astonished members of Congress below them, wounding five.

The nationalist perpetrators of this violence were fighting for the independence of their destitute territory, which until 1952 had been ruled from afar as a colony by an outside power. But the outside power that had ruled over them was neither an imperial power such as Great Britain nor a totalitarian regime like the Soviet Union. The outside power was the United States and it had governed the territory of these gunmen, Puerto Rico, ever since the island had been taken from Spain in 1898 after US victory in the Spanish-American War. The

---

[1] Aesop 1993, 388.

gunmen were the ideological descendants of independence advocates which at various times had been backed by the majority of the territory's population. By the time the aforementioned shots echoed through the Capitol Building, however, Puerto Rico was no longer a colony ultimately ruled by technocrats in Washington. Nor, however, was it fully independent. In 1952, through mutual agreement, US and Puerto Rican representatives brought into being a new constitutional order for the territory. Puerto Rico had been guaranteed some final decision-making powers and territorial sovereignty without being a state of the US federation, like Texas or California.[2] Territorial sovereignty can be described as a polity's powers of de facto and de jure priority in some respects over a territory.[3] It had become a partially independent territory (PIT) that had full and ultimate control over most of its domestic affairs, while many foreign policy and all military powers were left to the US.[4] With the entry into force of its partially independent status, Puerto Rico joined the ranks of numerous other similar nationalistically distinct territories in the world that are types of partially independent polities without being domestically incorporated into a federation.[5] Before this relationship with the US began in 1952, much like its other neighbors, Puerto Rico was destitute, weak, and insecure. Today, by contrast, Puerto Rico possesses a sophisticated and modern democracy. It has a gross domestic product (GDP) per capita that is more than five times higher than the average Latin American sovereign state and three times higher than its Caribbean sovereign state neighbors.[6] Puerto Rico is certainly no utopia; it has its own set of sometimes frustrating challenges. But it is a testament to how far this polity has come that the points of reference that some use for comparing the territory are parts of the United States (the world's wealthiest and most powerful country), rather than its more culturally, historically, and

---

[2] On the history of the constitutional development of Puerto Rico see Carr 1984, 17–72; Leibowitz 1989, 127–85; Lerner 1981, 125–34; Monge 1997, 1–140; and Reisman 1975, 2–35.

[3] Jackson 1987, 529; and Tilly 1990. Daniel Philpott observes that "the most traditional meaning" of sovereignty as emphasized by Thomas Hobbes and Jean Bodin refers to "the authority and effective control of a government within a state." Philpott 2001a, 300. There is, nevertheless, no consensus in the political science or legal literatures on the meaning of sovereignty. For those who doubt that a consistent definition can be established see Benn 1955, 501–5; Falk 1993, 854; and Oppenheim 1905, 103.

[4] On partial independence see, Rezvani 2012. For the nascent literature on the synonymous term of "federacy" see Anderson 2012; Coppieters 2001; Elazar 1991; 1993; 1994; 1997; Ghai 2000; Jakobson 2005; McGarry 2007; O'Leary 2001; 2002; 2005; 2013a; 2013b; Rezvani 2004; 2007a; 2007b; 2012; Stepan, Linz, and Yadav 2010; Stepan 2013; Stevens 1977; Watts 1996.

[5] The existence of such a partially independent polity harkens back to the overlapping jurisdictions before the advent of the modern state system. On neo-medievalism see, Barkin and Cronin 1994, 107–30; Bull 1977, 254–76; Cerny 1998, 36–64; Deibert 1997, 167–92; Lipschutz 1992, 389–420; Wæver 1996, 107–28; Wæver 1997, 321–63; Zielonka 2001, 507–36.

[6] UN Statistics Division 2009.

demographically similar neighbors. The transformation of Puerto Rico from a rebellious and destitute colony to a polity with high degrees of wealth, security, and guaranteed self-determination reflects a wider change that is occurring to the structure of the international system. This book will challenge prevailing assumptions in the international relations and comparative politics scholarship that sovereign states are preeminent and that they possess inviolable sovereignty. The widespread existence and advantages of partially independent territories present puzzling challenges to these assumptions. According to prevailing views, partially independent territories should simply not exist in light of the intrinsic interests of local populations and sovereign states. If a sovereign state promises to surrender some powers of autonomy to a distinct territory, why would the population that lives there trust the credibility of such commitments? Once such powers are promised, what would prevent a more powerful core state from arbitrarily taking them back? Conversely, fearing the possibility that partial independence might be a gateway to secession and full territorial fragmentation, why would a core state with a larger economy, population, and military be willing to surrender some sovereignty over part of its territory to a nationalistically distinct population?

Similar to other constitutive political forms in the international system from the emergence of the first polities in the form of city-states in 6000 BC to modern times,[7] partially independent territories (PITs) are defined by their distribution of jurisdictional priority over all other organizations within a specific territorial space.[8] Partially independent polities (such as Bermuda, Kurdistan, Scotland, Puerto Rico, Greenland, the historic British Dominions, as well as nearly 70 territories that have emerged since the nineteenth century) are (1) nationalistically distinct and (2) constitutionally differentiated territories that (3) share and divide sovereign powers with a core state.[9] Since they are not fully incorporated into the constitutional system of a core state, they are neither member-units of federations nor are they fully controlled parts of unitary states. Such PITs exercise a wide range of powers over domestic jurisdiction, some foreign matters, but not external military affairs.

---

[7] As Charles Tilly describes, these early city-states can be defined as "A priest-ruled capital surrounded by a tribute-paying hinterland" Tilly 1990, 252.

[8] By broadly defining a "state" as a political community that exercises jurisdictional priority in certain respects over all other organizational forms within a territory, Tilly 1990 provides a definition of the state that embraces a wide range of constitutive units of the international system, including historic fiefdoms, city states, city leagues, loosely configured empires, as well as the modern sovereign state and partially independent polities.

[9] On PITs see Rezvani 2012. For the synonomous term of "federacy" see Anderson 2012; Coppieters 2001; Elazar 1991; 1993; 1994; 1997; Ghai 2000; Jakobson 2005; McGarry 2007; O'Leary 2001; 2002; 2005; 2013a; 2013b; Rezvani 2004; 2007a; 2007b; 2012; Stepan, Linz, and Yadav 2010; Stepan 2013; Stevens 1977; Watts 1996.

Partially independent territories (like the Cayman Islands [UK] and Liechtenstein [Switzerland]) are some of the most sophisticated offshore financial centers in the world. A large percentage of the world's money supply passes through them.[10] Partially independent arrangements (like those for Northern Ireland [UK] and the Kurdish Territories [Iraq]) also serve as centerpieces of compromise for some of the world's most difficult nationalistic disputes.[11] The fate of such arrangements can have a pivotal impact on the likelihood of peace and war in important areas of the world. And partially independent polities also furnish military basing rights and preferential natural resource allocation to sovereign states that were once only available through forcible imperial control. The degree of international impact, global dispersion, constitutional innovation, stabilizing and destabilizing potential, and influence on the changing structure of the international system make PITs worthy of closer consideration within the comparative politics and international relations discourse.[12]

This book will argue that PITs tend to be accepted by distinct populations and core states because of the wealth, security, and self-determination advantages they provide for territories and core states. Their emergence is also associated with cataclysmic events that tend to sweep away core state norms that would otherwise oppose the division of sovereignty that gives rise to them. Consequently, pooled sovereignty and *partial* independence from an existing sovereign state—rather than full independence—may be a more advantageous institutional alternative for distinct minority populations striving for self-determination.[13] Formalized and credible cooperation can provide greater levels of security and wealth than the relative poverty, loss of control, divorce, and enmity that can result from full independence.

This introductory chapter will begin by summarizing the structural, economic, security, and geostrategic importance of these polities. It will then articulate the book's key questions, central arguments, and relationship to other literatures. The chapter will conclude with a summary of the book's remaining chapters.

---

[10] Palan 2002, 151–3.
[11] O'Leary et al. 2005.
[12] On such criteria to measure a polity's significance see Philpott 2001b, 29.
[13] On the phenomenon of pooled sovereignty see Keohane and Hoffmann 1991, 1–39; Philpott 2001b, 39–40; and Ruggie 1993, 172.

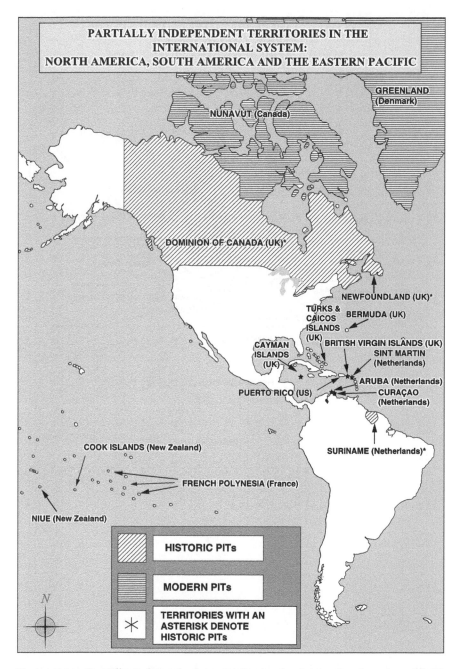

Figure 1.1a. Partially independent territories in the international system: North America, South America, and the Eastern Pacific

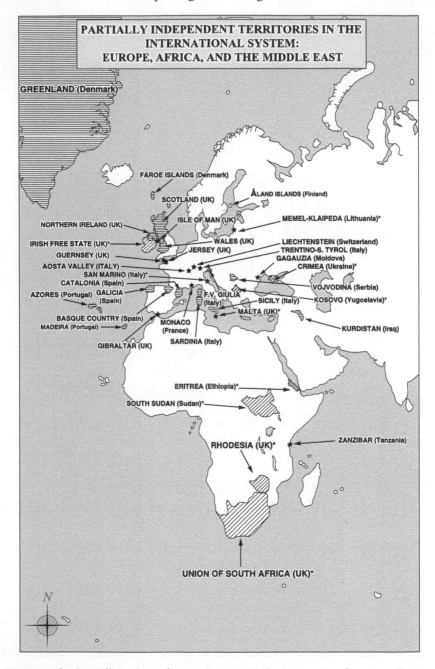

Figure 1.1b. Partially independent territories in the international system: Europe, Africa, and the Middle East

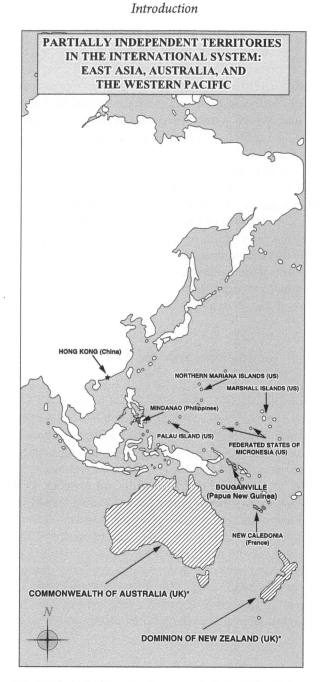

Fivure 1.1c. Partially independent territories in the international system: East Asia, Australia, and the Western Pacific

THEIR IMPORTANCE

In spite of their relatively small size (the average sovereign state has a population that is about 23 times larger),[14] PITs have capitalized on their range of sovereign powers and the synergies of partial integration with a larger sovereign state to become significant factors in international affairs in the areas of global finance, international security, and geostrategic capability. They are also adding to the diversity of polities within the international system as they increasingly proliferate throughout the international system at a rate that exceeds that of the rate of emergence of sovereign states (see Figures 1.3–1.5). But even if PITs did not filter trillions of US dollars through the international system; even if they did not serve as real or potential solutions to many of the world's most seemingly intractable disputes; even if they did not provide important geostrategic advantages to sovereign states without the disadvantages of imperialism, they would still arguably be important because of their implications for the structure of the international system.

International Systemic Amendment

Whenever a sovereign state divides and shares powers with another polity, it is arguably remarkable and momentous—and in light of prevailing views of sovereign state primacy and sovereign inviolability—surprising. Sovereign states are commonly recognized as the only systematically existent polity that exercises territorial sovereignty. Following the observation of the early twentieth-century sociologist Max Weber, many also emphasize that they exercise a monopoly on power rather than sharing and dividing it.[15] The international system's key socio-political principle, nationalism, is also often defined in terms of achieving full independence rather than self-determination that has some limitations in terms of its scope. The existence of PITs, however, contradicts these assumptions. They possess some, though not all, territorial sovereignty. They share powers with core states. And they embody a division of power that satisfies nationalistic self-determination without full independence. The increasing frequency of partial independence sets the stage for a changed ontological view of the international system in which the sovereign

---

[14] Most of the data taken for this statistic are derived from the World Development Indicator 2008.
[15] Weber 1964, 154.

state is not the only systematically present or increasingly sought after political alternative in possession of sovereign power.[16]

Accordingly, the structure of the post-Westphalian system has changed because these nationalistically distinct portions of state territory are increasingly breaking away from states into a partially sovereign constitutional orbit where the separated political space (the partially independent polity) is neither fully independent nor fully assimilated into the state with which it is associated. This therefore is a type of "neo-medieval" change that harkens back to the overlapping authority structures and sovereignties that existed before the seventeenth century in which sovereign states, city-states, city-leagues, loosely controlled empires, and still other entities competed for control.[17] And reflecting much of the literature on international hierarchy, the emergence of these polities emphasizes an erosion of a strict dichotomy between monolithically sovereign states surrounded by the pure anarchy of the international system without a world government.[18] Hence the nature of the system change described here is less one of total transformation and unit replacement, and more one of incremental amendment and unit diversification.

As distinct from this view, these governmental forms are sometimes dismissed as anomalies or exceptional cases that are incomparably unique to a particular state. Such a view is, however, mistaken. In his 1977 book, Hedley Bull was one of the earliest to point out the possibility of a form of "neo-medieval" change that is similar to what is described here.[19] "Perhaps," he said, "the time is ripe for the enunciation of new concepts of universal political organization which would show how Wales, the United Kingdom and the European Community could each have some world political status while none laid claim to exclusive sovereignty."[20] In the end however, although he raised this idea as a possibility, he concluded that the issue is moot because he believed that groups are not striving for such differentiated status. Furthermore, he emphasized secession (and the creation of sovereign states) rather than partial territorial integration, as the overriding principle. "Secessionist movements,"

---

[16] By "ontological view of the world system" I mean "the metaphysical concern with the essence" of the international system, especially the chief units that compose it. Landman 2000, 15. On ontology see also Lawson 1997, 15.

[17] E.g., Barkin and Cronin 1994, 107–30; Bull 1977, 254–76; Cerny 1998, 36–64; Deibert 1997, 167–92; Lipschutz 1992, 389–420; Wæver 1996, 107–28; Wæver 1997, 321–363; Zielonka 2001, 507–36.

[18] E.g., Cooley 2000/2001; 2005; Donnelly 2006; Hobson and Sharman 2005; Lake 1996; 1999; 2001; 2003; 2007; Nexon and Wright 2007.

[19] Bull 1977, 254–76. For later works on neo-medievalism, see Barkin and Cronin 1994, 107–30; Cerny 1998, 36–64; Deibert 1997, 167–92; Lipschutz 1992, 389–420; Wæver 1996, 107–28; Wæver 1997, 321–63; Zielonka 2001, 507–36.

[20] Bull 1977, 254–76.

Surpassing the Sovereign State

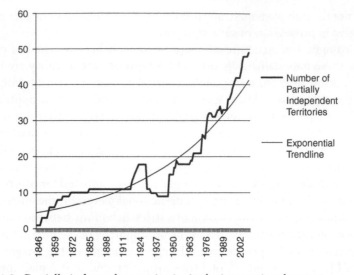

Figure 1.2. Partially independent territories in the international system
Data Source: See Appendix 1.

he pointed out, "like those that have given rise to the breakup of European empires, only confirm the institution of the sovereign state and do not bring it into question."[21]

Contrary to what Hedley Bull asserted, as Figure 1.2 indicates, the aspiration for partially independent arrangements is not just possible, it is already a fact. Since the nineteenth century, significant populations and leaders have aspired for and attained such a status. And although numerous states have seceded into full juridical independence as sovereign states, as the 66 partially independent polities listed in Appendix 1 illustrate, many others have opted for a partially sovereign status. Furthermore, a considerable number of examples exist where, although a partially independent arrangement has not yet emerged, populations and governments have aspired for such an accommodation and have initiated serious governmental negotiations (see Appendix 2). These polities are not therefore anomalous exceptions in the international system. They are numerous and increasing. And in some contexts they provide a tried and tested alternative to the sovereign state.

---

[21] Bull 1977, 254–76.

Offshore Finance

One of the functional explanations for the aforementioned unit diversification is the economic performance of many partially independent polities, which is particularly noticeable in the area of international finance. Among other things, PITs receive about US$3.5 trillion of the world's cross border loans.[22] This amounts to approximately 15% of all global lending. Over the past two decades, these claims have had a sevenfold increase, which mirrors the growth of global cross border banking activity (see Figure 1.3). According to data from the Bank for International Settlements (BIS), PITs also receive 76% of all loans that go to the world's offshore financial centers[23] (OFCs).[24]

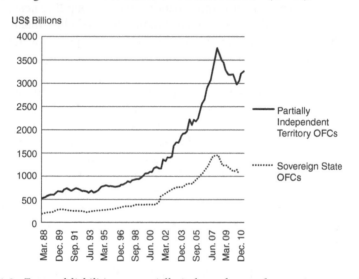

Figure 1.3. External liabilities to partially independent and sovereign state offshore financial centers

Data Source: Bank for International Settlements. 2011.

[22] See Bank for International Settlements 2011. The amount of cross border loans to PITs may actually be much higher than this number indicates. For example, data for Monaco, which is a widely acknowledged offshore financial center, are not included in the BIS data. Banking secrecy laws in various PITs may also hinder a full understanding of PIT financial data including liabilities.

[23] The BIS defines offshore financial centers as "an expression used to describe countries with banking sectors dealing primarily with non-residents and/or in foreign currency on a scale out of proportion to the size of the host economy." Bank of International Settlements 2008.

[24] There is no general agreement on what defines an OFC. Accordingly, different sources having varying lists of examples of such polities. While the BIS list is used here (because of the accessibility of the data that is associated with it), other lists, including one from the IMF, adds a number of further sovereign states (and PITs). The IMF list consists of: Andorra, Anguilla,

Observers have emphasized that when the states of the world have this level of financial exposure to a limited range of countries, the functioning and operation of the domestic systems of those countries can transmit shocks and benefits to other parts of the global economy.[25] The capabilities of PITs in this area are especially facilitated by the combination of their final decision-making powers over economic issues (which are guaranteed by a core state) and the public goods that the core state can facilitate with respect to the rule of law, regulatory standards, governmental accountability, security, and diplomatic protection.[26] Fully independent states in the relative anarchy of the international system do not normally receive such oversight and assistance. When an environmental disaster strikes, when corruption is rife, when crime is widespread, when an economic downturn occurs, when a coup threatens, (usually powerful) core states take a direct interest in the affairs of a PIT, much like they would with regard to the rest of their international legal space. Sovereign states do not have this form of insurance against the many dangers in the international system.

Some have also emphasized that the limited regulations and low taxes of OFCs mostly play a beneficial role for global finance through business and governmental competition with other jurisdictions.[27] Others however, including some G-20 leaders, scholars, and international organizations (such as the Organisation for Economic Cooperation and Development (OECD) and the International Monetary Fund (IMF)), have blamed OFC PITs for being a major cause for the 2008 global recession because of banking secrecy rules which prevented businesses and financial institutions from having information on the ability of banks to furnish credit and repay loans (Table 1.1).[28]

Aruba, Bahamas, Bahrain, Barbados, Belize, Bermuda, British Virgin Islands, Cayman Islands, Costa Rica, Curaçao, Cyprus, Dominica, Gibraltar, Grenada, Guernsey, Hong Kong SAR, Isle of Man, Jersey, Liechtenstein, Luxembourg, Malaysia, Malta, Marshall Islands, Mauritius, Nauru, Palau, Panama, St Lucia, St Vincent and the Grenadines, Samoa, Seychelles, Singapore, Sint Maarten, Switzerland, and Vanuatu. See International Monetary Fund 2004. Still others emphasize the need to include countries like the US (with tax advantages offered in states like Delaware) and UK to the list of tax havens. However, since the purpose of this study is to compare PITs to sovereign states, the BIS list is arguably the most attractive because it builds in a type of control by excluding relatively large states (like Switzerland, the UK, or the US).

[25] Dixon 2001, 105.

[26] See for example the UK, Secretary of State for Foreign and Commonwealth Affairs (1999) white paper which details such assistance to British territories.

[27] By competing with firms that are domiciled in OFCs, financial institutions of other countries are forced to become more efficient. Similarly, developed countries are pressured to reduce their rates of taxation, lest businesses continue to flee to OFCs where governments have intentionally crafted lower degrees of regulation and lower taxes to attract international business.

[28] On the role of OFCs see for example, Rawlings 2007; Palan 2002; 2003; Sharman 2006; and Webb 2004.

Table 1.1. Top offshore financial centers ranked by external liabilities (end 2011)

Offshore financial center	Polity type	External liabilities of reporting BIS banks Billions of US$
1. Cayman Islands	Partially independent territory	$1,919
2. Singapore	Sovereign state	$460
3. Hong Kong SAR	Partially independent territory	$454
4. Jersey	Partially independent territory	$399
5. Bahamas	Sovereign state	$356
6. West Indies UK*	PIT/state combination*	$233
7. Guernsey	Partially independent territory	$183
8. Curaçao	Partially independent territory	$103
9. Panama	Sovereign state	$90
10. Bermuda	Partially independent territory	$83

*West Indies UK refers to the Bank for International Settlement's aggregation of two PITs (Anguilla and the British Virgin Islands), one UK colony (Montserrat), and two former UK colonies that are now sovereign states (Antigua and Barbuda, and St Kitts and Nevis.)

Source: Bank for International Settlements 2011.

International Security

Still another functional explanation for the diversification of polities in the international system caused by partially independent polities are the roles they play in the area of international security. In addition to full independence, the issue of providing autonomous powers to nationalistically distinct territories has been one of the principal alternatives that governments and populations have debated and fought for in as many as 46% of the world's conflicts internal to states since the end of the Cold War.[29] Debates over the status of partially autonomous regions and nationalistically distinct territories have been among some of the most widely discussed controversies in international affairs in places such as the Palestinian Territories, Northern Ireland, the Basque Country, Tibet, South Sudan, Darfur, Kashmir, Kosovo, Taiwan, East Tamil, Aceh, Mindanao, the Karen region, South Ossetia, Abkhazia, Nagorno-Karabakh, the Atlantic Coast Territory, and many others. In all of these territories a distinctive allocation of autonomous power short of full independence has been a central issue because populations and core

---

[29] This estimate was obtained by first adding all territories known to have at least 25 battle deaths in a single calendar year, whether military or civilian, that are in Appendix 1 (PITs), Appendix 2 (autonomy negotiations), and Appendix 3 (sham-federacies). In total these territories amount to about 41 conflicts after 1989. This number is then divided by the 89 intra state conflicts from 1989 to 2006.

states have debated the possibility (see Appendix 2), aspired for it, or established such an arrangement (see Appendix 1). Within some states, PITs have been highly effective in stemming the tide of revolt and creating an environment of relative stability and effective governance.[30] In other states, however, while the effort to allocate some credible final decision-making powers to a territory may have created domestic harmony and peace for a time, in the end regional conflict, terrorism, state fragmentation and/or economic strife reasserted themselves.[31] In still other cases, although the possibility of such arrangements has been the subject of serious negotiations, partially independent arrangements have nevertheless not materialized, passing desires for limited independence on to future generations.[32] The effectiveness or ineffectiveness of partially independent arrangements is one of the most crucial factors in determining whether such regions will be characterized by peace and stability or by war and strife. When the powers of a PIT decay and when the institutions promised in the agreement between center and periphery unravel, war, terrorism, regional instability, and/or economic unrest can follow closely behind (as with Northern Ireland in 1972, South Sudan in 1982 and 2011, or Eritrea in 1955). Ignorance of the dynamics and nature of partially independent territories can therefore prove to be fatal.

[30] Examples include: the Åland Islands (Finland), Azores and Madeira (Portugal), Aruba (Netherlands), British Virgin Islands (UK), Channel Islands (UK), Cook Islands (New Zealand), Greenland (Denmark), Hong Kong (China), Faroe Islands (Denmark), Federated States of Micronesia (US), French Polynesia (France), Isle of Man (UK), Liechtenstein (Switzerland), Monaco (France), Netherlands Antilles (Netherlands), Niue (New Zealand), Northern Mariana Islands (US), Nunavut (Canada), Palau Islands (US), Puerto Rico (US), Scotland (UK), Trentino-South Tyrol (Italy), Wales (UK), and Zanzibar (Tanzania). Historic cases include: the Memel-Klaipeda Territory (Lithuania) and the British Dominions of Australia (UK), Canada (UK), Ireland (UK), New Zealand (UK), and South Africa (UK). For an exhaustive list of cases, see Appendix 1.
[31] Examples include: Buganda 1962–67 (Uganda), Eritrea 1952–55 (Ethiopia), Kashmir 1952–53 (India), Kosovo 1974–89 (the former Yugoslavia), Mindanao (the Philippines), New Caledonia (France), Northern Ireland 1921–72/1998–99 (UK), South Sudan 1972–83 (Sudan), and Tibet 1951–59 (China).
[32] Contemporary examples of negotiations proposing semi-sovereign status include: the 2002 negotiations for the semi-independent status of north Sumatra (Aceh) and West Papua (Irian Jaya) within Indonesia; 2002 UN negotiations for the semi-autonomous status of Western Sahara within Morocco; the 1999 Rambouillet self-rule proposals for Kosovo within Yugoslavia; UN negotiations for federal solutions in Cyprus; 1995 Hague negotiations between Armenia and Azerbaijan regarding Nagorno-Karabakh; the 1994 Meech Lake Accords for a "special society" status for Quebec within Canada; UN proposals for a semi-independent status for East Timor within Indonesia; the unimplemented 1957 Bandaranaike-Chelvanayagam Pact proposing federal arrangements for the Tamils in North and Eastern provinces of Sri Lanka; 1995 proposals from Sri Lankan President Chandrika Kumaratunge to give limited self-rule to the Tamils; talks over the status of Bougainville in Papua New Guinea; and proposals to provide an autonomous status for South Ossetia (Georgia) and Abkhazia (Georgia).

Geostrategic Capability

Partially independent polities (like Greenland [Denmark], Nunavut [Canada], and New Caledonia [France]) also furnish military basing rights, an extended maritime economic zone, and preferential natural resource access to sovereign states. Extended military capability and natural resources that were primary reasons for forcible imperial control are now available through the cooperation of a partially independent arrangement without the historic imperial problems of legitimacy and governance costs.[33] From the perspective of a core state, their limited jurisdiction over a PIT in areas such as external defense allows them to have distant military bases (or to contract with third party states to establish such bases) without many of the costs of imperial control.[34] The US has bases on Greenland (Denmark), the Azores (Portugal), Palau (US), Micronesia (US), the Mariana Islands (US), and Puerto Rico (US).[35] Other states also make use of the strategic location of PITs. France has used French Polynesia for nuclear tests. France also uses naval port facilities in New Caledonia. Britain has naval forces stationed in Gibraltar and at Faslane, Scotland. In light of the international struggle over arctic resources and the opening of the northwest passage due to the melting of sea ice, in 2007 Canadian leaders also announced plans for a deep water naval port facility at Nanisivik, Nunavut and an army arctic training base at Resolute, Nunavut.

Partially independent territories are also relatively numerous and globally widespread. From the historic British Dominions to the 2010 regimes for Curaçao and Sint Maarten (Netherlands) approximately 39 percent of all states in the world with populations above 4 million have either been constitutionally associated with PITs, have themselves been PITs at one time, and/or have had government-level negotiation for the creation of such an arrangement.[36] Partially independent territories are numerous in the sense that nearly 50 known cases exist today and nearly 70 have existed since the nineteenth century. This is more than the total number of sovereign states (56) just after World War II.

---

[33] For works that assess such factors as they relate to empire–colony relations see Cooley 2005; Motyl 1999b; and Peattie 1984.

[34] On the politics of basing rights that include some PITs see especially Cooley 2008.

[35] Although the US naval bases in Puerto Rico at Roosevelt Roads and on the island of Vieques have been removed by local request, the US army base of Fort Buchanan remains within the territory.

[36] The 63 states that have a population below 4 million were excluded in the analysis because they are less likely to have decentralized arrangements or nationalistic conflicts over internal territory due to their smaller size. Eleven states have themselves been PITs. Twenty-four states have

THE ACCEPTABILITY OF PARTIAL
INDEPENDENCE

This book will attempt to answer a range of questions, but the primary questions are these: why do local nationalistically distinct populations and core states accept partially independent unions? What makes a partially independent arrangement sufficiently credible so that local populations will be able to trust it? Equally, what makes a core state willing to part with some of its sovereignty amidst fears that its country will fully fragment? In order to answer these questions, answers need to be found to a number of supplementary questions on the structure of the arrangement, its causal effects, its origins, and its evolution.

Structural Questions

In order to understand the acceptability of a political arrangement, it is necessary to understand how it is distinguished from other alternatives. In a world of fully independent sovereign states, how can PITs exist and how are they differentiated from other polities such as sovereign states, colonies, and member-units of federations? According to a variety of literatures,[37] the possession of sovereignty (credible final decision-making powers) by a polity is critical for nationalistic stability, economic advancement, and good relations with neighboring polities. It is also often assumed that only sovereign states possess this power. In addition to differentiating these polities from other political forms, it is therefore necessary to underscore that PITs do not merely have delegated powers that can be taken away by the whim or fiat of another power. Rather, they possess mechanisms that deliver final decision-making powers that are credible (and therefore very difficult to take away).

---

had PITs within their international-legal borders. It should be noted, however, that a number of states such as the US, the UK, Denmark, the Netherlands, France and others have more than one PIT that they are associated with. Fourteen states have negotiated for a partially sovereign arrangement which were not associated with a PIT at some point or which were not themselves PITs in the past. The United Nations has 185 state-members when anomalous entities such as the Vatican and various PITs with membership are taken out. See US, Central Intelligence Agency 2006.

[37] The next chapter will discuss these literatures that include those that focus on nationalism, relational contracting, and market preserving federalism.

Questions of Relative Advantage

Still another set of questions that address the acceptability of partially independent unions deal with the arrangement's relative advantages. How do PITs compare to the alterative of full independence with respect to the performance of their economies, security, and self-determination? How is it that PITs in most cases have managed to not only maintain their status but multiply amidst the nationalistic, economic, and security threats that have divided, impoverished, and destabilized so many of the world's sovereign states? It is not an exaggeration to observe that much of the world that is governed by sovereign states is mired in deep poverty, insecurity, and varying degrees of repression. More than half of the population of the world lives on less than $2 per day; the twentieth century alone saw 237 wars and 115 million battle deaths with an additional civilian death total of near or equal size;[38] and more than 20% of the world's 337 ethnic groups have engaged in armed conflict from 1940 to 2000.[39] This degree of poverty, conflict, and nationalistic opposition in turn directly hampers the potential for even a well-meaning government to protect its citizens, provide basic services, foster economic development, and insure basic freedoms. This problem of states failing to provide basic welfare and security as well as having effective control and authority over their territories and population, is now widely recognized as a global problem. A literature on weak states has developed which emphasizes that large numbers of the sovereign states of the world are so destitute, unstable, and repressive that they pose a significant risk to the world's overall security in areas such as the spread of disease, terrorism, environmental degradation, transnational crime, and regional war.[40] In fact, in 2002 US President George W. Bush's National Security Strategy identified state failure as America's main threat. It also observed that in the face of such challenges some of the traditional tools of foreign policy, including deterrence and containment, were largely ineffective. In 2009, the Obama Administration also reiterated this concern.[41] Amidst these challenges, how can it be that PITs (without full military powers and only partial independence) not only survive but increasingly proliferate in the face of the challenges faced by sovereign states?

---

[38] See Sivard 1986, 26; and Tilly 1990, 67.

[39] Walter, 2006, 114.

[40] See for example, Commission on Weak States and US National Security 2004; Crocker 2003, 32–44; Fukuyama 2004; Hamre and Sullivan 2002, 85–96; Krasner and Pascual, 2005, 153–163; Patrick 2006, 27–53; Rice 2003; and Rotberg 2004–05, 71–81.

[41] US President Obama's Remarks at West Point 2009. As President Obama noted, "unlike the great power conflicts and clear lines of division that defined the 20th century, our effort will involve disorderly regions, failed states, diffuse enemies."

Questions of Origins and Evolution

The general resilience and proliferation of partially independent arrangements leads to another set of questions on the nature of their evolutionary dynamics. Under what conditions are they likely to begin? Under what conditions are they likely to be sustainable? Under what conditions are they likely to come to an end? What metric can make plausible predictions about the appropriateness of this type of union for the nationalistic, security, and economic challenges that culturally distinct territories and sovereign states face? What are some persistent conditions in which PITs tend to maintain themselves and come to an end, and under what conditions is it better to be fully independent as opposed to partially independent? For example, should territories such as Scotland, Hong Kong, Catalonia, Puerto Rico, Kashmir, the Palestinian Territories, Tibet, Taiwan, and the Jaffna Peninsula have full independence? Should they have a status as PITs? Should they embrace the status quo? This study will provide answers to such questions.

CENTRAL ARGUMENTS

Partially independent unions are accepted by nationalistically distinct local populations and core states because they deliver a wide range of unexpected advantages. For local populations they provide some real powers of sovereignty as well as an array of public goods that would be lost to independence. For core states they deliver cooperation and access to a range of important resources that might be lost to nationalistic opposition. Such factors result in improved economies, more security, and a better fulfillment of self-determination for local populations and core states than the alternatives of full secession or full assimilation.

In response to those who may, however, cast doubt on the existence of PITs or emphasize the advantages of full independence, this book will argue that (1) PITs in fact exist, (2) for relatively smaller polities they often represent a better "deal" (a more attractive set of alternatives for distinct minority populations) than full independence, and (3) the likelihood of the maintenance or failure of the polity can be determined by the capability of the core state to furnish the public goods that make an arrangement worthwhile.

Existence

In spite of the near absence of works that address the subject of PITs, a number of well-known authorities have, used the synonymous (but arguably more confusing) term of "federacy" in their publications.[42] For the most part, the only other studies that discuss the same type of political category are the area study literatures and the literature on "political autonomy."[43] This book attempts to build upon the excellent work in this growing literature, which mostly focuses on illuminating aspects of individual case studies. For such studies, PITs represent a category that allows for wider comparisons with similar polities that exist elsewhere. This study also attempts to build upon the work in this literature by further sub-dividing the forms that can fall under the umbrella of autonomous arrangements. A wide diversity of distinct political forms (including federation member-units, decentralized units in unitary systems, colonies, protectorates, associated states, sham federacies, international protectorates, and even sovereign states) have been referred to with terms such as "autonomy."[44] Such forms of political autonomy (which will be distinguished from PITs in Chapter 3 in greater detail), however, fail to fully describe the sovereign characteristics, nationalistic distinctiveness, and constitutional uniqueness of PITs.

A PIT is neither under the full authority of a central government (as in a unitary system) nor is it a member-unit (state, province, or *länder*) of a federation. Partially independent territories are (1) nationalistically distinct entities that are (2) constitutionally unincorporated into the core state with which they (3) divide and share sovereign power. In the majority of cases they possess

[42] The term "partially independent territory" has been used here because its meaning is arguably clearer and more intuitively obvious (even without further definition) as compared to the synonomous term "federacy". For the first use of "partially independent territory" see Rezvani 2012. The term "federacy" arguably suffers from being easily confused with distinct political forms like federations. Before any substantive discussion can begin, the use of federacy requires laborious efforts to (1) distinguish it from federations; (2) clarify that unlike federations it is not a type of sovereign state; and (3) show that it is a political form that can indeed be compared to sovereign states. Nevertheless, in spite of its arguable limitations, some scarce but admirable work has been done by scholars of comparative politics through the use of the term. The first time "federacy" was used was by Michael Stevens (1977), who described some of the constitutional commonalities among "associated states." Since that time, and especially in the past decade, there has been a growing use of the concept. Daniel Elazar (1991; 1993; 1994; 1997) devoted several pages to federacy in a number of works including his 1991 *Handbook of Federal, Confederal, and Autonomy Arrangements*. Brendan O'Leary (2001; 2005; 2013a; 2013b) applied the concept to Northern Ireland, to the Kurdish Territories of Northern Iraq, and to powersharing in general. Juan Linz, Alfred Stepan, and Yogendra Yadav (2010) and Stepan (2013) applied the concept to multinational democracies. For other sources that have used the concept see Anderson 2012, Coppieters 2001; Ghai 2000b; Jakobson 2005; McGarry 2007; Rezvani 2004; 2007a; 2007b; and Watts 1996.

[43] On "autonomy" see Ackrén 2009; Archer and Joenniemi 2003; Baldacchino 2006; Crawford 1979, 211; Dinstein 1981, 23–8; Hannum and Lillich 1980, 858–89; Hannum 1990, 4; Lapidoth 1997, 4; Rothchild and Hartzell 2000, 254–71; Safran and Máiz 2000; Sohn 1980, 58–68; Suksi 1998; Tkacik 2008, 369–401; Weller and Wolff 2005.

[44] Legal scholar Ruth Lapidoth emphasizes the cacophony of differing views and widely different definitions of "autonomy." Lapidoth 1996, 51–2.

almost total power over their domestic affairs, some power over foreign policy, but no power over the external use of the military.[45]

Powers of Sovereignty

Partially independent territories possess sovereign powers in the sense that they are not fully subordinate constitutionally to another power in the same way as a colonial possession or a sham autonomous region (sham federacy) within an empire. Instead, they have been constitutionally allocated some defensible, final control and authority over a range of issues, giving it de jure[46] and de facto[47] priority above all other organizations in some respects within a specific geographic space.[48]

This builds upon the widely held view among political scientists and legal scholars that sovereignty[49] is divisible rather than indivisible.[50] Even after the seventeenth century when the modern sovereign state system emerged, states have been dividing sovereignty between branches of government, with populations, by function, and between center and periphery (as with PITs).[51] From this perspective, sovereignty is a type of power that defines governmental forms that have degrees of de facto and de jure jurisdictional priority across human history, rather than an ahistorical description of the sovereign state itself.

Accordingly, this book codes polities as PITs only if some entrenchment mechanism exists to defend them from easy usurpation by the core state with which they divide and share powers.[52] This can be achieved through formal,

---

[45] "Domestic" powers refers to the exercise of effective control over the territory and population within the PIT's borders in certain respects. Krasner 1999; Lapidoth 1997; Tilly 1990.

[46] De jure authority as used here refers to a polity's constitutional recognition whether through formal (written) or informal (unwritten) rules. Authority is therefore not conceived as only a formal-legal phenomenon, since unwritten constitutional rules can also confer duties, rights, and obligations.

[47] De facto control as used here refers to a polity's actual final ability to control certain people or objects if its agents encounter them. This, however, does not mean that the authority with de facto control is omnipresent. A polity with de facto control over a territory may not control all goods, people, and currency that pass over the territory, but if it encounters such persons or objects it has the ultimate ability to control them. For the meaning and significance of such control see Jackson 1990; Krasner 1999; and Ottoway 2002, 1001–23.

[48] Tilly 1990.

[49] On sovereignty generally see for instance, Barkin and Cronin 1994; Bartleson 1996; Biersteker and Weber 1996; Bunck and Fowler 1994; 1996; Hall 1999; Hinsley 1986; Jackson 1999; James 1986; Krasner 1999; Philpott 2001b.

[50] See Agnew 2005; Bunck and Fowler 1996; Keene 2002, 44; Keohane 2003; Krasner 1999; Lake 2003, 309; Lake 2007; and Osiander 2001.

[51] Lake 2003, 309. See also Keene 2002, 44.

[52] On veto points and veto players in hierarchical arrangements see for example Spruyt 2005 and Tsebelis 1999.

conventional, and political-formal forms of entrenchment. These forms of entrenchment will be elaborated upon in greater detail in Chapter 3. Briefly, however, formal entrenchment exists when an enforceable legal rule is created by a core state with high levels of rule of law that makes the powers allocated to a PIT very difficult to change (beyond the fiat or simple majority decision of a legislature). High levels of rule of law can be confirmed though a World Governance Indicator rule of law ranking of about 70 or higher (which was around the range of Italy's ranking from 1998 to 2010).[53] There are a variety of formally entrenched guarantees that would tend to protect a partially independent arrangement from the unilateral fiat of one side or another, including supermajority voting in the central legislature, mutual core–PIT assent to changes in the arrangement, judicial review, and treaty guarantee by an outside sovereign state. In accordance with Table 1.2, most known PITs are formally entrenched in this way.

Conventional entrenchment also exists in high rule of law systems when non-legal rules (which are not formally created by a government) nevertheless allocate rights and duties within governments or between them.[54] The existence of this form of entrenchment of the powers of a PIT can be identified through precedents, informal agreements, and/or widely held constitutional mores that are publically acknowledged by a core state premier or high court. The British Dominions were, for example, first brought into being in 1846 after a division of powers was informally agreed upon by Canadian and UK leaders and when "responsible government" was first exercised in Canada.[55]

All of the PITs mentioned in Table 1.2 that are formally or conventionally entrenched are associated with core states that have relatively high levels of rule of law. If, however, the core state does not have this, an associated territory is not coded as a PIT unless there is clear evidence of robust political-formal entrenchment that adds further credibility to formal guarantees. Political-formal entrenchment exists when the formal commitments of low rule of law core states are supplemented by plausible threats of economic disaster, war, or territorial secession if commitments are usurped. Hong Kong, is for example a case in which political-formal entrenchment applies.[56] Hong Kong provides over 42% of China's foreign direct investment (FDI), which

---

[53] Rule of law rankings can be obtained from the World Governance Indicator. Kauffmann, Kray, and Mastruzzi 2008.

[54] On convention see especially Marshall 1984.

[55] On the widely acknowledged unwritten constitutional rules (convention) that nullified pre-existing colonial laws that applied to the historic British Dominions, see for instance, Marshall 1984 and Wheare 1949.

[56] See Rezvani 2012.

Table 1.2. Modern partially independent territories

Partially independent territory	Core state	Year of origin	Primary entrenchment	Partially independent territory	Core state	Year of origin	Primary entrenchment
Åland	Finland	1922	Formal	Kurdistan	Iraq	2004	Political-formal
Aosta Valley	Italy	1948	Formal	Liechtenstein	Switzerland	1919	Formal
Aruba	Netherlands	1985	Formal	Madeira	Portugal	1974	Formal
Azores	Portugal	1974	Formal	Marshall Islands	US	1994	Formal
Basque Country	Spain	1978	Formal	Micronesia[b]	US	1986	Formal
Bermuda	UK	1967	Conventional	Mindanao[c]	Philippines	1990	Political-formal
Bougainville	P. New Guinea	2004	Political-formal	Monaco	France	1861	Formal
British Virgin Is.	UK	2005	Conventional	New Caledonia	France	1988	Formal
Catalonia	Spain	1978	Formal	Niue	N. Zealand	1974	Formal
Cayman Islands	UK	1967	Conventional	N. Ireland	UK	1998	Conventional
Cook Islands	N. Zealand	1965	Formal	N. Mariana Is.	US	1978	Formal
Crimea[f]	Ukraine	1996	Political-formal	Nunavut	Canada	1999	Formal
Curaçao[a]	Netherlands	2010	Formal	Palau	US	1994	Formal
Faroe Islands	Denmark	1948	Conventional	Puerto Rico	US	1952	Conventional
French Polynesia	France	1977	Formal	San Marino	Italy	1886	Formal

Friuli-Venezia Giulia	Italy	1948	Formal	Sardinia	Italy	1948	Formal
Gagauzia	Moldova	1994	Political-formal	Scotland	UK	1998	Conventional
Galicia	Spain	1978	Formal	Sicily	Italy	1948	Formal
Gibraltar	UK	2006	Conventional	Sint Maarten[a]	Netherlands	2010	Formal
Greenland	Denmark	1979	Conventional	South Sudan[d]	Sudan	2005	Political-formal
Guernsey	UK	1744	Conventional	Trentino-S. Tyrol	Italy	1948	Formal
Hong Kong	China	1997	Political-formal	Turks & Caicos Is.[e]	UK	2006	Conventional
Isle of Man	UK	1886	Conventional	Vojvodina	Serbia	2009	Political-Formal
Jersey	UK	1744	Conventional	Wales	UK	2006	Conventional
				Zanzibar	Tanzania	1977	Political-formal

[a] In 2010 the Netherlands Antilles terminated and split into two different partially independent territories: Sint Maarten and Curaçao.

[b] "Micronesia" refers to the Federated States of Micronesia

[c] "Mindanao" refers to the Autonomous Region of Muslim Mindanao

[d] South Sudan's partially independent arrangement terminated in 2011 with full independence.

[e] In 2009 the constitution of the Turks and Caicos Islands was suspended by the British but then restored in 2012.

[f] Crimea's status as a PIT terminated in February 2014 by the military occupation and annexation of Russia.

Note: This table attempts to exhaustively articulate modern cases of partial independence. For an articulation that includes previous PITs see Appendix 1.

makes the territory (by far) the largest source of investment into China.[57] The ability of the territory to produce such economic outcomes is, however, dependent on the maintenance of its autonomous institutions, press freedom, rule of law, and civil liberties.[58] Because of the pivotal role Hong Kong plays in its economy, Beijing is dissuaded from maximalist usurpation of the powers that were allocated to the territory in the 1997 Basic Law.[59]

Constitutionally Unincorporated

Partially independent territories are also domestically unincorporated into the internal system of a core state in the sense that in significant respects they are not recognized "as an integral part" of the rest of the country.[60] They do not have the same powers, rights, and status as other parts of the core state with which they are associated. Consider for example the cases of Northern Ireland, Scotland, and Wales. They are certainly part of the United Kingdom in many respects. Nevertheless, a range of written and unwritten UK constitutional rules have conferred upon these territories a wide array of defensible powers[61] and rights that are not possessed within the rest of the UK (where the majority of citizens, wealth, and territory of the UK is concentrated). Citizens in Northern Ireland, Scotland, and Wales have two legislatures that make laws for them (e.g. the Northern Ireland Assembly and the Westminster Parliament make laws for citizens in Northern Ireland). Citizens in England, however, only have one parliament (the Westminster Parliament). Citizens in these territories vote for the members of their local parliament. The citizens of England cannot vote in these same territorial parliaments. Territorial legislatures then enact a host of distinctive laws that are applicable for their local populations and not other parts of the UK (e.g. Scotland's rules on higher education in Scotland). Territorial citizens are also empowered to vote for representatives in the UK parliament that vote on matters that at times only affect the citizens in England (this is known as the West Lothian Question). In sum, a distinct set of rights and status is conferred on these territories through the unique institutions that they possess, the distinct powers that have been allocated to them, and the geographically delimited applicability of

---

[57] Ministry of Commerce: Beijing 2009.

[58] Rezvani 2012.

[59] For valuable works that assess the Basic Law see for instance, Chan and Clark 1990; Ghai, 1999; and Lee and Wah 1988.

[60] This concept was articulated in the seminal US Supreme Court Case *Downes v Bidwell* 1901.

[61] For the constitutional conventions that make these powers defensible, please see the discussion of Sewel Conventions in Chapter 3.

the unique laws they create. A similar constitutionally unincorporated status applies to all PITs.

National Distinctiveness

In addition to their sovereign powers and constitutionally unincorporated status, PITs are also nationalistically distinct because in virtually every case they have distinct populations that believe that they (and not another national group) ought to govern the nature of their political reality within the confines of a specific territory.[62] The fulfillment of national self-determination is often (wrongly) conceived of as maximizing self-rule and sameness with sovereign statehood.[63] Ernest Gellner calls this culture-state congruence.[64] However, in light of the number of polities throughout the world that have rejected full independence as a means to satisfy their nationalism, a better way to conceive of the concept is by the degree that their national self-interest and sense of fairness is fulfilled.[65] Such fulfillment can be achieved through perceptions of increased security, economic benefit, or self-rule guarantees. In some cases, maximizing such self-interest may indeed entail sovereign statehood. In other cases, however, it may be better fulfilled by alternative institutional arrangements (such as partial independence).

Because PITs divide and share powers with a sovereign state they are plainly not fully independent. They are, however, also not mere colonies (for a full list of colonies after the beginning of the twentieth century see Appendix 4).[66] Similar to fully independent states they possess powers of territorial sovereignty (some de jure and de facto final decision-making powers in some

---

[62] This definition of nationalism draws on a similar though distinct definition from Gellner 1983, 1. A sampling of some of the most important works in the immense literature on nationalism includes, Anderson 1991; Breuilly 1982; Brubaker 1996; Chatterjee 1993; Gellner, 1983; Hall 1998; Hechter 2000; Hobsbawm 1992; Hroch 1985; Kymlicka 1995; Miller 1995; and Smith 1986.

[63] On the variable applications of the principle of self-determination short of full independence see for instance, Hannum 1990, 48–9 and Kirgis 1994, 304. See also Canada 1998.

[64] Gellner 1983, 1–2.

[65] Indeed the International Covenant on Economic, Social and Cultural Rights favors a similar view of self-determination that does not mention full independence as the ultimate objective. Article 1(1) describes self-determination as a right that entitles people to "freely determine their political status and freely pursue their economic, social and cultural development." See, UN, the UN International Covenant on Economic, Social and Cultural Rights 1976.

[66] Data on historic colonies used here was drawn from CIA World Factbook (<www.cia.gov/cia/publications/factbook/>); Encyclopedia Britannica 2010; Columbia Encyclopedia 2010; Goldsmith and He 2008, 609–11; History World (<www.historyworld. net>). Data on current colonies was drawn from Aldrich and Connell 1998, 12–15. With all of these sources, polities that were in fact PITs, sham-federacies, federation member-units, states, and de facto states were removed.

respects).[67] Crudely lumping such formidable and complex political entities into the same category as colonies, a category that existed within historic empires such as France, Britain, Spain, and the Soviet Union, creates a needless emotional diversion and adds little to our ability to understand the constitutional, economic, historical, and political significance of these organizational forms.[68]

Causation

As economist Oliver Williamson pointed out, it is insufficient "merely to acknowledge that the microanalytic details of organizations matter."[69] Instead he says, "the salient structural features of market, hierarchic, and quasi-market forms of organization need to be identified and linked to economic consequences in a systematic way." Similarly, with regard to political institutions, in addition to identifying them or pointing out their significance, specific forms need to be linked to the quality of their economic, security, and normative outcomes. A unified and complete theory of all political institutions should eventually address these concerns fully. This book will, however, focus on evaluating the relative merits of PITs as they compare to sovereign states.

In spite of the emphasis here on their advantages, PITs are certainly not panaceas for the problems of poverty, insecurity, and nationalism faced by the world's population. Nevertheless, when contrasted to the overall performance of sovereign states, these polities tend to be wealthier, more secure, and have more credible forms of self-determination.[70] Partially independent territories are especially suited to deliver such advantages better than the sovereign state.

First, partial independence provides a type of nationalistic compromise that the monopoly of control of sovereign statehood is hard pressed to deliver. Unlike sovereign states, which in many cases are exposed to internal and external challenges to their self-rule, the self-determination of PITs are guaranteed by one or more fully independent states.[71] Unlike federations, which

---

[67] Jackson 1987, 529; and Tilly 1990. For a bibliography of the widespread view in the political science and international law literatures that sovereignty is divisible, see Bunck and Fowler 1996.

[68] On hierarchal forms which include colonies, informal empires, and protectorates, see Cooley 2000/2001; 2005; Donnelly 2006; Hobson and Sharman 2005; Lake 1996; 1999; 2001; 2003.

[69] Williamson 1998, 15.

[70] The focus here on wealth and security as outcomes does not, however, deny the importance of other worthy outcomes such as health, education, inequality, political freedom, and civic duty as measures of well-being. Indeed, future studies should account for such factors.

[71] On the challenges that many sovereign states face with respect to maintaining self-rule see Jackson 1990.

can also at times possess some of these advantages, because PITs are constitutionally unincorporated they are often more feasible to implement. Unlike the establishment of a federation, they typically do not require a new constitution for the whole state, separate regional governments that territories may not want, and a one-size-fits-all distribution of powers that may be inappropriate for the needs of individual territories. The scope of powers of sovereignty of federation member-units are also distinct from those possessed by PITs, since (unlike federation member-units) PITs have foreign policy powers (including representation within international organizations as well as powers to negotiate some international agreements).[72] The attractiveness of PITs as compared to other alternatives is reflected explicitly in data from polling and referendums held in PITs such as the Netherlands Antilles, Aruba, Azores, Madeira, Puerto Rico, Greenland, Faroe Islands, Bermuda, the Isle of Man, Scotland, Sardinia, and New Caledonia in which PIT populations reject full independence in favor of their self-governing status.[73] It is also reflected implicitly in other PITs through party affiliations that reject full independence and other alternatives.

Second, their combination of local jurisdictional control over economic issues together with a wide range of public goods from a typically powerful core state allows vested interests, specialization, accountability, and competition that the centralized rule of a sovereign state often cannot provide. In region after region throughout the world, they tend to be wealthier—in many cases by a wide margin—because they benefit from the public goods of a core state, including credible self-rule guarantees, monetary transfers, cost free defense, preferential trade advantages, and proxy diplomatic assistance. Amidst these advantages, it is no accident that PITs have a GDP per capita (of $32,526) which is over three times higher than the average GDP per capita of sovereign states (of $9,779).[74]

And third, in an international system without an impartial world government, partial independence allows polities to have credible guarantees to improve security. They have a mutually agreed upon cooperative union with another sovereign state in which (1) the leaders of both sides have taken serious steps to come to terms with any preexisting distrust and nationalistic differences and (2) the core state they are associated with (which is often a

---

[72] For the membership of PITs in international organizations see Table 3.2 in Chapter 3.
[73] Aldrich and Connell 1998, 43–133.
[74] GDP data from 2008 using constant US dollars from 2005. UN Statistics Division 2009; European Commission 2009; World Bank national accounts data, and OECD National Accounts data files. When data were unavailable from these sources, individual territorial and core state governmental offices were consulted for Crimea, Nunavut, Mindanao, Kurdistan, and Vojvodina.

significant military power) furnishes their external defense. Unlike historic colonies, which were at the mercy of the self-interest of the military might of their core state, PITs possess credible guarantees against the arbitrary usurpation of powers that have been surrendered to them.

Modern sovereign states do not have these advantages. Sovereign states may recognize each other's external authority, but they do not constitutionally guarantee each other's powers.[75] France, for instance, recognizes the authority of other sovereign states (like the Solomon Islands), but it does not emphasize the inviolability of their powers in its own constitution (as it has done with PITs like New Caledonia and French Polynesia).[76] Fully independent states may agree to defend each other within an alliance (however historically precarious their promises have been in some cases), but for the purposes of mutual protection they do not see their ally's territory as tantamount to their own territory, much less furnish the entire cost of all defense.

Sovereign states may economically cooperate with one another, but they rarely display the same depth of economic integration, which can include customs unions, proxy diplomatic assistance, incentives for increased foreign direct investment, and large-scale fiscal transfers.[77] One example that displays proxy diplomatic assistance occurred in 2008 at a G-20 summit in London in which countries threatened to add Hong Kong (a PIT associated with China) onto an OECD blacklist of "harmful tax jurisdictions." Chinese President Hu Jintao reacted by forcing the states of the G-20 to remove Hong Kong from the blacklist by threatening not to endorse the meeting's proposed policies.

In other cases the assistance is more discrete as when PITs enjoy the benefits from international treaties (such as double taxation agreements [DTAs]) between their more powerful core state and other states in the international system. Double taxation agreements are bilateral treaties between states that intend to remove the possibility of a firm being taxed twice.[78] Offshore financial centers, however, use these treaties to prevent a firm from being taxed at all. Fearing this prospect, states like the US have canceled some of their DTAs with Caribbean sovereign states that have been known to be tax havens.[79]

---

[75] On the burgeoning literature on international hierarchy see Cooley 2000/2001; 2005; Cooley and Spruyt 2009; Donnelly 2006; Hobson and Sharman 2005; Lake 1996; 1999; 2001; 2003; 2007; 2009; Nexon and Wright 2007; and Weber 2000.

[76] May 1998 Nouméa Accord; 1958 Constitution of France, Articles 72–74, 76, and 77. As described in Article 74, the territory's constitutional acts can only be "amended … after consultation with the territorial assembly concerned."

[77] Again, these types of benefits mirror the advantages that member states have within the anomalous structure of the European Union.

[78] Braithwaite and Drahos 2000, 106.

[79] Eden and Kudrle 2005, 114.

Partially independent territories can, however, avoid this problem by "piggy-backing" on the DTAs that have been created between their core state and powerful states like the US.

In still other cases the protection is indirect, as when UK officials exert consistent pressure, and provide expertise and resources to develop policies (such as the rule of law, transparency, accountability, human rights, and freedom of information) that act to improve the reputation of associated self-governing territories in the eyes of the international community.[80] As a consequence of such cooperation, PITs are perceived as sharing the reputation of the core state. Foreign investment and other financial flows in turn tend to follow areas that are known for political stability and have a "good reputation."

Sovereign states are a product of the period from the fourteenth to the seventeenth century when modern nationalism did not exist,[81] globalization was in its infancy, and empires were on the rise.[82] Partially independent territories by contrast are a post eighteenth-century phenomenon. They have evolved to address the needs for nationalistic compromise, to capitalize upon the economic interdependency of globalization, and to provide advantages to sovereign states (such as preferential access to natural resources, distant military basing rights, and extended sovereign territoriality) that were once only available through forcible imperial control.

Put another way, "if you are interested in survival" amidst the dangers and challenges of the international system, the best way to survive is not necessarily "to have your own state and lots of power."[83] Indeed, the assertion that full independence represents the best of all political alternatives for security and survival (and wealth) is strangely inconsistent with some of the most important assumptions of realist scholars of international relations.[84] Realists are right to emphasize the many dangers and insecurities of the international system. But amidst their emphasis on such dangers in an international system without a world government, why do they paradoxically recommend that a polity be abandoned to it as a fully independent state? Why is it rational or in the best interest of a territory to embrace full independence if it puts them into the lawless, self-reliant, and fearful condition of international anarchy? The answer is that, such proponents of full independence assume away (or ignore) alternatives other than the sovereign state that can allow a territory

---

[80] UK, Scotland, Wales, and Northern Ireland. 1999.
[81] Benedict Anderson describes that the modern age of nationalism did not emerge until the eighteenth century. Anderson 1991.
[82] See for example Tilly 1990; Spruyt 1994b.
[83] On such pro-independence views see Mearsheimer 1995, 82–93.
[84] For a summary on such realist views see Doyle 1997, 41–8, 93–204.

to possess measures of sovereign powers while also partially escaping from aspects of international anarchy through institutionalized bonds with a larger sovereign state.

Evolution

Partially independent territories are in part a response to the dramatic change to the international system after the eighteenth century such as imperial fragmentation, economic globalization, widespread global poverty, and wars of nationalism. Against this backdrop, they begin because of (1) their advantages over other alternatives as well as (2) environmental shocks (such as wars or constitutional revolutions) that primarily afflict core states. These shocks sweep away preexisting perceptions and norms that would otherwise mitigate against allowing the arrangement to be established. The emphasis here on (1) organizational advantages and (2) environmental shocks as the focus for change builds upon concepts in the state formation literature that draw upon the evolutionary concepts of biologists Stephen Jay Gould and Niles Eldredge. Gould and Eldredge introduced the concept of "punctuated equilibrium" in which sudden and dramatic changes in the evolution of organisms lead to a "flurry of radical new forms" relative to preexisting capabilities.[85] They rejected a purely Darwinian process of natural selection which postulated that biological organisms necessarily evolve from more simple to more advanced stages.[86] Instead, they emphasized that preexisting forms (like the dinosaurs) were complex but, in spite of their highly evolved adaptations, were eliminated through environmental conditions (like cataclysmic asteroid strikes) which their advanced adaptations could not surmount. Hence, if such a theory of biological evolution is analogously applied to the arguments here, both unit advantages as well as environmental shocks must be taken into account to understand the emergence of PITs. It should, however, be noted that this book does not see the environmental shocks that have helped give rise to partially independent arrangements as necessarily leading to the extinction of the sovereign state (as with the extinction of the dinosaurs). As emphasized later in this book, the systemic change that is contemplated here envisions system amendment not unit replacement.

The arguments here therefore assume the bounded rationality of leaders and populations (in which choices are "intendedly rational, but only limitedly

---

[85] On this see for example Krasner 1984, 242–3 and Spruyt 1994b, 23–4.
[86] Gould and Eldredge 1977; and Gould 1982.

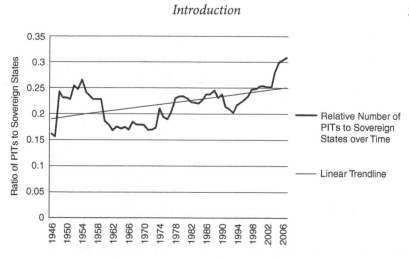

Figure 1.4. Relative frequency of partially independent territories 1946–2007

Sources: For partially independent polities see Appendix 1. For sovereign states see Correlates of War Project 2008.

so"[87]) as they attempt to maximize wealth, security, and credible control over their own affairs.[88] When all other things are equal, leaders and populations will generally select the institutional alternative that maximizes their wealth, security, and self-determination relative to available alternatives.

If these rationalist assumptions are true but PITs are, nevertheless, not more advantageous than sovereign states, it can be predicted that the relative frequency of these polities would decline. The opposite is however true. As Figure 1.4 shows, when a ratio is created out of the number of PITs as compared to the number of sovereign states for each year from 1946 to 2007, the relative frequency of PITs are rising.[89] Moreover, this trend accelerated after the Cold War as shown by Figure 1.5.[90] Another way to convey this finding is through the inverse trend of the ratio of sovereign states to territories as shown in Figure 1.6. In spite of the widespread observation that the number of sovereign states has

---

[87] Simon 1961, xxiv.
[88] In some sense this assumption mirrors the rationalist arguments of intergovernmentalist theories of political integration that debated European integration. See for example Hoffmann 1966, 862–915 and Morazvcsik 1998. As Chapter 3 will explain, however, the arguments presented here significantly depart from intergovernmentalism. Unlike intergovernmentalist theory, the "integrationist" arguments here propose that the locus of causality that produces integration primarily centers on the integrated political form (the partially independent arrangement) rather than the exclusive interests of the sovereign state (as argued by intergovernmentalist scholars).
[89] Standard deviation is 0.06.
[90] Standard deviation is 0.03.

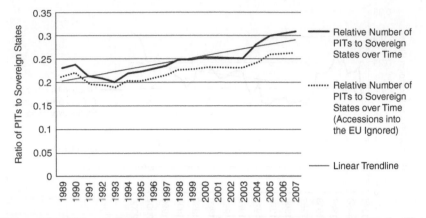

Figure 1.5. Rising Relative Frequency of partially Independent Territories Post Cold War

Sources: For partially independent polities see Appendix 1. For sovereign states see Correlates of War Project. 2008. Except where noted, countries that have acceded into the European Union are not coded as fully independent sovereign states.

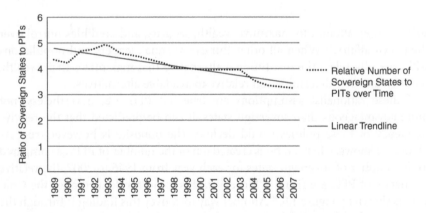

Figure 1.6. Fewer and fewer sovereign states relative to partially independent territories post-Cold War

Sources: For partially independent polities see Appendix 1. For sovereign states see Correlates of War Project 2008.

been rising rapidly, when compared to partially independent polities, their relative frequency has been declining since 1949 and especially since the end of the Cold War.[91] After 1989 the relative frequency of sovereign states has declined

[91] For those who emphasize the increasing number of states see especially Alesina and Spolaore 2003. See also Roeder 2007.

from being as high as five times as numerous as PITs to about three times as numerous in 2007.[92] The increasing frequency of these polities as an alternative to full independence sets the stage for a changed ontological view of the international system in which the sovereign state is not the only systematically present or increasingly sought after political alternative in possession of sovereign power.[93]

The conditions that cause the emergence of these polities are, however, distinct from the variables that cause their maintenance and potential termination. Accordingly, in spite of their advantages over full independence, there are nevertheless times when PITs come to an end (whether through secession or political assimilation by a core state). There are also times in which full independence may be a better alternative. As distinct from those that emphasize that nationalistically distinct populations tend to gravitate toward sovereign statehood, and by contrast to purely geographic, economic, or security explanations, it is argued here that the maintenance or termination of a PIT can be determined by whether the territory has a "good deal" (an equitable settlement). Partially independent territories trade full independence for partial independence so that they can obtain a wide range of scarcely available public goods (like external defense, a large single market, and judicial institutions for dispute resolution) from a more powerful core state. They accept giving up some powers because another larger state has the capacity to provide these services better or at a lower cost. The difference in power and responsibility in the relationship is therefore sustained and justified by a difference in capability. But when a PIT increasingly grows to a similar economic size as the core state, these differences in capability begin to disappear. The core state is less and less able to furnish public goods better than the territory could on its own. Under such circumstances, the difference in power seems increasingly unjustifiable and unfair. As a consequence of this, core states, which have economies that are too small in proportion to the PIT, are usually in a poor position to convince local nationalists that the arrangement is worthwhile. As this book will show, almost every case of maintenance and termination of PITs can be seen in this light.

This study predicts that this form of union will tend to be unworkable in those cases where the core state does not have sufficient capacity to deliver the economic, security, and self-determination advantages that typically characterize the relationship. Without such advantages, PITs will increasingly

[92] Standard deviation is 0.49

[93] By "ontological view of the world system" I mean "the metaphysical concern with the essence" of the international system, especially the chief units that compose it. On ontology see Landman 2000, 15; and Lawson 1997, 15.

drift toward full independence, which can lead to secession or incite political assimilation back into the core state. As will be illustrated later in the book, this core state capacity to deliver some of these advantages can be measured by the relative size of a core state economy as compared to the PIT with which it is associated.

PLAN OF THE BOOK

The objective of this book will be (1) to draw inferences based on samples of cases, (2) to establish relationships between variables, (3) to eliminate competing explanations, and (4) to demonstrate that the results are verifiable in the real world.[94] This introductory chapter has articulated some of the key constitutional, political, geographic, and demographic regularities of PITs and conveyed the book's chief puzzles and arguments. It has also summarized the regime's political, ontological, and epistemological importance. This book is the first work that systematically examines the existence, causal features, and evolution of PITs. By introducing PITs as distinct entities in international affairs and by illustrating the contributions that they make as compared to other alternatives, it is hoped that this work will induce reflection, debate, and further research on this understudied and underdeveloped area of international and comparative politics. The structural, causal, and evolutionary arguments are supported by fieldwork, new country-specific data, interviews with high ranking government officials, as well as the literatures of nationalism, federalism, constitutional law, comparative politics, international relations, international political economy, and area studies.[95] Ultimately, the evidence presented here will, nevertheless, be imperfect. Evidence that would confirm or disconfirm the arguments are constrained by the depth of information that can be provided on each case as well as data on the range of cases throughout the world as they compare to other polities. It is, therefore, by no means claimed that the analysis in this book is the final word on partially independent polities. Indeed, the arguments here are only the beginning of what it is hoped will be a larger effort and debate with regard to the effects of these political systems.

Chapter 2 will draw on the literatures of state formation, nationalism, market preserving federalism, and relational contracting to provide analytical

---

[94] Johnson, Joslyn, and Reynolds 2001.
[95] For this study, the author conducted fieldwork and interviewed senior leaders in the following governments: the Åland Islands, Bermuda, Canada, China, Finland, Hong Kong, Israel,

explanations of why PITs arguably cause levels of self-determination, wealth, and security that tend to surpass the sovereign state. It will then build upon functionalist, federalist, neo-functionalist, and intergovernmentalist theories of political integration to provide some conducive conditions that explain when these regimes tend to emerge, when they maintain themselves, when they come to an end, and when full independence may be a better alternative.

Parts II and III of the book will provide evidence to show that this book's arguments are likely to be true. Since a polity's jurisdictional priority (its sovereign powers) are critical for giving rise to the arguable advantages of PITs, Part II of the book will address the mechanisms that provide self-determination that is guaranteed by a core state. Chapters 3–6 will build upon the brief definitions offered in this chapter and illustrate the varying ways that PITs exist. Chapter 3 will set the stage for the other chapters by (1) placing these polities within the context of debates on the structure of the international system, (2) providing an overview of the various causal mechanisms through which the full universe of PITs have powers of territorial sovereignty short of full independence, and (3) distinguishing PITs from similar though distinct political forms.

Chapters 4 and 5 probe more deeply into the causal mechanisms that allow for PIT existence. These chapters intentionally select US and UK territories as their focus. In these chapters case studies have been selected according to (1) their "hardness" (the expectation on the part of some sources that they are not partially independent); (2) the existence of one or more counter equilibrium events (test events that challenge the purported sovereign powers of the territory);[96] (3) their global geographic dispersion; and (4) their differences over time on the independent variable (regime type)[97] as opposed to selecting on the dependent variable (the presence of economic, self-determination, and security advantages).[98] Such cases were therefore not selected because they fit the theory, but rather because they matched such independent criteria. Out of all PITs, Puerto Rico, the British Dominions, and Northern Ireland satisfy these criteria. The British Dominions were some of the first PITs in history that set the stage for a wide range of other future PITs. Puerto Rico is also a

Northern Ireland, Quebec, Puerto Rico, Scotland, the Palestinian Territories, and the United Kingdom.

[96] On such out-of-equilibrium events seek Lake 2009, 66–7. Here equilibrium refers to the status quo or systemic conditions. See also Gartzke 1999.

[97] Puerto Rico, for example, experienced colonialism, but after becoming a PIT has maintained its status. The British Dominions on the other hand went from colonial status, to becoming partially independent, to ultimately quitting their partial independence in favor of sovereign statehood.

[98] On the importance of avoiding research design by selecting cases on the dependent variable see Geddes 1990, 131–50.

paradigmatic case that illustrates how PITs deliver advantages to post-imperial states without the disadvantages of imperialism. Chapters 4 and 5 will also illustrate entrenchment through unwritten rules and the little understood transition that takes place from a relationship mostly characterized by pure self-interest to one that is defended by unwritten constitutional rules. Such cases are therefore critical for testing the arguments presented here.

Chapter 6 will further clarify the self-determination that can be provided to autonomous arrangements by distinguishing PITs from cases of "sham federacy." Sham federacy exists when the effort (or psuedo-effort) of providing a semi-independent status results in a form of neo-colonialism. This chapter emphasizes the perils that core states and local populations encounter when territories do not have credible self-determination. The chapter will also answer questions that have been raised in the literature on imperialism and what the future of empires and imperial control may be.[99] Even as the numbers of traditional colonies and empires have largely come to an end, this chapter will illustrate a significant increase of modern neo-colonial patterns under the cover of a partially autonomous arrangement that does not meaningfully exist.

Part III of the book will provide empirical support for the wealth, security, and integration causal claims of the book presented in Chapter 2. Chapter 7 will illustrate the historical emergence, strengths, and weaknesses of sovereign states. Such an analysis is important for understanding the interests and capabilities of core states (which are an integral part of partially independent unions) and for illustrating the weaknesses of sovereign states in modern times as they compare to partially independent arrangements.

Chapter 8 will draw on the universe of cases of PITs and sovereign states throughout the world to examine their comparative economic and security performance. The chapter will make use of matching techniques and case studies to produce an "apples-to-apples" comparison to show that PITs tend to have significant advantages over their demographically similar sovereign state counterparts. It will also refute counterarguments such as the claim that the causal relationship proposed here is in fact reversed. Someone may, for example, hypothesize that rather than PITs tending to create security and economic advantages, the opposite may be true: security and economic advantages may in fact cause PITs to emerge. Accordingly, Chapter 8 will provide a range of reasons to explain why such a critique arguably does not apply to the arguments here.

---

[99] For works that have dealt with such questions see for example, Barkey 1994; Daniels and Kennedy 2002; Galtung 1971; Motyl 1997, 19–29; 1999a; 1999b; Spruyt 2005; and Tilly 1997, 1–11.

Chapter 9 will then build upon the theory of integration presented in Chapter 2 and provide empirical illustrations of the conducive conditions for PIT maintenance and termination. Lastly, Chapter 10 will make a number of concluding observations on the impact of partial independence on international structure, its use as an alternative to full independence, its challenges in spite of its advantages, and its implications for state failure and state building.

2

Partial Independence Advantages and Evolution

> Huge sections of the world's population have won the right of self-determination on the cruelest possible terms: they have been simply left to fend for themselves. Not surprisingly, their nation-states are collapsing.
>
> —Michael Ignatieff [1]

It is common for observers to see no other viable contemporary alternative to sovereign statehood. In accordance with the 1933 Montevideo Convention, a sovereign state is a polity that possesses (1) a territory, (2), a population, (3) a government [with sovereignty over the territory and population], and (4) foreign affairs capability [which includes full diplomatic relations and the ability to engage in war within the confines of international law].[2] Sovereign states are seen as peerless and incomparable to other political forms besides themselves. As Jennifer Milliken and Keith Krause have emphasized "it has been the state—and not some other form of political organization—that has been promoted as *the* answer to addressing social and economic upheaval, conflict and war."[3] In those cases where state institutions lose control of their territory, when they fail to provide security, deliver essential services, or collapse amidst the challenges that assail them from the international system, the institutions of the sovereign state are not themselves rejected in favor of another alternative—because there often does not seem to be (or is not) any alternative. Indeed, most political forms such as federation member-units or decentralized territories such as cities, counties, departments, etc. are fully incorporated into

---

[1] Ignatieff 1993, 8.

[2] Montevideo Convention on the Rights and Duties of States 1933. A PIT by contrast has a formal division of sovereignty with a core state, does not possess full foreign affairs capability, and often shares and divides a limited range of domestic powers.

[3] Milliken and Krause 2002, 762. Italics not added.

a sovereign state's domestic system. Because these units are incorporated into a sovereign state, their populations exercise the same rights and privileges of citizenship. And although colonies exist outside of a state's constitutional system, they are by definition under the full sovereignty of a core state.[4] It is therefore common to see the sovereign state as a type of clay that does not change its essential reality whatever shapes its various parts may take. Furthermore, observers praise how the clay has in some cases been sculpted into a masterpiece or condemn how in other cases it has been turned into a failure, but the comparative qualities of the clay itself are not questioned. While there are some rare exceptions where full independence is in fact rejected (as with the emergence of European integration in which members have surrendered part of their sovereignty to Brussels) sovereign statehood is an institution that is often seen as beyond reproach for lack of alternatives.[5]

The seeming absence of other political mediums that provide meaningful comparisons to the performance of sovereign states, however, presents ontological problems. As any good consumer knows, limiting one's self to a particular purchase (such as a bicycle) without externally validating the decision by considering the potentialities of a distinct product (like a car) can have disadvantages.[6] Even the best bicycle does not have the same capabilities of a car (and vice versa). But perhaps even more importantly, in a world where the bicycle is seen as the only mode of transportation, it may be difficult imagining capabilities that surpass it. Similarly, there are advantages of not limiting ourselves to the sovereign state and examining the relative merits of other options as well.

In order to determine the merits of other alternatives to the sovereign state, one however needs to consider a number of issues. First, do alternatives really exist?[7] If other alternatives are mere theories, incomparably unique cases, or visions for the future, one may indeed be stuck. The next chapter and the rest of Part II of the book will therefore take up this question by expanding on the preliminary account of the existence of PITs provided in Chapter 1. Second, if alternatives do exist, do they really have advantages? What is the logic and

---

[4] Doyle 1986, 12.

[5] In addition to structures such as the European Union, scholars of international hierarchy have also underscored the existence of shared sovereignty between states with respect to assets such as military bases. See for example Cooley and Spruyt 2009.

[6] Comparing sovereign states to themselves has the advantages of internal validity (through a greater understanding of one type of political form). Such internal comparisons within a single category, however, suffer from the absence of external validity (in which a political form is compared against distinctive political systems). Barrington 2011, 19.

[7] The term "alternative" here does not suggest that PITs have the ability to replace all sovereign states. Systemic amendment rather than unit change is the form of change that will be emphasized here. For many local populations and core states, the choice is indeed between the alternatives of secession for a territory and the existence as a partially independent polity.

performance record behind them? This chapter will begin by providing the logic behind the relative advantages of PITs as compared to sovereign states, beginning first with an examination of the relative deficiencies of sovereign states. Such weaknesses will be further elaborated in Chapter 7. Third, even if other alternatives exist that have advantages, under what conditions are they feasible? One may discover the existence and excellent performance of a distinct alternative, but then be disappointed to discover that it is prohibitively costly or too inconvenient to use. This chapter will therefore also address other forms of integration such as federations and explain why they are often less feasible than PITs. Lastly, if an alternative option does indeed exist, has advantages, and is relatively feasible, under what conditions can it be obtained? What sustains it? And under what conditions does it cease functioning? This chapter will therefore conclude by examining conditions in which PITs emerge, maintain themselves, and sometimes come to an end as well as the conditions that can in some cases make full independence a better option. Part III of the book will provide evidence to support these claims.

SOVEREIGN STATE DEFICIENCIES

Some have asserted that the sovereign state as an institution is generally in decline.[8] This view has in significant ways not stood the test of time. Powerful states still play an overridingly important role in the international system in spite of the existence of various significant transnational forces and actors, which in any case do not possess constitutionally allocated sovereign power.[9] Sovereign states are also geographically ubiquitous and are not likely to be replaced by a distinct organizational form anytime soon.[10] Nevertheless, after the eighteenth century, many sovereign states have experienced significant challenges that have diminished their capabilities. Post eighteenth-century international norms, nationalism, and economic market conditions have in many cases weakened their ability to provide economic growth, security, and legitimacy. Sovereign states are fourteenth-century innovations that exist within the very different conditions of the twenty-first century. The sovereign state remains the world's preeminent political entity. But in the post-World War II period, it now presides over a world that has been riven by disastrous

---

[8]   See, Herz 1957, 473–93; Herz 1968; Vernon 1971.
[9]   See Krasner 1991, 336–66; and Thomson and Krasner 1989, 198.
[10]   Even in the case of the EU or PITs, sovereign states have not been fully replaced since they exercise overlapping jurisdictions with either Brussels or a PIT.

internal war and endemic poverty.[11] Some, however, still contend that states generally have more strengths than weaknesses. James Malloy for example asserts that states are "characterized by strong and relatively autonomous governmental structures that seek to impose on the society a system of interest representation based on enforced limited pluralism."[12] Nevertheless, the fact remains that since 1945, 73 sovereign states have experienced civil war, and excluding China, about 40% of the world's population of 6.5 billion lives on less than $2 per day.[13] States that are riven by such poverty and insecurity are commonly viewed as "abnormal." They are considered as polities that need to be built back up to resemble "normal," strong states like Japan, the United States, or Sweden. Weakness among sovereign states (not strength) is, however, the new normal condition that prevails in the international system for most states that have emerged after the nineteenth century—especially when contrasted to distinctive organizational forms such as PITs.

One bipartisan panel of former and current US government leaders and academics, the Commission on Weak States and US National Security, observed that "weak and failed states are particularly prevalent among the 70-plus low-income countries.... They are failing to control their territories, meet the most basic needs of their citizens, and provide legitimacy that flows from effective, transparent governance."[14] Institutions such as the World Bank, Britain's Department for International Development, and former and current US policy makers have arrived at similar conclusions.[15] In light of these numbers, state weakness, failure, and weakness is relatively common—especially for newly independent states.[16]

The existence of weak sovereign states in various parts of the world amidst the world's new challenges is, however, no accident.[17] As will be discussed in greater detail in Chapter 7, international anarchy threatens them externally.

---

[11] In addition to the period since 1945, during the past few centuries wars between and within states have been fought in increasing numbers and have resulted in increasing levels of destruction and loss of life within sovereign states. The eighteenth century recorded approximately 68 wars and 4 million dead, and the nineteenth century witnessed 205 wars with 8 million killed. But the twentieth century saw 237 wars and 115 million battle deaths with an additional civilian death total of near or equal size. Sivard 1986, 26 and Tilly 1990, 67. More recently, while major wars between great powers have greatly declined since World War II, the number of wars within sovereign states has increased.

[12] Malloy, 1977, 4. Also quoted in Migdal 1988, 6.

[13] Stiglitz 2006, 11.

[14] Commission on Weak States and US National Security 2004, 2.

[15] World Bank 2002; and UK, British Department for International Development 2005, 27–8.

[16] Milliken and Krause 2002, 766.

[17] Scholars distinguish between varying levels of statehood inadequacy. State failure occurs when a state loses its sovereign authority and control over its territory, population, and external relations. This can be a partial loss of control and authority, as with Pakistan's loss of authority and control over North and South Waziristan. Robert Rotberg also refers to collapsed states, in

The post-eighteenth-century force of nationalism divides them from within. And the demands of international market conditions strain them both inside and out. Some sovereign states have had the institutional strength to overcome and master these challenges, but many have not. Sovereign statehood has delivered benefits to countries such as America, Japan, and Switzerland, but it has also sunk many of the world's other nationalistically distinct territories into an abyss of internal conflict, external insecurity, and economic poverty.[18] This book will argue that PITs have in some respects evolved to overcome the challenges that have faced many of their fully independent counterparts.

COMPENSATING FOR SOVEREIGN STATE WEAKNESS

For core states, full independence for minority populations may mean the loss of an extended economic zone, strategically important territory, military bases, and natural resources. On the other hand, however, the imposition of their own sovereign state on an unwilling nationalistically distinct population can unleash the complications of imperialism, including violence, governance, and/ or legitimacy costs. While sovereign states often tend to monopolize political control within their borders, PITs are often the embodiment of nationalistic compromise.[19] While sovereign states are in a condition of relative anarchy, PITs have the advantages of a wide range of economic, security, and politically ori-ented public goods from a large and usually strong core state. While sovereign states have few guarantees that their regimes will be compromised by internal or external adversaries, PITs have powers that are externally guaranteed.

Liberty and Self-determination Advantages through Nationalistic Compromise

Some of the first identifiable PITs (like the historic British Dominions detailed in Chapter 4) emerged in the nineteenth century amidst the aforementioned

---

which states such as Somalia may succumb to periods in which the official government has virtu-ally no authority and control structures. Rotberg 2002, 85–96.

[18] For sources in the literature on decolonization that confirm this see for example Jackson 1987, 519–49.

[19] Sociologist Max Weber (1964, 154) defined the sovereign state as a "human community that successfully claims the monopoly of the legitimate use of physical force."

backdrop of sovereign state disadvantages. Their ability to exist in the first place, however, is in some sense puzzling. If sovereign states are often defined by their tendency to monopolize all control within their borders, why would they paradoxically be willing to divide some sovereignty with another entity? As will be discussed below, many sovereign states have come to realize that it is more advantageous to compromise with distinct populations through the use of partially independent arrangements rather than face secessionist revolts, possible full fragmentation of their territorial space, and/or the consequent diminishment of their resources.

Sovereign states were built to exclude all other internal competitors. This however drives a wedge between contending nationalist populations within states, creating an ideological impetus for the majority of the world's civil wars since the end of World War II.[20] Accordingly, theories of nationalism tend to support the view that the sovereign state is challenged by its tendency in many cases to extend the state's monopoly of control over nationalistically distinct territories.[21] As a result of these challenges, the existence of a political compromise, such as a partially independent arrangement, that allows *limited areas* of full independence to national groups who are troubled by their lack of self-rule means that a nationalistically distinct population can realize the ideal of self-determination short of having their own sovereign state.[22] Under these circumstances a core state can also potentially benefit by avoiding the costs of unwanted control and potential full territorial fragmentation. The path of least resistance sometimes results in the creation of a partially independent arrangement where a territorially-bounded national population is granted *some* powers of sovereignty without full independence.

The essence of national self-determination is when a distinct population determines the nature of its own existence, regardless of the governmental form. Full independence is therefore not the ultimate fulfillment of national self-determination if it does not fulfill a population's economic, political, and security self-interest. Indeed, the process of sharing and dividing sovereignty can deliver substantial advantages that may not be realized through full independence. This logic is supported by the seventeenth-century philosopher John Locke. Locke argued against the emotional and illusory advantages of the

---

[20] For data on the wars of nationalism, which constitute the majority of wars that have taken place since 1945, see Cederman et al. 2009b; Gleditsch et al. 2002; and Roeder 2007, 5.

[21] See Anderson 1991; Armstrong 1982; Breuilly 1982; Brubaker 1996; Chatterjee 1993; Gellner 1983; Hechter 2000; Hall 1998; Hobsbawm 1992; Hroch 1985; Kymlicka 1995; Miller 1995; Smith 1986.

[22] The existence of PITs provides answers to dilemmas in democracy theory regarding the problem of culture–state incongruence as discussed in the literature on nationalism. On problems of culture–state incongruence in the literature on nationalism see Gellner 1983; Hall 1998; Hechter 2000.

anarchical "state of nature" conditions that prevail amidst full independence in which there is no higher government. He says that:

> If man in the state of nature be so free, as has been said; if he be absolute lord of his own person and possessions, equal to the greatest, and subject to no body, why will he part with his freedom? Why will he give up this empire, and subject himself to the dominion and control of any other power? To which it is obvious to answer, that though in the state of nature he hath such a right, yet the enjoyment of it is very uncertain, and constantly exposed to the invasion of others: for all being kings as much as he, every man his equal, and the greater part no strict observers of equity and justice, the enjoyment of the property he has in this state is very unsafe, very unsecure. This makes him willing to quit a condition, which however free, is full of fears and continual dangers: and it is not without reason, that he seeks out, and is willing to join in society with others, who are already united, or have a mind to unite, for the mutual preservation of their lives, liberties, and estates...[23]

Sovereign states are compromised internally because they often tend to monopolize territorial control. This results in self-determination movements that are destabilizing for both sovereign states as well as nationalistically distinct minority populations. It was the fear of such absolute and unchecked control by imperial powers that helped lead to the moral outrage which in turn contributed to the development of the post-World War II norm against colonialism.[24] By contrast, PITs are advantaged internally since they embody overlapping jurisdiction and compromise on territorial control. This can result in moderated self-determination movements. Not everyone, however, agrees with the conclusions of scholars of nationalism. A relatively new literature has emerged which emphasizes that internal war is more a product of poverty and greed rather than a desire to achieve nationalistic ideals.[25] For proponents of such theories the wealth producing features of partially independent arrangements, which sovereign states alone often do not possess, may be of interest.

Wealth Advantages through Market Preserving Federalism

There are still other puzzles with regard to the existence of PITs. For example, why should a core state settle for dividing and sharing some sovereignty and

---

[23] Locke 1690/1980, 65–6.

[24] See Crawford 2002; Jackson 1993.

[25] On poverty and greed as a source of internal war, see Collier et. al. 2003; Fearon and Laitin 2003, 75–90; and Nagel and Olzak 1982, 127–43; Ragin 1979; Rudolph and Thompson 1985, 291–311.

delivering expensive public goods to a distinct population? When resources are always relatively scarce, why is it worth it for a core state to hand over such benefits to a potentially resentful nation in the periphery? With respect to this problem, the market preserving federalism (MPF) literature[26] emphasizes that markets, competition, and investment tend to flourish within both sovereign states and their associated territories when areas within the state have "primary regulatory responsibility" over their economic affairs that is credibly shielded from interference by a central government.[27]

Barry Weingast, for example, observes that "thriving markets require not only the appropriate system of property rights and a law of contracts, but a secure political foundation that limits the ability of the state to...remove its earlier grant of authority to the lower levels."[28] Weingast postulates that MPF was one of the primary causal factors in producing England's industrial revolution in the eighteenth century, America's subsequent rise as an economic superpower, and China's economic ascent after the late 1970s. After local jurisdictions within such countries were institutionally protected from state interference, they developed powerful vested interests to create policies that would compete with other jurisdictions for increasing levels of investment and growth.[29] Given such incentives, the local leaders in these jurisdictions created low taxation, flexible employment, and favorable development policies that were designed to attract and maximize outside investment.[30] Meanwhile the central government provided an umbrella of public goods, which included a common market and a single monetary framework.[31] Additionally, autonomous local jurisdictions were shielded at the national level from rent-seeking leaders and special interests that hamper investment, productive capacity, and free competition in order to satisfy their own particularistic interests.[32] The net result was not only more prosperous territories, but a critical mass of local jurisdictions that were intercompeting and therefore more efficiently

---

[26] The emphasis on constitutional credibility of PITs reinforces the MPF literature by providing an additional political form to analyze. On market preserving and fiscal federalism see, Buchanan 1995, 19–28; Mossberger, 1999, 31–50; Qian and Weingast 1997, 83–92; Rodden and Rose-Ackerman 1997, 1521–72; Rose-Ackerman 1980, 593–616; Rubinfeld 1997, 1581–92; Strumpf 2002, 207–41; Tiebout 1956, 416–24; Weingast 1995, 1–31; Zodrow 1983.

[27] Weingast 1995, 4.

[28] Weingast 1995, 1.

[29] The emphasis on the market-type competition of local jurisdictions (which are analogous to firms), public goods like education, roads, and police protection (which are analogous to products), and levels of taxation (which are analogous to prices) are drawn from the seminal work of Tiebout 1956.

[30] Weingast 1995, 8.

[31] Weingast 1995.

[32] Brennan and Buchanan 1980, 13–33.

designing policies to maximize their own relative advantages.[33] This then led to overall levels of spectacular growth for countries, such as America, China, and England.

While the MPF literature is usually applied to federations that meet its criteria, the same arguments can be applied to partially independent arrangements, since in most cases they have the critical elements of MPF as described by Weingast.[34] These include autonomous regional control,[35] regulatory responsibility over the local economy, and a common market with a core state.[36] An MPF theory, which accounts for PITs, therefore provides the theoretical basis to expect relatively high levels of economic growth for PITs, which sovereign states that exist within international anarchy in many cases cannot achieve.[37] While many sovereign states have at least the same potential of a PIT to craft their own distinct economic policies, they nevertheless usually do not benefit from the same level of public goods that are provided through institutionalized linkages with a core state (unless of course they are able to join an anomalous structure like the European Union or until other regionally or globally sovereign structures appear in the future). These public goods often include

---

[33]   For a classic article on this subject see Tiebout 1956, 416–24.

[34]   Weingast 1995, 4–5.

[35]   Riker 1975, 93–172.

[36]   Weingast's first and second criteria (autonomous regional control and two governments ruling over the same people) are satisfied by partially independent arrangements because first, they have a wide range of autonomous control (final decision-making powers) over their affairs and second, such powers are defended (and made credible) by mechanisms of constitutional entrenchment that prevent the core state from recentralizing control by fiat. Partially independent arrangements also satisfy Weingast's third and fourth criteria (primary regulatory responsibility over the economy and a common market), because in most cases they benefit from a larger state's provision of public goods, which frequently includes a common market, while also being freed from core state interference to craft competitive taxation, employment, and developmental policies.

[37]   The only criteria of MPF which PITs sometimes do not possess is Weingast's criteria of a hard budget constraint, in which they would be unable to print or borrow money. In relatively rare cases some PITs like Hong Kong and Bermuda print their own currency but since their currencies are pegged to the US dollar they are limited in their ability for currency devaluation. Some PITs also have the ability to borrow and have the capacity to accept fiscal transfers from the core state. According to Weingast, a hard budget constraint provides incentives for better fiscal decisions because a sub-unit is unable to bail itself out by borrowing. While there may be some truth to this point, critics have, however, pointed out that this last criterion is too rigid. See Rodden and Rose-Ackerman 1997, 1557–6. Most modern federations (including those which Weingast includes within his MPF framework), such as Australia, Canada, Germany, and the United States provide large redistributive grants and financing (referred to as "cooperative federalism") in which the federal government attempts to limit inequality and stabilize potential systemic crisis. See Elazar 1991, 65. Additionally, China, which Weingast describes as a *"de facto* federation," also provides such redistribution, transferring vast sums of capital from more wealthy areas such as Shanghai to less well off landlocked regions such as Henan province. Relaxing this criterion therefore helps reinforce the causal connections within Weingast's own MPF theory.

a common market, fiscal protections, external defense, shared governmental representation, as well as the stamp of legitimacy that can come from being linked to an established great power.

The presence of credible local autonomy together with the provision of public goods from a core state leads to an increased ability to specialize and compete with other jurisdictions. Under such conditions, as Charles Tiebout argued, localized governments benefit from many of the advantages that are obtained by firms operating in market economies.[38] Residents are like customers. The services the local government provides are like products. The chamber of commerce is the marketing department. And taxes are the polity's product costs. These localized governments then compete for additional taxpayers and investors through more attractive services and varied taxation policies. Similar to firms in a market economy, the net result is then increased specialization and competition as they relate to other parts of a state (or other parts of the international system), which is advantageous to local governments as well as core states.

By contrast, rather than benefiting from public goods from a core state, fully independent states in many respects have to "do it all," which inhibits specialization. Modern polities are forced to navigate a wide range of complex challenges (in areas such as international finance, monetary policy, diplomacy, internal security, external defense, human rights, public relations, free speech, urban planning, trade, rule of law, corruption, political accountability, environmental policy, infrastructure, representation, transportation, and still other sectors). Sovereign states in international anarchy without a world government are certainly not completely on their own in all of these areas. However, the degree of collaboration and mutual assistance on such issues that prevails between core states and PITs usually far surpasses the relatively solitary existence of fully independent states. Some may, nevertheless, challenge this by arguing that some sovereign states benefit from free trade areas, alliances, foreign aid, etc. A free trade area, however, does not provide the same advantages as a single market, wherein a customs union (in which there is a common external tariff) is added to the free flow of goods and labor. An alliance does not have the advantages of a great power viewing an invasion of a PIT as an invasion of their own territory. And the foreign aid that states provide to other states is much smaller than the fiscal transfers that they provide to jurisdictions within their own international legal space (which often includes PITs).

---

[38] Tiebout 1956, 416–24.

Still another example of a public good possessed by PITs as compared to sovereign states applies to disaster response. When disaster strikes in a sovereign state, humanitarian intervention by outside states is often seen as a right but not a duty. As Michael Walzer observes it is "no one's duty in particular, so in fact the brutalities and oppression of international society are more often denounced than interdicted."[39] It would naturally be better if this were not the case for weak sovereign states. The situation is, however, quite different for PITs. The manmade disasters that one can observe in many weak and failed states—invasion, genocides, coups, famines—are inconceivable in PITs for a variety of reasons. Among other things, while the rest of the international community may stand by to ponder their rights, core states are not only authorized, but have a duty to intervene.

Similar to an individual in a preindustrial society that requires a diversity of skill sets in order to survive, sovereign states often need to furnish much of their own defense, regulation, diplomacy, and reputational credibility. Additionally, by virtue of their full independence, in many cases, other than their own domestic system, they have no assured tariff-free markets, no external single market, no guaranteed fiscal safety net, and no shared institutions that provide direct collaboration with other states. When states are forced to increase their range of responsibilities in this way, it reduces the resources that they can devote to areas where they have a comparative advantage. Sectors that may have benefited from increased government investment are weakened. With respect to this, economists have long emphasized the importance of abandoning the autonomy of full economic self-sufficiency as a chief factor that led to various revolutions in economic affairs, including the industrial revolution. As eighteenth-century economist Adam Smith wrote:

> The tailor does not attempt to make his own shoes, but buys them of the shoemaker. The shoemaker does not attempt to make his own clothes, but employs a tailor. The farmer attempts to make neither the one nor the other, but employs those different artificers. All of them find it for their interest to employ their whole industry in a way in which they have some advantage over their neighbors, and to purchase with a part of its produce, or what is the same thing, with the price of a part of it, whatever else they have occasion for.[40]

Importantly, with respect to these points Adam Smith added that, "What is prudence in the conduct of every private family can scarce be folly in that of a great kingdom."[41]

Hence, whether at the individual or policy levels, relinquishing control over some issues and allowing other actors to do the job can have important

---

[39] Walzer 1997, 107.   [40] Smith 1776/1904, 34.   [41] Smith 1776/1904, 34.

economic advantages. After being freed from the burdens of some aspects of statecraft by a core state that shares and shoulders some of the responsibilities, territories can better afford to devote more resources toward policies that create increased specialization and competitiveness. Many PITs have, for example, focused their limited resources on bolstering their financial services, tourism, or natural resource sectors. Sovereign states often do not have the luxury or resources to make such commitments. This in turn can explain the economic success that many PITs have had as compared to their demographically similar sovereign state counterparts (as detailed in Chapter 8).

Security and Credible Commitment through Relational Contracting and Norms

Still another puzzle with regard to the existence of PITs relates to the fears of weaker populations that they will be exploited by a larger and stronger core state. If a nationalistically distinct population does indeed accept a partially independent arrangement, what will prevent the core state from arbitrarily changing its mind, usurping its commitments, and engaging in full domination? Why should they believe that they will not be exploited and subjugated like the colonies of the past?

As described previously, theories of nationalism can be used to predict that PITs can in some cases furnish liberty and self-determination better to some populations than the institutions of the sovereign state alone. Market preserving federalism theories can also be used to forecast that PITs will tend to attain greater degrees of wealth than sovereign states that do not benefit from the public goods of a higher government. Similarly, observations from the literature on relational contracting and constructivism can be used to emphasize the institutions that partially independent arrangements possess to promote norms such as trust, duty, predictability, fairness, communication, and mutual support that can deliver a greater sense of confidence that each side will honor its side of the bargain.[42]

The relational contracting literature emphasizes the deficiencies of polities in the anarchic international system in which there is an absence of an impartial third party that can enforce agreements (such as a world government).[43] In significant ways relational contracting and many constructivist studies have

---

[42] On relational contracting see especially Lake 1999; Williamson 1985.
[43] For works that discuss the lack of credible commitment between ethnic groups as a contributing factor that can lead to violence see Bartkus 2001; Fearon 1994; Fearon 1995, 379–414; Hardin 1995, 143; Lake and Rothchild 1996, 48–52.

an overlapping focus with the scholarship on nationalism with respect to the need for self-determination to reduce interethnic conflict. Works on nationalism, however, often put an emphasis on the need for self-determination as an end unto itself to overcome cultural-political controversies surrounding the distribution of powers within distinct territories.[44] By contrast, the literatures on relational contracting and constructivism tend to focus on the problems and structure that arise out of the international system.

In the international system without a world government, there is no impartial arbiter to monitor and enforce a potential agreement between different actors and conditions of fear and mistrust greatly hamper the possibility of cooperation and/or reconciliation.[45] Jeffrey Frieden has emphasized the dangers and contractual vulnerabilities of stateless ethnic minorities under the control of distinct majority populations.[46] In anarchy, a commitment problem arises from "private information about resolve or capability and incentives to misrepresent these,"[47] "a third party not being available to guarantee agreements," and a lack of trust that arises from "a structure of preferences and opportunities, that gives one party an incentive to renege."[48]

When faced by such inconveniences of anarchy and decentralization, contracting scholars argue that governmental cooperation can be enforced in interethnic agreements through political checks and balances.[49] These include electoral rules, group vetoes, and central government power sharing.[50] They can also include an ethnic balance in police and military forces as well as minority control over economic assets that are important to the national government.[51] In addition to these methods, the structures within a partially independent arrangement also offer a similar though distinct set of structures. Partially independent arrangements depart from a condition of pure anarchy by providing credible commitments between a core state and a nationalistically distinct region.[52] This can in turn overcome the insecurity problems postulated by the relational contracting literature.

---

[44] See for example Gellner 1983 and Hechter 2000.
[45] For an excellent description of this conundrum see Walter 1997, 335–64.
[46] Frieden 1994.
[47] Fearon 1995, 409.
[48] Fearon 1995, 406.
[49] On the political checks and balances of ethnic power giving rise to credible commitments see Fearon 1995 and Lake and Rothchild 1996, 49.
[50] See Sisk 1995; Horowitz 1985; and Lijphart 1967. On veto players see Tsebelis 1999.
[51] Adam and Moodley 1993, 226–50.
[52] The study of PITs compliments the literature on international hierarchy in some respects. The existence of PITs underscores much of what the hierarchy literature supports, namely that the global anarchy that some international relations theorists (such as neo-realists) argue in

These arrangements depart from a condition of pure hierarchy (in which a dominant power rules over a subordinate as with a colony or protectorate) since the territory possesses some measures of de facto control and de jure authority on some matters over a geographic area (territorial sovereignty). This mirrors the emphasis that scholars in the state formation literature put on many of the polities that competed with the sovereign state before the seventeenth century, such as fiefdoms, as having "non-hierarchical" characteristics, because on a range of matters they held jurisdictional priority over other polities.[53] Partially independent unions are therefore better conceived of as a hybrid between hierarchy and anarchy that Daniel Deudney in his analysis of America's constitutional development calls "negarchy."[54] "Negarchy" he says, "is the arrangement of institutions necessary to prevent simultaneously the emergence of hierarchy and anarchy.... Thus understood, negarchy is a third—and liberal—structural principle of political order, along with hierarchy and anarchy."[55] Indeed, as the rest of the chapters of this book will emphasize, when territories like Puerto Rico compelled the US to remove its Naval base on the island of Vieques in 2003, when G-20 countries were unable to subdue the tax haven status of various PITs in 1998 and 2007, when Hong Kong compelled China to retreat from imposing unpopular national security laws in 2003, sovereign states failed to exert a dominant status.

As Part II of the book will illustrate, a defining characteristic of partially independent arrangements is that they possess mechanisms that make the final decision-making powers that have been constitutionally allocated to them by agreement very difficult to usurp and therefore credible. For fiefdoms in the medieval ages, this degree of de facto political and military control could be seen as real and credible vis-à-vis a core state by the high walls of the vassal lord's fortress and the brute force of an army. Accordingly, PITs embody such forms of credibility. But instead of the protective structures of castle walls, PITs are protected by formal, conventional, and political-formal constitutional entrenchment that make it very difficult for their powers to be taken away by the fiat of other polities. Such entrenchment creates conditions that affirm that no other polity but the PIT has final de facto control and de jure authority over many of the powers that have been allocated to it.

---

favor of is not pure. On international hierarchy see Cooley 2000/2001, 2005; Cooley and Spruyt 2009; Donnelly 2006; Hobson and Sharman 2005; Lake 1996, 1999, 2001, 2003, 2009; Nexon and Wright 2007; Weber 2000.

[53] For example, some of the powers exercised by the fiefdom's rulers were non-hierarchically arranged as they related to the monarchy, see Spruyt 1994b.

[54] Deudney 1995, 208.

[55] Deudney 1995, 208.

In sum, according to the relational contracting literature, sovereign states are compromised internationally since an impartial body (such as a world government) often does not exist to enforce agreements within their nationalistically distinct territories. By contrast, PITs address this deficiency because their constitutional entrenchment delivers trust, reassurance, and enforceability. The strength of such commitments in turn reassures territories that (1) the core state will abide by the terms of their arrangement and deliver public goods (including external defense), and (2) that the territory will maintain its local de jure and de facto jurisdiction, which can act to prevent core–PIT hostility.

The Applicability of Partially Independent Territory Advantages to other Polities and their Feasibility

Some may point out that other forms of integration also embody many of the aforementioned advantages. Other divided sovereignty arrangements (such as federations, EU-style regional integration, and potential world government) can in some cases make up for sovereign state deficiencies in ways that mirror those of the pooling of sovereignty between core states and PITs.[56] The argument here, however, is not that PITs have self-determination, wealth, and security advantages above all other forms. Instead, the intention is to make the more modest claim that they often tend to be better than full independence. Indeed, the aforementioned advantages of PITs are in many cases also applicable to other forms of political integration (whether one is considering EU-style regional integration, the establishment of a federation, or even world government).[57] Nevertheless, whatever advantages these other forms of divided sovereignty may share with PITs, their structural distinctiveness may cause them to be rejected because of their frequent infeasibility.[58]

Political integration can be described as the process and outcome of dividing and sharing of sovereign powers between distinct territorial units.[59] Apart

[56] For a compelling comparison between the arguable advantages of a future world state as compared to the sovereign state see, for example, Tamir 2000, 244–67.

[57] On the establishment and value of world government see Cabrera 2010; Copp 2005; Craig 2003, 2008; Deudney 2007; Etzioni 2004; Singer 2002; Tamir 2000, 244–67; Wendt 2003, 491–542.

[58] On political integration see Caporaso 1997; Deutsch et al. 1957; Haas 1968; Hesse and Wright 1996; Hoffmann 1966, 862–915; Levi 1990; Lindberg and Scheingold 1970; Mattli and Slaughter 1995, 183–90; Mitrany 1966; Morazvcsik 1998; Rosamond 2000, 175; Tranholm-Mikkelsen, 1991, 11–25; Wallace 1994, 9.

[59] To some degree this definition draws on the definition of integration provided by Ernest Haas (1968, 16). The definition, however, omits Haas's reference to a shared loyalty to a common center. There have been a significant number of cases (as in the Azores or Puerto Rico) in which under a partially independent arrangement the prevalence of secessionism within a territory has given way to a strong and widespread sense of core state nationalism in addition to the preexisting territorial

from Europe itself, thus far no efforts at a regional integration on the European model have been successful, much less world level political integration in the form of a world government (although it should be noted that the establishment of bodies such as the United Nations Security Council, the International Criminal Court, and the World Trade Organization are perhaps significant steps in that direction).[60]

The establishment of federations for sovereign states also presents challenges that often exceed that of bringing into being a PIT.[61] Federations have relatively high start-up costs.[62] Because they require two levels of government for most regions of a state, many unitary states have rejected the revolutionary, system-wide changes and costs that are necessary for their establishment. The creation of a federation requires that some territories have distinct regional governments that they have rejected. It also necessitates a new Constitution and a new federal government that people in some cases do not want. In the United Kingdom, for example, most of the historic proposals for transforming the country (and their historic empire) into a federation have been rejected for such reasons.[63]

By contrast, under a partially independent arrangement, if a state without a federation wants to allocate some credible final decision-making powers to a specific territory, it does not have to undergo the revolutionary transformation of creating a federation over most of the state just to satisfy the distinctive desires of self-determination of only one part of the country. And even if a sovereign state already has a federation, core state authorities may have little desire to politically assimilate a nationalistically, economically, and politically distinct enclave into a preexisting federation. This, for example, was the case in the early 1950s, when some members of the US Congress expressed reluctance with fully incorporating Puerto Rico, because of its cultural distinctiveness, its relative economic underdevelopment, and the opposition in the territory to full incorporation as a federation member-unit.[64] Apart from core state

nationalism. Nevertheless, unlike a federation or the federalizing institutions of European integration, a partially independent arrangement does not have a second level of overarching government. In partially independent arrangements, there may be some collective institutions in certain cases, such as a specially created constitutional court, but in most cases collective institutionalization comes in the form of mutual representation in each other's legislatures or executive departments. A sense of shared loyalty is therefore omitted as a necessary condition for political integration. The definition offered here is also similar to Leon Lindberg and Scheingold's (1970, 46) definition of integration, but for similar reasons it omits an emphasis on a "collective arena."

[60]   Caporaso 1997; Rosamond 2000, 175; Wallace 1994, 9.

[61]   On federations see especially Dahl 1986, 114; Elazar 1997, 239; Lijphart 1999, 186–8; Rector 2009; Riker 1975, 101; Stepan 2001, 6; Wheare 1956, 32.

[62]   Rector 2009, 135.

[63]   On this see especially Kendle 1989.

[64]   Leibowitz 1989, 127–85.

interests, nationalistically distinct territories also tend to favor a distribution of powers and set of institutions that are custom made to their interests rather than having to accept the "one size fits all" package of powers that is often distributed amongst federation member-units.[65] Such territories are in some cases more interested in a specific agreement, set of powers, and status that are more customized to their specific historic, cultural, political, and/or economic condition.

There are also difficulties with establishing federations in light of the inevitable inequalities between members who fear exploitation. As Chad Rector describes, small states that are considering such a union fear exploitation by more powerful states. As a hedge against their weakness and vulnerability, they demand "contrived symmetry" (degrees of shared control and economic redistribution), which large states often reject.[66]

By contrast to such inequality problems, PITs are designed for and are arguably sustained by asymmetry and inequality. They tend to maintain themselves when inequality prevails and paradoxically tend to terminate when growing equality in terms of size and capability emerges. As will be elaborated later in this chapter (and especially in Chapter 9), equality, not inequality, is arguably more of a threat to the arrangement.

Adding to the infeasibility of federations are cases in which a number of territories favor the creation of such a union, but the rejection of federation by one member results in the defection of all. This, for example, occurred with the failed formation of the East Africa Federation, in which the largest political parties of Kenya and Tanzania favored federation, but those in Uganda did not.[67] Similarly, Trinidad changed its preference for being part of the ill-fated Federation of the West Indies in the Caribbean when it became clear that Jamaica would not join.[68] By contrast to these conditions, when the union is bilateral (as with a core–PIT union) there are fewer veto players and thus a lower likelihood of defection. Indeed, from the ashes of the aforementioned failed efforts to form federations, a number of partially independent arrangements emerged and have sustained themselves, including unions between Tanzania and Zanzibar and the Cayman Islands and the UK.

---

[65]   Riker 1975, 93–172. It may be worth reemphasizing that the comparison here is to PITs that have a distinct set of powers, rights, and status as they relate to a core state. In comparison to a centralized unitary government, however, a federation allows for a great deal of diversity. Member-units have their own governments and can for example create their own distinct laws. On this see for example Hooghe and Marks 2003, 233–43.

[66]   Rector 2009.

[67]   Rector 2009, 136.

[68]   Rector 2009, 159.

Additionally, unlike most constitutionally incorporated federation member-units, PITs are also able to capitalize on their own powers of foreign relations by engaging in a wide range of agreements with other countries in areas such as trade and finance. For example, many of the PITs that are associated with the UK (such as Bermuda, the Cayman Islands, the Isle of Man, and the Channel Islands) have negotiated their own Tax Information Exchange Agreements with other countries.[69] This potentially improves their ability to not only attract entrepreneurs and investments from elsewhere within a country, but from other areas around the world (for the membership that partially independent arrangements have in international organizations that provide such foreign relations, see Table 3.2). Such advantages add to the degree that PITs can be tailored to the economic, security, and nationalistic interests of distinct populations in ways that federation member-units typically do not.[70] Hence, although other forms of integration may benefit from many of the self-determination, wealth, and security advantages discussed in the previous sections, as compared to the creation of a PIT, they may be less feasible to implement.

In sum, as compared to partially independent arrangements, federations (and other formulations such as the application of the EU model or world federation) have high start-up costs, which often inhibit their feasibility. However brilliant their solutions for many of the problems of self-determination, poverty, and insecurity throughout the world, relative infeasibility will inhibit the solutions they can potentially provide. By contrast, core–PIT unions are tailor-made to the specific political, nationalistic, and economic interests of a region rather than a framework that demands revolutionary state-wide transformation. They also tend to sustain themselves (rather than unravel) in the presence of the often inevitable inequality of capability between the polities that are involved. Furthermore, as bilateral unions, they involve fewer veto players that have precipitated mass defection and unraveling of other potential federations. And unlike most federation member-units they have their own foreign affairs capability which provides a potentially greater fulfillment of local self-determination. These factors in turn allow core–PIT unions to respond to international challenges in ways that may be better adapted to the challenges of economic globalization, ethnic nationalism, and relative international anarchy. Rather than applying a one size fits all framework, economic

---

[69] Foot 2009, 10.

[70] It may be instructive to note that there are rare cases in which member-units of federations do possess some limited powers of foreign affairs, such as Tatarstan in Russia. Nevertheless (unlike partially independent polities) such territories are still incorporated as an integral part of their state Hughes 2001, 36–68.

globalization demands public goods and local autonomy that are specialized for the needs of specific regions. Rather than being a hostage to other units that may influence the terms of the arrangement or defect, the presence of international anarchy necessitates conditions that are more agreeable for the formation of credible commitments by both sides. And rather than suffering from problems of inequality, which are sometimes problematic for federal unions, an allocation of powers that is tailor-made to a territory's interests can better fulfill the specific self-determination interests and perceptions of fairness of local groups.

THE EMERGENCE OF PARTIALLY INDEPENDENT TERRITORIES

PITs emerge for the same general reasons that sovereign states arose: a combination of (1) institutional natural selection and (2) norms-resetting catastrophe. These arguments draw on contemporary theories of biological evolution and the excellent work of political scientists that have drawn from such studies.[71]

Alternative Possible Explanations

The previous sections have argued that PITs tend to surpass sovereign states in a variety of ways. They tend to be more feasible than other divided sovereignty arrangements. Their powers are externally guaranteed. They avoid the defects of imperialism. And together with a core state they often obtain joint gains[72] through public goods, nationalistic compromise, standardization, and lower governance costs. Such factors tend to translate into better economic, security, and self-determination outcomes within the much changed conditions since the nineteenth century. As a consequence of these advantages, it is tempting to argue that PITs emerge solely because of a type of natural selection in which more institutionally fit and advantaged forms are selected by leaders and populations above others. Such a view would be similar to federalist theories of integration that have been applied to Europe's path toward increasing integration.[73] Federalist theories emphasize the inherent benefits of a constitutional division of power as a focal point that tends to cause further political integration.

---

[71] On this see for example Krasner 1984, 242–3 and Spruyt 1994b, 23–4.
[72] Hart 1995, 47–51.
[73] On federalist theories of integration see Hesse and Wright 1996; Levi 1990.

While such a view is arguably applicable to the emergence of PITs in significant ways, by itself it is an insufficient explanation. Many territories and core
states throughout the world could benefit from partially independent unions
and yet they have not come into being. Similarly, numerous sovereign states
that have failed to provide basic levels of welfare and security have not evolved
into PITs. Furthermore, many populations throughout the world still aspire
for full independence (perceiving that it is the answer to many of their problems) even while there are widespread examples of failure. Some of the same
conditions exist with regard to regional integration. Many regions throughout
the world could arguably profit from EU-style integration which has provided
greater security and single market benefits since the first institutions were put
into place with the European Coal and Steel Community in 1952.[74] But the
EU remains a *sui generis* example of sovereignty pooling that has not spread
to other parts of the globe.[75] (The fact that PITs have, however, spread to many
areas of the world offers an opportunity to contribute to further understanding the origins of political integration.) Furthermore, as discussed in greater
detail in Chapter 9, there are rare cases in which a core–PIT division of power
can in fact cause political integration to diminish (rather than increase) as federalist theories would predict. For example, consistent with federalist theories,
Canada's post 1846 partially independent arrangement with the UK provided
significant advantages to the Canadians in the latter half of the nineteenth
century. Contrary to federalist theories, however, after the beginning of the
twentieth century many of Canada's leaders increasingly rejected the arrangement. The division of powers itself, which is the key causal element of federalist theories, became a bone of contention. In light of the absence of cases of weak
sovereign states opting for status as a PIT, the persistence of popularity among
some populations in favor of full independence, and cases in which the federal
bargain itself has been a source of dispute, federalist theories are by themselves
therefore insufficient to take into account the varying views of leaders and the
conditions in which they may reject the division of powers.

[74] Philpott 1999, 577.
[75] Given the unique *sui generis* nature of the European Union as the only instance in the
world of regional integration that pools sovereignty between a central government and a series
of sovereign states, the rich corpus of regional integration literature has repeatedly lamented the
absence of other instances of integration where existing theories can be applied and tested. The
existence of partially independent arrangements, however, presents a widespread dataset of cases
where theories of integration can potentially apply. Federalist, functionalist, neo-functionalist,
and intergovernmental theories of integration that have often been used to predict and chart the
course for European institutions could therefore potentially be employed to explain the rise of
partially independent territories. On the *sui generis* status of European integration see Caporaso
1997; Rosamond 2000, 175; Wallace 1994, 9.

Some related views (which have also been used to predict European integration) are equally tempting.[76] One popular view is the neo-functionalist theory of
integration.[77] According to this view, initial economic and political integration
between polities acts as a trigger that inevitably causes still more "spillover" of
integration into new domains of responsibility and geographic regions.[78] Another
view of the emergence of divided sovereign arrangements is intergovernmentalism.[79] This view argues that integration emerges because of the self-interested
decisions of sovereign state leaders (rather than the deterministic processes of
spillover or the inherent attractiveness of federal divisions of sovereign power).[80]

Integrationalist Arguments

The integrationalist theory introduced here has both similarities and differences with each of the other theories, but the causal focus is neither the

---

[76]　Two prominent theories (functionalist theories and transactionalist theories) that have
been used to attempt to predict the course of events in Europe have been excluded here as theories of integration because they do not focus on providing explanations for polities that have
decided to divide and share sovereign power. Functionalist theories emphasize the importance
of high levels of economic interdependence that tend to cause a fading importance of preexisting
political institutions and the rise of those that satisfy economic needs. While economic interdependence may indeed have an important role in moderating relations between distinct polities
(whether they are sovereign states or PITs), it is nevertheless well established that the predictions
of functionalist theorists that sovereign states would fade away have not come to pass. By contrast, the arguments here emphasize the sustained importance of political actors as rational decision makers. On functionalist theories of integration see Mitrany 1966. Similarly, Karl Deutsch's
theory of transactionalism has also been excluded as a theory of integration because he sees
integration as a "security community" of peaceful independent states rather than those that have
partially abolished fully independent state structures in favor of pooled sovereignty. Integration
he says is "the attainment, within a territory, of a 'sense of community' and of institutions and
practices strong enough and widespread enough to assure, for a 'long' time, dependable expectations of 'peaceful change' among its population." Deutsch et al. 1957.

[77]　For earlier neo-functionalist arguments see especially Haas 1968 and Lindberg 1970. For
newer variants see Tranholm-Mikkelsen, 1991, 11-25; Mattli and Slaughter 1995, 183-190.

[78]　Neo-functionalist theories of integration have been vigorously criticized for their determinism, in which they predict that initial political and economic integration necessarily unleashes
further integration that is out of the hands of decision makers to stop. As the economic historian
Alan Milward has written, such theories of integration suffer from "greatly exaggerating the inca-
pacity of the state." Milward asserts that it is sovereign state self-interest that produces integration
rather than the inevitable, determinism of spillover. "From the beginnings of detailed research
into the origins of the European Community" he says, "it became clear that nation-states had
played the dominant role in its formation..." Milward 2000, 10.

[79]　For earlier intergovernmental arguments see especially Hoffmann 1966, 862–915. For a
newer variant see Moravcsik 1998.

[80]　Intergovernmentalists like Andrew Moravcsik emphasize the economic advantages that
tend to accrue from integration (through single markets, monetary stability, mutual aide, etc.).
Mirroring the views of relational contracting scholars he observes that such advantages are,

Table 2.1. Comparative emergence causality of theories of integration

Theory of political integration	Causal variable
Federalist	Self-interest determinism: when a federal bargain is initiated its inherent benefits will cause automatic appeal, which then results in political integration
Neo-functionalist	Spillover determinism: when an act of political integration occurs, more integration necessarily follows
Intergovernmentalist	Sovereign state material self-interest: divisions of sovereignty and political integration will occur when sovereign states believe that their interests will be satisfied by an integrated union
Integrationalist	Institutional natural selection plus norms resetting catastrophe cause divisions of sovereignty and political integration

irresistible advantages of the bargain of federalist theories, the inevitable spillover of neo-functionalist theories, or the economically focused self-interest of sovereign states of intergovernmentalist theories (Table 2.1). Instead, the focus is on the availability of an equitable settlement for both a core state and territory based on both self-interested material calculations as well as the availability of normative conditions that are triggered by catastrophic events (punctuated equilibrium described below). Hence, similar to federalist theories, the view here is that partially independent unions do indeed have inherent advantages. But unlike federalist theories, such advantages are not deterministic—normative barriers can prevent actors from capitalizing on the benefits of the regime. Similar to neo-functionalist theories, the view here is that spillover does occur. But the spillover that takes place is not inevitable—it is a byproduct of core states and territories choosing to adopt integration because of their self-interest and normative conditions.[81] Similar to intergovernmentalist theories, the view

however, jeopardized by sovereign states that may usurp their commitments. He says that "to secure the substantive bargains they had made, finally, governments delegated and pooled sovereignty in international institutions for the express purpose of committing one another to cooperate." Morazvcsik 1998, ch. 1. For related views that apply relational contracting concepts to integration see Cooley and Spruyt 2009 and Rector 2009.

[81] While PITs are indeed spilling over internally within some states (as when after 1982 territories in Spain demanded *"café para todos"* (coffee for all) in response to the partially independent arrangements that were at first uniquely created for the Basque Country, Catalonia, and Galicia). They are also spilling over externally in the rest of the world (in terms of their precipitous growth since the nineteenth century). On the other hand, in other areas of the world they are not spilling over. In China, for example, the core state's hope that their vision of "one country, two systems" would spill over from Hong Kong to Taiwan has not yet materialized.

here is that actors respond to self-interest, but the actors involved include not only sovereign states—they also include the PIT. And without a revolutionary trigger event that is able to overcome preexisting norms that are hostile to divisions of sovereignty, actors are unable to act upon the self-interest that allows them to capitalize on the advantages of partially independent unions.

Accordingly, after examining the genesis of these arrangements, an arguably more accurate explanation emerges of the origins of PITs. Biologists such as Stephen Jay Gould and Niles Eldredge have acknowledged some aspects of Darwinian views which argue in favor of the survival of the fittest, in which organisms with better adaptations are more likely to survive.[82] What such scholars do not accept, however, is a purely deterministic (or ladder) view of natural selection in which evolution only takes place from more simple to more advanced organisms. What is missing is the role played by "punctuated equilibrium" in which sudden and dramatic changes lead to a "flurry of radical new forms" relative to their preexisting capabilities.[83] According to Gould and Eldredge, the fossil record indicates that most organisms remain in an equilibrium condition of stasis (in which they exhibit very little genetic variation overtime). Dramatic and sudden events, however, such as cataclysmic meteor strikes or widespread volcanic eruptions, disrupt the preexisting dominance of other life forms. This then makes way for the evolution of new organisms that are able to better master the new environmental conditions. Similarly, just as human beings or dinosaurs could not have evolved without the catastrophes that eliminated the dominance of preexisting life forms, some forms of human institutions (even those that are better adapted to prevailing conditions) cannot assert themselves without human catastrophes that sweep away (or "reboot") preexisting norms, expectations, and incentives. These crises can create political windows of opportunity within which more advantageous alternatives will have a chance to survive and establish themselves.

Accordingly, the origins of PITs almost always coincide with a catastrophic event or crisis that applies between a potential core state and a potential PIT. Such a crisis reorders perceptions, norms, and creates a political window of opportunity for the advantages of these arrangements to be utilized. It could be the threat to the core state of territorial fragmentation because of war with another breakaway territory (as with the emergence of the British Dominions after the loss of

---

And while there are significant numbers of PITs spread across the globe, very few of them have spilled over into South America, Africa, and the Middle East. The spillover that does exist for PITs therefore appears to be motivated less by an automatic and inevitable process (as viewed by neo-functionalists) than by the self-interested decisions of territorial leaders and sovereign states that have decided to adopt such an arrangement under some circumstances.

[82]   Gould and Eldredge 1977; Gould 1982.
[83]   Spruyt 1994b, 23–4.

the Thirteen Colonies or the emergence of Gagauzia after Moldova's war with Transnestria). It could be a surge in local nationalism that threatens the possibility of the territory's own full independence (as with the emergence of Northern Ireland and the Irish Free State in the early 1920s after the local backlash against the British following the 1916 Easter Uprising). It could be a revolutionary core state regime change that creates new opportunities for a division of power (as with the emergence of Hong Kong after the 1997 core state handover from the UK to China). It could be a creeping rise in the popularity of a secessionist party that threatens the fragmentation of the core state (as with the specter of the Scottish Nationalist Party helping to trigger British devolution in 1998 or the rise of the Parti Québécois helping to trigger Canada's 1982 constitutional entrenchment of treaties made with indigenous leaders in Nunavut). It could be the historical memory of actual fragmentation that results in new norms and standard operating procedures for preventing such a possibility (as with Denmark's 1918 loss of Iceland resulting in changed attitudes toward Greenland and the Faroe Islands as well as the conventional entrenchment of British Territories in the twentieth century after the loss of empire). Or it could be a combination of such factors. Indeed this mirrors the experience of the emergence of European integration, whose revolutionary pooling of sovereignty was punctuated by a history of devastating war that culminated with World War II.[84]

The presence of a more advantageous institutional alternative alone does not seem to be enough for change. One of the greatest dangers that humanity faces in the twenty-first century and beyond is the stagnant nature of sovereign state adaptation in the face of exponential technical and scientific development. Many listlessly wonder if humanity will ever be able to overcome the moral, self-rule, security, and resource collective action challenges that continue to threaten a planet mostly ruled by sovereign states. Sovereign states, nevertheless, remain in a state of relative stasis; after seven centuries, they have not evolved into a substantially different entity than their existence in the fourteenth century. However, there is a major exception to this. When core state leaders are made to confront terrible possibilities (such as war, territorial fragmentation, hurting stalemates, or other revolutionary change), the power of entrenched lobbies, dogmatic ideologies, and dominant norms, which are sometimes obstacles to rational change, can be neutralized in favor of institutional alternatives (such as partially independent arrangements) that are more suitable to fulfilling interests amidst the new prevailing conditions.[85]

It may, however, be useful to note a number of limitations to these observations. In order for a crisis to act as a trigger, a bilateral crisis must apply with

[84] Dinan 2005, ch. 1.
[85] For a compelling analysis, which also focuses on overcoming veto players, but as it applies to issues of decolonization, see Spruyt 2005.

respect to both a potential core state and a potential PIT. The creation of a PIT therefore does not arise in a wide range of catastrophic events (such as wars, environmental destruction, institutional collapse, economic disorder, etc.) that assail various parts of the globe. This perhaps explains why PITs tend not to emerge amongst failed states even while in some cases a mutually beneficial union could be created between them and another larger state. Rather, they tend to occur in cases where there has already been a deep and preexisting interaction whether through imperialism, overlapping nationalism, or war.[86]

It is also important to note that meteor strikes and the process of natural selection were not the only factors that helped give rise to humans or dinosaurs. Similarly, the combination of PIT institutional advantages with a crisis that assails a potential core and PIT are necessary but not sufficient conditions for their emergence. The fact that PITs often tend to beat out other institutional alternatives such as statehood and colonialism when local populations are given a choice, does not mean that even more attractive alternatives (such as full independence under some conditions) could not present themselves. As the next section and later chapters will emphasize, there are indeed times (such as when a core state increasingly lacks the capability to provide public goods) in which full independence tends to be a more satisfactory alternative.

Furthermore, conditions of bounded rationality can also prevent the emergence of PITs. Factors such as misunderstanding and lack of information make it impossible to guarantee that people and leaders will always be presented with a PIT as a choice. This perhaps explains why even more former colonies did not opt for a PIT amidst the mass decolonization and collapse of the European empires in the twentieth century. In light of the catastrophic performance of many former colonies since independence, however, some PIT leaders often justify their continued status by making their own observations of the plight of many of these sovereign states that remain weak or failed.[87]

THE MAINTENANCE OF PARTIALLY
INDEPENDENT TERRITORIES

As distinct from other theories of integration, the arguments presented here focus on not just how and when divisions of sovereignty occur but

---

[86] This point bears some similarity to Phillip Roeder's (2007) analysis of the modern origins of sovereign states because of the historic legacies of colonialism. The emphasis here, however, is a preexisting connection (which also includes war, full territorial assimilation, and overlapping nationalism) rather than necessarily preexisting colonial institutions, which as Roeder emphasizes sets the stage for greater degrees of future power.

[87] Author's interviews in Bermuda 2011.

the conducive conditions that cause them to maintain themselves and possibly fail.[88] Whether in the natural or social sciences, the factors that produce a phenomenon are not necessarily the same as those that sustain it.
In light of the above analysis on the emergence of PITs, it is tempting to conclude
that PITs sustain themselves mainly because of self-interested core–PIT calculations in reaction to punctuated equilibrium. Such factors do not, however, provide
an adequate explanation of the maintenance of these arrangements, especially in
light of a significant number of cases where such material advantages have declined
overtime while the risks and costs associated with the partnership have continued.
The deterioration of PIT advantages and fading memories of the revolutionary conditions that caused its emergence do not by themselves tend to induce regime failure. The argument here is that in order for a more accurate explanation, such purely
self-interested justifications should in many cases be wedded to normative factors.[89]

Possible Alternative Explanations

There are a number of other plausible explanations that might be considered
conditions that would tend to sustain or end a partially independent arrangement. One could plausibly speculate that core state wealth (as measured by GDP
per capita), rule of law (as measured by the World Bank's governance indicator),
military might (as measured by military spending), or geographic proximity
with the PIT could all be used to predict the maintenance or failure of PITs. Each
of these views postulates that relatively high degrees of such factors might work
to maintain the relationship between a PIT and a core state while their absence
would weaken it. However, none of these factors systematically[90] apply.

Among modern PITs that have maintained themselves for more than ten
years, in some cases PITs have a higher GDP per capita than the core state (as
in Hong Kong, Lichtenstein, the Cayman Islands, Monaco, etc.), while in others the PIT's GDP per capita is lower (as in Greenland, Puerto Rico, French
Polynesia, Netherlands Antilles,[91] and the Cook Islands). Similarly, some core

---

[88]   Interestingly, there is a scarcity of theories of integration that attempt to address such conditions. This may stem from the unique instance of European integration as well as the European
Union's continued enlargement since 1952 that may lead to perceptions that such a theory is not
needed. The present analysis will, however, examine conducive conditions in which PITs tend to
maintain themselves and potentially fail.

[89]   For works that similarly emphasize constructivist characteristics with regard to international hierarchy see Donnelly 2006, 2009; Hobson and Sharman 2005; Kang 2004, 2010; Keene
2002, 2007; Sharman 2011.

[90]   Here the word "systematic" refers to factors that "are persistent and have consistent consequences when the factors take a particular value. Nonsystematic factors are transitory: we cannot
predict their impact." King et al. 1994, 62.

[91]   In 2010 after mutual agreement with the Netherlands, the Netherlands Antilles has split
into two separate PITs: Curaçao and Sint Maarten.

states have a high rule of law ranking (such as the UK, the US, France, and the Netherlands) while others have a low or weak rating (such as China, Papua New Guinea, Tanzania, the Philippines, and Ukraine). Some core states have relatively high military spending (such as the US, China, the UK, and France) while others have much lower levels. Some PITs are distant from the core state (such as the Cayman Islands, Palau, New Caledonia, Faroe Islands, and Aruba), while others are territorially contiguous (such as Scotland, Sardinia, Gagauzia, Hong Kong, Nunavut, and Liechtenstein). Similar variation on GDP per capita, rule of law, military spending, and geographic proximity also apply to history's PITs that have come to an end. Each of these factors is therefore not persistent with respect to the maintenance or termination of partially independent arrangements.

Still another explanation is that PITs sustain themselves so long as the material self-interest that launched the relationship persists. They then unravel when such material self-interest disappears. Such a view also does not seem applicable to these regimes. While the arrangement is often initially characterized by dramatic events that allow the core state to capitalize on advantages provided by the PIT, in the long run PITs vary in terms of the advantages that they provide to the core state. Some do indeed continue to provide material advantages that are similar to those that launched the relationship. Hong Kong, for example, continues to serve as the world's largest source of foreign direct investment into China. Nunavut continues to provide Canada with preferential access to vast natural resources. Such material advantages could be viewed as providing a type of political-formal entrenchment (as distinct from entrenchment from purely legal or unwritten rules), which make an arrangement very difficult to change because of material influence. In other situations, however, the same material advantages that existed at the start of the arrangement no longer apply. This is for example the case with Puerto Rico (which was previously a more valuable military basing area on the approaches to the Panama Canal) or the Åland Islands (as a demilitarized zone which prevented a foreign power from using the islands as a staging area for an invasion of Finland). These latter territories now no longer provide the core states with the same level of advantages that existed in past periods. And while Bermuda and the Cayman Islands play important roles for diverting vast capital flows to London, British leaders have expressed concerns about the political and economic fallout for the UK that these territories might create. As a 1999 British white paper indicated with respect to these risks:

> Failure to tighten regulation could affect the stability of and confidence in financial markets and expose the UK to international criticism and to potential contingent liabilities. Furthermore, it could undermine our ability to combat financial

fraud, money laundering, terrorist funding and tax evasion, and undermine the effectiveness of financial sanctions. It could also undermine the UK's ability to press for higher standards of global financial regulation, and to encourage greater regulatory cooperation.[92]

If political-formal entrenchment (through the security or economic advantages that a territory provides) was the chief source for the maintenance of the arrangement by the core state, in light of the diminishing advantages that these territories provide in some cases, one could expect that many more arrangements would unravel at the behest of the core state. Examples of this are, however, difficult to find. While there are cases of territories quitting the arrangement (as with the historic British Dominions), there are almost no examples of core states doing this.[93]

The Marriage Metaphor

The argument here, therefore, combines both self-interest and normative rules to explain how these arrangements sustain themselves and potentially end. Since firms are especially known for advancing material interests, an even better analogy for the operation of core–PIT unions that embodies the argument here is the institution of marriage. While marriage no doubt has material advantages, it is also known for its application of values and norms.[94] Similar to negarchical core–PIT unions, in marriage both members make formal commitments and divide and share obligations, while maintaining aspects of their own independence. Material interests are certainly very important. As Chad Rector describes, polities can possess relationship specific assets, which are resources that are "more valuable while cooperation persists."[95] Relationship

---

[92] UK, Secretary of State for Foreign and Commonwealth Affairs, 1999.

[93] Perhaps one example of a core state quitting an existing PIT would be the UK's termination of Northern Ireland's arrangement in 1972 with the emergence of civil unrest in the territory. But there are two reasons why this is not a good example of a core state quitting an arrangement. First, the UK did not quit Northern Ireland in the sense that it did not abandon it to the anarchy of the international system (as with many imperial powers toward their colonies). Rather the UK retained control and continued to pour resources into the territory. Second, even while it terminated the arrangement for Northern Ireland, it presided over creating a new one for the territory in 1998.

[94] The fact that marriage is used to emphasize the operation of norms and values certainly does not mean that norms and values do not apply in business relations. On the contrary, as Williamson (1973, 1985, 1998) has emphasized, formal enforcement and moral rules (in addition to self-interest) are critical to reducing the possibility of market failure. While such factors also apply to firms, marriage arguably provides a better analogy for the salience of normative and value oriented behavior.

[95] Rector 2009, 16.

specific assets (like shared income, a home, belongings, and children) no doubt can play important roles in improving the credibility of mutual commitments. By holding such assets "hostage,"[96] commitments will tend to be upheld lest they be lost through divorce. Nevertheless, while the loss of such assets may be one factor, it is however not a good explanation for how marriage is normally sustained (at least healthy marriages). It is also arguably not the way core–PIT relations are usually maintained.

Again it is accepted here that such material factors play a necessary role when "unwedded" polities are considering the merits of the initial bond. However, for the maintenance of the relationship, even more important than such material elements are the values that are employed. More than income or belongings being held hostage, effective relationships (whether with marriages or partially independent unions) are fueled by trust, duty, fairness, communication, and mutual support. Although such factors can be manifested in many ways, such norms can be operationalized in core–PIT relations in the following ways: duty comes from constitutional commitments, trust from entrenched (very difficult to change) enforcement mechanisms, predictability from increasing behavioral precedents, fairness from a justifiable division of responsibilities based on capability, communication from shared institutions, and mutual support from outside assistance or fiscal transfers. Marriage is distinguishable from other relations among individuals (such as friendship or fleeting romantic interaction) by a commitment to such values. While they may indeed be imperfectly applied on occasion, the point is that marriage has these components while other more casual relations usually do not. Similarly, core–PIT relations are not perfect. Indeed, just as with married couples, some core states and territories apply such principles more effectively than others.

Limits and Modifications to the Marriage Metaphor

There are some important ways in which marriage departs from core–PIT relations as an effective model. Unlike marriage relationships, in which the partners involved by and large have equal potentialities,[97] core–PIT relations are built upon an inequality of capability. The difference in capability facilitates

---

[96]   On this as it applies to federal relations, see Rector 2009.

[97]   There is no doubt that societal constraints (such as gender prejudice) can unfairly hamper the potentialities of partners in marriage. The assumption here, however, is that if these constraints were absent, their capacities are by and large equal, in as much as both men and women have attained the highest degrees of achievement in all fields. Indeed, reflecting the arguments presented here, when women are treated unequally while their potentialities are the same this can create a strong sense of injustice.

the relationship. This is a major way in which the arguments presented here differ from those made about European institutions or federations, in which the inequality of power is often seen as a source of division and potential antagonism, in which the greater power of one party threatens the other.[98]

Mirroring symbiosis in the natural world, whether with the relationship between a sea anomie and a clown fish or between a cleaning wrasse and a shark, many forms of symbiosis are successful because of their differences of capability and power (rather than their equality). PITs are typically much smaller than the core state. They do not have the same amount of resources. By themselves they are less likely to have economies of scale (which is the condition in which the cost of economic and policy output decreases with an expanding scale of production).[99] Faced with such potential economic and security burdens as a small independent state, the likelihood of specialization is generally lower since investments in human capital and infrastructure need to be spread over a much larger scope of industries and political competencies (such as defense). From the perspective of a distinct territory it therefore makes sense for the core state to be responsible for expensive external defense and proxy aspects of trade and financial representation. Partially independent territories also have much to gain from the larger state's single market, citizenship privileges, emergency fiscal transfers, and internal constitutional guarantees. For their part, core states in many cases gain security and economic advantages from the arrangement, but exchange very little foreign affairs and domestic capabilities.

Much like individuals that give up some of their sovereignty in the state of nature (while nevertheless retaining enforceable rights and autonomy) in order to be part of civilization, PITs therefore share and divide aspects of sovereignty in exchange for the public goods that the larger core state provides. Accordingly, the sovereignty differential (the distribution of powers) in the relationship is therefore justified by a capability differential (the distribution of abilities and resources). From the perspective of the PIT, all other things equal, so long as this distinction persists, the relationship will be perceived as fair and therefore maintain itself. If, however, over time the capability differential equalizes, the sovereignty differential will be increasingly difficult to sustain. The capability differential tends to equalize when the PIT is increasingly able to provide the same level of public goods as the core state and conversely when the core state is increasingly hard pressed to furnish the same relative level of benefits. The benefits of defense, the advantages of a wide citizenship, the relative size of the single market, and other benefits will

---

[98] See Moravisik 1998; Rector 2009.   [99] Stimpert and Laux 2011, 47–56.

all shrink in comparison to what the territory could provide itself if it were to be on its own. This is more than a matter of loss of material benefits. It is a matter of fairness and (increasingly unjustifiable) inequality. The territory will more and more question not only the usefulness but the equitability of the relationship. This will in turn fuel opposition by local nationalists who will call for a better fulfillment of self-determination. Secession will therefore become more likely. If as a result of this, it is the territory's expressed will to leave, normative biases against departure will no longer apply with the same force.

The erosion of the norms against departure are not only caused by increasing equalization of capacity. Such change is also a function of the identity difference that prevails between both entities—while the nationalistic territorial reference in the relationship for the territory is the territory itself, the core's territorial reference is the overall state, which often overlaps with the territory. The core state however does not have the same impetus for change. The values perceptions and point of view of each policy is based on their differing national geographic references. For the PIT, their nationalistic perceptions tend to be "self-regarding"—their primary national geographic reference focuses on its own domestic territory. The "homeland" of Bermudans is Bermuda. The homeland of the Kurds are the Kurdish Territories. Its most salient values perceptions, such as its sense of fairness over the distribution of powers, is therefore in relation to its own territory. For the core state, however, nationalistic perceptions are "other-regarding"—their national geographic reference embraces the entirety of its international legal space, which eventually often includes the PIT. American leaders see its territories as part of America. British leaders see its territories as part of Britain.[100] This especially applies when the core state extends full citizenship to the citizens of PITs as has occurred with the US in Puerto Rico and the Northern Mariana Islands from the beginning or in Britain with its overseas territories after 2002.[101] The most salient values perceptions of the core state, such as its own sense of fairness, equitability, and identity is therefore in relation to perceptions of all parts of its state. Overtime what may have been an initial self-interested phase of extending a PIT status gives way to a variant of unwritten rules that already apply to the larger

---

[100]   Authors interviews 2011.

[101]   Largely in response to fears that there would be a mass exodus of Hong Kong citizens to the UK in the lead up to the changeover of the core state from Britain to China, the UK formulated a much more restrictive British Dependent Territories Citizenship after 1981, which applied to its territories excluding the Isle of Man, Guernsey, and Jersey. This status largely prevented a right of abode in the UK together with the privileges of working, free movement, and European Union benefits that it entails. In 2002, however, this ended, allowing the populations in British territories the same level of British citizenship as those in the core state.

state.[102] Unilaterally spinning off and deserting the territory against its will into full independence based on cold material calculations of economic or security self-interest becomes highly doubtful. Such abandonment becomes nearly as absurd as spinning off parts of the core state for the same reasons. Here again the marriage or family analogy becomes relevant. Just as there is a normative bias against abandoning one's long-time spouse or children because they provide less material advantages, there is a similar normative bias against doing so in the context of the core's relations with a territory. The equitability of the deal will, however, hinge on the presence of a substantial core–PIT capability difference that justifies the difference in sovereignty. As long as this substantial capability difference prevails and the core state is able to provide public goods advantages that a territory would have difficulty furnishing for itself, local populations and leaders will see the arrangement as fair.[103]

As long as a PIT has an equitable deal, the nationalism of the leaders and population of PITs will continue to be reassured and contained. It will convince them not to call for a continued drift toward full independence. Hence, the "other-regarding" nationalism of core states generally neutralizes it as a potential source of PIT secession. If tendencies toward secession materialize, they are generated from the PIT's self-regarding nationalism. When, however, the capability of the core state to furnish public goods erodes, the likelihood that nationalism will burst through its institutional confines will increase. In some cases a core state can attempt to prevent a rupture by adding further advantages to the arrangement. But the success of this effort depends upon the willingness for additional core state sacrifice as compared to the size of the nationalistic flood. Partially independent territories are therefore increasingly likely to emerge and maintain their status as the ability of the core state to furnish public goods is relatively large. They are, however, increasingly likely to fail as the ability of the core state to furnish public goods is relatively small.[104]

In other words, it can be postulated that as the size of the PITs GDP approximates that of the core state, the attractiveness and maintenance of the partially

---

[102] In a study of the Netherlands Antilles, Cook Islands, and the Faroe Islands, Jason Sharman (2011) observes that the balance of advantages in such arrangements often weigh more heavily with the territory rather than the core state. He emphasizes the importance of norms (rather than the interest of the core state) for maintaining the arrangements. But as distinct from the theory here, he argues that core states "self-identify as good international citizens, innocent of *realpolitik* motivations," which prevents them from quitting the arrangement. See Sharman 2011, 15.

[103] Chapter 9 will operationalize the degree of "substantial" capability difference that is required.

[104] Hooghe and Marks (2003) have emphasized the important advantages that central governments can play by providing economies of scale with their public goods. The argument presented here attempts to take this a bit further by acknowledging that the resulting advantages and viability of the partnership can erode with the decline of such scale.

independent arrangement will be in jeopardy. As will be described in greater detail in Chapter 9, this can be measured by dividing the core's GDP by the territory's GDP, which provides what can be called the core–PIT GDP ratio. The core–PIT GDP ratio is a conducive indicator similar to some indicators in other fields (like the price earnings ratio in the field of finance). It predicts the conditions that *tend to* lead to something rather than necessarily predicting such a result in all cases. As a consequence, the causal factors discussed here that have brought PITs into being, have sustained them, and in rare cases have led to their termination are neither necessary (the absence of causal variable A precludes the outcome B) nor sufficient (A insures the outcome B).[105] Instead, they are contributing or conducive conditions (A's presence increases the likelihood of B).[106]

In sum, as the core-PIT GDP ratio decreases and approaches near parity with the core state, the core has decreasing resources to deliver an attractive package of benefits to dissuade the PIT from secession. Partially independent territory termination is therefore increasingly likely. As the core to territory GDP ratio increases and moves away from parity with the core state, the core has increasing resources to deliver an attractive package of benefits to dissuade the PIT from secession. All other things being equal, PIT termination is therefore increasingly less likely.

As Chapter 9 will illustrate, measurements of the relative size of the core state as compared to the PIT correctly predict most of the PITs that have come to an end. This theory is also consistent with most of the partially independent arrangements that have emerged and maintained themselves. It can also serve as a reference to help determine conducive conditions for the appropriateness of PITs that have been proposed for the future in some of the world's most important real or potential flashpoints, such as Taiwan, Kashmir, the Palestinian Territories, and still others.

CONCLUSION

This chapter developed a causal story that explains (1) why states are weak; (2) why PITs have some important advantages over them; (3) why other negarchical alternatives are often less feasible; (4) why PITs emerge; and (5) why they maintain themselves and sometimes fail. In addition to these factors,

---

[105] On necessary and sufficient conditions see, Abernethy 2000, 25.
[106] On conducive conditions see, Abernethy 2000.

however, PITs underscore some significant changes to the structure and evolution of the international system. The next chapter will therefore illustrate how PITs contradict some widely held assumptions in the scholarly literature about unit composition and the structure of the international system.

Partially independent unions are usually born from dramatic events that pave the way for territories and states to capitalize on their economic, security, and self-determination benefits. If not disrupted by interest-oriented differences in the first few years, overtime the self-interest that launches the relationship often comes to be defined by trust and is sustained through the core state's sense of inclusive identity and the territory's sense of fairness. It is the ability of many core states and territories throughout the world to maintain this sense of identity and fairness that has allowed partially independent arrangements to surpass the performance of sovereign states in significant respects.

These arrangements are, however, not invincible and appropriate in every situation. In spite of the defensibility of the powers that are divided and the advantages that they provide, if the sense of fairness and shared identity between core and territory becomes weakened—and especially if the territory no longer sees the arrangement as fair—the relationship will have a tendency to unravel. Some arrangements are especially vulnerable in the first few years of a relationship (before rules have had a chance to be solidified by time, precedent, and attendant constitutional mores.) If either side—but especially the core state—repeatedly oversteps the bounds of its core–PIT agreement, the relationship could gradually slide into a sham federacy. (Sham federacies are neo-colonial polities with all the trappings of a PIT, except they do not have mechanisms that produce core–PIT credible commitments. These arrangements will be the subject of Chapter 6.)

While there can be great advantages when people manage to divide and share some sovereign powers in a partially independent arrangement, it is nevertheless not a panacea for the world's problems. Failed states will, for example, not normally have the ability to transform into PITs, nor will prospective core states always be able to join with a weaker state in this type of union just because it offers potential mutual advantages. The empirical record shows that the evolutionary advantages of PITs must be married to revolutionary events of core–PIT punctuated equilibrium before such a union can be viable. The emergence of PITs also does not overthrow the international system through unit replacement as sovereigns states did when they beat out competing polities from the fourteenth to the eighteenth centuries. Indeed, PITs by definition cannot exist without being associated with an existing sovereign state. In spite of these points, however, the argument in this book is that partial independence represents a real and often superior alternative to statehood.

This chapter has built on the literatures of nationalism, MPF, and relational contracting to illustrate the logic and theoretical justification of why PITs cause nationalistic accommodation, security, and economic growth. It has also built on theories of political integration as well as the assumptions and regularities addressed in Chapter 1 to provide a set of arguments that sets forth some conducive conditions for the origins, maintenance, and possible termination of PITs. Critical to these literatures, however, is the ability to produce credible commitments between distinct populations. Part II will therefore draw on empirical cases to explain the mechanisms which produce credible commitments between PITs and core states. The next chapter will begin by distinguishing PITs from other political units and placing them into the context of existing debates about the nature of sovereignty and the structure of the international system.

Part II

Self-determination

3

Domestic and International Structural Amendment

With the Americans to feed us and the British to defend us, who needs independence?

—Sir John Swan, Premier of Bermuda, 1982

International relations theorists have struggled to develop explanations of change in the international system that might theorize how views of state-centered organization could be altered or amended.[1] A deep and beneficial literature has provided explanations for the development of the sovereign state.[2] But the central focus of this literature has been on where the state system has come from rather than on post-seventeenth-century phenomena (such as nationalism and globalization) that might point to where such a system is now going.[3] Others, especially in the 1960s and 1970s sought to argue that the state system is indeed changing, since the sovereign state is becoming increasingly irrelevant.[4] But this view has arguably not stood the test of time as the state still seems to be overridingly important in the international system in spite of the existence of various significant transnational forces and actors, which in any case do not possess constitutionally allocated sovereign power.[5] Still others have rightly pointed out that the emergence of the pooled sovereignty of European integration is an example of the emergence of a new form of territorial sovereignty.[6] As indicated previously, territorial sovereignty can be described as a polity's powers of de facto and de jure

---

[1] See Dessler 1989; Gilpin 1981; Ruggie 1989; 1993; Waltz 1979; Wendt and Duvall 1989; Wendt 1987.

[2] See, Hall 1985; 1986; Skocpol 1985; Spruyt 1994a; 1994b; Strayer 1970; Tilly 1990.

[3] Anderson 1991.

[4] See Herz 1957, 473–93; 1968; Vernon 1971.

[5] See Krasner 1991, 336–6; and Thomson and Krasner 1989, 198.

[6] See Keohane and Hoffmann 1991, 1–39; Philpott 2001b, 39–40; Ruggie 1993, 172.

priority in some respects over a territory.[7] But while it may be true that other forms of regional integration are emerging, as with the case of the North American Free Trade Agreement (NAFTA), the Southern Common Market (Mercosur), the Asia Pacific Economic Cooperation (APEC), and the Association of South East Asia Nations (ASEAN), nevertheless, no regional organization—apart from the European Union (EU)—has been able to manifest attributes of territorial sovereignty.[8] And so, given the seeming absence of other organizational forms that currently compete with states for sovereign power, some scholars have concluded that states are the sole constitutive unit of the international system. Sovereign states are seen as the only systematically present repositories of territorially-based sovereignty.[9]

As distinct from the aforementioned views, this book suggests that a newly apparent, widespread, and partially independent governmental form has in fact emerged in the international system which is a constitutive unit of the international system and successfully competes with sovereign states for territorial control. The competition that takes place between PITs and sovereign states is not usually an adversarial contest. Indeed core–PIT relations are frequently characterized by mutual agreement and cooperative synergy. The competition that does, however, exist is between the alternatives of sovereign statehood (whether through secession or political assimilation) as compared to the alternative of partial independence. The existence of such a polity arguably leads to a changed ontological view of the world system, which is similar in some respects to the overlapping sovereignties before the advent of the modern state system in the seventeenth century.[10] These PITs,[11] possess measures of credible jurisdictional priority and have reshaped and unbundled the sovereign territoriality of many states.[12] This therefore leads to an amendment to the structure of the international system, in which PITs are partially breaking away from sovereign states into a partially independent orbit of their own in the twilight between full independence and full assimilation.

[7] See, e.g., Bunck and Fowler 1996; Jackson 1987, 529; Tilly 1990. See also Barkin and Cronin 1994; Bartleson 1996; Biersteker and Weber 1996; Hall 1999; Hinsley 1986; Jackson 1999; James 1986; Philpott 2001a, 297–324; 2001b.

[8] Caporaso 1997; Rosamond 2000, 175; Wallace 1994, 9.

[9] See Spruyt 1994b, 3–6; and Wendt 1999, 9–10.

[10] By "ontological view of the world system" I mean "the metaphysical concern with the essence" of the international system, especially the chief units that compose it. On ontology see Landman 2000, 15; Lawson 1997, 15.

[11] For the nascent literature (including those who have used the synonymous term "federacy") see Anderson 2012; Coppieters 2001; Elazar 1991; 1993; 1994; 1997; Ghai 2000; Jakobson 2005; McGarry 2007; O'Leary 2001; 2002; 2005; 2013a; 2013b; Rezvani 2004; 2007a; 2007b; 2012; Stepan, Linz, and Yadav 2010; Stepan 2013; Stevens 1977; Watts 1996.

[12] On "unbundling" of territory see Ruggie 1993, 165.

Central to this international structural amendment (as well as the wealth, security, and evolutionary causal assertions of this book) is that PITs possess some powers of territorial sovereignty. Accordingly, this chapter will focus on the credibility and nature of the powers possessed by PITs as compared to other polities in the international system. It is important to inquire into the means that exist to make the powers that have been allocated to a putative PIT difficult to take away, defensible, real, and not mere paper promises that are unilaterally changeable by the whim of a core state. Such credibility mechanisms overcome what Barry Weingast calls "the fundamental political dilemma of an economic system" in which a sovereign state "strong enough to protect property rights and enforce contracts is also strong enough to confiscate the wealth of its citizens."[13]

Weingast points out the gap in the literature on such issues. "One of the central limits of the literature," he observes, "is that few scholars actually provide a complete analysis of any mechanism purported to provide such credible commitments."[14] He also emphasizes that "we remain remarkably ignorant about how constitutions affect credible commitments to secure economic rights and, more generally, limited government."[15] Similarly, economists, such as Nobel laureate Oliver Williamson, also emphasize the need for political, moral, and formal credibility mechanisms to overcome the problems of anarchy.[16] This second part of the book will therefore attempt to address this epistemological gap as it relates to the jurisdictional priority (the credible final decision-making power) that is at the root of the wealth and security advantages that PITs tend to possess.

This chapter will begin by comparing the existing international system to the preexisting era in world affairs in which there were overlapping sovereignties. This will set the stage for elaborating upon the characteristics that distinguish PITs from other polities in the international system as a modern version of overlapping jurisdiction. Because of the critical role played by territorial sovereignty emphasized by the arguments on nationalism, market preserving federalism, and relational contracting made in Chapter 2, the chapter will also map out some of the formal and informal causal processes through which partially independent arrangements produce final decision-making powers that are credible.[17] The next chapters in Part II will attempt to widen an understanding

---

[13] Weingast 1995, 3.
[14] Weingast 1995, 3.
[15] Weingast 1995, 3.
[16] See Williamson 1973, 1985, 1998.
[17] The terms "partially independent *arrangement*" and "sham federacy *arrangement*" are used to denote the union between a sovereign state and a partially independent polity or sham federacy unit. When, however, the term "arrangement" is omitted in favor of "unit," "polity," or simply referring to these regimes as PITs or sham federacies, reference is being made to the territorially fixed, defined, and constitutionally differentiated PIT or sham PIT.

of constitutional credibility and self-determination through case studies on the concept of conventional entrenchment, the limits of partial independence, and sham federacy. Part III will then turn to the empirical economic, security, and evolutionary characteristics of PITs.

INTERNATIONAL ORDER AND CHANGE

Some scholars, especially international relations realists such as Kenneth Waltz, have reacted to polities with distinctive allocations of territorial sovereignty by ignoring them and choosing to see sovereignty as either being monolithically attributable to the sovereign state as a whole or not at all.[18] As described by Hans Morganthau "if sovereignty means supreme authority, it stands to reason that two or more entities—persons, groups of persons, or agencies—cannot be sovereign within the same time and space."[19] This view is similar to the age-old idea of *imperium in imperio*: two sovereign authorities cannot coexist within one polity.[20] By contrast to this, much of the legal and political science literature adopts the view that sovereignty is not only attributable to a state as a whole but can be divided.[21] It can be horizontally divided between branches of government within a polity as well as vertically divided between distinct yet overlapping polities.[22] From this perspective, sovereignty is a type of power that defines governmental forms that have degrees of de facto and de jure jurisdictional priority across human history, rather than an ahistoric description of the sovereign state itself. Powers of supreme (or final) authority and control have been applied by scholars of state formation to the first city-states

---

[18] Bunck and Fowler 1996, 64. Bunck and Fowler describe what is referred to here as "monolithic sovereignty" as "chunk sovereignty." The word "chunk," however, is arguably more of a metaphor that conveys a piece of something (which is the opposite of what Bunck and Fowler are trying to convey) rather than a form that is indivisible. The word "monolithic" is therefore used here instead.

[19] Morgenthau 1948/1993, 341.

[20] Rakove 1996, 182.

[21] See Agnew 2005; Bunck and Fowler 1996; Keene 2002, 44; Keohane 2003; Krasner 1999; Lake 2003, 309; 2007; Osiander 2001.

[22] Although populations and branches of government can possess some sovereign powers within the internal framework of a territorial unit, they are not themselves constitutive units of the international system comparable to sovereign states and PITs. As the historic composition of fiefdoms, city-states, loosely configured empires, city-leagues, and territorial states have shown, while powers of sovereignty may be a necessary characteristic for a constitutive unit, it is not sufficient. In order to exist as a constitutive unit, overarching dominion (rather than an existence as one element within a government) over a particular territory and unit-to-unit interaction with other territorial entities is also arguably required.

in 6000 BC and to some of the organizational forms in the present, as described in this chapter.[23] By asserting that such sovereign powers can only be held by sovereign states and by assuming that this power cannot be divided, monolithic sovereignty theorists miss an understanding of how other actors that possess this power affect international affairs. They also deny an understanding of how the structure of the international system has changed in the past and continues to change as the future unfolds. In the final analysis, the monolithic view of sovereignty is historically, politically, and constitutionally more myth than reality. Even from as early as the fifteenth century, those such as Dutch Jurist Hugo Grotius acknowledged that sovereignty can be divided.[24]

Unlike many neo-realists, constructivist scholars of international relations perceptively recognize that sovereignty and the structure of the international order are subject to change.[25] Before the seventeenth century, sovereign states did not have a monopoly of territorial control and external jurisdiction.[26] As Joseph Strayer and Dana Munro explained, this pre-seventeenth century period was a "patchwork of overlapping and incomplete rights of government."[27] Perry Anderson also described it as a systemic environment in which "different juridical instances were geographically interwoven and stratified, and plural allegiances, asymmetrical suzerainties and anomalous enclaves abounded."[28] It was a condition in which "few authorities held" total "supremacy within a territory."[29] In nascent sovereign states like France, Spain, England, and other areas of Europe before the seventeenth century, there could simultaneously be a king in a particular region in addition to elements of the nobility, papacy, loosely configured empires, city-states, and still other entities that were also to one degree or another in control of the same territorial space. Nascent sovereign states during this period were similar to Swiss cheese[30] in which the royal-controlled domains (the solid cheese) were pock marked by holes in which they were compelled to share control with warlords and other actors. Under these circumstances of overlapping authority the sense of what was "international" and what was "domestic" was impossible to discern.[31] The word "international" (and other qualities that are associated with it) would

---

[23] Tilly 1990. John Ruggie 1983 has also emphasized that in different historic eras such powers give rise to a "hegemonic form" of political relations.

[24] Lake 2003, 309. See also Keene 2002, 44.

[25] See Dessler 1989; Jackson 1993, 111–38; Kratochwil 1986; Lustick 1993; Onuf 1989; Philpott 2001a, 297–324; 2001b, and Ruggie 1993.

[26] Anderson 1974; Ruggie 1993, 149; Strayer 1970; Strayer and Munro 1959.

[27] Strayer and Munro 1959.

[28] Anderson 1974.

[29] Philpott 2001a, 310.

[30] Spruyt 1994b.

[31] Holzgrefe 1989, 11–26; Kratochwil 1986, 27–52; Ruggie 1983, 261–85; Spruyt 1994b, 12.

only become relevant after states largely excluded all other competing forms of territorial sovereignty after the seventeenth century.

Constructivists also recognize the importance of constitutive rules—the foundational rules of the international system that "define the holders of basic authority and their most essential prerogatives."[32] According to John Ruggie, and much of the state formation literature, the differentiation of polities should therefore not be ignored. Others such as Robert Gilpin sustain this view.[33] Gilpin concedes that sovereign states are not the only possible constitutive unit and indeed argues that the most fundamental form of change in the international system is that of unit change. This perspective has set the stage for a number of scholars to argue in favor of the EU as a modern—albeit sui generis—example of a multiperspectival polity.[34] Multiperspectival polities are governmental forms that have overlapping territorial control similar in some sense to the diverse entities that competed with the state before the advent of the modern state system in the seventeenth century.[35] The point here is that the same argument may also be used as the basis for seeing partially independent polities in a similar light.

DISTINGUISHING PARTIALLY INDEPENDENT TERRITORIES FROM OTHER GOVERNMENTAL FORMS

Partially independent territories are nationalistically distinct polities that share and divide some sovereign powers with a sovereign state (a core state) while being constitutionally unincorporated. For a summary of how the aforementioned features of PITs compare to other political forms see Table 3.1. They possess most of the powers over their domestic affairs, some powers over foreign policy, but no powers over the external use of the military. "Domestic" powers refer to the exercise of effective control over the territory and population within the PIT's borders in certain respects. [36] Although external defense and forms of diplomatic relations are exercised on their behalf by a core state, PITs frequently negotiate their own treaties with other states and are members

---

[32] Philpott 2001a.
[33] Gilpin 1981.
[34] Dessler 1989, 441–73; Ruggie 1989, 21–35; Wendt 1987, 335–70; Wendt and Duvall 1989, 51–73.
[35] Ruggie 1993, 172.
[36] Krasner 1999; Lapidoth 1997; Tilly 1990.

Table 3.1 Defining characteristics of partially independent territories as compared to other polities

	Legally allocated final decision-making powers	Constitutionally unincorporated within a core state	Nationalistically distinct	Presence of entrenched powers	Some authority *and* control over foreign affairs
Partially independent territories	Yes	Yes	Yes	Yes	Yes
Sovereign states	No	No	Yes	Yes and no**	Yes
Colonies and protectorates	No	Yes	Yes	No	No
Federation member-units	Yes	No	Yes and no*	Yes	No
Sham federacies	Yes	Yes	Yes	No	No
De facto states	No	Yes	Yes	Yes and no**	No
Warlords	No	Yes	Yes and no	No	No

* Member-units within ethnofederations (like Switzerland) are nationalistically distinct. Those within more culturally homogenous federations (like the US federation) are not.

** While sovereign states and de facto states do not have powers that are constitutionally guaranteed by a core state, they may have domestic constitutions that guarantee powers as well as some external guarantees from third party states. For example, the de facto state of Taiwan is to some degree protected by guarantees from the United States in the 1979 Taiwan Relations Act that it will defend the territory if attacked.

of international organizations that are usually reserved for sovereign states. For example, many of the PITs that are associated with the UK (such as Bermuda, the Cayman Islands, the Isle of Man, and the Channel Islands) have negotiated their own Tax Information Exchange Agreements with other countries.[37] Furthermore, as illustrated by Liechtenstein and Monaco's membership in the United Nations, Hong Kong's membership in the International Monetary Fund (IMF), or Åland's membership in the Nordic Council, the majority of PITs are also members of international organizations. (For a comprehensive listing of membership of PITs in 103 of the world's international organizations see Table 3.2).

Partially independent territories are nationalistically distinct because they have distinct populations that believe that they (and not another national group) ought to govern the nature of their political reality within the confines of a specific territory. This definition of nationalism is based on a similar though distinct definition from Ernest Gellner.[38] Gellner's definition acknowledges the essential combination of a cultural, territorial, and political unit, but nevertheless conceives of nationalism as ultimately aspiring toward the attainment of sovereign statehood (culture–state congruence). The definition offered here, by contrast, leaves open the possibility that national groups may choose an alternative that best suits their interests (whether such an alternative is sovereign statehood or some other outcome such as partial independence).[39]

Partially independent territories are also constitutionally unincorporated in the sense that they have a distinct set of constitutional rules that apply to them as compared to those that prevail within the core state with which they are associated.[40] The institutions of unincorporated polities do not have the same rights, status, and powers when compared to other areas of the core state. Indeed, this has been a common feature among colonies, in which the imperial metropole applied one set of rules to its home territory (which often included human rights protection and democratic representation) while the populations of periphery territories were bereft of such benefits. A similar distinction prevails between core states vis-à-vis PITs. The US Supreme Court conveyed this reality when it declared that such units are constitutionally "unincorporated" and therefore not recognized "as an integral part" of the rest of the country.[41] They are "foreign in a domestic sense."[42] Hence, in both unitary states and federations, PITs have a distinct set of constitutional rules that apply to them as opposed to other areas of the core state.

---

[37] Foot 2009, 10.   [38] Gellner 1983, 1
[39] Gellner 1983.   [40] For a similar conclusion see Cooley 2005, 27–8.
[41] See *Downes v Bidwell*, 1901.   [42] *Downes v Bidwell*, 1901.

Table 3.2. Partially independent territories diplomatic interaction as measured by international organization membership

Partially independent territory	International organization membership and interaction	Index of international organizations that have partially independent polities as members
Åland Islands	EU (Representation), NC	ACP (African, Caribbean and Pacific Group of States)
Azores	EU (Representation)	AC (Arctic Council)
		ADB (Asian Development Bank)
		APEC (Asia-Pacific Economic Cooperation)
Aruba	Caricom (observer), ILO, IMF, INTERPOL, IOC, ITUC, UNESCO (Associate member), UNWTO (Associate member), UPU, WCL, WFTU, WMO	AT (Antarctic Treaty)
		CARICOM (Caribbean Community)
		CE (Council of Europe)
		CW (Commonwealth)
Basque Country	EU interaction (Delegation of the Basque Country to the EU)	CTBT (Comprehensive Nuclear Test Ban Treaty)
		EBRD (European Bank for Reconstruction and Development)
		EFTA (European Free Trade Association)
		EU (European Union)**
Bermuda	Caricom (Associate member), Interpol (Subbureau), IOC, ITUC, OECD (Interaction), UPU, WCO, WFTU	FAO (Food and Agriculture Organization)*
		IAEA (International Atomic Energy Agency)
		ICAO (International Civil Aviation Organization)
		ICC (International Criminal Court)
Bougainville	N/A	ICJ (International Court of Justice)
		ICAO (International Civil Aviation Organization)
		ICRM (International Red Cross and Red Crescent Movement)
Catalonia	EU interaction (Delegation of the Government of Catalonia to the EU)	IFAD (International Fund for Agricultural Development)
		IFRCS (International Federation of Red Cross and Red Crescent Societies)
		IHO (International Hydrographic Organization)

(*Continued*)

Table 3.2. (Continued)

Partially independent territory	International organization membership and interaction	Index of international organizations that have partially independent polities as members
Cayman Islands	Caricom (Associate member), CDB, INTERPOL (Subbureau), IOC, UNESCO (Associate member), UPU, WFTU	ILO (International Labor Organization) IMF (International Monetary Fund) IMO (International Maritime Organization)* IMSO (International Mobile Satellite Organization)
Cook Islands	ACP, ADB, CW (Associate Member), CTBT, FAO, ICAO, ICC, ICRM, IFAD, IFRCS, IMO, IMSO, IOC, OPCW, PC, PIF, RCRC, UNESCO, WHO, WMO	INTERPOL (International Criminal Police Organization) IOC (International Olympic Committee) IPU (Inter-parliamentary Union) ITSO (International Telecommunications Satellites Organization)
		ITU (International Telecommunication Union) ITUC (International Trade Union Confederation) LU (Latin Union) MIGA (Multilateral Investment Geographic Agency)
Faroe Islands	AC, FAO (Associate member), IMO (Associate member), NC, NIB, UPU	NC (Nordic Council) NIB (Nordic Investment Bank) NPT (Nuclear Non-Proliferation Treaty) OECD (Organization for Economic Cooperation and Development)**
French Polynesia	FZ, ITUC, PC, PIF (Associate member), UPU, WMO	OIC (Organization of the Islamic Conference) OIF (International Organization of the French-speaking World) OPCW (Organization for the Prohibition of Chemical Weapons) OSCE (Organization for Security and Cooperation in Europe)

Table 3.2. (Continued)

Partially independent territory	International organization membership and interaction	Index of international organizations that have partially independent polities as members
Gagauzia	N/A	PCA (Permanent Court of Arbitration) PC (Pacific Community) PIF (Pacific Islands Forum)* RCRC (Red Cross and Red Crescent)
Greenland	AC, IMF, IOC, NC, NIB, UPU	UN (United Nations) UNCTAD (United Nations Conference on Trade and Development) UNESCO (United Nations Educational, Scientific, and Cultural Organization) UNICEF (United Nations Children's Fund)
Guernsey	OECD (Interaction), UPU, British-Irish Council	UNIDO (United Nations Industrial Development Organization) UNPO (Unrepresented Nations and Peoples Organization) UNWTO (United Nations World Tourism Organization)*
Hong Kong	ADB, APEC, BIS, ICC, IHO, IMF, IMO (Associate member), IOC, ITUC, WCO, WMO, UNWTO (Associate member), UPU, WCL, WFTU, WMO, WTO	UPU (Universal Postal Union) WB (World Bank) WCL (World Confederation of Labor)
Isle of Man	British-Irish Council, OECD (Interaction), UPU	WCO (World Customs Organization) WFTU (World Federation of Trade Unions) WHO (World Health Organization)
Jersey	British-Irish Council, OECD (Interaction)	WIPO (World Intellectual Property Organization) WMO (World Meteorological Organization)
Kurdish Territories	UNPO	WTO (World Trade Organization)

(*Continued*)

Table 3.2. (Continued)

Partially independent territory	International organization membership and interaction	Index of international organizations that have partially independent polities as members
Liechtenstein	CE, CTBT, EBRD, EFTA, IAEA, ICJ, ICC, ICRM, IFRCS, INTERPOL, IOC, IPU, ITU, ITSO, NPT, OPCW, OECD (Interaction), OSCE, PCA, RCRC, UN, UNCTAD, UPU, WIPO, WTO	
Madeira	EU (Representation), UNWTO (Associate member)	
Marshall Islands	ACP, ADB, FAO, IAEA, ICAO, ICC, IFAD, ILO, IMO, IMF, IMSO, INTERPOL, IOC, ITU, NPT, OPCW, PC, PIF, UN, UNCTAD, UNESCO, WB, WHO, UNWTO (Associate member), WTO	
Micronesia	ACP, ADB, CTBT, FAO, ICAO, ICRM, IFRCS, IMF, IOC, ITU, ITSO, NPT, OPCW, PC, PIF, RCRC, UN, UNCTAD, UNESCO, WB, WMO, WHO	
Monaco	AT, CE, CTBT, FAO, IAEA, ICAO, ICC, ICRM, IFRCS, IHO, IMSO, IMO, INTERPOL, IPU, ITU, ITSO, LU, NPT, OIF, OIC, OPCW, OSCE, RCRC, UN, UNICEF, UNCTAD, UNESCO, UNIDO, UNWTO, UPU, WIPO, WMO, WHO	
Netherlands Antilles	INTERPOL, ILO, IMF, IOC, UNESCO (Associate member), UNWTO (Associate member), WCO, WMO, WTO	
New Caledonia	ITUC, PC, PIF (associate member), UPU, WFTU, WMO	
Niue	ACP, CW (Associate Member), FAO, IFAD, OPCW, PC, PIF, UNESCO, WMO, WHO	
Northern Ireland	EU interaction (The Office of the Northern Ireland Executive in Brussels), British-Irish Council	
Northern Mariana Is.	PC, UPU	

Table 3.2. (Continued)

Partially independent territory	International organization membership and interaction	Index of international organizations that have partially independent polities as members
Nunavut	N/A	
Palau Islands	ACP, ADB, APEC, CTBT, FAO, IAEA, ICAO, ICRM, IDA, IFC, IFRCS, IMF, IOC, IPU, ITU, MIGA, OPCW, PCA, PIF, UNICEF, UN, UNCTAD, UNESCO, WB, WHO	
Puerto Rico	Caricom, FAO (Associate member), (Observer), INTERPOL (Subbureau), IOC, ITUC, UNWTO (Associate member), UPU, WCL, WFTU	
Scotland	EU interaction (Scottish Government European Union Office), British-Irish Council	
Trentino-South Tyrol	N/A	
Vojvodina	EU interaction (Vojvodina Representation Office)	
Wales	EU interaction (Welsh Government European Union Office), British-Irish Council	
Zanzibar	AU, FAO (Associate member), INTERPOL, OIC, UN, UPU, UNPO, WHO	

Data drawn from <http://www.worldstatesmen.org/> and the CIA's World Fact Book, 2008.

* Regular and Associate memberships as the case may be.

** Formal governmental interaction without membership.

Hence PITs are (1) nationalistically distinct, (2) constitutional unincorporated, and (3) possess some authority and control over foreign affairs. As discussed in greater detail in the next sections, PITs also possess powers of sovereignty through (4) legally allocated final decision-making powers (whether by statute, judicial decision, executive order, or constitutional provision) that are (5) entrenched (which means that there is a mechanism in place that defends such legal promises from usurpation by the arbitrary whim of the core state). In addition to defining PITs, these features can also be used to distinguish them from other polities in the international system. Just as there was a wide variety of distinctive governmental forms that existed before the advent of the modern state system (such as fiefdoms, city-leagues, city-states, and loosely configured empires), a wide range of entities also exist today that are unincorporated into the normal constitutional system of a sovereign state. A variety of such political forms, including sovereign states, autonomy, segment states, devolution, colonies, protectorates, associate states, and federation member-units fail to embody the characteristics of PITs articulated above and in Table 3.1.

Sovereign States

As illustrated in Table 3.1, PITs are not fully independent sovereign states because they formally divide what would otherwise be their sovereignty with a core state. Of special interest on this issue is a series of polities, like the Federated States of Micronesia, Palau, Liechtenstein, Monaco, and the Marshall Islands that are recognized by the United Nations as sovereign states while in fact they divide and share sovereignty with another state. It is arguably important to look beyond official titles for evidence of a territory's status. As a range of scholars have confirmed, such arrangements are not sovereign states.[43] They do not conform to widely recognized definitions of sovereign statehood (as with the Montevideo definition that was provided at the outset of Chapter 2). While they retain nearly all of their domestic sovereignty, they have ceded some of their diplomatic capabilities and all of their external defensive capabilities to a core state. For example, with regard to the case of Liechtenstein, international law scholar Ruth Lapidoth observes that since "Liechtenstein has transferred a considerable part of its powers to Switzerland" it is not fully independent.[44] Rather than being fully independent, Liechtenstein's transfer of defense and many foreign affairs powers to Switzerland makes it partially independent—it is nationalistically distinct, constitutionally unincorporated into Switzerland, and possesses some but not all sovereignty that it would otherwise possess if it were a fully independent sovereign state. Similarly, in spite of their membership and recognition by international organizations such as the United Nations, Micronesia, the Marshall Islands, and Palau each have provisions in their compacts with the US that allocate sovereignty over military and some foreign affairs matters to America. In Palau's Compact of Free Association, for example, it says that "the Government of the United States has full authority and responsibility for security and defense matters in or relating to Palau."[45] Nor

---

[43] See e.g. Elazar 1994, 132; Korn 1991, 191–3.

[44] Lapidoth 1997, 62–3.

[45] Palau, Compact of Free Association 1986 (Amended in 2003), Section 311.

are PITs de facto states (like Taiwan, Nagorno Karabakh, or Abkhazia) because their powers are guaranteed by a core state and they possess both control and authority over some foreign affairs issues (such as membership in international organizations and the ability to conclude foreign trade agreements).[46]

Autonomy

Partially independent territories are also distinct from a wide range of other political forms that have been referred to with terms such as "autonomy." Indeed, scholars emphasize the cacophony of differing views and widely different definitions of "autonomy."[47] "Autonomy" can, for instance, refer to the transfer of rights to individuals.[48] As with the concept of personal (or cultural) autonomy, it can exist when autonomous powers are allocated to a distinct group on the basis of group membership rather than territorial location.[49] It can mean the absence of the imposition of power by a great power over one or more states in the international system.[50] It can refer to the powers exercised by colonies, although final decisions are in the hands of the central state.[51] It can refer to territories, such as the Palestinian Territories (1995–2001) that have final decision-making powers, but do not have a mechanism to entrench the powers that they exercise.[52] The term "segment state" is a similarly broad category that includes a wide range of constitutionally asymmetric and nationalistically distinct territories.[53] It combines distinctive regimes like colonies, protectorates, and PITs into a single category. Still another term like this is "devolution" which is frequently used to denote the delegation of *non*-sovereign power to a territory as well as the allocation of a limited range of autonomous powers.[54]

Colonies

Similar to PITs, colonies are polities that are nationalistically distinct and constitutionally unincorporated. However, unlike PITs, which have powers of domestic sovereignty in some categories, the full constitutional powers of

---

[46] On de facto states seek King 2001, 524–52.
[47] See for example Lapidoth 1997, 51–2.
[48] See Dahl 1982, 196–7.
[49] See Lapidoth 1997, 37–40. The condition for Eastern Slavonia (Croatia) after 1998 is perhaps an example of what Ruth Lapidoth calls personal autonomy. On this see Caspersen 2003.
[50] See Merom 2003, 113.
[51] See Cooley 2005.
[52] On autonomy see also Hannum 1990.
[53] See Roeder 2007.
[54] See Bogdanor 1999, 2–3 and 293.

colonies are under the ultimate control of another state.[55] For an exhaustive list of these polities after 1945 see Appendix 3. Examples of modern colonies include Christmas Islands (Australia), Torros Straight Islands (Australia), Cocos Islands (Australia), Anguilla (UK), Montserrat (UK), South Georgia (UK), South Sandwich Islands (UK), St. Helena (UK), Pitcairn Island (UK), Virgin Islands (US), Guam (US), French overseas departments (Guadeloupe, French Guiana, Martinique, and Réunion), and French territorial collectivities (Mayotte and Saint-Pierre-et-Miquelon). Although today France accords its remaining nationalistically distinct territories with a package of representation and rights that is more similar to what is applied in France itself as compared to the past, Robert Aldrich and John Connell still observe that the status of these overseas territories possess attributes of constitutional asymmetry since they are not identical to governmental sub-divisions within France itself.[56]

Protectorates

With regard to protectorates, much of the literature sees them as fully subordinate and constitutionally unincorporated territories which exercise delegated powers over most of their internal affairs, while their external relations and defense are exercised by their core state.[57] In other words, protectorates are essentially colonies except they have been delegated a much wider range of powers over their internal affairs. Full sovereignty, however, remains with the core state. Examples include those within the British Empire such as Aden, the Maldives Islands, the Malay states, the British Solomon Islands, Tonga, British Somaliland, Buganda, and Zanzibar.[58] Within empires, such as that of Great Britain, the constitutional status of protectorates were very similar to colonies, since the powers of a protectorate are vulnerable to usurpation by the fiat of their core state.[59] Partially independent polities are also

---

[55] On defining elements of colonies and empires see for example Aldrich and Connell 1998; Armstrong and Read 2000, 285–306; Barkey 1994; Bertram 2006; Daniels and Kennedy 2002; Doyle 1986, 12; Galtung 1971; Motyl 1997; 1999a; 1999b; Oostindie 2006, 609–26; Spruyt 2005; Tilly 1997. In the British Empire, for example, this status was relatively unambiguous. See Maitland 1908, 339–41. Colonies were culturally distinct territories whose powers were under the control of an imperial power. Such territories did not share the same constitutional space as the empire's metropolitan territory. States like Britain maintained a wide range of liberal constitutional guarantees and representation for citizens within the United Kingdom, while subjects within Britain's far flung colonies were forced to reconcile themselves with separate systems.

[56] See Aldrich and Connell 1992, ch. 3.
[57] See for example Lake 1999; and Wight 1952, 5–11.
[58] Wight 1952, 5–11.
[59] See Martel 1993, 204.

not international protectorates under the ultimate control of the international community. Under its present status, Bosnia, for example, is not a partially independent unit since (1) its final decision-making powers are in the hands of the international community (under the auspices of the United Nations), although nominally there is internal self-governance within the territory, and (2) its juridical association is with the international community rather than with a sovereign state.[60]

Associate States

With regard to "associate states," these polities are usually PITs with wide powers. This term, which is used in the international law discourse, generally applies to decolonized territories that have full internal sovereignty (and in some cases limited powers of foreign relations), but have chosen to surrender military and diplomatic powers of external security to another state.[61] Modern associate states include the Marshall Islands (US), the Federated States of Micronesia (US), the Palau Islands (US), and the Cook Islands (New Zealand). Not all associate states are, however, PITs, and not all PITs are associate states. Associate states are not PITs if their powers are not entrenched. Such entrenchment does not exist if they are therefore able to unilaterally secede from their association with a central state by fiat or a simple majority decision of their legislature (core–PIT unions are by contrast constitutionally entrenched.) Partially independent territories are not associate states if they have no experience as a colony or if their representatives were not a party to the arrangement in which they surrendered their powers of defense.[62]

Federations and Federation Member-units

A federation is a political union between a central (federal) government that divides and shares some credible final decision-making powers with a series of periphery member-units.[63] Whether they are more symmetrical or more asymmetrical in structure, a "federation" describes the organizational robes that

---

[60] See especially Bose 2002, chs 1, 2, and 5. On the similar case of Kosovo after 1999 see Yannis 2004, 67–81. The same can also be said for the autonomous enclave of the Brcko District, which is within Bosnia and Herzegovina and therefore under the ultimate authority and control of the international community's High Representative.

[61] On associate states see for example Lapidoth 1997; Mautner 1980, 305; Stevens 1977, 117–203.

[62] Lapidoth 1997.

[63] For some of the most widely cited definitions of federations and federalism see Dahl 1986, 114; Elazar 1997, 239; Lijphart 1999, 186–8; Riker 1975, 101; Stepan 2001, 6; Wheare 1956, 32.

some sovereign states (and indeed some PITs like the historic British Dominion of Canada or the Netherlands Antilles) have chosen to wrap themselves in to organize themselves internally.[64] Similar to the relationship between a person's head and body, the two vertically organized parts of a federation, the federal government and the member-units, are parts of a single entity.[65] The federal government's powers, status, and leadership is drawn from and inextricably derived from the constitutionally incorporated member-units. Consequently, it is constitutionally inseparable from the states, *länder*, or provinces from which its powers and leadership are derived. Partially independent territories are, however, not member-units of federations (or sham federations).[66] As illustrated in Figure 3.1, partially independent arrangements also do not have a second level

---

[64] A perfectly symmetrical federation would be one in which the powers and status of each of its member-units were constitutionally identical. See Stepan 2001. This is contrasted with a perfectly asymmetrical federation in which the member-units are constitutionally different and have few characteristics in common.

Consider the constitutional structure of Canada. At first glance Canada's federation may appear to be more asymmetrical because of the cultural distinctiveness of some of Quebec's institutions. Canada, however, is mostly a constitutionally symmetrical federation since the provinces within its federal union have nearly identical final decision-making powers and status. This symmetry is true even in the case of Quebec, which compared to the other provinces has its own distinctive immigration, health care, pension, transportation, taxation, and education systems that differ greatly from other provinces in the rest of Canada. In spite of this apparent distinctiveness, Canada's 1867 and 1982 Constitutions allow the other provinces a similar degree of distinctiveness. Canada's other provinces have, however, not chosen to exercise their powers in these areas in the same way as Quebec.

It should be noted that there are four byzantine and relatively inconsequential exceptions to this constitutional symmetry of Quebec and Canada's other provinces. The four most noteworthy provisions that make Quebec legally distinct from Canada's other provinces are as follows: (1) Section 133 of the Constitution Act of 1867 (the Constitutional document that brought Canada into being) that mandates the use of both French and English in Quebec's laws as well as in court and legislative proceedings. (This provision, however, imposes bilingualism in such matters on Quebec in the interests of Canada's Anglophones rather than providing any special privileges for the French-speaking majority of Quebec). (2) The second of these provisions is Section 93 of the Constitution Act of 1867, which discusses the rather archaic matter of denominational rights between Protestants and Catholics. (3) The third distinctive provision is Section 23(1)(a) of Canada's Constitution Act of 1982 which provides parents in all provinces but Quebec the option of sending their children to English schools. (4) The only other major distinctive provision is Canada's Supreme Court Act which mandates that Quebec have three Supreme Court Justices, which, given Quebec's relative population within the Union, does not seem to provide any particularly significant prejudice for or against the province's status within the Canadian federation. These four constitutional stipulations constitute the main ways that Quebec is legally distinct from its nine other provincial counterparts.

[65] For observations on America's federal member-units existing under a single system after the US Civil War see, Deudney 1995, 191–228.

[66] An example of a sham federation would be the former Soviet Union in which wide ranging powers were constitutionally allocated to Union Republics while no discernible entrenchment mechanisms existed that credibly shielded these member-units from Moscow's arbitrary interference. For more on this see Roeder 1991, 196–232.

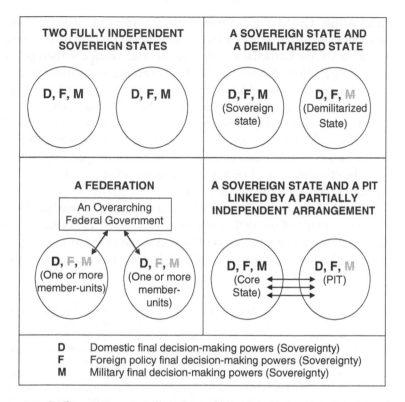

TWO FULLY INDEPENDENT SOVEREIGN STATES	A SOVEREIGN STATE AND A DEMILITARIZED STATE
D, F, M D, F, M	D, F, M (Sovereign state) D, F, M (Demilitarized State)
A FEDERATION An Overarching Federal Government — D, F, M (One or more member-units) D, F, M (One or more member-units)	**A SOVEREIGN STATE AND A PIT LINKED BY A PARTIALLY INDEPENDENT ARRANGEMENT** D, F, M (Core State) ⟷ D, F, M (PIT)

D	Domestic final decision-making powers (Sovereignty)
F	Foreign policy final decision-making powers (Sovereignty)
M	Military final decision-making powers (Sovereignty)

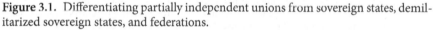

Figure 3.1. Differentiating partially independent unions from sovereign states, demilitarized sovereign states, and federations.

of federal government. Instead two polities, which would otherwise be fully independent, share and divide a range of sovereign powers with one another.

Puerto Rico is, for example, not a "state" of America's federal union. Indeed, most PITs are associated with unitary states (like the UK or Finland) that do not have a second level of country-wide government and a series of federal member-units, which are essential characteristics of federations. Hence regions such as Quebec, Bavaria, Tatarstan, California, Slovenia (within the former Yugoslavia), and the federation member-units of still other federations are constitutionally incorporated as member-units and are therefore not PITs.[67] While Quebec (Canada) is not a PIT[68] since it is a member-unit

---

[67] On federalism see Elazar 1997, 239; Riker 1975, 101; Stepan 2001, 6; Wheare 1956, 32.

[68] For Quebec, the constitutional reality is that its distinctive exercise of powers in immigration, health care, pension, taxation, civil law, and education, are by and large equally granted by Canada's constitution to the other provinces as well. The other provinces have simply chosen not

(province) within Canada's federation,[69] the arrangement between Canada and the territory of Nunavut is a partially independent arrangement.[70] In their 1982 Constitution, the Canadians made a momentous change to their political order by adding Section 35. Section 35 formally entrenches treaties made with its indigenous populations, which included the 1993 Nunavut Land Claims Agreement made with the Inuits of Nunavut.[71] This PIT comprises nearly half of the Arctic and approximately one quarter of Canada's land mass and the Inuit who govern this territory also comprise 85% of the population. This polity has measures of credible final control over its own laws, policing, taxation, education, health care, natural resources, and other affairs, while not existing as one of Canada's federation member-units.[72]

Even if some federation member-units (such as a German *Länder* like Bavaria) possess a wider range of domestic sovereignty than some PITs (like Scotland and Wales), it does not change the fact that they are very much distinct political forms. As illustrated in Table 3.1, unlike PITs, federation member-units are

to exercise powers in the same way as Quebec. For example, in the case of Quebec's powers of taxation, Section 92 of the Constitutional Act of 1867 makes clear that all of Canada's provinces possess powers of direct taxation (Canada, The 1867 Constitution Act (The 1867 British North America Act)). Canada's other provinces have simply opted not to implement this provision in the same way that Quebec has. According to Section 92 they are free to alter their form of taxation in line with that of Quebec if they so choose. Therefore, Quebec's unique exercise of power is a difference in substance rather than the structural allocation of power in Canada's Constitution. With the exception of the few powers that make Quebec legally distinct as noted in fn 63, the Canadian provinces are by and large legally symmetrical. The reason why Quebec superficially seems different in a legal sense is only because it has decided to exercise its powers differently, a decision that the other Canadian provinces in accordance with Canada's Constitution could equally make if they opted to do so. Quebec, therefore, is deprived of two central features of PITs: a separate constitutional allocation of power by the central government as distinct from other regions of the state and a non-federal member-unit status within the state. (Author's interviews with Canadian and Quebec legislative leaders October 2003.)

[69] Indeed, it was the near absence of constitutional distinctiveness, and not its abundance, that was one of the factors that led to the 1988 Meech Lake and the 1992 Charlottetown Accords, which called for Quebec to be constitutionally transformed into a "special society" (Simeon 2004). Although these accords were ratified by the leaders of Quebec and Canada's other provinces, they failed to be ratified by referendum among Canada's population. Had these efforts succeeded, however, Canada would have indeed been transformed into a much more asymmetrical federation. To its preexisting powers as a regular member-unit of Canada's federation, Quebec would have gained the power to veto constitutional amendments, obtain greater powers over immigration, and secure extra limitations on central government power to attach conditions to federal grants (Simeon 2004, 107). Under such conditions, however, it would still have been a member-unit of Canada's federation and thus technically not a PIT.

[70] Nunavut, Nunavut Implementation Commission 1995; Hawkes 2001, 153–61.

[71] The arrangement for Nunavut (which was carved out of the Northwest Territories) was agreed upon with Inuit representatives and ratified by the Canadian Parliament under the 1993 Nunavut Act and entered into force in April 1999.

[72] Burrows 2012; Curry 2004; Hawkes 2001, 153–61.

constitutionally incorporated as an integral part of a sovereign state where they have the same rights, status, and powers as other parts of the country. Also unlike PITs, most federation member-units do not possess foreign affairs capabilities, such as membership of international organizations or limited treaty-making capability that are common among PITs.[73] A PIT's status might also blur with that of federation member-units in states where there is disagreement whether a federation (and membership in a federation) in fact exists. For example, for those who argue that Spain is a federation, Catalonia, the Basque Country, and Galicia would be federation member-units and thus not PITs.[74] For those, however, who argue that Spain is not a federation, the aforementioned territories would arguably seem to be PITs within a decentralized unitary state, since they have credible final decision-making powers allocated to them.[75] In either case, however, from October 1979 to April 1983, Catalonia, the Basque Country, and Galicia were the only self-governing arrangements in a more unitary Spain in which other regions of the country were ruled more centrally from Madrid. These three PITs were like islands of partial independence within a sea of centrally controlled territory. After 1983, however, when the institutions of Spain's other autonomous communities were entered into force, their status as PITs began to blur as the distinctive centrally controlled sea of territory around them adopted degrees of autonomy more and more like their own.[76] Nevertheless in as much as Catalonia, the Basque Country, and Galicia are nationalistically distinct, in possess formally entrenched powers, and retain much of their constitutionally unincorporated status within a country that is arguably not a full-fledged federation, they are coded here as PITs.

Sham Federacies

If a polity accords with most of the characteristics of a PIT mentioned in Table 3.1, but nevertheless does not have any form of entrenchment, it is referred to here as a "sham federacy." Sham federacies, such as the Autonomous Region of Tibet (China) or the Chittagong Hill Tracts (Bangladesh) are nationalistically distinct and constitutionally unincorporated polities that have been nominally allocated some autonomous powers which can be arbitrarily changed or rescinded by the core state.[77] For an exhaustive list of these polities

[73] It may be instructive to note that there are rare cases in which member-units of federations do possess some limited powers of foreign affairs, such as Tatarstan in Russia. Nevertheless (unlike PITs) such territories are still incorporated as an integral part of their state, see Hughes 2001, 36–68.

[74] See Agranoff 1994, 61–89; Linz 1989, 260–326.

[75] See Colomer 1998, 40–52; Russell 2001, 111.

[76] See Colomer 1998, 40–52.

[77] Sham federacies are externally dominated in the sense that they do not have any real ownership over the powers that have merely been delegated to them.

after 1945 see Appendix 2. Sham federacies are also the subject of Chapter 6. By contrast, colonies are nationalistically distinct and constitutionally unincorporated polities whose constitutional powers are unambiguously under the control of the core state. America's Indian territories are sham federacies, since they are not member-units of America's federation, they have been legally promised powers, but (as will be explained in greater detail in Chapter 6) their powers are bereft of any discernible credibility mechanisms that make those powers defensible and very difficult to change.[78] Similarly in the People's Republic of China, the Special Administrative Region of Macau as well as an additional 45 "autonomous" regions are also sham federacies since they have been nominally allocated a wide range of final decision-making powers without any discernible means to make those powers credible. By contrast, Hong Kong is a PIT since the final decision-making powers that were allocated to it in the 1997 Basic Law are made credible through the political influence it arguably exercises over the Chinese core state.[79]

As with other large categories (whether with other polities such as sovereign states or any form of objective reality such as chairs or dogs) in spite of the features that they share, PITs themselves vary in significant ways. For example, while they all have degrees of foreign representation, the degree of this representation can be different. Some like Liechtenstein and the Marshall Islands have seats in the United Nations (UN). Others like Hong Kong do not (although Hong Kong is a member of more than seventeen international organizations including the World Trade Organization [WTO] and the IMF). On this see Table 3.2. Still other PITs, like Scotland, have less elaborate foreign functions (with formal representation limited to the EU, the core state with which it is associated [the UK], and foreign trade offices). And while all PITs possess a wide range of powers over their domestic affairs (as with their consistent ability to elect their own legislatures that possess a wide range of credible final decision-making powers), this too varies from case to case. For example, while Puerto Rico's government appoints justices in its local judiciary,[80] the Åland Island's judiciary is controlled by the core

---

[78] The new found economic prosperity and delegated powers of many Indian territories masks the reality that the US Congress seems to still retain all final decision-making powers ("plenary power") over these territories, which it exercises. For an excellent account of this see Aleinikoff 2002, 95–121. For a sampling of modern US Supreme Court cases that have also confirmed this see for example, *Santa Clara Pueblo v Martinez*, 1978; *United States v Wheeler*, 1978; and *Washington v Confederated Bands and Tribes of the Yakima Indian Nation*, 1979. On the status of the Indian Territories see also Pommersheim 1995; Wallace 1999; Wilkinson 1987.

[79] Rezvani 2012, 93–122.

[80] As Puerto Rico's Constitution says, "The Legislative Assembly may create and abolish courts, except for the Supreme Court, in a manner not inconsistent with this Constitution, and

state (Finland).[81] Similarly, while Bermuda locally elects its premier, the chief executive of Hong Kong is appointed by the core state (China).

The point here, however, is not to create a category where the identified units are identical in every way (this would not only be impractical, but in significant ways, useless). Scholars of comparative politics have long emphasized the methodological necessity of capitalizing on a unit's differences (from one to another or within the same category) to arrive at conclusions and knowledge.[82] Nor is the intention to arbitrarily single out characteristics and identify a phenomenon for its own sake. Instead, the point is to classify a distinctive unit of the international system that has a combination of characteristics that matters for various problems in global politics including nationalistic conflict, poverty, security, and international systemic change.

TERRITORIAL SOVEREIGNTY AND POWERS OF PARTIAL INDEPENDENCE

As discussed above, PITs amend the structure of the international system. Widely held assumptions about the structure, unit types, and allocation of sovereign power in global politics need to be altered in light of the widespread existence of PITs. A similar amendment has, however, also occurred within the structure of sovereign states themselves. When sovereign states are associated with PITs, the core state no longer has a monopoly of legitimate control within their international legal space. Final authority and control over some issues is shared and divided within the partially independent union rather than being exclusively controlled by a core state. If, for example, one ventures to question police or other local officials in Scotland, Hong Kong, Puerto Rico, Iraqi Kurdistan, or other PITs about whether they take their orders from their respective core state capitals (London, Beijing, Washington DC, Bagdad, etc.), many of them will react with an incredulous or dismissive scoff. But in addition to the final control in some respects that is exercised by PITs, they also

---

shall determine the venue and organization of the courts." Puerto Rico, The Constitution of the Commonwealth of Puerto Rico 1952, Article 5, Section 2. "Judges shall be appointed by the Governor with the advice and consent of the Senate." Puerto Rico, The Constitution of the Commonwealth of Puerto Rico 1952, Article 5, Section 8.

  [81] Åland, Act on the Autonomy of Åland 1991/1997, Section 27:23.

  [82] Much work in comparative politics has been based on John Stuart Mill's method of difference (which identifies different features across similar units) and the method of similarity (which identifies similar features across different units). On this method see Faure 1994, 307–22; Landman 2000, 27–32; Przeworski and Teune 1970.

possess final authority that is made credible by constitutional entrenchment. After briefly discussing the defining elements of PITs, the remainder of this chapter will discuss the nature of their sovereign powers and elaborate upon the credibility producing mechanisms that they possess.

As indicated previously, PITs are (1) nationalistically distinct and (2) constitutionally unincorporated organizational forms that share and divide some (3) credible final decision-making powers (some territorial sovereignty) with a sovereign (core) state.[83] Such PITs exercise a wide range of powers over domestic jurisdiction, some foreign matters, but not external military affairs.

When considering partially independent arrangements, it is important to bear in mind that a territory does not have some powers of independence just because there is a formal division of power between a core state and an associate territory or that such a division of power consists of some final decision-making powers.[84] Beyond these characteristics, credibility is necessary. The final decision-making powers that are allocated to the territory need to be defensible and very difficult to take away. Something must exist to make such promises difficult to change or remove. If either party to the arrangement can unilaterally usurp, change, or alter a territory's status by fiat, and/or without great difficulty, it can neither be a partially independent arrangement nor can there be real self-determination.[85] While it is possible for both sides to violate a core–PIT arrangement, in light of the smaller size of territories, it is especially important to illustrate mechanisms that prevent usurpation by the core state. If the powers that have been allocated to a territory are vulnerable to usurpation, the sense that an arrangement is truly a compromise between full independence and full assimilation will be significantly weakened. Under such conditions, the principle of nationalism, which says that a culturally distinct people ought to be able to rule their own affairs within a specific territory, will be violated.[86] Furthermore, market preserving federalism's requirement for local economic jurisdiction will be transgressed. And the relational contracting emphasis on checks and balances will be compromised.

---

[83] On PITs (also referred to as federacy) see Anderson 2012; Coppieters 2001; Elazar 1991; 1993; 1994; 1997; Ghai 2000; Jakobson 2005; McGarry 2007; O'Leary 2001; 2002; 2005; 2013a; 2013b; Rezvani 2004; 2007a; 2007b; 2012; Stepan, Linz, and Yadav 2010; Stepan 2013; Stevens 1977; Watts 1996.

[84] On final decision-making powers see Riker 1975, 93–172.

[85] On differing forms of self-determination see Kirgis 1994, 310. Similar to nationalism, self-determination is a political principle that emphasizes that a culturally distinct group ought to rule over itself and control its destiny within the confines of a particular territory. For the purpose of this study, aspirations for nationalism and self-determination can be seen as synonymous.

[86] Gellner 1983, 1.

Accordingly, it is arguably important not to confound the concept of delegation with territorial sovereignty.[87] Whether with individuals or polities, there is an important distinction between borrowing and owning, assisting and appropriating, and renting and stealing that does not seem to be recognized in some of the literature. Reflecting other definitions used in the sovereignty literature, Daniel Philpott observes that "the most traditional meaning" of sovereignty (as emphasized by early philosophers such as Thomas Hobbes and Jean Bodin) refers to "the authority and effective control of a government within a state."[88] Accordingly, territorial sovereignty can be described as a polity's jurisdictional priority through its de facto control and de jure authority in some respects over a territory.[89] De jure authority as used here refers to the constitutional recognition of a polity's powers whether through formal (written) or informal (unwritten) rules. As elaborated further below, authority is therefore not conceived as only a formal-legal phenomenon—unwritten constitutional rules can also confer duties, rights, and obligations.[90] De facto control as conceived here refers to a polity's actual final ability to control certain people or objects if its agents encounter them. This, however, does not mean that the de facto control that rulers may possess is omnipresent. A polity with de facto control over a territory may not control all goods, people, and currency that pass over the territory, but if it encounters such persons or objects it has the ultimate ability to control them.[91] The authority and control components of sovereignty can be further subdivided into internal applications (which apply within the polity's domestic jurisdiction) and external applications (which apply to relations with other polities in the international system).[92] These sovereignty distinctions can be used to map out varying polities in the international system as distinct from PITs (see Table 3.3).[93]

[87] For an assessment of the difference between these distinct concepts see also Lapidoth 1997.

[88] Philpott 2001a, 300. On sovereignty see also, Bartleson 1996; Bunck and Fowler 1996; Krasner 1999; Jackson 1999. There is, nevertheless, no consensus in the political science or legal literatures on the meaning of sovereignty. For those who doubt that a consistent definition can be established see Benn 1955, 501–5; Falk 1993, 854; Oppenheim 1905, 103.

[89] For those who apply similar definitions see Jackson 1987, 529; and Tilly 1990.

[90] For a sampling of some of the key sources on unwritten rules see, Bogdanor 1995; Brazier 1994; 1997; Dicey 1885/1982; Forsey 1984; Heard 1991; Jennings 1959; Keith 1935b; Marshall 1984; Munro 1975; Wheare 1949. For a seminal account of the application of unwritten rules within the United States see Horwill 1925.

[91] Even powerful states like the US do not have the omnipresent capability to control all goods, people, and currency that passes over its territory. For the meaning and significance of such control see Jackson 1990; Krasner 1999; Ottaway 2002, 1001–23.

[92] For a bibliography of the widespread view in the political science and international law literatures that sovereignty is divisible, see Bunck and Fowler 1996. Some areas of jurisdiction, such as control over international business, may of course blur the distinctions between internal and external applications of territorial sovereignty.

[93] For other efforts to create a similar taxonomy of polities see especially Elazar 1994; Lake 2003.

Table 3.3 Territorial polities and their sovereign and delegated powers as compared to the sovereign state*

Power Type		Sovereign state**	Partially independent territory	Federal member-unit	De facto state	Warlord	Protectorate	Colony	Sham federacy
Credible final decision-making (sovereign) power	External control	X	(X)		X				
	External authority	X	(X)						
	Internal control	X	X	(X)	X	(X)			
	Internal authority	X	X	(X)	X				
Delegated power	External control		(X)				(X)		
	External authority		(X)				(X)		
	Internal control						X	(X)	(X)
	Internal authority						X	(X)	(X)

Polity category

X = Full or a preponderance of powers

(X) = Partial allocation of powers

* This table represents a generalization of the powers of the polities described. There may be variations in individual cases.

** This category also includes alliance and confederal relationships that sovereign states have with one another in which they delegate some powers to another state or body but retain a right of exit from the arrangement and unanimity decision making.

While accepting the concept of divided sovereignty, this book nevertheless rejects the notion that since sovereignty can be viewed as divisible it can as a consequence refer to virtually any type of authority relationship of one pol- ity over another: both final control and authority are arguably necessary on a particular issue for sovereignty to exist.[94] As some have rightly noted, "purely coercive relationships—as when a mugger demands 'your money or your life'—are characterized by power, but they are not authoritative."[95] While such a criminal may well have control, the mugger does not have de jure authority and therefore does not possess sovereignty. This condition applies to de facto states (such as Taiwan or Northern Cyprus) since they are bereft of external diplomatic authority through their absence of international legal recogni- tion by other sovereign states.[96] De facto states are polities with most of the trappings of full independence except international recognition.[97] They may have de facto control over the ability to represent themselves to other poli- ties although they do not have authority (recognition). For example, although Taiwan is not recognized as a sovereign state by the US and extended full dip- lomatic recognition, Taiwan nevertheless has representatives in the US, as with the Taipei Economic and Cultural Representative Office in Washington DC. Such external authority (if they had it) could potentially win them greater lev- els of security and diplomatic advantages.

This book, however, also rejects notions of sovereignty that only empha- size de jure authority without de facto control. Some of the literature seems to ignore this flip-side to the sovereignty coin. Purely authoritative relation- ships—such as those that exist with some failed sovereign states, sham federa- cies, or even the defunct League of Nations—do not signify control.[98] As Inis Claude once wrote when referring to those who were tasked with first setting up the constitutional authority relationships of a political system,

[94] Motyl 2006, 229–49.

[95] Lake 2007, 51.

[96] On de facto states see King 2001, 524–52. Further examples of de facto states include Abkhazia (vis-à-vis Georgia), the FARC territory (vis-à-vis Columbia), the Jaffna Peninsula (vis-à-vis Sri Lanka) before the 2009 Sri Lankan military invasion of the area, Nagorno-Karabakh (vis-à-vis Azerbaijan), the Somaliland Republic (vis-à-vis Somalia), South Ossetia (vis-à-vis Georgia), and Transnistria (vis-à-vis Moldova).

[97] It may be useful to note that although de facto states do not have sovereignty over foreign affairs, they do indeed have such sovereignty (both de facto control and de jure authority) over other issues, such as domestic affairs.

[98] This is the problem that failed states have since they have international and external author- ity with a loss of internal control. As Marina Ottaway has pointed out, although such states may be constitutionally recognized they have little capacity for effective administration. Ottaway 2002, 1001–23.

> Founding fathers are among the most frustrated and double crossed heroes of history: they can state the purposes of the institutions that they create, but they cannot determine these purposes or control the course of development of those institutions.... They can only launch the institutional ships, which are then tossed on the seas of history, driven by the winds of political forces, and steered by a succession of men who have their own ideas about where they want to go.[99]

Parties to any agreement, whether they are partners in business, domestic institutions, or polities in the international system may recognize an authority relationship; they may even at first believe that they are bound by the rules that they create. But as scholars of constitutions and politics have long recognized, when these actors encounter de facto control and interests that are consistently at odds with that authority, the de jure authority designations that they have created will break down and give way to a newly defined order.[100] This newly defined order will then either be based upon the violations themselves, which will give way to a new set of customs and authority relationships, or the contrary practices will result in a *non liquet* (a state of disarray in which authoritative relations are not clear).[101] The idea that effective sovereignty can be attained by authority relationships alone is therefore questionable. Both de facto control and de jure authority are arguably necessary for powers of sovereignty to be attained on specific issues.

When former colonies or protectorates, such as the Åland Islands, the historic British Dominions, or Puerto Rico, are provided with entrenched constitutional guarantees that their powers cannot be easily taken away, they become partially independent polities.[102] Because they have de jure authority and de facto control over a range of decisions upon which they make the final decisions, they have powers of territorial sovereignty while colonies, protectorates, and other decentralized arrangements do not (see Table 3.3). Decentralized relationships in the international system are certainly worthy of study.[103] But

---

[99] Claude 1956/1984, 6.

[100] For a sampling of scholars that have made these types of arguments in the context of unwritten constitutional rules see Bogdanor 1995; Brazier 1994; 1997; Dicey 1885/1982; Forsey 1984; Heard 1991; Jennings 1959; Keith 1935b; Marshall 1984; Munro 1975; Wheare 1949. For a seminal account of the application of conventional rules within the United States see Horwill 1925.

[101] Glennon 2003, 16–35.

[102] Much of the literature sees protectorates as constitutionally unincorporated territories which exercise delegated powers over most of their internal affairs, while their external relations and defense are exercised by their core state. See for example Lake 1999; Martel 1993, 204; Wight 1952, 5–11. In other words, protectorates are essentially colonies except they have been delegated a much wider range of powers over their internal affairs. On other relationships between European powers and their protectorates, see Martel 1993, 204.

[103] On the importance of examining the decentralization between the US and other sovereign states see, Lake 2007.

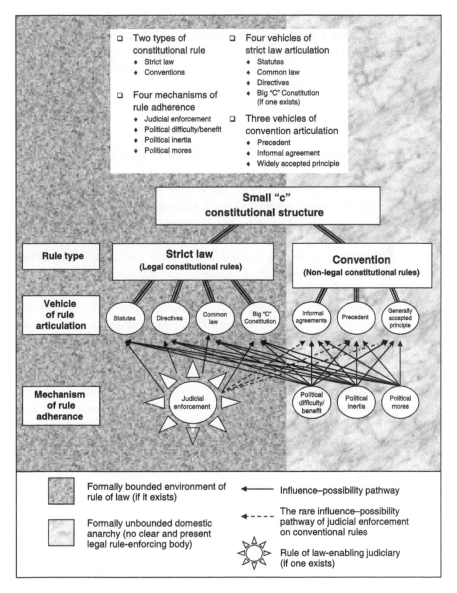

Figure 3.2. Constitutional structure

since decentralized jurisdictions do not have final authority and control, they should be distinguished from relationships in which powers of sovereignty are shared and divided.[104] As this book argues, this issue is not merely a matter

---

[104] See Lapidoth 1996.

of semantics or a topic of only academic interest. As discussed in the previous chapter, as the literatures on nationalism, market preserving federalism, and relational contracting argue, a polity's ability to have credible final
decision-making powers over their affairs can provide significant economic,
security, and political advantages.

CREDIBILITY PRODUCING MECHANISMS

Again, in order for credibility to exist, some force or mechanism must be in
effect to prevent the core or associated territory from changing the division of
power that they have agreed upon by fiat or through a simple majority decision. If an arrangement is constitutionally embedded or entrenched, it refers
to the result that occurs from a mechanism or force that makes a constitution very difficult to change.[105] Here the term "constitution" refers to a polity's set of government-regulating and government-establishing rules.[106] Like
some other sources in the literature, big "C" Constitution is used here to indicate a formally-entrenched written Constitution and its amendments (such as
America's 1787 Constitution), and little "c" constitution is used to express the
meaning of government-establishing and regulating rules in general, which
include written rules (including the formally entrenched big "C" Constitution)
as well as unwritten rules.[107] Constitutional rules that act to establish and regulate government can be divided into two categories: strict law (legal rules) and
convention (non-legal "unwritten" rules) (see Figure 3.2).[108] Rules are established, obligatory, and enforceable principles of behavior. Credibility mechanisms consist of formal, conventional, and/or political-formal entrenchment
of a constitution.

Formal-Legal Entrenchment

The most straightforward type of constitutional entrenchment is that which
is unambiguously written down in the constitutional instrument between a

---

[105] On veto points and veto players in hierarchical arrangements see, e.g., Cunningham 2006;
Hallerberg 2002; O'Reilly 2005; Spruyt 2005; Tsebelis 1999.
[106] Wheare 1949, 6.
[107] Fallon 2000, 112. It may be instructive to note that the total written constitutional documents of the US include those which exist at the federal, state, and territorial levels.
[108] Wheare 1949, chs 1–2.

PIT and a core state. In fact, most known PITs are entrenched in this way (see Table 3.4 at the end of this chapter). There are a variety of legal guarantees that would tend to protect a partially independent arrangement from the unilateral fiat of one side or another, including supermajority change, mutual assent, judicial review, treaty guarantee, and mutual consultation.[109]

Supermajority Change

Perhaps the most well-known type of formal entrenchment (used in federations like the US or Germany) is referred to here as *supermajority change*. With supermajority change, a constitution is made very difficult to alter because more than a majority vote is required for a core or associate legislature to change the partially independent arrangement.[110] Partially independent territories such as the Åland Islands[111] (Finland), Azores and Madeira[112] (Portugal), Catalonia[113] (Spain), Gagauzia[114] (Moldova), Nunavut[115] (Canada), and Zanzibar[116] (Tanzania) are entrenched through supermajority change provisions within a core state Constitution.

[109] Mutual consultation is provided by specifying in the arrangement the need for the central government to seek the advice of, or to consult with, the PIT authorities before any changes are made. The Åland Islands and Greenland are examples of a PIT with mutual consultation provisions. See Lapidoth 1997, 70–7, 143–51. This type of mutual consultation entrenchment is very much distinct from mutual assent provisions since only *advice-seeking* is necessary rather than the *agreement* of both sides. Even with the need to consult, a central government could, for example, conceivably seek the advice of a PIT and then undertake exactly the type of actions that the PIT government opposes. For this reason, by itself mutual consultation is not sufficient to make an arrangement credible. On the other hand, it could be argued that this type of entrenchment does indeed create some difficulty for the arrangement to be changed in the sense that it can provide delays and the possibility of the territory lodging its protest as well as mobilizing opposition against the impending legislation. It is, however, considerably weaker than most of the other forms of entrenchment.

[110] Such a supermajority could be accomplished, for example, by a 2/3, 3/4, 4/5, etc. vote in the legislature or by referendum.

[111] Åland, Act on the Autonomy of Åland, 1997, Section 69.

[112] Portugal, Constitution of Portugal 1974, Article 288.

[113] Spain, Constitution of Spain, 1978, Article 167; Catalonia, Catalan Statute of Autonomy, 1979, Section 4, Article 56. From October 1979 to April 1983 Catalonia (together with the Basque Country and Galicia) were the only federal arrangements in Spain. After 1983, however, when the self-governing institutions of Spain's other autonomous communities entered into force, Catalonia's status as a PIT began to blur considerably. See Colomer 1998, 40–52.

[114] See Moldova, Constitution of the Republic of Moldova, Article 111(1). The 1994 "Law on the Special Juridical Status of Gagauzia" passed by the Moldovan Parliament also specifies that a three-fifths majority is necessary in Moldova's Parliament for any changes to Gagauzia's powers. See Neukirch 2002, 105–23. See also Suksi 1998, 160.

[115] Canada, The Constitution Act, 1982, Section 35.

[116] Tanzania, Constitution of the United Republic of Tanzania, 1995, Article 97(1b).

Mutual Assent

A second type of formal entrenchment is through formally-specified *mutual assent* provisions. With mutual assent a core–associate arrangement cannot be altered except through the simple majority agreement of the legislatures of the central government and the PIT. Partially independent territories with mutual assent provisions include the Åland Islands,[117] the Northern Mariana Islands,[118] and Trentino-South Tyrol.[119]

Judicial Review

A third type of formal entrenchment can be provided by some independent party (usually a judicial body) to be assigned a role in policing the arrangement. Such *judicial review* is done through a body with the power to declare void or unconstitutional the actions of any party that violates the arrangement. This type of entrenchment works well when the provisions of the constitutional arrangement are further entrenched by supermajority change provisions. Otherwise, the policing role of a judiciary (or some other independent body) could theoretically be circumvented through simple majority legislation. In any case, however, even when supermajority change provisions do not exist, such judicial review can still be an effective means to prevent officials within government—whether by deterrence or actual use of such a process—from overstepping their duly allocated powers. Partially independent arrangements that have forms of judicial review include, the Åland Islands[120] (Finland), Catalonia[121] (Spain), Gagauzia[122] (Ukraine), Greenland[123] (Denmark), the Faroe Islands[124] (Denmark), Micronesia[125] (US), the Netherlands Antilles[126] (the Netherlands), Puerto Rico[127] (US), and Scotland[128] (UK). For examples of the legal provisions

---

[117] Åland, Act on the Autonomy of Åland, 1997, Section 69.
[118] Northern Mariana Islands, Covenant to Establish a Commonwealth of the Northern Mariana Islands in Political Union with the United States of America, 1976, Section 105.
[119] Wolff 2004, 72.
[120] Lapidoth 1997, 70–7.
[121] Colomer 1998, 40–52.
[122] Suksi 1998, 160.
[123] Foighel 1980, 91–108; Lapidoth 1997, 143–51.
[124] Lapidoth 1997, 112–15.
[125] Leibowitz 1989, 596–601.
[126] Hannum 1990, 347–52.
[127] Rezvani 2007, 115–40.
[128] Bogdanor 1999, 205–9.

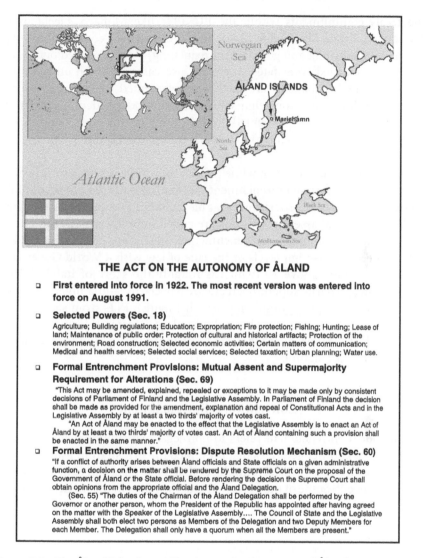

THE ACT ON THE AUTONOMY OF ÅLAND

- First entered into force in 1922. The most recent version was entered into force on August 1991.

- Selected Powers (Sec. 18)

  Agriculture; Building regulations; Education; Expropriation; Fire protection; Fishing; Hunting; Lease of land; Maintenance of public order; Protection of cultural and historical artifacts; Protection of the environment; Road construction; Selected economic activities; Certain matters of communication; Medical and health services; Selected social services; Selected taxation; Urban planning; Water use.

- Formal Entrenchment Provisions: Mutual Assent and Supermajority Requirement for Alterations (Sec. 69)

  "This Act may be amended, explained, repealed or exceptions to it may be made only by consistent decisions of Parliament of Finland and the Legislative Assembly. In Parliament of Finland the decision shall be made as provided for the amendment, explanation and repeal of Constitutional Acts and in the Legislative Assembly by at least a two thirds' majority of votes cast.

  "An Act of Åland may be enacted to the effect that the Legislative Assembly is to enact an Act of Åland by at least a two thirds' majority of votes cast. An Act of Åland containing such a provision shall be enacted in the same manner."

- Formal Entrenchment Provisions: Dispute Resolution Mechanism (Sec. 60)

  "If a conflict of authority arises between Åland officials and State officials on a given administrative function, a decision on the matter shall be rendered by the Supreme Court on the proposal of the Government of Åland or the State official. Before rendering the decision the Supreme Court shall obtain opinions from the appropriate official and the Åland Delegation.

  (Sec. 55) "The duties of the Chairman of the Åland Delegation shall be performed by the Governor or another person, whom the President of the Republic has appointed after having agreed on the matter with the Speaker of the Legislative Assembly.... The Council of State and the Legislative Assembly shall both elect two persons as Members of the Delegation and two Deputy Members for each Member. The Delegation shall only have a quorum when all the Members are present."

Figure 3.3. The Åland Islands and The Act on the Autonomy of Åland

of one PIT—the Åland Islands—that exemplifies each of the aforementioned formal entrenchment mechanisms see Figure 3.3.

Treaty Guarantee

Another type of formal entrenchment, *treaty guarantee*, can be provided by formal diplomatic obligations and guarantees between polities. Much like the treaty commitments within the EU, PITs like Monaco, Liechtenstein, Micronesia, Palau, Marshall Islands, and still others have constitutional (government establishing and government regulating)[129] rules spelled out in treaties with associated core states. There are also cases in which other existing entrenchment mechanisms are further supplemented by core state treaties with other third party sovereign states. Partially independent arrangements whose powers are supplemented in this way include the Åland Islands (Finland), Hong Kong (China), Northern Ireland (UK), and Trentino-South Tyrol (Italy).[130]

Strictly speaking, however, while polities may indeed have a variety of the aforementioned formal entrenchment mechanisms, for the purposes of this study, only core-PIT associations that have either (1) supermajority change and/or (2) mutual assent provisions are coded here as formally entrenched PITs. Furthermore, formal entrenchment is itself only considered credible if the core state has high levels of the rule of law with a World Governance Indicator ranking above 70 (which is roughly the score of Italy).[131] These more limited criteria hopefully create greater clarity and a higher standard for constitutional protection. They also distinguish PITs from sham federacies, which in some cases have been allocated weak forms of formal entrenchment, such as legal promises that can be changed with a simple majority fiat of a core state legislature.

Conventional Entrenchment

Conventional entrenchment refers to non-legal constitutional rules (such as the widely acknowledged rules that prevented the British from usurping powers from the historic British Dominions) that make an arrangement very difficult to change.[132] Some of the most well-cited scholars in the modern literature

---

[129] Wheare 1949, 6.

[130] On the application of treaty guarantee in such cases see Chan and Clark 1990, 259–88; Lapidoth 1997, 70–7; O'Leary 2001, 53–89; and Wolff 2004, 57–76.

[131] Kauffmann et al. 2008.

[132] The term "convention" used in the literature on the topic refers to unwritten constitutional rules rather than a meeting of officials to draft or change a written Constitution as with the "Constitutional Convention of 1787." In this book the term "convention" and "unwritten constitutional rule" will be used interchangeably. On convention in Britain see Bogdanor 1995; Brazier 1994; 1997; Marshall 1984; Munro 1975, 218. On convention (unwritten constitutional rules) in the United States see Ackerman 1991, 44–50, 81–130; Bryce 1895, 391–407; Fallon 2000, 119; 2001; Fisher 2003; Foley 1989; Grey 1975, 703–18; 1978, 843–93; 1988; Horwill 1925; Munro 1930, 1–23; Sherry 1987, 1127–77; Strauss 1996, 877; Tiedeman 1890; Whittington 1999; Wilson 1908; Wilson 1992, 645.

on conventions have defined conventional rules in different ways.[133] British jurist A. V. Dicey referred to them as "customs, practices, maxims, or precepts" that constitute a type of binding "constitutional or political ethics."[134] Canadian scholar Eugene Forsey described them as "the acknowledged, binding, extra-legal customs, usages, practices and understandings by which our system of government operates."[135] Geoffrey Marshall, in his seminal book, *Constitutional Conventions*, summarizes the relative consensus in the literature on the most basic meaning of convention. He defines conventions as "non-legal rules of constitutional behavior…that define major non-legal rights, powers and obligations of office-holders in the three branches of government, or the relations between organs of government."[136]

Conventions are not only applicable to states such as the United Kingdom,[137] but they also apply to virtually all states, including the United States.[138] In the United States for instance, unwritten constitutional rules establish informally binding norms of behavior among leaders.[139] They help regulate the division of power between Congress and the executive over foreign affairs.[140] They confer powers upon governmental branches, such as the Congressional Commerce Clause powers that are arguably derived from constitutional norms rather than exclusively from the written text of the Constitution.[141] They serve as an important source from which the judiciary draws to formulate some of their most significant judgments.[142] And, as discussed in greater detail in Chapter 5, they make the powers that were formally-allocated to Puerto Rico in 1952 very difficult to change.

---

[133] On the widely acknowledged unwritten constitutional rules that nullified preexisting colonial laws that applied to the historic British Dominions, see for instance, Evatt 1967; Forscy 1943; Keith 1912/1927; Leacock 1907, 355–92; Marshall 1984; Wheare 1949. The British Dominions were first brought into being in 1846 when "responsible government" was first exercised in Canada. This status came to an end in 1931 with the Statute of Westminster when by and large the full range of sovereign powers were surrendered to Australia, Canada, New Zealand, South Africa, the Irish Free State, Malta, and Rhodesia.

[134] Dicey 1885/1982.

[135] Forsey 1943.

[136] Marshall 1984, 3, 210.

[137] Bogdanor 1995; Brazier 1994; Marshall 1984; Munro 1975, 218.

[138] Ackerman 1991, 44–50, 81–130; Bryce 1895, 391–407; Fallon 2000, 119; 2001; Fisher 2003; Foley 1989; Grey 1975, 703–18; 1978, 843–93; 1988; Horwill 1925, 1–23; Sherry 1987, 1127–77; Strauss 1996, 877; Tiedeman 1890; Whittington 1999;Wilson 1908; Wilson 1992, 645; .

[139] The United States is in part used as an example here because it is the core state of the case of Puerto Rico that will be explored in Chapter 5.

[140] Casper 1976, 463; Koh 1990; Paul 1998, 671; White 1999, 1.

[141] Ackerman 1984, 1013, 1053–5, 1069–71; Epstein 1987, 1387; and Fallon 2001, 115.

[142] For examples of this see Fallon 2001; Grey 1975, 703–18; Levinson 1998; Rubenfeld 1995, 1119; Strauss 1996, 877.

As illustrated by Figure 3.2, just as with written rules, conventions are made up of: (1) their vehicle of rule articulation (the outward manifestation of the rule) and (2) the mechanisms that enforce the rule and therefore make it real and credible. Like written rules, conventions may be broken and violated. But as long as the rule (1) has a *reason*, (2) is *articulated* by some means (whether by precedents, generally accepted principles, or informal agreements) and (3) is supported by an informal *enforcement* mechanism, it can be said that a conventional rule exists.[143] Informal enforcement mechanisms such as deeply held political mores, political difficulties/benefit, and/or custom (political inertia through repeated precedent) play an effective role in creating a sense of mutual expectation and constitutionally oriented obligation. Similar to formal entrenchment, conventional entrenchment is itself only considered credible here if the core state has high levels of rule of law with a World Governance Indicator ranking above 70.[144]

Similar also to the more narrow operationalization of formal entrenchment mentioned in the previous section, the presence of such conventional rules which act to entrench a polity's powers from arbitrary core state interference are coded by (1) a high court that informally acknowledges the operation of such territorial protections, or (2) the informal acknowledgment by the core state's executive branch that such rules are in fact in operation. For example, although no amendments have been made to America's Constitution with respect to the operation of the Congress's plenary power over territories, nevertheless the US Supreme Court has acknowledged in a non-legal (dicta) statement that, "Puerto Rico, like a state [of the Union] is an autonomous political entity, 'Sovereign over matters not ruled by the Constitution....'"[145]

A number of modern PITs associated with the United Kingdom also have written constitutional rules that are not in force and are nullified by unwritten conventional rules. For example, the 1998 Scotland Act (which is the body of legislation that transferred a wide range of powers to Scotland) clearly and openly emphasizes the concept of British Parliamentary Sovereignty. Parliamentary sovereignty is a concept that asserts that the British Parliament—and no other entity—is sovereign within the United Kingdom. Section 28(7) of the 1998 Scotland Act makes the following statement: "This section does not affect the power of the Parliament of the United Kingdom to make laws for Scotland."[146] On its surface, such a declaration makes clear

---

[143] The aforementioned three-part assessment of identifying a conventional rule is a modification of Sir Ivor Jennings's tripartite account of the establishment of convention accepted by the Canadian judiciary in 1981. Jennings 1959, ch. 3.
[144] Kauffmann et al. 2008.   [145] *Rodriguez v Popular Democratic Party*, 1982.
[146] UK, Scotland Act 1998.

that the center–periphery arrangement between Scotland and Westminster has not really allocated any final decision-making powers to Scotland because Westminster still retains the power to legislate for Scotland whenever and however it chooses. If, however, the center were to take actions that would significantly displease Scotland's population (such as arbitrarily exercising Section 28) this may translate rapidly into increased support for the Scottish National Party (SNP) whose ethno-centric platform openly advocates Scottish secession.[147] The SNP has grown from an insignificant band of fringe radicals with barely even two locally elected candidates in 1955 to becoming the largest party in Scotland after overtaking the Labour Party in the elections of 2011.[148] Accordingly, one of the purposes of the 1998 Scotland Act was to allocate powers to Scotland that would stem the tide of Scottish secessionism. Among the states of the world that have partially independent arrangements within their international-legal boundaries, few are more aware of the possibility of politically damaging hostility, rebellion, and secession than the United Kingdom. Indeed, the British political agenda since the eighteenth century has been dominated by questions of how to prevent territories from seceding into independence.[149]

Hence, mirroring the experience of other partially independent polities that have been associated with the UK, there were increasing calls for constitutional conventions to shield Scotland (as well as Wales and Northern Ireland) from arbitrary core state interference. One such suggestion was made in 1998 in the British House of Lords by Lord John Sewel, who was the Under Secretary of State for Scotland.[150] He suggested that British Laws should only apply to Scotland with the consent of the newly created Scottish Parliament. Subsequently, his suggestion was in fact implemented in the form of what became known as the "Sewel Coventions" (or legislative consent motions) in which the Scottish Parliament would need to pass a motion before a British law could apply to areas that were within the legislative competency of Scotland.[151] In 1999, the UK government then enshrined these protections in a non-legal Memorandum of Understanding (MoU) with the territorial governments of Scotland, Northern Ireland,[152]

---

[147] Bogdanor 1999, 120–2.
[148] *Evening Express* 2012.
[149] For an overview of this see especially Kendle 1989.
[150] See UK, House of Lords *Parliamentary Debates* 1998.
[151] Cairney 2006, 434; Winetrobe 2001, 287.
[152] The Memorandum of Understanding that articulated the conventional entrenchment between the UK and Northern Ireland, Scotland, and Wales, however, ceased to apply to Northern Ireland during its suspensions from February to May 2000, August 2001, December 2001, and from October 2002 to May 2007 when the core state reestablished central control. The core state suspensions were a result of local militants failing to relinquish their weapons as per the terms of the 1998 Belfast Accords. However, Northern Ireland's Assembly was restored

and Wales[153] in which it confirmed that conventional rules would operate to limit the arbitrary usurpation of powers.[154] The MoU confirmed that "the UK Government will proceed in accordance with the convention that the UK Parliament would not normally legislate with regard to devolved matters except with the agreement of the devolved legislature."[155] The application of unwritten constitutional rules therefore nullifies the legal rules that one might infer from formal provisions, such as Section 28 of the 1998 Scotland Act.

There are also signs that the use of unwritten constitutional rules to entrench the arrangements between erstwhile imperial powers and colonies is expanding, especially with respect to British overseas territories. Since the late 1990s there is evidence that constitutional conventions have been increasingly migrating to former British colonies that combine a representative legislature with a status as an established offshore financial center.[156] Britain's highest constitutional court for overseas territories and crown dependencies is the Judicial Committee of the Privy Council (JCPC) in London.[157] In the 2005 case *Al Sabah v Grupo Torras et al.*, the court confirmed that, in spite of the British Parliament's legal supremacy, British overseas territories with their own representative governments are shielded by constitutional convention against unilateral British legal interference.[158] Speaking for the Court on the status of the Cayman Islands and other similarly situated territories, Lord Walker made the following observation:

> The Westminster Parliament's supreme legislative competence has in practice been more and more constrained by two factors. One has been an increasingly strong Constitutional convention...not to interfere, unasked, in the laws of Commonwealth countries which enjoyed representative government. The

in May 2007 after the October 2006 St. Andrews Agreement. Additionally, the convention that mandates legislative assent before core state decisions can apply to powers allocated to Northern Ireland has also been restored. On this see for example, Birrell 2007, 305.

[153] Unlike most other partially independent polities, Wales is unable to create primary legislation. With the passage of the 2006 Government of Wales Act, a limited degree of legislative powers were however added. See Wales, Welsh Assembly Government, 2006.

[154] For the Memorandum of Understanding see UK, Scotland, Wales, and Northern Ireland. 1999, ¶13. This commitment to protection by conventional rules is known as the "Sewel Convention" and is named after Scottish official Lord Sewel.

[155] Memorandum of Understanding see UK, Scotland, Wales, and Northern Ireland. 1999, ¶13.

[156] Antoine 2008, 14.

[157] The JCPC is the highest court for British Territories (Bermuda, Cayman Islands, British Virgin Islands, Turks and Caicos, Gibraltar, Crown Dependencies (Jersey Guernsey, and Isle of Man), and devolved regions (Northern Ireland, Scotland, and Wales).

[158] Antoine 2008, 14.

other has been the courts' long standing practice, in construing statutes of the Westminster Parliament, of presuming that their intended territorial extent is limited to the United Kingdom, unless it is clear that a wider extent is intended.[159]

In light of such an acknowledgment, conventional rules can also be seen to apply to the British Virgin Islands and Gibraltar, which combine local representative government with a status as a significant offshore financial center.[160] Similar cases of conventionally entrenched territories include the Isle of Man (UK),[161] Jersey (UK),[162] Guernsey (UK),[163] Faroe Islands (Denmark),[164] Greenland (Denmark),[165] as well as the historic British Dominions of Australia, Canada, the Irish Free State,[166] New Zealand, Malta, Rhodesia, and South Africa before 1931.[167]

Political-formal entrenchment

Lastly, in addition to formal-legal and conventional entrenchment, political-formal entrenchment refers to territories whose legal powers have been made very difficult to change through the consistent application of political power.[168] While this form of entrenchment is more difficult to systematically code, it arguably exists and can be ascertained through more detailed single case study analysis. It is referred to as political-formal entrenchment because promises of final decision-making power, which by themselves are insufficient because of a core state's low rule of law ranking, are nevertheless made credible by high levels of political influence. Such entrenchment can be identified when compelling evidence is provided of high levels of political pressure (such as

[159] Quoted in Antoine 2008.
[160] Antoine 2008.
[161] McKercher 2000, 95. See also Grahl-Madsen 1988, 297.
[162] On the constitutional conventions that make core state interference difficult see Williams 1972, 275; and Grahl-Madsen 1988, 297.
[163] Grahl-Madsen 1988.
[164] Denmark's legislative acts that have allocated powers to Greenland and the Faroe Islands are increasingly seen as "'Constitutional Laws' on a level superior to ordinary Parliamentary Acts." See Suksi 1997, 113. Home Rule Act of the Faroe Islands, No. 137 of March 23, 1948; Parliamentary Act No. 103 From July 26, 1994, Act No. 79 of May 12, 2005 on The Assumption Act of Matters and Fields of Responsibility by the Faroese Authorities.
[165] Lapidoth 1997, 143–51, 172–85.
[166] Calvert 1968.
[167] On the widely acknowledged unwritten constitutional rules that nullified the preexisting colonial laws that applied to the British Dominions, see for instance, Keith 1935b and Wheare 1949.
[168] On forms of political-formal entrenchment (rather than necessarily constitutional entrenchment) with regard to ethnic disputes see Fearon 1994. For an especially useful analysis of federal relations based on political-formal entrenchment see Rector 2009.

economic disaster, state fragmentation, and/or war) that would thwart a core state from usurping powers.

As mentioned in Chapter 1, the otherwise flimsy legal promises that China has made to Hong Kong (in the Hong Kong Basic Law and by treaty with the United Kingdom in the 1984 Sino-British Joint Declaration) are made credible and real by the arguable economic disaster that would result if Beijing usurped the territory's autonomous powers.[169] Similarly, in addition to the final decision-making powers allocated to the Kurdish Territories by Iraq in the 2004 Iraqi Transitional Administrative Law, Turkish leaders have vowed to invade the Kurdish Territories if PIT leaders declare independence.[170] Similar threats of plausible war, territorial fragmentation, and/or economic disaster underpin the constitutional relations between Moldova and Gagauzia, the Philippines and Mindanao, Tanzania and Zanzibar, Vojvodina and Serbia, and Bougainville and Papua New Guinea.

As discussed earlier, polities can possess relationship specific assets which are resources that are "more valuable while cooperation persists."[171] While a partially independent arrangement maintains itself, core states can, for example, benefit from preferential natural resources, military basing rights, and in some cases large-scale financial flows. Such resources are also held hostage by the arrangement and are subject to being lost if the arrangement is usurped. In some cases, however, the salience of such defenses are less noticeable because constitutional rules (whether formal or conventional) may provide a more codified, public, and officially sanctioned set of protections.

In connection with forms of entrenchment, one might wonder if a core state that has a low rule of law ranking can make credible commitments that would entrench the powers allocated to a territory.[172] What are the distinguishing features between a sham federacy (which has all the features of a PIT except for entrenched powers) and a real PIT? With respect to this, some may point out that because of their higher levels of rule of law, the constitutional commitments that core states like France, the US, or Finland make to territories should be more believable than commitments made by countries like the Philippines, China, Sudan, Ethiopia, and Tanzania where the degree of rule of law has been called into question.[173] While this may be true to a certain extent, there are a number of issues to bear in mind.

---

[169] See Rezvani 2012.
[170] O'Leary 2005.
[171] Rector 2009, 16.
[172] Rule of law rankings can be obtained from the World Governance Indicator. Kauffmann et al. 2008.
[173] See Kauffmann et al. 2008.

First, in spite of their high rule of law ranking, countries like France and the US have a history of broken agreements and have established a number of sham autonomous arrangements (see Chapter 6). Therefore, while a high rule of law ranking may provide some confidence that a core state will adhere to its constitutional commitments, it is nevertheless not a sufficient predictor for determining agreements that are defensible from core state usurpation. Beyond having an association with a high rule of law core state, to avoid a sham federacy status the commitments made by these core states need to surpass mere promises that can be changed by fiat or a simple majority decision (as with the aforementioned formal, conventional, or political-formal forms of entrenchment).

Second, some arrangements made under difficult and demanding circumstances between low rule of law core states and territories appear to last for significant periods of time without a pattern of core state usurpation. About one-fifth (13) of PITs have been associated with low rule of law core states (see the political-formally entrenched PITs in Table 3.4 at the end of this chapter.) Of these, more than half (seven) have not experienced termination and continue to the present day.[174] And the average life of the remaining (six) PITs that terminated lasted on average about ten years.[175] Although the termination of their arrangements was often associated with armed conflict, an average period of a decade that resulted in cooperation should arguably not be discounted, especially when real or potential wars are averted. And while PITs associated with low rule of law core states may have less credible degrees of formal-legal and conventional entrenchment, they may have robust political-formal entrenchment. For example, in the Hong Kong–China relationship, although China is not known for its high degrees of rule of law, nevertheless, as indicated previously, the core state is dependent upon Hong Kong's economy.[176] This therefore prevents the otherwise human rights abusing and authoritarian Chinese Central Government from engaging in a pattern of usurpation that would undermine the arrangement.[177] Low rule of law core states should therefore not be dismissed out of hand as incompetent with regard to credible commitments.

---

[174] These territories are: Bougainville–Papua New Guinea (2004–present), Kurdistan–Iraq (2004–present), Vojvodina–Serbia (2009–present), Gagauzia–Moldova (1994–present), Muslim Mindanao–Philippines (1990–present), Zanzibar–Tanzania (1977–present), Hong Kong–China (1997–present).

[175] These territories are: South Sudan–Sudan (2004–11), South Sudan–Sudan (1972–83), Kosovo–Yugoslavia (1974–89), Vojvodina–Yugoslavia (1974–89), Eritrea–Ethiopia (1952–5), and Crimea–Ukraine (1996–2014).

[176] Rezvani 2012.

[177] Rezvani 2012.

The analysis here therefore assumes that one can indeed have greater confidence in the credibility of commitments when a core state has relatively high degrees of rule of law. Nevertheless, political-formal entrenchment is still possible between low rule of law core states and territories if the entrenchment can be corroborated by evidence of high levels of political influence (as with war, economic disaster, or territorial fragmentation) that act to stay the hand of a potentially usurping core state.

The Overlapping Nature of Entrenchment Mechanisms and the Demonstration Effect

Chapter 2 described the dramatic events that are often associated with the emergence of PITs. These stormy incidents (whether they consist of wars or revolutions) sweep away preexisting norms and rules, and redirect the leaders of core states and territories onto a new course in which they can capitalize on the advantages of a partially independent union. Such dramatic events can, however, also create a type of demonstration effect, which can illustrate the political damage that may assail core states and territories. The political damage that these leaders witness, can in turn incentivize them to not disrupt the integrity of an existing arrangement lest they too become subject to such political misfortunes.

For example, Britain's damaging loss of the American Thirteen Colonies and the increasing numbers of violent revolts by both Anglophone and Francophone Canadians during the first half of the nineteenth century demonstrated the damaging consequences of usurping its commitments to its settled colonies (which would come to be known as the British Dominions) and its other modern day partially independent arrangements.[178] Similar stories can be told of Moldova's war with the breakaway territory of Transnistria (which led them to consider the compromise of a partially independent arrangement with Gagauzia),[179] Dutch wars with the Dutch East Indies (which led to PITs for the Netherlands Antilles, Aruba, and Surinam),[180] France's many wars including those in their sham federacies of Indo China (which were formative events that set the stage for PIT status for New Caledonia and French Polynesia),[181] and Yugoslavia's devastating

---

[178]   On this point see Ferguson 2002, 90 and Wilton 1995, 111–36.
[179]   See Roper 2010, 101–22.
[180]   See Oostindie 2006, 614.
[181]   Herring 1979, 4.

wars and loss of its breakaway provinces, including the 1989 cancelation of Kosovo's partial independence that led to the forfeiture of that territory (which set the stage for the rump state of Serbia to reinstate Vojvodina's PIT status). Such political self-interest (in the form of fear of the negative repercussions of war, full secession, and negative economic consequences) on the part of core states and potential PITs leads to the formal legal agreements that give rise to partially independent arrangements.

Overtime as these rules crystalize into the psyche of the polities involved, unwritten rules develop.[182] As described in greater detail in the following chapters, in time a new basis for the arrangement is often established that rests more on unwritten or written constitutional rules than the self-interested protections of political pressure alone. One-time or intermittent demonstrations of political power can therefore ultimately lead to rules that operate even in the absence of the consistent application of clear and present political self-interest. America no longer has the same strategic interest in Puerto Rico (which was more strategically important before the end of the Cold War). Britain no longer has the same strategic interest in Bermuda (which was once its critical Atlantic military base). The Netherlands no longer views the Curaçao and Sint Maarten as critical to its geopolitical interests. While there are indeed some advantages for the core states to hold onto these territories, it is difficult to look only to core state self-interest (in the form of losing relationship specific assets) to justify their continued union. The point here is that formal and unwritten rules now defend these arrangements. They can play a critical role for defending the arrangement even when one side or another does not have strong materially based self-interest in the core–PIT relationship.

Formal, conventional, and political-formal entrenchment are therefore not mutually exclusive. In fact, in order to have effective formal-legal guarantees, either conventional or political underpinnings are often necessary. Countries without a strong internal tradition of unwritten rules, such as newly independent states, may have more difficulty entrenching partially independent arrangements with constitutional rules.[183] Without the prevalence of a significant chain of precedents, informal agreements, and/or deeply held constitutional principles to reinforce formal legal entrenchment, the possibility for the usurpation of the arrangement may be greater. Similarly, in order to have effective conventional guarantees, politically

---

[182] On such crystallization of practices or "usage" into unwritten rules see Wheare 1949.
[183] North 1993, 20.

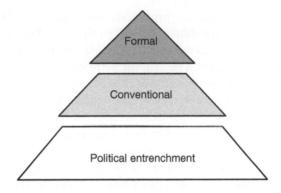

Figure 3.4. The entrenchment pyramid

entrenched underpinnings may be necessary (at least initially). Indeed, a glance at the list of sham federacies in Appendix 3 indicates that sham federacies are much more commonly associated with rule of law abusing authoritarian states as compared to core states associated with PITs that have higher rule of law ratings.

The mutual interdependence of these forms of entrenchment can be illustrated in the entrenchment pyramid illustrated in Figure 3.4, in which the top levels of entrenchment are supported by the lower levels. For example, although the partially independent arrangement between the Åland Islands and Finland provides far reaching formal entrenchment, Åland's formally entrenched association with Finland was initially solidified by the archipelago's strategic importance and the perceived danger on the part of Finnish leaders that adversarial powers could use the islands as a staging area for invasion. Finland insisted that the Åland Islands were a geographically natural part of its territorial space that could threaten its national security if held by a foreign power. It claimed that foreign "possession of the Islands would place Finland at the mercy of any Power which held, or was allied with a Power holding, the Islands."[184] The threat of such an invasion is now, however, gone. The strength of the arrangement now rests upon its formal legal entrenchment, which is reinforced by unwritten constitutional rules in the form of precedent. The deterrent effect provided by political damage evolved into formal legal entrenchment followed by

---

[184] Quoted in Barros 1968, 251.

conventional rules that make a partially independent arrangement very difficult to usurp. Although unwritten or political-formal entrenchment may exist for a particular PIT, the most salient element of entrenchment may, however, be the formal elements because of their written and often more public nature.

In spite of the frequent overlapping nature of entrenchment mechanisms, there are, however, partially independent arrangements where there is no formal entrenchment. Only conventional and political-formal entrenchment may apply. Table 3.4 therefore codes the form of entrenchment of a particular case based on the highest degree of formal entrenchment it has received. As far as the effectiveness of entrenchment, the main conclusion one can take away from these cases is that forms of entrenchment vary according to their robustness. Accordingly, the present study attempts to apply the stronger variants of entrenchment rather than those that are weaker. Formal legal entrenchment that consists of mutual agreement and supermajority change is stronger than weaker assurances, such as mutual consultation (which in many cases have been made to sham federacies). Conventional entrenchment that is characterized by long held precedent, the application of similar rules elsewhere in the polity, and multiple branches of government that have acknowledged its operation are stronger than mere claims of constitutional morality. Political-formal entrenchment that has the potential to throw the polities involved into economic disaster or war is obviously stronger than mere inconvenience. A final point to consider is that however robust such entrenchment mechanisms may be, they are not invincible. Whatever the prevailing strength of such entrenchment, in much of the same way that these regimes came into being in the first place, new forms of punctuated equilibrium can overthrow them. Such disasters are, however, rare. An arguably more likely possibility for their unraveling or maintenance is articulated by the integrationalist theory discussed in Chapter 2 and illustrated in Chapter 9 of the book.

CONCLUSION

Most views of international structure and sovereignty acknowledge the overriding importance of the supreme power held by sovereign states. They recognize how this power has made the citizens of states safer, how it has provided them with the dignity of self-determination, and how it has been a means of influence in the international system. But by not recognizing the existence of other systematically apparently polities that also possess this power, most of them overlook additional ways that these same outcomes are manifested, but by a political form other than the sovereign state. It may be possible to distinguish three constitutionally unincorporated polity forms in addition to the sovereign state that contain attributes of territorial sovereignty. In each case, while both supreme control and authority exists, the degree of sovereign power is not complete and is controlled by one or more associated sovereign states. First, there are de facto states, such as Taiwan, Nagorno-Karabakh, and Abkhazia.[185] Unfortunately, however, most of these polities have been racked with deep problems of insecurity as they relate to their preexisting sovereign state. Second, is the example of the EU, which possesses measures of both internal and external control and authority, although the authority that it possesses is not complete. But as mentioned earlier, the EU is an anomaly since other regional organizations have not yet been able to manifest attributes of territorial sovereignty. Finally there are partially independent polities, which are systematically present on almost every continent. And far from being disadvantaged as compared to sovereign states, the next chapters will show how in important ways they are in certain respects a more attractive option.

Given the emergence of partially independent polities, the structure of the international system is changing to accommodate threats created by nationalism, globalization, and international insecurity. The combination of powers of sovereignty together with partial integration with another sovereign state provides advantages to partially independent polities to respond to these forces in international affairs that the sovereign state by itself cannot achieve. Reflecting the marriage analogy presented in Chapter 2 in which PITs and core states maintain their relationship based on the informal norms that prevail between them, the following chapters will illustrate the normative underpinnings of PITs by illustrating the unwritten conventional rules that in many cases underpin their status.

---

[185] On de facto states seek King 2001, 524–52.

Table 3.4 Partially independent territory constitutional entrenchment

PIT	Core state	Primary type	Sources of entrenchment articulation
Guernsey and Jersey 1744–Present	UK	Conventional	*Pipon v Pipon* (1744) in which an attorney general confirmed that, "the laws of [Guernsey and Jersey] are separate, distinct, and independent of the laws of England..."[a]
Canada 1867–1931 (United)	UK	Conventional	1839 Durham Report; Dominion-UK Imperial Conferences held in 1887, 1894, 1897, 1902, 1907, 1911, 1921, 1923, 1926, and 1930*
Newfoundland 1855–1934	UK	Conventional	1839 Durham Report; Dominion-UK Imperial Conferences held in 1887, 1894, 1897, 1902, 1907, 1911, 1921, 1923, 1926, and 1930.* In 1933 the Newfoundland legislature voted to become a directly-controlled UK Crown Colony
New Zealand 1856–1931	UK	Conventional	1839 Durham Report; Dominion-UK Imperial Conferences held in 1887, 1894, 1897, 1902, 1907, 1911, 1921, 1923, 1926, and 1930*
Monaco 1861–Present	France	Formal	Constitution of the Principality 17 December 1962 (as amended by Law 2 April 2002) Article 8 "The present treaty may be modified by common consent of the parties" (The Principality of Monaco and the French Republic)
San Marino 1862–Present	Italy	Formal	1862 Treaty with Italy (later amended)[b]
Australia 1900–1931 (United)	UK	Conventional	1839 Durham Report; Dominion-UK Imperial Conferences held in 1887, 1894, 1897, 1902, 1907, 1911, 1921, 1923, 1926, and 1930*

(Continued)

Table 3.4. (Continued)

PIT	Core state	Primary type	Sources of entrenchment articulation
South Africa 1910–1931 (United)	UK	Conventional	1839 Durham Report; Dominion-UK Imperial Conferences held in 1887, 1894, 1897, 1902, 1907, 1911, 1921, 1923, 1926, and 1930*
Isle of Man 1886–Present	UK	Conventional	Conventional entrenchment enshrined in precedent since the 1765 Isle of Man Purchase Act[c]
Malta 1919–1931	UK	Conventional	1839 Durham Report; Dominion-UK Imperial Conferences held in 1887, 1894, 1897, 1902, 1907, 1911, 1921, 1923, 1926, and 1930*
Liechtenstein 1919–Present	Switzerland	Formal	Customs Treaty Between Switzerland and Liechtenstein of 29 March 1923 (later amended) creating a customs and monetary union with Switzerland. Article 42: "Changes to this contract may be agreed by mutual consent without formal notice." Article 43 designates an independent dispute resolution mechanism for the interpretation of the treaty.d Convention may however play the primary role in entrenching the 1923 arrangement. Switzerland also conducts some diplomatic relations on behalf of Liechtenstein.
Northern Ireland 1920–1972	UK	Conventional	Conventional entrenchment enshrined in precedent since the 1920 Government of Ireland Act until the Stormont Parliament's suspension in March 1972.[e]
Irish Free State 1921–1931	UK	Conventional	1921 Anglo-Irish Treaty, Article 1. 1839 Durham Report; Dominion-UK Imperial Conferences held in 1887, 1894, 1897, 1902, 1907, 1911, 1921, 1923, 1926, and 1930*

Table 3.4. (Continued)

PIT	Core state	Primary type	Sources of entrenchment articulation
Åland Islands 1922–Present	Finland	Formal	1920 Act on the Autonomy of Åland 1920, Sections 60 and 69. "This Act may be amended, explained, repealed or exceptions to it may be made only by consistent decisions of Parliament of Finland and the [Åland] Legislative Assembly." 2000 Constitution of Finland, Section 121
Rhodesia 1923–1931	UK	Conventional	1839 Durham Report; Dominion-UK Imperial Conferences held in 1887, 1894, 1897, 1902, 1907, 1911, 1921, 1923, 1926, and 1930*
Memel-Klaipeda 1924–1939	Lithuania	Formal	The substantial powers and democratic institutions that were allocated to Memel (over areas such as economic development, police, cultural matters, taxation, and others) were entrenched by a set of relatively novel instruments.[f] These included supermajority change guarantees. In order for changes to happen to the 1924 Statute, Memel's Chamber of Representatives had to provide a three-fifths majority. Furthermore, with the petition of a certain number of Memel citizens and/or members of the Chamber of Representatives, a successful popular referendum with two-thirds in favor was also needed for change. Moreover, Article 38 of the Statute specifies the simple majority mutual assent of the Legislative Assembly of Lithuania to any changes that are approved by Memel.

(Continued)

Table 3.4. (Continued)

PIT	Core state	Primary type	Sources of entrenchment articulation
Faroe Islands 1948–Present	Denmark	Conventional	1948 Home Rule Act of the Faroe Islands, Article 1; 1994 Denmark Parliamentary Act No. 103; 2005 Denmark Parliamentary Act No. 79.[g] A working group of lawyers appointed by the Danish government in July 1985 concluded that the state of Denmark "is certainly empowered to transfer all or part of its sovereignty. The Faroese Home Rule arrangement is just an example of a partial transfer of sovereignty to the Home Rule authorities, which according to the Home Rule Act have legislative power in matters of special concern."[h]
Trentino-South Tyrol, Sardinia, Sicily, Friuli-Venezia Giulia, Aosta Valley 1948–Present	Italy	Formal	1947 Constitution of Italy, Article 116. "Friuli-Venezia Giulia, Sardinia, Sicily, Trentino-Alto Adige/Südtirol and Valle d'Aosta/Vallée d'Aoste have special forms and conditions of autonomy pursuant to the special statutes adopted by constitutional law…"
Puerto Rico 1952–Present	US	Conventional	In non-legally binding dicta in 1982, the US Supreme Court confirmed that "Puerto Rico, like a state, is an autonomous political entity, 'Sovereign over matters not ruled by the Constitution…'"[i] For a similar view see *United States v Quinones* 1985, 42
Eritrea 1952–1955	Ethiopia	Political-formal	UN Resolution 390A, 5th Assembly—1950, implemented 1952
Netherlands Antilles 1954–2010	Netherlands	Formal	Netherlands Antilles, Charter for the Kingdom of the Netherlands (1954), Articles 12 and 18

Table 3.4. (Continued)

PIT	Core state	Primary type	Sources of entrenchment articulation
Surinam 1954–1975	Netherlands	Formal	Netherlands Antilles, Charter for the Kingdom of the Netherlands (1954), Articles 12 and 18
Cook Islands 1965–Present	N. Zealand	Formal	New Zealand, 1965 Cook Islands Constitution Act Commencement Order; New Zealand, 1964 Cook Islands Constitution Act, Article 46[j]
Bermuda 1967–Present	UK	Conventional	Bermuda Constitution Act of 1967 / Bermuda Constitution Order 1968[k] *Al Sabah v Grupo Torras et al.* 2005[l]
Cayman Islands 1967–Present	UK	Conventional	Cayman Islands (Constitution) Order 1972 (1972 No. 1101) *Al Sabah v Grupo Torras et al.* 2005[m]
South Sudan 1972–83	Sudan	Political-formal	1972 Addis Ababa Agreement, Article 2
Azores and Madeira 1974–Present	Portugal	Formal	1976 Constitution of Portugal, Articles 6 and 288
Niue 1974–Present	N. Zealand	Formal	Niue Constitution Act 1974 (Public Act 1974, No. 42) The Niue Constitution Act surrenders virtually all internal powers to the territory.[n] Article 6 of the Constitution Act allocates foreign and military powers to the central state.[o] Provided that it is able to surmount a two-thirds vote in its Assembly and a two-thirds majority of voters in a referendum, Niue can also change its constitution or even terminate its relationship altogether with New Zealand.
Kosovo 1974–1989	Yugoslavia	Political-formal	1974 Constitution of the Socialist Federal Republic of Yugoslavia, Part I, Articles 1–5, 18

(Continued)

Table 3.4. (Continued)

PIT	Core state	Primary type	Sources of entrenchment articulation
Vojvodina 1974–1989	Yugoslavia	Political-formal	1974 Constitution of the Socialist Federal Republic of Yugoslavia, Part I, Articles 1–5, 18
French Polynesia 1977–Present	France	Formal	1958 Constitution of France, Articles 72–74[p]
Zanzibar 1977–Present	Tanzania	Political-formal	1977 Constitution of the United Republic of Tanzania, Chapter I, Part I; Chapter 4. The Second Schedule, list 2 also confirms that any amendment to the powers allocated to Zanzibar requires support "by two-thirds of all Members of Parliament from Mainland Tanzania and two-thirds of all Members of Parliament from Tanzania Zanzibar."
Basque Country 1978–Present	Spain	Formal	Spain, Constitution of Spain, 1978, Article 167
Galicia 1978–Present	Spain	Formal	Spain, Constitution of Spain, 1978, Article 167
Catalonia 1978–Present	Spain	Formal	Spain, Constitution of Spain, 1978, Article 167
Northern Mariana Islands 1978–Present	US	Formal	Northern Mariana Islands, Covenant to Establish a Commonwealth of the Northern Mariana Islands in Political Union with the United States of America, 1976, Section 105
Greenland 1979–Present	Denmark	Conventional	1979 Home Rule Act; Act on Greenland Self-Government[q]
Aruba 1985–Present	Netherlands	Formal	Netherlands Antilles, Charter for the Kingdom of the Netherlands. 1954. Article 12 and 18
Micronesia, Federated States of 1986–Present	US	Formal	Federated States of Micronesia, Compact of Free Association. 2003. Title Four, Article III

Table 3.4. (Continued)

PIT	Core state	Primary type	Sources of entrenchment articulation
New Caledonia 1988–Present	France	Formal	May 1998 Nouméa Accord; 1958 Constitution of France, Articles 74, 76, and 77. As described in Article 74, the territory's constitutional acts can only be "amended...after consultation with the territorial assembly concerned."
Mindanao, Autonomous Region of Muslim 1990–Present	Philippines	Political-formal	1986 Constitution of the Philippines, Article 10 Section 15
Gagauzia 1994–Present	Moldova	Political-formal	Art. 111 of Constitution of Moldova, 1994 and "Law on the Special Juridical Status of Gagauzia (Gagauz Yeri)" requiring a three-fifths majority in the Moldovan Parliament for changes in the law[r]
Marshall Islands 1994–Present	US	Formal	Marshall Islands, Compact of Free Association. 2003. Title Four, Article III
Palau Islands 1994–Present	US	Formal	Palau Islands, Compact of Free Association. 1994. Title Four, Article V, Section 452
Hong Kong 1994–97	UK	Conventional	1994 Hong Kong Electoral Reform
Crimea 1996–2014	Ukraine	Political-formal	Chapter X of Constitution of Ukraine, 1996
Hong Kong 1997–Present	China	Political-formal	1997 Hong Kong Basic Law; 1984 Sino-British Joint Declaration
Northern Ireland and Scotland 1998–Present	UK	Conventional	1999 Memorandum of Understanding and Supplementary Agreements between the United Kingdom Government, Scottish Ministers, the Cabinet of the National Assembly for Wales. "The UK Government will proceed in accordance with the convention that the UK Parliament would not normally legislate with regard to devolved matters except with the agreement of the devolved legislature."[s]

(Continued)

Table 3.4. (Continued)

PIT	Core state	Primary type	Sources of entrenchment articulation
Nunavut 1999–Present	Canada	Formal	Canadian Constitution 1982, Section 35; Constitution Act, 1993 (Nunavut Act); 1993 Nunavut Land Claims Agreement
Kurdistan 2004–Present	Iraq	Political-formal	2004 Transitional Administrative Law; 2005 Constitution of Iraq, Articles 117, 121, & 141
Bougainville 2004–Present	Papua New Guinea	Political-formal	Section 219 of the 2004 Constitution of the Autonomous Region of Bougainville Constitution specifies supermajority entrenchment.[t]
South Sudan 2005–11	Sudan	Political-formal	May 26, 2004 "Protocol between the Government of Sudan (GOS) and the Sudan People's Liberation Movement (SPLM) on Power Sharing." Sudan, The Interim National Constitution of The Republic of the Sudan 2005, Part 17, Article 224 and Part 16
Gibraltar 2006–Present	UK	Conventional	Gibraltar's 2006 Constitution; Judicial Committee of the Privy Council's 2005 case *Al Sabah v Grupo Torras et al.*[u]
British Virgin Islands 2005–Present	UK	Conventional	Judicial Committee of the Privy Council's 2005 case *Al Sabah v Grupo Torras et al.*[v]
Wales 2006–Present	UK	Conventional	2006 Government of Wales Act (which established a local legislature with primary legislative powers). 1999 Memorandum of Understanding and Supplementary Agreements between the United Kingdom Government, Scottish Ministers, the Cabinet of the National Assembly for Wales. "The UK Government will proceed in accordance with the convention that the UK Parliament would not normally legislate with regard to devolved matters except with the agreement of the devolved legislature."

Table 3.4. (Continued)

PIT	Core state	Primary type	Sources of entrenchment articulation
Turks and Caicos Islands 2006–09/2012– Present	UK	Conventional	Judicial Committee of the Privy Council's 2005 case *Al Sabah v Grupo Torras et al.*[w]
Vojvodina 2009–Present	Serbia	Political-formal	Serbia, Constitution of the Republic of Serbia 2006, Articles 176–187 specifying supermajority, judicial review, and some mutuality provisions. Statute of the Autonomous Province of Vojvodina 2009. Adopted by the Assembly of Vojvodina on October 2008 and by the National Assembly of Serbia in November 2009.
Curaçao 2010–Present	Netherlands	Formal	Netherlands Antilles, Charter for the Kingdom of the Netherlands (1954), Article 12 and 18
Sint Maarten 2010–Present	Netherlands	Formal	Netherlands Antilles, Charter for the Kingdom of the Netherlands (1954), Article 12 and 18

* On the widely acknowledged unwritten constitutional rules that nullified preexisting colonial laws that applied to the historic British Dominions, see for instance, Evatt 1967; Forsey 1943; Keith 1912/1927; Leacock 1907, 355–92; Marshall 1984; Wheare 1949.

[a] On the constitutional conventions that make core state interference difficult see Grahl-Madsen 1988, 297; Williams 1972, 275.

[b] See Willoughby and Fenwick 1919, 79. See also Lapidoth 1997, 63–4.

[c] McKercher 2000, 95. See also Grahl-Madsen 1988, 297.

[d] Liechtenstein, 1923 Customs Treaty.

[e] Among the widespread acknowledgment of Northern Ireland's conventionally entrenched status, for one of the best accounts see Calvert 1968. See also Marshall 1984, 201–2.

[f] On Memel's status in general see Lapidoth 1997, 77–85 and Hannum 1990, 379–84.

[g] See Suksi 1997, 113. Faroe Islands, Denmark Parliamentary Act No. 103 1994. July 26; Faroe Islands, Denmark Parliamentary Act 2005. No. 79.

[h] Poulsen 1988, 340–1. For others that reflect this view see also Harhoff 1988, 293.

[i] *Rodriguez v Popular Democratic Party* 1982.

[j] Hannum 1990, 384–89. New Zealand, Cook Islands Constitution Act 1964. No. 69.

[k] See Davies 1995, 132–3.

[l] Antoine 2008, 14.

[m] Antoine 2008, 14.

[n] Niue, Niue Constitution Act. 1974.

[o] New Zealand Act No. 42, Article 6.

(*Continued*)

Table 3.4. (Continued)

[p] France's Constitution (as per Article 89) can be amended only after approval of both of its assemblies and approval by French referendum. It can also be amended if the President of the Republic submits the amendment to the National Assembly for a three-fifths majority vote.

[q] See Suksi 1997, 113; Harhoff 1993, 504.

[r] See Neukirch 2002, 105–23

[s] See also Winetrobe 2001, 287; and Cairney 2006, 434.

[t] Constitution of the Autonomous Region of Bougainville, 2004.

[u] Antoine 2008, 14.

[v] Antoine 2008, 14.

[w] Antoine 2008, 14.

4

Civil Order through Conventional Rules in the British Context: The British Dominions and Northern Ireland

Without a change in our system of government, the discontent which now prevails will spread and advance....The governor...should be instructed that he must carry on his government by heads of departments, in whom the united legislature shall repose confidence; and that he must look for no support from home in any contest with the legislature, except on points involving strictly imperial interests.

—Lord Durham, from his 1839 report (the Durham Report) to the British Parliament, in which he recommends that Britain's governor in Canada adopt a curtailed role similar to the constitutional monarchy with respect to the British Parliament.

I yet see such formidable obstacles to the disavowal of [the] policy [of cabinet government] that I lean to the opinion that we must avow and adopt it.

—Lord Stanley, British Colonial Secretary, in an October 1842 letter to the British Prime Minister in which he recommends that local affairs in Canada should be governed by the territory's elected cabinet rather than the British Governor.

In April 1849 widespread rioting broke out in the largest cities of the British territory of Canada. In the territory's capital, Montreal, the violence was especially fierce. Nationalists openly burned an effigy of the British-appointed governor-general, Lord Elgin, and then directly attacked the governor-general himself by stoning his carriage after it emerged from the houses of government.[1] Afterwards mobs unleashed their fury upon the territory's parliament

---

[1] On the political violence during this time in Canada see Wilton 1995, 111–36.

buildings and burned them down.[2] Relative peace only emerged after large numbers of imperial troops managed to quell the disturbances. The perpetrators of the 1849 riots, however, were not nationalists who wanted Canada to be independent, such as those who had perpetrated another set of rebellions in 1837. Instead, these were British loyalists who were angry about the reconfirmation of a new political status for Canada because of a decision made by Lord Elgin in April 1849 with the full approval of Britain's central government in London. To the great disappointment of the British loyalists, the governor-general's actions had proven that Canada was no longer a colony ultimately under the full power of Britain. Nor, however, was it fully independent. Canada had arguably become one of the first partially independent arrangements in history. The autonomy that was surrendered to the territories within Canada (and then later to still other colonies like Australia, Ireland, New Zealand, and South Africa) after the middle of the nineteenth century meant that the British metropole was constitutionally barred from unilaterally interfering in many of the internal workings of these PITs.[3] As is widely acknowledged in the constitutional law and political science literatures, on such issues they—and not Britain—had sovereign power.[4]

Autonomy created a compromise between full domination and full independence that arguably worked to quell the type of violent nationalism that eventually led to the secession of the Thirteen North American colonies. Indeed, much of the armed conflict throughout the world since that time and especially since the end of the Cold War has been domestic in nature, and much of this conflict has been a result of ethnic populations striving for self-determination.[5] For nearly a century the nationalistic compromise embodied by these partially independent arrangements arguably worked to prevent the violence and territorial fragmentation experienced by other empires. As historian Niall Ferguson observed with respect to the capital cities of the historic UK PITs of New Zealand, Australia, and Canada, "there would be no Battle of Lexington in Auckland; no George Washington in Canberra; no declaration of independence in Ottawa."[6]

---

[2] After this action, Canada's capital was moved from Montreal to Ottawa.

[3] For a bibliography and description of the widespread view in the political science and international law literatures that sovereignty is divisible rather than only attributable to states as a whole, see e.g., Bunck and Fowler 1996, 70–82.

[4] On the widely acknowledged unwritten constitutional rules that nullified the preexisting colonial laws that applied to the British Dominions, see for instance, Evatt 1936; Forsey 1943; Keith 1928; Leacock 1907, 355–92; Marshall 1984; Wheare 1949.

[5] Cederman et al. 2007; David 1997, 552–76; Gleditsch et al. 2002.

[6] Ferguson 2002, 90.

This chapter seeks to illustrate the unwritten rules that provide credible commitments for PITs, which fully independent polities in the relative anarchy of the international system do not possess. Such an analysis will build upon the formal entrenchment mechanisms discussed in Chapter 3. The focus of the chapter will be on the conventional entrenchment mechanisms between the UK and the British Dominions, which were among history's first PITs.[7] While unwritten constitutional rules usually exist to some degree in most partially independent arrangements, core–PIT entrenchment in the UK context does not include formal legal entrenchment. This therefore allows one to examine the effects of this form of entrenchment in relative isolation. This chapter will also examine the British Dominions and Northern Ireland as case studies because they have been challenged by counter equilibrium events. Counter equilibrium events are circumstances that threaten to usurp the otherwise credible commitments of an arrangement.[8] One can then make inferences of the operation of similar entrenchment mechanisms in other cases based on the outcomes of such challenges. In addition to discussing some of the counter equilibrium events that applied to the British Dominions, toward the end of the chapter similar events that apply to Northern Ireland will also be addressed. As distinct from those that argue that such counter equilibrium events undermined the autonomous powers of these territories, it will be argued that they illustrate institutional mechanisms—which sovereign states often do not possess—that protect territories from threats to democracy and civil disorder.

As the first known and identifiable PITs in history, PITs associated with the United Kingdom were used as models by a wide range of future states that sought to establish such arrangements. Puerto Rico (US) (and by extension other PITs associated with the United States) were modeled after the British Dominions.[9] The Åland Islands (Finland) was modeled after the autonomous arrangements for the Channel Islands (UK).[10] Future UK territories, whether one considers the historic proposals for Irish "Home Rule" or the modern

[7] A sampling of some of the key sources on the unwritten rules of constitutional behavior known as "convention" include, Bogdanor 1995; Brazier 1994; 1997; Dicey 1885/1982; Forsey 1984; Heard 1991; Jennings 1959; Keith 1935b; Marshall 1984; Munro 1975; Wheare 1949. For a seminal account of the application of conventional rules within the United States see Horwill 1925. As mentioned earlier, in this book associations are only coded here as conventionally entrenched partially independent arrangements when the core state's high court or executive leaders have informally acknowledged the bindingness of core–PIT conventional rules.

[8] On such out-of-equilibrium events seek Lake 2009, 66–7. Here equilibrium refers to the status quo or systemic conditions. See also Gartzke 1999.

[9] Leibowitz 1989.

[10] On the original use by Finns of the constitutions of the Channel Islands and the Isle of Man see Barros 1968, 216.

overseas arrangements (such as Bermuda (UK) and the Cayman Islands (UK)) were also modeled after the historic Dominions.[11] Still other countries have borrowed labels associated with them such as "home rule," "free state," and "regional autonomy" as public relations smoke screens for territorial arrangements that do not have any discernible entrenchment of their powers (as discussed in Chapter 6). An analysis of UK territories therefore provides a broader understanding of a wide range of PITs that have used them as historic antecedents.

Examining the British Dominions are also especially useful in this sense since they are a "hard" case in which one might expect that an argument in favor of partial independence might be dismissed in light of the many advantages these territories had *after* independence. As will be illustrated in Chapter 9, however, the argument that centers on the quality of the deal between the core state and the PIT overcomes such challenges—after the beginning of the twentieth century the UK was increasingly unable to furnish a set of public goods to British Dominions such as Canada that succeeded in persuading local nationalists that partial independence continued to be more favorable than sovereign statehood. Qualitative analysis will therefore be used here to understand many of the specific historic, economic, and political mechanisms that clarify how effects are exerted for making sovereignty work and not work for societies.

The chapter begins by summarizing the events which gave rise to the British Dominions. It will describe the logic behind the rejection of other alternatives in favor of partial independence. It will then illustrate the causal mechanisms which allow for such credibility even without effective formal legal entrenchment. The chapter will go on to briefly discuss the entrenchment mechanisms for other partially independent arrangements that are associated with the United Kingdom. Lastly, the chapter will address some of the counter equilibrium events that have assailed the British Dominions as well as Northern Ireland and discuss their outcomes.

THE EMERGENCE OF THE BRITISH DOMINIONS

Several decades after the cataclysmic loss of the Thirteen North American Colonies and another damaging war with the Americans in 1812, the British anxiously observed a new revolutionary movement emerging in the Canadian colonies among both Anglo and French Canadians. Canada was ceded to the

---

[11] Morton 1995, 75.

British by the French in 1763 after the British success in the French and Indian War. After a number of years of military rule, a civil government was established in 1764, but without a legislature (the idea of creating a legislature at this time was viewed by the British Parliament as "inexpedient").[12] The territory was instead ruled by a British-appointed governor and a legislative council, which would be chosen by the governor. After the US War of Independence, however, Parliament passed the Constitutional Act of 1791, which divided Canada into two colonies, Upper Canada (Ontario) and Lower Canada (Quebec), and granted each its own democratically-elected legislature, in addition to the governor and the legislative council. More than many colonies, Canada was seen at the beginning of the nineteenth century to be a bastion of British loyalty. Among other things, from the time of the American Revolution, Canada had benefited from the emigration of a stream of British nationalists who rejected the secession of the Thirteen Colonies. Canada's democratic assemblies were nevertheless under the ultimate control of the British central government. British Laws had made it clear that ultimate sovereignty rested with the central government. The life line of this control that connected Britain with such colonies were the centrally-appointed governors who exercised absolute power and legal omnipotence on behalf the central state. Instructions (referred to as "advice") would be given directly from British ministers to the governors whom they had appointed in these territories.[13] Just as the British monarch in old times had autocratic powers to unilaterally dismiss ministers, dissolve parliament, or call up the military to do their arbitrary bidding, so too did the British central government with respect to colonial possessions such as those in Canada. Acting through the governors that they had appointed, their powers were seen to be virtually unlimited. The British central institutions were fully sovereign. In spite of the large influx of British loyalists after the American Revolution, the complaints that resulted from such a form of autocratic governance were, however, all too familiar. Many Canadians resented having a legislative council and governor that was accountable, not to their own democratically-elected House of Assembly, but instead to a distant and high-handed central government in London.

In 1837 culturally French *Québecois* in Lower Canada, as well as swelling numbers of Anglophone Canadians in Upper Canada who had sympathy with the revolutionary path of the United States, revolted. As British subjects, Canadians in both its upper and lower territory wanted no more and no less than the form of government that was in operation within the metropole itself.

---

[12] Leacock 1907, 359.
[13] As Phillips et al. describe, "Her Majesty's pleasure would be made known on the advice of the Secretary of State." See Phillips et al. 2001, 783.

They wanted their executive branch, which was composed of a governor[14] and a legislative council chosen by him, to be responsible to the local legislature, rather than to the distant and autocratic central government. This was little different than the responsibility the British cabinet had to Parliament instead of to the whims of the British monarch (as was the case in centuries past).

Hence, in the version of this system that the Canadians proposed, cabinet governments would rise and fall according to the confidence the territorial Parliament had in their leadership, rather than the autocratic dictates of the core state. This form of governance (which would constitute the conventional entrenchment mechanisms that the territory would eventually adopt) was also known as "responsible cabinet government."[15] The governors' actions on most internal matters would be subordinated to the will of the territorial cabinets that could command a majority of their parliament rather than to the central government ministers in London.[16]

This constitutional shield proposed by the Canadians was, however, only a mirror of the protective mechanisms that have prevented Britain's monarchs from usurping the powers exercised by ministers who command a majority within the British Parliament. Anyone with a cursory familiarity with British democracy knows that the British Queen does not control the United Kingdom's military. It is also well known that unlike the old days of absolutism, the Queen can no longer dismiss Parliament at her whim. Nor can she remove the Prime Minister by her decree. This, however, is not what current British law says. Modern *legal* rules in the United Kingdom say that she can indeed do all of these things. A long tradition of common law (judge-made law) makes it clear that Britain's monarch possesses what are called "prerogative powers" (such as the power to dismiss Parliament, to dismiss the Prime Minister, to veto legislation, and to control the military).[17] These prerogative powers represent the residue of formal-legal powers that remain in the hands of the monarch from what was once full legal sovereignty. Although the Queen legally possesses these powers, they are almost all nevertheless controlled by the Queen's ministers (who command a majority within the British Parliament) and not the Queen herself. The irony of such informal rules of convention is that legal rules that completely contradict them are on the books. But in the case of the Queen's prerogative powers, it is not legal rules that regulate governmental institutions; it is the rules of convention instead. Therefore, with respect to

---

[14] In Lower Canada the governor was referred to as lieutenant-governor. In Upper Canada the governor was referred to as governor-general.

[15] On responsible government in the British Dominions see especially, Keith 1928.

[16] Phillips et al. 2001, 787.

[17] Marshall 2002, 6.

this area of Britain's constitution, written legal rules are dormant, suspended, nullified, and "frozen." What can be called a "written constitutional vacuum" pervades this area of Britain's written constitutional documents. Within this constitutional space powerful conventional rules (as opposed to written laws) allocate the exercise of executive functions to the Queen's ministers, instead of the Queen herself.

Even in this circumstance, however, the Queen as an individual with free will may still attempt to use her vast and draconian, legally-allocated powers. Since prerogative powers such as the monarch's legal ability to veto (refuse royal assent to) legislation has not been used since 1707, such an action would of course generate a constitutional crisis. She may decide to unilaterally dismiss Britain's Prime Minister. She may call up the military and order them to do her bidding. She may veto a bill duly passed by Parliament. However, in accordance with Figure 3.2, if she were to take such a bold course of action without proper cause (such as preventing imminent civil war or a *coup d'état*), it is clear that she would be assailed on all sides by *informal* constitutional enforcement mechanisms. The Queen, of course, does not risk chastisement from a formal-legal constitutional enforcement mechanism such as a written rule that may prohibit her action or from a mechanism such as a strong form of judicial review. The Queen, after all, would be well within the law with respect to carrying out such actions since the use of such power has been legally allocated to her.

Instead of formal-legal enforcement, informal enforcement mechanisms help to create compliance with the rules of convention. In addition to bearing the moral burden (political mores) of undermining Britain's democratic institutions and going against the political inertia of nearly two centuries of political practice (precedent), she would risk inciting popular opinion against her (political difficulty). And as has been shown over centuries of political practice within the United Kingdom, when sufficient popular antagonism is generated because of the monarch's arbitrary and unpopular actions, Parliament takes measures (as with the 1689 Bill of Rights) to formally limit the powers possessed by the monarch. The Queen may risk losing some of her legally-held prerogative powers or even risk her position as monarch. It is consequences such as these that prevent the monarch from thawing out her frozen powers.

With such rules already prevailing in Britain's central government, for more than a decade before 1837 Lower Canada's Patriot Party (under the leadership of Louis-Joseph Papineau) and Upper Canada's Reform Party (with leaders such as William Lyon Mackenzie) had lobbied the British Government to establish responsible government, but to no avail. One year after another the British Central government acting through their powerful colonial governors rejected proposals for such reforms within both of Canada's provinces. After March 1837 when the stamp of British intransigence with regard to such reforms seemed complete, Papineau shed non-violent tactics and turned to support the organization of a paramilitary body called the *Société des Fils de la Liberté*, which took its name from the revolutionary Sons of Liberty organized by Samuel Adams during the US War of Independence.[18] Recruits were enlisted. Militias were organized. A weekly manifesto was published. But before the militants could fully launch their revolutionary plans, the territorial Lieutenant-Governor Archibald Acheson, the second Earl of Gosford, issued warrants for the arrest of twenty-six high-ranking Patriot leaders. Papinueau and others fled into exile in America. Other leaders however stayed behind to fight a series of mostly unsuccessful battles with British troops and to endure acts of harsh British repression, which included the burning and raising of rebellious villages and the arrest of hundreds of rebels, many of whom were deported to the penal colony in Australia or executed for treason.[19]

Meanwhile in Upper Canada, in December 1837 reformist Canadians, who shared the desire for responsible government with the *Québecois* rebels in Lower Canada,[20] organized a rebellion of their own after receiving news of the attempts to arrest Patriot leaders. Led by a Scottish-born member of the Upper Canadian legislature and former mayor of Toronto, William Lyon Mackenzie, a small army of 1,000 men was organized to march on and overthrow Upper Canada's colonial government.[21] In addition to these potentially destabilizing conditions, the British also were well aware of American expansionist desires to annex the vast Canadian territory; a desire that was clearly expressed in Article XI of America's Articles of Confederation. They were therefore anxious that the United States not exploit the growing revolutionary spirit in Canada to once again attempt to capture the territory as they had already attempted in 1812 when a 12,000-man American army was defeated by British forces.[22]

British leaders wondered whether other British-settled colonies would now follow America's lead into independence.[23] Some feared that this was a clear sign of impeding full fragmentation of the overseas empire. Something had

---

[18] For an account of the 1837 rebellion see Greer 1993.

[19] Greer 1993.

[20] For a number of years before 1837 reformists in Upper Canada had urged the implementation of responsible government. This was enshrined in a 1835 document, the Seventh Report on Grievances, which was presented to the assembly of Upper Canada. The report said that "one great excellence of the English constitution consists in the limits it imposes on the will of a king by requiring responsible men to give effect to it. In Upper Canada, no such responsibility can exist. The lieutenant-governor and the British ministry hold in their hands the whole patronage of the provinces: they hold the sole Dominion of the country and leave the representative branch of the legislature powerless and dependent." Quoted in Leacock 1907, 361–2.

[21] On the political violence during this time in Canada see Wilton 1995, 111–36.

[22] Ferguson 2002, 90.

[23] Ferguson 2002.

to be done to prevent events like America's Battle of Lexington (which helped trigger the American Revolution) from being repeated in yet other British Territories such as Australia, New Zealand, South Africa, as well as Canada.[24] The British responded to these fears by suspending Lower Canada's constitution in January 1838 and dispatching John Lambton, the Earl of Durham, to investigate the causes of the Canadian rebellion and to recommend solutions.

The British witnessed the abundant success of federalism in the United States in overcoming many of the problems of governing a vast and heterogeneous land. Indeed, some suggest that a similar form of governance be adopted for the British Empire. Politicians and a variety of commentators put forward a diversity of proposals.[25] However the idea of making such a fundamental change was mostly greeted with hostility and fear.[26]

Skeptics emphasized that a federation on the US model would demand splitting the whole empire into a number of separate semi-independent units, which would greatly sap Britain's power, confuse its decision making, and make it more vulnerable to attack. Unitary government was seen to be more conducive to unity, cohesion, and organizational efficiency than federation. And while such a solution might have suited the demands of self-determination within the settled colonies of the empire, to the minds of many, it did not make sense to saddle England (which had by far the largest concentrations of population and wealth) with localized legislatures and other institutions that the regions within it neither requested nor needed. As British jurist A. V. Dicey would later argue, a federation would deprive "English institutions of their elasticity, their strength, and their life; it weakens the Executive at home, and lessens the power of the country to resist foreign attack."[27] Like most central governments, British leaders were also naturally reluctant to throw away their advantages and sovereignty over their subordinate colonies. Some also thought it would be unfair for Britain, which was far more wealthy and populous, to have somewhat of an equal status with much poorer and weaker polities. Many also broadly rejected the creation of a federation as "unsuited to the historical traditions and to the genius of Great Britain."[28]

In spite of this rejection of federation for the empire, the problem of nationalism and imperial cohesion remained. British statesmen held fast to the notion of unlimited British Parliamentary sovereignty over its territories. As the British experience with America's revolution indicated, however, local populations greatly resented being arbitrarily interfered with by an outside

---

[24] Ferguson 2002, 92.
[25] For an account of such proposals see Cheng 1931; Kendle 1989, 8–31; Tyler 1938.
[26] For a description of such criticisms see Kendle 1989, 17–23.
[27] Quoted in Kendle 1989, 22.   [28] Quoted in Kendle 1989, 23.

power. Eighteenth-century British parliamentarian Sir Edmund Burke mirrored this sentiment before the British Parliament while America was reacting negatively to Britain's unilateral decision to impose a stamp tax. He pointed out that "if, intemperately, unwisely, fatally, you sophisticate and poison the very source of government by urging subtle deductions and consequences odious to those you govern from the unlimited and illimitable nature of supreme sovereignty, you will teach them by these means to call that sovereignty itself in question."[29] As Burke surveyed the unfolding events in their once loyal colonies, he observed that "when you drive him hard, the boar will surely turn upon the hunters."[30] "If that sovereignty and their freedom cannot be reconciled," he asked' "which will they take?"[31] He answered that "no one will be argued into slavery."[32]

The Partial Independence Compromise

After being dispatched to Canada to examine the nature of the Canadian revolt and possible solutions, statesmen like Lord Durham concluded that if Britain were to maintain its empire—and the stability of its political and economic commitments within its numerous territories—steps needed to be taken to deal with the divisive effects of centralized rule in the midst of the menace of nationalism within the periphery territories. This was especially true with regard to the more politically and economically sophisticated colonies settled with British citizens. Something had to be done to cool the inflammatory notion that the central government's sovereignty was unlimited and it had the right to do whatever it wanted with its inferior colonies. Under such circumstances, as Burke warned the British Parliament, "they will cast your sovereignty in your face."[33]

After six months of investigation, Lord Durham presented his report to the British Parliament in 1839.[34] This report has been hailed by later historians as "the book that saved the Empire."[35] Lord Durham observed that "without a change in our system of government, the discontent which now prevails will spread and advance."[36] The central change that Durham suggested provided a constitutional framework through which partial independence would ultimately emerge with the establishment of responsible government. In such an arrangement,

---

[29] Burke 1964, 110–11.   [30] Burke 1964.   [31] Burke 1964.
[32] Burke 1964.   [33] Burke 1964.
[34] For more details on the events which led to Lord Durham's report see Craig 1963, 257–70.
[35] Ferguson 2002, 91.   [36] Quoted in Leacock 1907, 363.

the governor...should be instructed that he must carry on his government by heads of departments, in whom the united legislature shall repose confidence; and that he must look for no support from home in any contest with the legislature, except on points involving strictly imperial interests.[37]

Mirroring numerous compromises that would take shape between core states and PITs around the world, the compromise that was arrived at delivered some of the benefits of a federation without its infeasible characteristics. For these settled colonies, which would eventually be called the self-governing Dominions, there would be no federation government at the center in London; no newly-created, coequal parliament for Britain, no federation member-unit status for the colonies, and by and large the British Parliament would continue as it had before. What would change, however, was that the settled colonies would be provided with their own powers of internal self-government. Military policy, "imperial" affairs, and many foreign policy issues would still be held in the hands of the British central government. And unlike member-units in the US federation whose status was formally-entrenched, these arrangement would be entrenched by the vague, yet often very important, informal rules known as convention.[38] Just as conventional rules shielded the British Cabinet and Prime Minister from the arbitrary whims of the monarch, conventional rules came to shield the self-governing Dominions from unilateral central government usurpation.

Conventionally-entrenching responsible government (cabinet government) first came to be established in Nova Scotia in 1846 and Canada in 1847, but then spread to significant numbers of other British territories throughout the globe (see Table 4.1).[39] Many of the territories where such governmental forms were established integrated into larger agglomerations such as the federation of Canada in 1867, the federation of Australia in 1900, and the Union of South Africa in 1909. Newfoundland,[40] New Zealand, and the Irish Free State retained their separate status (Figure 4.1).

No constitutional breakthrough was necessary; only the application of a credibility-enhancing mechanism that was already at work within Britain's

---

[37] Quoted in Leacock 1907, 364.

[38] The application of such conventional entrenchment to partially independent arrangements is also part of the focus of the next chapter.

[39] On the self-governing status of the British Dominions see for instance, Evatt 1936; Forsey 1943; Keith 1928; 1932; 1935a; 1935b; 1948; Leacock 1907; Wheare 1949.

[40] In 1933, Newfoundland decided to return to being a colony. This decision by the parliament of Newfoundland was based on its financial difficulties, with millions of dollars of debt from the First World War as well as the trials of the Great Depression. In 1946, however, it joined the Canadian federation.

Table 4.1 Emergence of partially independent territories within the British Empire through grant of ministerial responsibility*

Partially Independent Territory	Date of origin
Nova Scotia	1846 (Merged into Canada in 1867)**
Canada (Ontario and Quebec)	1847**
Prince Edward Island	1851 (Merged into Canada in 1867)
New Bruswick	1854 (Merged into Canada in 1867)**
Victoria	1855 (Merged into Australia in 1900)
New South Wales	1855 (Merged into Australia in 1900)
Tasmania	1855 (Merged into Australia in 1900)
South Australia	1855 (Merged into Australia in 1900)
Newfoundland	1855 (Merged into Canada in 1949) In 1933 the legislature voted to become a directly-controlled UK Crown Colony.
Dominion of New Zealand	1856
Queensland	1859 (Merged into Australia in 1900)
Dominion of Canada	1867
Manitoba	1870 (Added to Canada)
British Columbia	1871 (Added to Canada)
Cape Colony	1872 (Merged into South Africa in 1909)
West Australia	1890 (Merged into Australia in 1900)
Natal	1893 (Merged into South Africa in 1909)
Commonwealth of Australia	1900
Saskatchewan	1905 (Added to Canada)
Alberta	1905 (Added to Canada)
Transvaal	1906 (Merged into South Africa in 1909)
Orange Free State	1907 (Merged into South Africa in 1909)
Union of South Africa	1909
Malta	1919†
Irish Free State	1921
Rhodesia	1923††

* Adapted in part from Scott 1919, vi–vii.
** Wheare 1949, 47–8.
† Keith 1912/1927, 50.
†† Keith 1912/1927, 37.

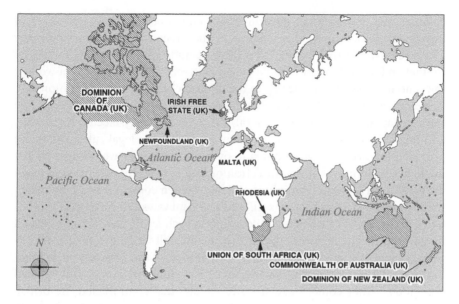

Figure 4.1 Historic British Dominion partially independent territories

central government. As Lord Durham himself explained in his report, "It needs no change in the principles of government, no invention of a new constitutional theory, to supply the remedy which would, in my opinion, completely remove political disorders. It needs but to follow out consistently the principles of the British constitution."[41] Convention would now be used to nullify the legal powers of the British Parliament, monarch, and territorial governor-generals as they related to these territories in much the same way that the British monarchs are limited from interfering in the affairs of the British Parliament. By applying its monarch-limiting rules to itself vis-à-vis its territories, the British achieved the compromise of nullifying its coveted Parliamentary sovereignty on some issues without providing full independence.[42]

The irony of such partially independent arrangements, however, was that—similar to the aforementioned relationship between the British Parliament and monarch—the establishment and entrenchment of their final decision-making powers were through unwritten rather than written constitutional rules. Rather than formally abrogating the British Parliament's existing laws which had established the centrally-controlled institutions within these one-time

[41] Quoted in Leacock 1907, 363.
[42] For a useful critique on the existence of British Parliamentary sovereignty see Elliott 2004, 545–52.

colonies, the new form of government would superimpose a new layer of unwritten conventional rules on top of the preexisting colonial structure. These rules would shift power from the autocratic governor to the territorial cabinet and legislature and would suspend, freeze, and nullify the powers of the central state from interfering in the domestic affairs of the Dominion.

Hence, all of the key pre-existing colonial institutions including the centrally-appointed governor-general, the democratically-elected legislature, and the cabinet would therefore remain. And all of the legal rules which had provided for Britain's autocratic rule over the territories would also be left unchanged. No moves in the direction of legally nullifying them were taken until 1931. All of these Dominions still had written constitutional laws which made it clear that a territory was still in significant ways subject to the omnipotence of the central authority.[43] According to such *legal* rules, acting through its governor in the territory, the British retained all vital powers of constitutional change.[44] They could arbitrarily strip leaders of their powers by dismissing them.[45] They could reserve (suspend) and disallow (annul) duly passed legislation.[46] They could make any and all laws that contradicted the British

[43] For many of the key constitutional documents for the Dominions of Canada, Australia, South Africa, New Zealand, and Newfoundland, including the Letters Patent, Instructions, Commission, and Dormant Commissions, see Keith 1928, 1561–613.

[44] Keith 1928, 1146–7. Australia and Canada could make no changes to their constitutional acts (the 1867 British North America Act and the 1900 Constitution of the Commonwealth of Australia) without a new law from the British Parliament. Interestingly, Canadian provinces (especially Quebec) were jealous of their own powers as federal member-units and wanted it this way so that the Canadian federal government would have less direct access to the levers of constitutional change to usurp their powers. Similarly, the Irish Free State's powers, which were specified in their 1921 treaty with Britain, could not be changed except by mutual assent. And while the unitary Dominions of New Zealand, South Africa, Newfoundland, Malta, and Southern Rhodesia had limited powers of constitutional change, they were not able to enlarge their powers or alter their status unilaterally. See Keith 1928, 1147.

[45] One of the Australian constitutional documents, the 1900 Letters Patent, which directly mirrors—in many cases word for word—the other "Letters Patent" of the other Dominions makes this clear. Article IV of the 1900 Australian Letters Patent, for instance, says: "The Governor-General may, so far as We Ourselves lawfully may, upon sufficient cause to him appearing, remove from his office, or suspend from the exercise of the same, any person exercising any office or place under the State, under or by virtue of any Commission or Warrant granted, or which may be granted, by Us, in Our name, or under Our authority." Reprinted in Keith 1928, 1570.

[46] With the power of disallowance the monarch (on the advice of British Ministers) could disallow (annul) laws passed by the territorial legislature. With respect to the powers of disallowance see the 1852 New Zealand Act, Section 55; the 1867 British North America Act (Canada), Section 56; the 1900 Constitution of the Commonwealth of Australia, Section 59; and the 1909 South Africa Act, Section 65. See also UK, The Report of the Conference on the Operation of Dominion Legislation and Merchant Shipping Legislation 1929, 175.

Under the similar but distinct power of reservation, the Dominion's governor-general could choose to not give his assent to a bill duly passed by the Dominion legislature and instead bring it before the British monarch to decide on its fate with the advice of British Ministers. With

Parliament's laws that explicitly applied to a territory invalid and void.[47] They could dissolve the territorial parliament.[48] They could overrule judicial decisions made in the territory. And they could control local military forces and foreign relations.

What would change, however, was that with the establishment of "responsible government" (or cabinet government), the powers of the central state would now be nullified with respect to the majority of domestic issues. This nullification went into effect by dispatch from the central government's Secretary of State to the territorial governor. Under the previous colonial constitutional order, the governor had served as the central state's eyes, ears, sword, and the chief means of the central government's autocratic control over its possessions. Under the new constitutional order however, by order from the central state, most of the governor's legal powers would be invalidated and power would now shift to the territorial cabinet and parliament. In the words of Lord Durham, the Secretary of State would instruct the territorial governors "to secure the co-operation of the Assembly in his policy, by entrusting its administration to such men as could command a majority."[49] With such instructions the governors would surrender domestic affairs to ministers who could command the loyalty of the majority of the democratically-elected territorial legislature. The territorial legislature's relationship with the central government through its governor-representative would be modeled on the relationship between the British Parliament and its monarch. As British Colonial Secretary, Lord Stanley, affirmed with regard to Canada's Prime Minister: "the prime minister of that colony is to advise the governor on every occasion, and his advice is to be explicitly followed."[50] With respect to the majority of domestic issues, the governor-general's position would therefore be relegated to that of a mere figurehead.[51]

respect to such legal powers of reservation see the 1852 New Zealand Act, Sections 55 and 59; the 1867 British North America Act (Canada), Sections 55 and 57; the 1900 Constitution of the Commonwealth of Australia, Sections 58 and 60; the 1909 South Africa Act, Sections 64 and 66; and the Constitution of the Irish Free State, Article 41. See also UK, The Report of the Conference on the Operation of Dominion Legislation and Merchant Shipping Legislation 1929, 177.

[47] This was set down in the British Parliament's 1865 Colonial Laws Validity Act. See UK, The Report of the Conference on the Operation of Dominion Legislation and Merchant Shipping Legislation 1929, 183–7.

[48] Article V of the 1900 Australian Letters Patent, for instance, reflects this saying: "The Governor-General may on Our behalf exercise all powers under The Commonwealth of Australia Constitution Act, 1900, or otherwise in respect of the summoning, proroguing, or dissolving the Parliament of Our said Commonwealth." Reprinted in Keith 1928, 1570–1.

[49] Reprinted in Wheare 1949, 45–6. See also Keith 1948, I, 137.

[50] Quoted in Leacock 1907, 372.

[51] As detailed above there is general agreement among scholars of a consistent record of conventional rules serving as an effective shield for PITs to keep the possibility of UK legal

Political incentives, political inertia, and deeply held political principles were the forces that have consistently shielded the British Parliament from interference by the monarch through modern history. These same forces shielded the self-governing Dominions from interference by the British central government. In accordance with Figure 3.2, the political incentives were made available by the specter of revolution, imperial fragmentation, and lobbying by elements from the periphery territories. The political inertia was supplied by the strong central government tradition of adhering to precedent. And the deeply held political principles were furnished by the abhorrence that had evolved—especially after the loss of the Thirteen North American Colonies—of usurping democracy in territories settled by British citizens. Because of such informal enforcement mechanisms, these territories would have powers that were real, credible, and very difficult to take away. While not being fully independent states, they would attain their own internal self-determination. Under such circumstances, these territories ascended from being mere colonies to becoming PITs.

THE RECORD OF CREDIBLE COMMITMENTS

Apart from some rare exceptions, the historical record shows that Britain's powerful legal rules were indeed held at bay by conventional rules with great consistency.[52] The adherence to such convention is reflected in the well-established precedents of noninterference by the central state and in the informal agreements that were articulated in the many imperial conferences attended by imperial and Dominion representatives.[53] Indeed, it eventually came to be that

interference at bay. Nevertheless, there are a few rare exceptions, notably in Canada and Australia, in which Dominion governors exercised powers against the advice of local ministers in their role as constitutional guardians. In spite of these exceptions, most observers who have studied the matter acknowledge the consistent application of conventional rules. See Evatt 1936; Marshall 1984; Phillips et. al. 2001.

[52] See Evatt 1967; Forsey 1943; Keith 1928; Leacock 1907, 355–92; Keith 1928Marshall 1984; Wheare 1949.

[53] Accordingly, the history of precedents show that the central government's power of disallowing legislation was almost never exercised. Phillips 2001 et al., 788. At the 1930 Imperial Conference it was further reconfirmed that "The power of disallowance can no longer be exercised in relation to Dominion legislation." Quoted in Wheare 1949, 127. The last time it was exercised in Canada was in 1873. See UK, The Report of the Conference on the Operation of Dominion Legislation and Merchant Shipping Legislation 1929, 175. The last time it was exercised in New Zealand was 1867. See UK, The Report of the Conference on the Operation of Dominion Legislation and Merchant Shipping Legislation 1929, 176. And it was never exercised with respect to Australia or South Africa. See UK, The Report of the Conference on the

the central government would take no unilateral action, whether with its legal control over the governor-generals or its powers to change legal constitutional rules without the explicit consent of the Dominions.[54] As Geoffrey Marshall described, "one function for convention has always been that of controlling the impact of the traditional legal doctrine of the supremacy of Parliament".[55] The operation of binding convention rendered the strict law statutes of the British Parliament as they pertained to the Dominions inoperable or frozen. As will be argued in the next chapter, a similar state of affairs also applies to the relations between Puerto Rico and America. With respect to rendering void territorial laws that contradicted laws made by the British Parliament, this is an area where the central government did indeed exercise its legal power over the Dominions, especially in the late nineteenth century. But it did so primarily with regard to issues outside of the domestic jurisdiction of the Dominions' territory.[56]

Operation of Dominion Legislation and Merchant Shipping Legislation 1929. With respect to the central government's power of reservation (reservation is the governor's suspension of duly passed legislation until the British monarch can decide upon it under the advice of the British Ministers), the operation of responsible government mandated that the power of reservation only be exercised with the Dominion's permission. Phillips et al. 2001, 788. In the 1930 Imperial Conference the existing convention of non-central government reservation of bills was reconfirmed: "His Majesty's Government in the United Kingdom will not advise His Majesty the King to give the Governor-General any instructions to reserve Bills presented to him for assent." Quoted in Wheare 1949, 130. Even the territorial governor himself came to be appointed by (on the direct "advice" of) the territorial ministers and the central state made it clear that "he is not the representative or agent of His Majesty's Government in Great Britain or of any Department of that Government." See UK, the Report of the Inter-Imperial Relations Committee, Imperial Conference 1926, 164. The British government mandated, however, that when such an appointment was made, that it be an official that was acceptable to both local political parties.

[54] In a 1929 Imperial Conference, the Central government declared that "it would not be in accordance with constitutional practice for advice to be tendered to His Majesty by His Majesty's Government in Great Britain in *any matter* appertaining to the affairs for a Dominion against the views of the Government of that Dominion." (emphasis added.) See UK, The Report of the Conference on the Operation of Dominion Legislation and Merchant Shipping Legislation 1929, 180.

[55] Marshall 1984, 201.

[56] Such extraterritorial issues included competencies in the areas of deportation, marriage, criminal law, shipping, air navigation, fisheries, taxation, and the enforcement of laws against smuggling and unlawful immigration. As late as 1928 Arthur Berriedale Keith wrote that "Not a single Dominion has passed a Bill regarding international matters to which any Imperial Government could possibly take exception, save Newfoundland, and her legislation in 1907 was promptly overridden by an Imperial Order in Council under an Imperial Act" Keith 1928, 1147. While the exercise of its powers of invalidating laws under the 1865 Colonial Validity Act had increasingly been confined to an ever narrowing field (so as to not antagonize the Dominions), the exercise of such powers was at last informally renounced by the central government in 1929. "We are of opinion that the recognition of the powers of a Dominion to legislate with extra territorial effect should not be limited either by reference to any particular class of persons (e.g. the citizens of the Dominion) or by any reference to laws ancillary to provision for the peace,

Dominion powers were at first mostly confined to domestic issues. Diplomacy (including commercial treaty-making powers, fiscal autonomy including the power to impose tariffs, and decisions of war and peace) were in the hands of the central government. Overtime, however, external powers were granted to them. In 1871 they were provided with powers to represent themselves in negotiating their own commercial treaties.[57] In 1878 they acquired their own fiscal autonomy.[58] In 1879 Canada—soon followed by Australia and New Zealand—imposed its first tariffs on British goods.[59]

Nevertheless, with regard to wars that Britain was engaged in, while the Dominions were not obligated to commit troops without their consent, they also acknowledged that they did not have the freedom to remain neutral. In the Canadian House of Commons in 1910 Canadian Premier Sir Wilfrid Laurier made the following statement:

> *If England is at war we are at war and liable to attack.* I do not say that we shall always be attacked, neither do I say that we would take part in all the wars of England. That is a matter that must be determined by circumstances, upon which the Canadian Parliament will have to pronounce and will have to decide in its own best judgment.[60]

Hence, while Canada asserted a right of consultation before participation in a British war (which was indeed respected), it was nevertheless not neutral.[61]

After World War I, Australia, Canada, New Zealand, and South Africa were recognized individually as members of the League of Nations. In time, the Dominions were also granted their own separate armed forces. In 1918, for instance, after contributing great material resources and over one million soldiers in support of the Empire during World War I, the central government agreed to separate Dominion navies after Dominion ministers rejected central government proposals for a united navy.[62]

Ultimately, however, a turning point came in 1931 when Dominions were by and large granted independence with the 1931 Statute of Westminster (a British law).[63] Section 2 of the Statute put down in legal terms that Dominions

---

order, and good government of the Dominion..." See UK, The Report of the Conference on the Operation of Dominion Legislation and Merchant Shipping Legislation 1929, 182.

[57] Ferguson 2002, 208.
[58] Ferguson 2002.
[59] Ferguson 2002.
[60] Quoted in Keith 1928, 1553–4. Emphasis added.
[61] Keith 1928, 1554.
[62] UK, Naval Defense and Dominion Autonomy: Memorandum of Dominion Ministers 1918, 11.
[63] The text of the 1931 Statute of Westminster is reprinted in Wheare 1949, 308–12.

have extraterritorial legislative powers. Section 3 made it clear that no laws of any Dominion would be rendered void because they contradicted statutes of the British Parliament. And Section 4 formalized the rule that "no act of Parliament of the United Kingdom" would "extend, or be deemed to extend, to a Dominion as part of the law of that Dominion" without its permission. With the addition of full external powers and the guarantees attached to them, the Dominions appeared to be more like independent states.[64] It is of course the case that on paper the British still had significant legal powers over the Dominions.[65] In practice, however, these powers were nullified to such an extent that the likelihood that they would be exercised against the will of any of the Dominions appeared absurd.[66] This mirrored the perceived absurdity of the British monarch arbitrarily taking up the reins of power against the will of Parliament within the United Kingdom. Hence, while the Irish Free State (called Eire after 1937) only formally achieved its independence in 1949,[67] the Union of South Africa in 1961,[68] the Dominion of Canada in 1982,[69] the Commonwealth of Australia in 1986,[70] and New Zealand in 1996,[71] for the purposes here, the status as a PIT came to an end when the Dominions achieved full control over their armed forces and diplomacy in addition to their internal sovereignty.[72]

Alleged Counter Equilibrium Challenges

In spite of the relative consistency with which conventional rules enforced the Dominion–UK partially independent union, a number of alleged challenges assailed the credibility of UK commitments in the first part of the twentieth century. The controversies centered on the repeated refusal of UK appointed-Dominion governors to grant legislative dissolutions to PIT legislatures that made the request. Such dissolutions occur from time to time in

---

[64] On the end of Dominion status see Scott 1945. See also Phillips et al. 2001, 788.

[65] As K. C. Wheare argued, "But it is necessary to emphasize that, in enacting section 4, the United Kingdom Parliament has not attempted in strict law to diminish or abolish its power to legislate for the Dominions. Section 4, as has been emphasized, is not a rule restricting power, it is a rule of construction," Wheare 1949, 150–157.

[66] On this subject, see, e.g., Marshall 1984, 201.

[67] See Ireland, Republic of Ireland Act 1948 and United Kingdom, Ireland Act 1949.

[68] South Africa applied provisions of its own 1934 Status of the Union Act as part of its process of independence. See Phillips et al. 2001, 789.

[69] See, United Kingdom, Canada Act 1982.

[70] See, United Kingdom, Australia Act 1986.

[71] See, New Zealand, 1996 Constitution Act.

[72] For a description of each of the aforementioned acts, see Phillips et al. 2001, 790–5.

parliamentary democracies, in which prime ministers request dissolutions of the legislature, which would result in new elections. Generally, such dissolution of the legislature (and the new elections that would necessarily follow) can sometimes serve an important role in parliamentary democracies by appealing to the electorate to determine the balance of representation in response to legislative debates. It will, however, be argued here that these refusals of the UK-appointed governors to grant these dissolutions were not in fact illegitimate core state usurpations of power and as a consequence did not undermine the credibility of core–PIT conventional entrenchment. Indeed, far from representing usurpations of the UK–Dominion union, these cases illustrate constitutional protections possessed by PITs that fully independent states do not possess.

Formally the monarch had the power to refuse "advice" of ministers for legislative dissolutions. By convention, however, in most cases the monarch was duty bound to abide by such "advice." Accordingly, in most cases monarchs and UK-appointed Dominion Governors would grant a prime minister's request for dissolution. In the first part of the twentieth century, however, some observers became troubled by what appeared to an inconsistency. Before World War II in the UK, dissolution was only refused on one occasion—in 1910.[73] In the British Dominions, by contrast, while there were 110 grants of dissolution, there were also 51 cases in which British Governors refused.[74] Some of these refusals also occurred after 1910, such as one especially notable case in Canada in 1926 (which helped trigger sentiments in favor of full secession). In light of such refusals there were accusations that the British were inappropriately (and in light of the record of dissolution in the UK) unfairly interfering in Dominion affairs. Some critics of these actions asserted that the monarch-appointed governors should always abide by the advice of the cabinet. They also argued that the dissolution, which would lead to a fresh appeal to the electorate, was always justified.[75]

Much of the scholarship on this issue, however, argues in favor of the constitutionality of such refusals by (1) pointing to the undesirable potential for an unlimited power of dissolution to harm the separation of power between the executive and legislative branches and by (2) emphasizing that the Dominion governors correctly applied the same conventional rules in the UK and the Dominions.[76] As distinct from the critics of the dissolution refusals, who evidently believed that any refusal of such a dissolution was a violation of the rules, there has been a long-held view that prime ministers do not have an unlimited power of dissolution. Accordingly, in both the UK and the Dominions, conventional rules demanded that dissolutions should be refused

---

[73] Forsey 1943, 65.   [74] Forsey 1943.
[75] Forsey 1943, 85–6, 258.   [76] See, e.g., Evatt 1936; Forsey 1943.

(1) when an alternative government is available to take up the reins of power (which is especially possible in a democracy with more than two main political parties), (2) when a dissolution is used by the prime minister to forestall a motion of no confidence, or (3) if there is no great public policy issue at stake.[77]

One can point to classic observations by those such as British Parliamentarian Sir Edmund Burke who emphasized the harmful effects that an unfettered power of dissolution would have on the separation of powers[78] between the cabinet and the main body of the legislature:

> If our authority is to be held up when we coincide in opinion with his Majesty's advisers, but is to be set at naught the moment it differs from them, the House of Commons will shrink into a mere appendage of administration, and will lose that independent character which…enables us to afford a real, effective and substantial support to his government.[79]

Mirroring this, Herbert Evatt emphasizes that an unfettered use of such power would result in "defamation and intimidation and the deliberate inculcation of disillusion and disgust" resulting in "the very means of first delaying and ultimately defeating the true popular will, and so represent a triumph over, and not a triumph of, the electorate."[80] From this perspective dissolutions are a blunt and disruptive tool, which many have feared could relegate democratically elected members of a legislature into "mere creature(s) of the cabinet."[81]

Eugene Forsey also clarifies that the different frequency of refusal of dissolution in the UK as compared to the Dominions was more a result of the prevalence of multiparty systems in the Dominions (as distinct from the mostly two-party system in the UK), which increases the chance that one of the aforementioned conditions for dissolution refusal would be met.[82] Namely, a multiparty system increased the chance that an alternative government that controlled a majority of seats could take up the reins of power. In order for a change of government to be achieved, a competing party would need to have the largest share of members of parliament. This is very hard to achieve in democracies like the UK with only two main parties, which under most circumstances would require an absolute majority in parliament.[83] As the number of parties that are represented in parliament increases, however, the ability of

---

[77] See Evatt 1936, 109; Forsey 1943, 263–4.
[78] On the separation of powers within the UK see Tomkins 2007, 255–92.
[79] Quoted in Forsey 1943, 9.
[80] Evatt 1936, 109.
[81] Forsey 1943, 258.
[82] Forsey 1943.
[83] While there have indeed been smaller third parties that are represented in the British Parliament (such as the modern day Liberal Democratic party) these third parties tend to be dwarfed by the two dominant parties (such as the modern day Labour and Conservative parities).

a single party to have the most representatives also increases. Hence, since the Dominions tended to have multiparty (rather than two party) systems, it was much easier than in the UK to form an alternative government. And since the availability of an alternative government was one of the long accepted reasons for refusing a dissolution request, many more dissolution refusals resulted in the Dominions. The Dominion Governors were therefore not applying a double standard in which rules were being applied differently in the UK as compared to the Dominions. Forsey makes the following observations:

> The apparent differences in practice are explicable almost entirely in terms of different circumstances. In most cases of refusal of dissolution overseas the existence of a multiple-party system, or the presence of Independents in sufficient numbers to hold the balance of power, or the looseness of party organization, and the fact that all alternatives had not already been tried, gave reasonable ground for believing that an alternative Government could carry on with the existing House.[84]

Hence, in light of these observations, in spite of the abdication of most of their preexisting imperial powers, the monarch-appointed governors still retained a type of constitutional guardian role with respect to the Dominion PITs in rare cases. In other words, the monarch-appointed governor was relegated in almost all circumstances to acting as a symbolic figurehead except for circumstances in which they acted as guardians of the constitutional order. Under such conditions they had an exercisable mandate to protect the constitutional order by suspending the actions of local officials who threatened to overthrow deeply held and widely acknowledged democratic principles. Moreover, while there have been disagreements between scholars as to the justification of some dissolution refusals (Forsey, for example, believed that the 1926 refusal by Canada's governor to dismiss the legislature was justified, while Keith disagreed),[85] these disagreements usually center around the correct application of constitutional rules rather than questioning the need for an institutional actor to act as a polity's constitutional guardian. Indeed, the utility of the mostly figurehead, constitutional guardian role of Dominion governor is underscored by the practice of commonwealth countries even after 1931 (when they became more similar to fully independent states).[86] Well after 1931, former dominions such as Canada, Australia, and New Zealand continued to maintain a watered down version of the constitutional guardian role played by the monarch-appointed governor.[87] In sum, far from seeing the Dominion

---

[84] Forsey 1943, 70.
[85] See Keith 1935a, 56–8; and Forsey 1943, ch. 6. See also Marshall 1984, 19–44.
[86] Keith 1935a, 392.
[87] In fact as late as 1975 in a bold and controversial move, the governor-general of Australia Sir John Kerr exercised normally dormant prerogative powers by dismissing the government of Gough Whitlam. Kerr (who himself was a Whitlam appointee) made this decision amidst

governor's refusal of dissolutions as an illegitimate core state usurpation of powers, such actions were arguably the outcome of an institution designated to defend the arrangements against the illegitimate executive dominance that threatened to undermine the separation of powers. Such actions constituted the use of rare emergency powers by an institution designated by conventional rules to uphold democratic principles

Emergency Powers within well Institutionalized Sovereign States and Partially Independent Territories

Similar to most PITs, well institutionalized sovereign states have emergency rules that apply when extraordinary conditions emerge. Such rules *temporarily* allocate authoritarian powers to a leader or institution in order to restore order. It should of course be acknowledged that when such emergency rules are applied, there is room for abuse by the actors that are empowered to preserve order. But just as we do not jump to the conclusion that a sovereign state is necessarily a failed state or an authoritarian regime because of the exercise of such powers, it can also be misleading to arrive at such conclusions with PITs. Indeed, the practice of overriding preexisting constitutional rules in clear cases of emergency is similar to the practice of many well established constitutional systems, such as those that exist with the United Kingdom's central institutions.

The fact that Britain's monarch retains vast and draconian legal powers is not merely an anachronistic remnant of past ages that has lost its relevance. On the contrary, it now serves as a fail-safe and insurance mechanism for preventing unlikely catastrophic events. As already mentioned, over time Britain's monarch has retained many legal prerogative powers (like the power to dismiss the prime minister, dissolve the parliament, control the military, and pardon offenders).[88] In practice, however, conventional rules mandate that such powers are under the control of parliamentary ministers.[89] The monarch is therefore bound by conventions to obey the "advice" of the parliamentary leaders on such issues. However, scholars of British constitutional law point out that there are modern circumstances in which Britain's monarch could justifiably exercise hitherto dormant legal powers to dissolve Parliament, refuse assent

---

deadlock between the Australian Senate (which had cut off treasury funds (blocked supply) to the government) and the Prime Minister (who refused to either resign or to call for a dissolution of the lower house). See Marshall 1984, 27–8.

[88] Bagehot 1928, 287.
[89] Marshall 1984, 19.

to a bill, or even command the military in extraordinary circumstances.[90] Representing the opinion in much of the literature, Eric Barendt confirms this:

> It may be that even now a Monarch would be justified in withholding Royal Assent if [Parliament's] enactment were to pose a clear danger to public order, or if the two Houses of Parliament had passed without good reason a Bill to postpone a General Election. In both these cases the Monarch might be acting constitutionally if she ignored the government's advice, since Assent would be refused to preserve public order or, in the second situation, democratic values.[91]

No one, however, suggests that as a result of being able to use these powers in extraordinary circumstances that consequently Britain's parliament, its ruling ministers, and other institutions do not have their own constitutional vitality and final decision-making powers. On the contrary, the historic reality and long-held view that prevails among British leaders and scholars is that the monarch's legal powers are very much limited by unwritten constitutional rules.[92]

The latter point is especially relevant for the discussion here since some may be tempted to mistakenly interpret the intervention or possibility of intervention by such a constitutional guardian (especially if it is appointed by the core state) as seeming evidence of the sham status or unentrenched nature of a partially independent arrangement. However, so long as the actor's actions are strictly constrained by established constitutional rules and it is indeed acting to prevent extraordinary events (such as those that are mentioned above), the termination (or possible termination) of a partially independent polity's powers for the purpose of preventing grave events does not necessarily indicate illegitimate termination, or that forms of entrenchment did not exist.

On the contrary, such actions are often designed with the intention of restoring the partially independent arrangement together with its security, political stability, and/or the core–PIT division of power. When civil disorder is sustained and uncontrollable, when officials flagrantly breach democratic principles, or when there is a *coup d'état*, sovereign states are sometimes unable to surmount such challenges. Internally, they often do not have the necessary resources, and externally, other states have no duty to help them. In some cases the result is the economic dislocation, political paralysis, and the perpetual violence of state failure in which political institutions are sovereign in name only. For PITs, however, opportunists that seek to foment violence, destabilize

---

[90] On this see Evatt 1936, 200; Forsey 1943, 104.
[91] Barendt 1998, 112.
[92] See Bogdanor 1995; Brazier 1994; 1997; Forsey 1984; Dicey 1885/1982; Heard 1991; Jennings 1959; Keith 1935b; Marshall 1984; Munro 1975; Wheare 1949.

institutions, or threaten the core–PIT division of power must not only contend with the partially independent polity's institutions and resources, but those of the core state as well.

Civil Disorder and Suspension in Northern Ireland as an Exception to Conventional Entrenchment?

Another challenge to the existence of the credibility of conventional entrenchment among British territories came in 1972 and in 1998 in the case of Northern Ireland's partially independent arrangements when the British government suspended the territory's legislature.[93]

Legislative Suspension in Northern Ireland

The PIT the UK first established for Northern Ireland in 1920 was a direct institutional successor to the British Dominions. English and Irish leaders had conceived of separate and autonomous institutions without full secession for Northern Ireland as a way to satisfy the local Protestant majority (which tended to favor continued union with the United Kingdom) as well as the local Catholic minority (which tended to favor union with Ireland). Since the partially independent arrangement that was created for Canada had a history of moderating tensions between local French and Anglophone populations as well as yielding stable core–PIT relations, leaders such as British Prime Minister William Gladstone who had created the architecture for Northern Ireland's "home rule" institutions looked to Dominions such as Canada as models.[94] Similar to the Dominions, Northern Ireland's conventionally entrenched status from 1920 to 1972 was also widely acknowledged.[95]

However, in April 1972 after five decades of existence, the British central government unilaterally suspended Northern Ireland's Stormont Assembly. When this happened, some cast doubt upon the entrenchment of the arrangement. In light of the unilateral suspension, critics assumed that the central government could at any time suspend Northern Ireland's institutions based on the core state's self-interest. In the view of some observers, the suspension therefore seemed

---

[93] For valuable works on devolution for Northern Ireland, principles of federalism, and by inference partial independence, concerning the twentieth century and after see, Bank 1971; Bogdanor 1999; Burrow and Denton 1980; Drucker and Brown 1980; McGarry 2001; McGarry and O'Leary 1995a; 2004.

[94] Morton 1995, 34.

[95] Among the widespread acknowledgment of Northern Ireland's conventionally entrenched status, for one of the best accounts see Calvert 1968. See also Marshall 1984, 201–2.

to indicate that entrenchment never existed in the first place. Consequently, Northern Ireland was merely a decentralized territory with delegated power rather than a territory that had credible final decision-making powers.

As elaborated in Chapter 6, some instances of core state interference may indeed signal the preexisting weakness (or non-existence) of entrenchment. In the case of Northern Ireland in 1972, however, the suspension did not occur because the core state engaged in an exercise of arbitrary powers when conditions in Northern Ireland violated its self-interest. Instead, consistent with Eric Barendt's interpretation of the British monarch's powers to assert control over the Parliament amidst "a clear danger to public order," the suspension represented an exceptional case of emergency conditions amidst a widespread breakdown in public order.[96] At the time of the decision, the province was indeed plagued by intense civil unrest, large scale sectarian confrontations, increased Irish Republican Army (IRA) recruitment and terrorist attacks, escalating clashes with the police and military, and the eventual massacre of thirteen Catholic demonstrators in Derry on January 1972 known as "Bloody Sunday." Indeed, Northern Ireland's Assembly itself was not innocent with respect to much of the chaos in the territory. In 1929 for instance, the unionist majority voted to repeal the system of proportional representation that had been guaranteed by the British Parliament's Government of Ireland Act of 1920.[97] Under the new majority-rule conditions, the result was that most of the Catholic minority became even more excluded from their participation in the government.[98] The Assembly's Protestant-dominated Unionist government was also largely responsible for the inflammatory decision to reintroduce the policy of internment without trial in August 1971, which was implemented by the unionist dominated police force (the Royal Ulster Constabulary).[99] Under these conditions it can be argued that suspending the legislature was justified on grounds of preserving public order and preventing a further escalation of widespread sectarian violence.

Just as with well institutionalized sovereign states, when real civil disorder presents itself or there is a potentially damaging breakdown of constitutional principles, the suspension of normal constitutional rules by a constitutionally appointed actor does not necessarily constitute an inappropriate breech

---

[96] Barendt 1998, 112.

[97] Section 5 of the 1920 Act attempts to prevent any law that would "either directly or indirectly...establish or endow any religion, or prohibit or restrict the free exercise thereof, or give a preference, privilege, or advantage, or impose any disability or disadvantage, on account of religious belief or religious or ecclesiastical status..." Furthermore "any existing enactment by which any penalty, disadvantage, or disability is imposed on account of religious belief or on a member of any religious order as such shall, as from the appointed day, cease to have effect in Ireland." Reprinted in Keith 1928, 317–18.

[98] Hannum 1990, 232. See also Northern Ireland, Fair Employment Agency 1978.

[99] For an analysis of the policing practices during this time see Farrell 1984. See also Spjut 1986, 712.

of the partially independent arrangement. A range of rare and extraordinary conditions exist in which the suspension of local governmental functions can in fact be in the interest of both core and territory. This is especially true when the institution is strictly constrained by a core state or PIT that is well institutionalized (i.e. with a relatively high World Governance Indicator rule of law rating [higher than 70]). As US Supreme Court Justice Robert Jackson once said when considering the issue of emergency powers as it has applied to the experiences of Weimar, Germany, the French Republic, and Britain:

> ...emergency powers are consistent with free government only when their control is lodged elsewhere than in the Executive who exercise them...with all its defects, delays and inconveniences, men have discovered no technique for long preserving free government except that the Executive be under the law, and that the law be made by parliamentary deliberations.[100]

When extraordinary events arise, such institutions can intervene to authorize the suspension of governmental functions, policies, or actions that threaten the constitutional order while operating within the constraints of strict law or conventional rules.

Hence, as distinct from the sham federacies discussed in Chapter 6, cases of suspension of powers can be viewed as benign if (1) they are in response to emergency circumstances such as a breakdown of civil order and/or the violation of deeply held democratic principles, (2) they are the outcome of prearranged constitutional rules designed to preserve security, political stability, and the core–PIT division of power and (3) the powers being exercised are ultimately vested in an institution distinct from the actor exercising the emergency powers. If such principles apply, the suspension of normal constitutional rules arguably does not necessarily violate the long-term spirit of a partially independent arrangement and should not necessarily be interpreted as usurpation (illegitimate termination). On the contrary, such mechanisms serve the interests of PITs by acting to restore order and/or security. Ultimately, in 1998 with the passage of the Belfast Agreement, a new partially independent arrangement was reestablished for the territory.

When Intervention does not Create a Rule: Northern Ireland after 1998

Although they are rare, there are additional cases in which core or partially independent governments engage in actions that result in the suspension of

---

[100] *Youngstown Sheet and Tube Co. v Sawyer* 1952, 652, 655.

a partially independent arrangement, but do not necessarily result in a sham federacy or a binding precedent that prevents the reestablishment of the arrangement in the future. People can, after all, break rules without necessarily calling into question the authority of rules. When someone commits a crime like theft, the crime that has been committed does not necessarily mean that there was no rule against theft in the first place. Nor does it necessarily set a precedent that rules against theft will not apply in the future. Even in well institutionalized countries, people break rules without tarnishing the ability of institutions to maintain order. A similar principle applies to the contravention of a constitutional rule by a government. As Sir Ivor Jennings has said with respect to conventional rules:

> Conventions grow out of practice. Their existence is determined by precedents. Such precedents are not authoritative like the precedents of a law court. There are precedents which have created no conventions, and there are conventions based on precedents which have fallen into desuetude.... Not every precedent creates a rule...[101]

If, however, more than one rule is repeatedly broken, one may begin to question the authority of the prevailing institutional order. Hence, many observers see the decisions of the US Supreme Court as credible and authoritative in spite of the existence of various exceptional cases in which their rulings have been disobeyed. One such case occurred in the middle of the nineteenth century when US President Andrew Jackson blatantly refused to abide by an interpretation by the US Supreme Court in which it judged that the policy of forcible removal of Cherokee Indians from their homeland in Georgia was unconstitutional.[102] On the other hand, the repeated and widespread violations by sovereign states of the UN Charter's rule of non-intervention have caused some scholars to call the Charter's rules into question.[103]

Perhaps one example of the ability of a partially independent arrangement to maintain significant degrees of authority after the contravention of agreed rules was the case of Northern Ireland from 1999 to 2006. During this period when local parties had violated the terms of the Belfast Agreement by failing to

---

[101] Jennings 1936, 5. Also quoted in Forsey 1943, 72.

[102] Jackson may have thought that the Supreme Court's judgment was senseless and may have been willing to ignore clear precedents. Surrounded as he was by popular approval of his Indian removal policies, perhaps informal enforcement mechanisms did not weigh very strongly on his lack of obedience. But it can nevertheless be assumed that if he had considered the precedents, reasons, and the costs of non-adherence to the Supreme Court's ruling more carefully, he would have (or should have) obeyed. In spite of Jackson's actions, the stable obedience of Presidents to the Supreme Court's rulings—even when obedience may not have been part of a popular policy and no *formal* checks have been available to stop such an action—has been borne out by the test of time and history. See *Cherokee Nation v Georgia*, 1831. See also *Johnson v M'Intosh*, 1823 (Marshall Chief Justice). This latter case enunciates a doctrine of limited Indian title to land.

[103] See Glennon 2003, 16–35.

relinquish their weapons, there was at least one occasion in which the British government failed to abide by its commitments in the Belfast Agreement to consult with the Irish Government and local political parties before departing from the terms of the arrangement. Subsequent events, however, indicate that this British violation was (1) isolated and (2) in reaction to sui generis events that are arguably not likely to reemerge.[104] Before elaborating upon these points, the events which led to this decision and the outcomes that were eventually achieved will be briefly described.

The Belfast Agreement and the Rebirth of Northern Ireland's Partially Independent Arrangement

On April 10, 1998 the UK and Ireland together with most of Northern Ireland's political parties (with the notable exception of the Democratic Unionist Party) put a decisive end to most of Northern Ireland's historic violent conflict by agreeing to create a partially independent arrangement in the Belfast Agreement (also known as the Good Friday, Stormont, Northern Ireland Peace, or British-Irish Agreement).[105] In addition to existing as an agreement between a core state and a territory, the agreement was also notable for being a treaty between the UK and another sovereign state (the Republic of Ireland). While hoping to build on the challenges of the past, the parties to the Agreement reaffirmed their commitment to stability and progress:

> The tragedies of the past have left a deep and profoundly regrettable legacy of suffering. We must never forget those who have died or been injured, and their families. But we can best honour them through a fresh start, in which we firmly dedicate ourselves to the achievement of reconciliation, tolerance, and mutual trust, and to the protection and vindication of the human rights of all.[106]

The Agreement was then approved by Northern Ireland voters in a referendum on May 23, 1998. It was also approved in a separate referendum by voters in the Irish Republic on the same day. It was then put into legal effect by the British Parliament in the 1998 Northern Ireland Act.[107] In accordance with the stipulations in the Belfast Agreement, the 1998 Northern Ireland Act allocated

---

[104] Some might also attempt to argue that the British failure to consult with parties before suspending the Stormont Assembly was justified because it was in response to extraordinary security threats. Unlike the case in Northern Ireland when the Assembly was suspended in 1972, this latter claim is rejected here since there did not seem to be any real or imminent breakdown in civil order as a result of the IRA not giving up its weapons after 1998.

[105] Northern Ireland, Belfast Agreement 1998.

[106] Northern Ireland, Belfast Agreement 1998, Section 1(2).

[107] UK, Northern Ireland Act 1998.

decision-making powers to the executive and legislature within Northern Ireland, providing them with wide ranging powers over the territory in areas such as health, education, social services, agriculture, environment, finance, economic development, and transportation.[108] Ultimately, the aforementioned agreements entered into force in December 1999 when the Northern Ireland Assembly was able to reconvene.

Weapons Decommissioning, Political Gridlock, and Core State Intervention

Unfortunately, however, in spite of its hopeful start, during much of the next seven years until 2007, the agreed division of power was not fully implemented. Mutual hostility between the territory's main political parties created gridlock and the failure of paramilitary groups to relinquish their weapons created obstacles. Among other things, the Belfast Agreement had been predicated on IRA weapons being dismantled or destroyed.[109] As the Agreement affirms, "All participants accordingly reaffirm their commitment to the total disarmament of all paramilitary organizations… and to use any influence they may have, to achieve the decommissioning of all paramilitary arms within two years following endorsement in referendums North and South of the agreement…"[110] Hence, according to the terms of the agreement, paramilitary groups like the IRA had a deadline of May 22, 2000 to fully disarm (which was exactly two years after the Agreement was endorsed in North and South referendums). However, after the initial implementation of the agreement, when it seemed clear that the IRA would not disarm, the core-appointed Secretary of State Peter Mandelson suspended the Stormont Assembly in February 2000, which was three months before the disarmament deadline specified in the Belfast Agreement.[111]

When the core state took this action they seem to have violated their commitments in the Agreement in a number of ways. First, as already indicated, the British action was premature since the IRA had a few more months to decommission their weapons.[112] Second, and most importantly, the British

---

[108] UK, Northern Ireland Act 1998.

[109] Northern Ireland, Belfast Agreement 1998, Section 7.

[110] Northern Ireland, Belfast Agreement 1998, Section 7(3).

[111] Gormley-Heenan 2008, 228. This action seems to have been precipitated by the threat by Northern Ireland's First Minister David Trimble to resign if the IRA did not follow through with the decommissioning of its weapons.

[112] Brendan O'Leary also contests the constitutionality of the British power of suspension itself. He points out that Northern Ireland's new constitutional order did not include the equivalent of the Section 75 clause (the legal supremacy clause equivalent to Scotland's Article

failed to engage in three-way dialogue with the Irish Government and parties in the Assembly before it resorted to suspending the Assembly as it committed to do in the Validation, Implementation and Review (VIR) section of the Belfast Agreement.[113] This section of the agreement reads as follows:

> If difficulties arise which require remedial action across the range of institutions, or otherwise require amendment of the British-Irish Agreement or relevant legislation, the process of review will fall to the two Governments in consultation with the parties in the Assembly. Each Government will be responsible for action in its own jurisdiction.[114]

The decision to suspend the Assembly did not, however, seem to involve consultation with parties in the Assembly or the Irish Government.[115]

Given these violations, some observers asserted that the entire arrangement would afterward be vulnerable to the unfettered and arbitrary interference by the British government. Brendan O'Leary asserted that "The act of suspension…has made it plain that every aspect of the Agreement is vulnerable to Westminster's doctrine of parliamentary sovereignty."[116] "Everything in the Agreement" he said, "is revisable by the current Westminster Parliament, and any future Parliament, irrespective of international law, or the solemn promises made by UK negotiators in the run-up to, and in the making of, the Agreement."[117] Dissenting British Members of Parliament (MPs) made similar critiques. One MP, John McDonnell, said the following:

> The Secretary of State is able by order not just on this occasion, but on future occasions, to suspend the Assembly and all the mechanisms associated with the agreement without full and adequate debate. There is no review element on revocation or restoration. It is government by order. There is no power in the legislation for consultation with the Irish Government.[118]

---

28), which existed in the Government of Ireland Act of 1920. Similar to Scotland's Article 28, Section 75 emphasized the core state's supreme legal powers. Without the presence of such a legal clause, Professor O'Leary maintains that the core state could not override its commitments in the Agreement and suspend the Assembly. O'Leary's argument rests on the view that the Belfast Agreement (as a treaty between two sovereign states) provided formal entrenchment mechanisms that the UK was obliged to obey. O'Leary makes an excellent point, but evidently from the UK's perspective the constitutionality of their actions seems to flow more from their own domestic statutes and conventional rules. In most of the other territories associated with the UK full legal powers to intervene remain intact, although (except for extraordinary cases) they are shielded by conventional rules.

[113] O'Leary 2001, 67.
[114] Northern Ireland, Belfast Agreement 1998, Section 11(7). Also quoted in O'Leary 2001, 67.
[115] O'Leary 2001, 66–9.
[116] O'Leary 2001, 68.
[117] O'Leary 2001.
[118] McDonnell 2000.

The Core State's Isolated Violation

While it seems to be clear that the British did indeed violate the terms of the Belfast Agreement when it suspended the Assembly in February 2000, nevertheless, in light of subsequent events there are reasons to doubt that these British violations damaged the ability for the Northern Ireland–UK arrangement to be entrenched through conventional rules. First, Britain's failure to engage in three-way dialogue appears to be isolated. Indeed, in the 2000 Northern Ireland Act which the UK enacted in conjunction with the February 2000 suspension, there does indeed seem to be an effort to codify the "review element" that John McDonnell mentions. For example, Section 2 of the Act codifies the necessity of implementing the VIR section of the Belfast Agreement to end the suspension.[119]

Furthermore, in accordance with these commitments, later interventions to reconstitute the Assembly and to suspend it in reaction to the weapons decommissioning violations of the Belfast Accords were done in consultation with the Irish government and local political parties. After the February 2000 suspension, the Assembly was allowed to reconvene in May 2000 when the IRA pledged to put its weapons "verifiably beyond use." Nevertheless, actual decommissioning by the IRA continued to be delayed.[120] As a result of these delays, the Assembly was briefly suspended twice more in 2001, in August and October. Shortly before these suspensions in 2001, however, media reports widely reported vigorous three-way consultations that occurred between British Prime Minister Tony Blair, Irish Prime Minister Bertie Ahern, and the Assembly's parties.[121] For example, the BBC reported that between July 22–27, 2001,

> The British and Irish governments spend the week putting together an intricate package as a "make or break" deal to be presented to the pro-agreement parties. Prime Ministers Tony Blair and Bertie Ahern insist that it will be the only document on offer and will not be open to negotiation.[122]

And even after concerns over the possibility of the IRA spying in the legislature led to the Assembly's fourth suspension in October 2002, three-way dialogue did not stop. In October 2003 for example the BBC observed "weeks of top-level negotiations between Sinn Fein and the Ulster Unionists, as well as the British and Irish Governments."[123] Ultimately, the IRA finally signaled an

---

[119] See UK, Explanatory Notes to Northern Ireland Act 2000, Section 2, in which it refers to the necessity of a "review."
[120] Independent International Commission on Decommissioning Report 2005.
[121] BBC News 2001.
[122] BBC News 2001.
[123] BBC News 2003.

end to its military campaign in July 2005.[124] And after four years of investigation, the cases against those who were accused of IRA spying at Stormont were dropped in December 2005.[125]

Perhaps the most significant effort by the British to implement the VIR section was the remarkable St Andrews Agreement on October 13, 2006 in which British and Irish governments as well as the representatives of Northern Ireland's political parties worked out a historic deal. At that meeting Northern Ireland's largest (and mutually hostile) political parties, Sinn Féin and the Democratic Unionist Party, agreed to join with each other in a power sharing government.[126] These events in turn led to the restoration of the Assembly in May 2007.

In light of these events, one can conclude that the pressure the UK government put on the contending parties by suspending institutions ironically contributed to (or at least did not prevent) the eventual restoration and strengthening of local institutions. Hence, given the frequent and vigorous three-way consultations that the UK government engaged in after 2000, the failure of the UK government to consult with the Irish government and the Northern Ireland Assembly seems to be isolated to the events that surrounded the February 2000 suspension.

One can, nevertheless, question the right of the British to suspend Northern Ireland's legislature on each of the four occasions from 2000 to 2002. This capability was not after all explicitly mentioned in the Belfast Agreement (although it was specified in the 2000 Northern Ireland Act). It was also not in response to any widespread large-scale breakdown of civil order or violent coup (however much some may have felt threatened by the IRA's weapons). Nevertheless, with respect to the core state suspensions after March 22, 2000 they were responding to clear violations of the Belfast Agreement through the failure of the IRA not to decommission its weapons. Furthermore, although suspension may not have been explicitly granted to them, the Agreement nevertheless allowed them to take "remedial action" in accordance with the three-way consultative procedure mentioned above, which they made reference to in the 2000 Northern Ireland Act and subsequently implemented.

As far as the view that Northern Ireland is now vulnerable to the arbitrary whims of the UK Government as a result of the British February 2000 suspension, this also does not seem to be consistent with the facts of the UK–Northern Ireland relationship. Indeed, there are clear signs that the territory is shielded by the same "Sewel" legislative consent motions (discussed in Chapter 3) that

---

[124] Gormley-Heenan 2008, 228.   [125] Gormley-Heenan 2008.
[126] Coakley 2008, 98–112.

apply in Scotland.[127] Interestingly, Lord Sewel's idea for legislative consent motions seems to have been taken from the experience of Northern Ireland's partially independent arrangement (albeit the one that existed from 1920 to 1971.)[128] Furthermore, the relatively isolated British violation in 2000 should also be weighed against the high degrees of consistency with respect to adhering to constitutional rules that have been observed by scholars, leaders, and other observers within Britain's own horizontal government and in its relations with its associated territories.[129]

Hence, the circumstances that led to the British violations in 2000 are arguably *sui generis*. While it is in theory possible that paramilitaries associated with the Assembly's political parties may rearm themselves, observers (such as Northern Ireland's Independent Monitoring Commission) have predicted that the economic, security, and self-determination advantages offered by the arrangement will make this issue less likely to reemerge.[130] A number of factors provide hope for political stability including IRA weapons decommissioning, the reduction of British forces in the territory, the power-sharing government, the territory's gradual economic improvement after 1998, and the increasing support by both sides for reconciliation. As scholars such as John Coakley have affirmed, "Northern Ireland has yet another safeguard against a return to violence. *It is not a sovereign state* and therefore possesses a paradoxical resource absent in many other cases of violent ethnic conflict."[131] Coakley points out that unlike a fully independent state, real or potential violent opportunists will tend to be dissuaded from forcing a political settlement on Northern Ireland because they understand that they will ultimately also have to face the considerable resources of the core state in the event of another breakdown of civil order.[132]

CONCLUSIONS

The use of conventions has significant advantages. These rules provide binding constitutional entrenchment when formal-legal agreement is unlikely or not

---

[127] On this see for example Birrell 2007, 305.

[128] Birrell 2007.

[129] The World Governance Indicator 2008 ranking for the United Kingdom as it applies to the rule of law is 93, which is one of the highest in the world, putting it in league with the United States (93), the Netherlands (93), and Germany (94). See Kauffmann et al. 2008.

[130] Kaufmann et al. 2008. Northern Ireland's Independent Monitoring Commission is composed of governmental representatives of British, Irish, Northern Ireland, and US governments. For Independent Monitoring Commission reports see <www.independentmonitoringcommission.org>.

[131] Coakley 2008, 106. Italics added.

[132] Coakley 2008.

possible. Conventional rules also supply the flexibility for future constitutional change if the political environment on the periphery significantly shifts. This is reflected by the success that the Dominions had with regard to securing ever increasing and unprecedented powers as their influence and needs increased. Lastly, conventional rules reinforce the outcome and principle-oriented spirit of a constitutional arrangement. As imperial and Dominion leaders conveyed in a 1929 inter-imperial conference:

> It [convention] has provided a means of harmonizing relations where a purely legal solution of practical problems was impossible, would have impaired free development, or would have failed to catch the spirit which gives life to institutions. Such conventions take their place among the constitutional principles and doctrines which are in practice regarded as binding and sacred whatever the powers of Parliaments may in theory be.[133]

This was amply illustrated by the series of events that first gave rise to responsible government for Canada and ultimately the rest of the Dominions. The Dominions, at least initially, were less concerned by the outward legal manifestations than by the substance of the powers that they actually exercised. The imperial government for its part was unoffended (and to a large degree unaffected) by sovereignty being credibly exercised on the periphery so long as the preexisting legal trappings remained unchanged and it did not have to endure the humiliation of further imperial disintegration. The conventional rules that the governor-general must assent to the advice of the territorial ministers or that the central government must not intervene in the domestic affairs of the Dominions provided the outcome of domestic sovereignty without having to surmount the legal obstacles of legally defining it. British Prime Minister Lloyd George conveyed this in 1921 to the British House of Commons:

> What does "Dominion status" mean?...It is something that has never been defined by an Act of Parliament, even in this country, and yet it works perfectly....In practice it means complete control over their own internal affairs without any interference from any other part of the Empire. They are the rulers of their own hearth—finance, administration, legislation...and the representatives of the Sovereign will act on the advice of the Dominion Ministers.[134]

Furthermore, after the establishment of responsible government, the central government-appointed governor still served as an important link of communication between center and periphery. The governor also retained the ability to use his reserve powers when events threatened the constitutional status of

---

[133] UK, The Report of the Conference on the Operation of Dominion Legislation and Merchant Shipping Legislation 1929: Article 56.
[134] UK, The Rt. Hon. D. Lloyd George, House of Commons 1921, 84.

the self-governing region (as in the case of a *coup d'état*, widespread violence, or the usurpation of democratic principles), while the mostly subordinated role of the governor made him less provocative to local nationalism.

Although the Dominions did eventually all become independent states, the initial arrangements that were established for these territories were not created to be interim steps toward statehood as some have implied.[135] They were instead designed to hold the British Empire together and stem the tide of territorial fragmentation which largely began with the secession of the Thirteen American Colonies. The shattering of other empires, the catastrophic history of nationalistic rebellion within settled colonies, the failure of other means of constitutional accommodation within the British Empire, the attractive compromise between full assimilation and independence, and the early and persistent lobbying of the Canadians in the mid to late nineteenth century were some of the key reasons for the emergence of partial independence in Canada (and by association the PITs that emerged elsewhere within the British Empire). But, as the relative benefits of association began to wane for the largest Dominion, Canada, the arrangement failed to rein in the powerful feelings of nationalism. This then precipitated calls for increasing powers of full independence which eventually culminated in the secession of all the Dominions. Nevertheless, conventional entrenchment ultimately succeeded in extending the life of the British Empire's territorial integrity for many decades. Significant and powerful territories that, like the Thirteen Colonies, may well have seceded into independence remained united and closely allied with one another, contributing their militaries, political prestige, and, at times, their economic resources to a common political union. And revolts in colonies like Canada became distant memory.

The British Dominions in the late nineteenth and early twentieth century were similar in many ways to Puerto Rico's status today. Puerto Rico is self-governing internally while some foreign and all military powers are in the hands of the core state. It was designed as an indefinite solution rather than as an interim arrangement that would lead to independence. And its powers were entrenched by conventional means in spite of the fact that legal rules that contradicted the unwritten rules are still on the books. The next chapter attempts to reinforce the arguments presented in this chapter by focusing on the conventional rules that apply between America and the territory of Puerto Rico.

---

[135] On such a suggestion see, Fliess 1952, 652.

5

From Secessionism to Mutual Agreement in the American Context: The Case of Puerto Rico

> Some of us confused love of the homeland with the narrow and bitter concept of the national state. We felt that love of Puerto Rico had as a necessary corollary the desire for separate independence.... What had seemed to be an integral idea—the homeland and separate independence—turned out to be two conflicting ideas: one, acceptable as an abstract idea; the other, a mortal enemy of the people.... Obviously, the United States could not maintain its present good economic treatment of Puerto Rico, which is vital to our continued development, if we acquired a status which had all the legal paraphernalia of separate independence.[1]
>
> —Luis Muñoz Marín, the first elected Governor of the Commonwealth of Puerto Rico.

Puerto Rico is another example of a conventionally-entrenched PIT. The focal point around which the politics of this nationalistically-distinct island group of 3.9 million US citizens has revolved for more than a century has been the issue of the territory's political condition.[2] This was the case from even before the US takeover of the territory after the 1898 Spanish-American War. After America's occupation and annexation of the territory, its status was an international badge of dishonor for America when categorizing Puerto Rico as a colony seemed inescapable.[3] Even as Presidents, such as Woodrow Wilson, lectured other countries about the instabilities of imperial control and the need

---

[1] Muñoz Marín 1953, 1. Also quoted in Gatell 1958, 43.

[2] On the history of the constitutional development of Puerto Rico see especially Leibowitz 1989, 127–85; Monge 1997, 1–140. See also Carr 1984, 17–72; Lerner 1981, 125–34; Reisman 1975, 2–35.

[3] On the history of the constitutional development of Puerto Rico see Carr 1984, 17–72; Leibowitz 1989, 127–85; Lerner 1981, 125–34; Monge 1997, 1–140; Reisman 1975, 2–35.

for self-determination, Puerto Rico remained an example of naked American colonialism. Since 1952, however, after its "commonwealth" regime was established, the issue of what Puerto Rico is and how to describe it has been at times bitterly debated by scholars and Puerto Rico's three main parties, which themselves center their political platforms on a hoped-for future status option. Each party is to one degree or another dissatisfied with the island group's present political condition and uses its vision of what Puerto Rico is now as a stick to win over local, US, and even international actors to their favored constitutional preference.[4] Advocates of a modified version of the present status quo (the Popular Democratic Party) have historically argued that after 1952 a "compact" was created between the US and Puerto Rico that legally bound both sides to receive each other's consent before any changes are made to Puerto Rico's post-1952 constitutional order. Both independence advocates (the Independence Party) and those who favor remaking the territory into a state of America's federation (the New Progressive Party) reject this view and argue that the decades since Puerto Rico's new regime began in 1952 have changed nothing. According to such views, Puerto Rico is still a mere colony of the US under the absolute (plenary) power of Congress. These latter views have in turn been sustained by much of the scholarly literature on the topic.[5] Such views, however, are politically, constitutionally, and historically incorrect. Puerto Rico is neither a mere colony nor are its powers formally safeguarded by a "compact" created in 1952. Instead, similar in significant respects to the historic British Dominions in the late nineteenth and early twentieth centuries, Puerto Rico's powers are rendered difficult to change by unwritten constitutional rules. Puerto Rico is best described, not as a colony or as some other governmental form, but as a conventionally-entrenched PIT.

Together with the British Dominions and Northern Ireland, the Puerto Rico case has been selected on the basis of (1) its hardness (which in this case is the view among some scholars that Puerto Rico is a mere colony); (2) the existence of counter equilibrium events; (3) its geographic spread relative to cases in Chapter 4; and (4) its differences over time on the independent variable (regime type [whether with its existence first as a colony and then as a PIT]) as opposed to selecting on the dependent variable (the presence of economic, self-determination, and security advantages).

---

[4] For a notable case of how such views have affected US leaders see the Hearings Before the House Committee on Resources 1997, 40–445.

[5] See for instance, Aleinikoff 2002, 77; Cabranes 1978–79, 68; Fliess 1952; Helfeld 1952; 1985; Torruella 1985, 167–200. For arguments on the unconstitutionality of final decision-making powers being allocated to territories such as Puerto Rico based on the Constitution's Presidential Appointment Clause rather than the Territorial Clause see Lawson and Seidman 2004, 124–38.

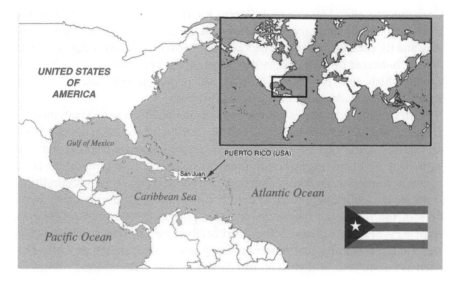

Figure 5.1. Puerto Rico

Puerto Rico's Constitutional Development

Before the modern US–Puerto Rico constitutional relationship was established in 1952, Puerto Rico was subjected to much of the same forcible cultural indoctrination and political assimilation as other territories acquired by the United States in its expansion westward. Through the brilliance of its federation government, established in 1787, the United States was remarkably able to achieve dominance over a vast territory which had previously been controlled by the British, French, Spanish, Mexicans, and a multitude of indigenous populations, and successfully overcome much of the destabilizing nationalistic hostility that plagued and fragmented other empires. For a number of decades after the Spanish-American war, however, the US flirted with self-damaging, European-style imperialism.[6] Its stabilizing federation-formula was therefore not extended to Puerto Rico.

From even before the US took control of the territory in 1898, Puerto Rico's uncommon strategic utility to the United States was recognized. A military foothold that was 1,000 miles southeast of Florida in the Caribbean would reinforce the policy emphasized by the 1823 Monroe Doctrine of preventing other powers from meddling in the Western hemisphere (Figure 5.1).[7]

---

[6] On America's new empire-building strategies during this time see Merrill and Paterson 2005, 290–357.

[7] Roman 1997, 1149.

Consequently after America took Puerto Rico in 1898, the United States built a range of sizeable military installations on the one hundred mile long territory and its associated islands. The value of Puerto Rico as a strategic asset was further bolstered by the territory's location on the approaches to the Panama Canal, which after the canal's costly construction in 1914 became one of America's vital trade and transportation lifelines.[8]

Such strategic advantages alone were not enough, however, to convince the United States to grant more powers to the territory. Like many great powers around the world that held colonies, US leaders viewed a colonial status as expedient for furthering national interests, such as policing important trade routes, regardless of a territory's subordinate political and economic condition.

While the tenth amendment of the US Constitution makes clear that members of the federation (states) have some powers of domestic sovereignty, Article IV, Section 3, clause 2 (the "territorial clause") by contrast makes clear that Congress has absolute power (plenary power) over non-state territories, such as Puerto Rico, that exist within America's international-legal confines:

> The Congress shall have Power to dispose of and make all needful Rules and Regulations respecting the Territory or other Property belonging to the United States; and nothing in this Constitution shall be so construed as to Prejudice any Claims of the United States, or of any particular State.

In a nineteenth-century case, the Supreme Court also affirmed this by making clear that Congress's "sovereignty over them [is] complete."[9] Through simple majority legislation, it was decided that the US Congress has the power to make and unmake rules for the territorial legislatures.

Accordingly, as with other territories in US history (such as those that included indigenous Indian populations), the Hispanic population of Puerto Rico was subjected to a systematic policy of cultural and political assimilation. Policies were put into effect, for instance, to introduce English as the only medium of communication in schools in a territory where the only language that was spoken was Spanish.

---

[8] Fernandez 1996, 58.

[9] *Late Corp. of the Church of Jesus Christ of Latter-Day Saints v United States*, 1889, 42. A well-known counterexample to this view was set forth by the Supreme Court in *Dred Scott v Sandford* in which it was argued that the territorial clause only applied to territories that were in the possession of the US when it became independent, and territories acquired afterwards would be governed under the provisions of the Constitution that apply to admitting new states. *Dred Scott v Sandford*, 1856, 438–39, 443; Aleinikoff 2002, 75–6. This view however was neither sustained by Supreme Court decisions before or after *Dred Scott*. See for instance, *Dorr v United States*, 1904, 140; *Sere v Pitot*, 1810, 337; *American Ins. Co. v Canter*, 1828, 542. See also Aleinikoff 2002; Leibowitz 1989, 140–55.

The political machinery which would govern the newly acquired territory was set up by Congress in 1900 with the passage of the Foraker Act. The statute established a Governor, an eleven-man executive council, a thirty-five-person assembly (the House of Delegates), and an elected Resident Commissioner who would speak for Puerto Rico in the US House of Representatives.[10] The problem, however, in the eyes of most Puerto Ricans was that the governor was appointed by the US President, the executive council consisted mostly of non-Puerto Rican appointees, the assembly's powers were subject to US Congressional veto, and the Resident Commissioner was deprived of voting privileges in America's Congress.

In a series of now infamous 1901 cases, known as the Insular Cases, the Supreme Court debated what would be done with the densely-populated territories acquired after the 1898 Spanish-American War and decided that Puerto Rico was an "unincorporated" territory.[11] Unlike incorporated territories where residents would have the full rights of the Constitution extended to them and which would eventually become states of the Union, unincorporated territories have a distinct set of rights, powers, and status. In the version of unincorporation set forth in the Insular Cases, territories like Puerto Rico only had basic protection from the Constitution, such as the writ of *habeas corpus*, prohibition against cruel and unusual punishment, and protection against unreasonable searches and seizures.[12] Otherwise, such territories are subject to the full and unfettered power of Congress. In his dissenting opinion in a 5–4 decision, Justice Harlan complained in one of the cases that,

> The concurring opinion...assumes that Congress is not bound, in those territories or possessions to follow the rules...prescribed by the Constitution....That theory assumes that the Constitution created a government empowered to acquire countries throughout the world, to be governed by different rules than those obtaining in the original states and territories, and substitute for the present system of republican government, a system of domination over distant provinces in the exercise of unrestricted power.[13]

For the first few decades after the US takeover of Puerto Rico, the territory was beset by economic squalor at relatively the same status as Haiti and some of the other similarly poor areas in the Caribbean. American direct rule initially did little to change these circumstances. Economic backwardness remained and sometimes worsened.

---

[10] Leibowitz 1989, 141.

[11] *Downes v Bidwell*, 1901, 294. For an excellent discussion of the Insular Cases see Leibowitz 1989, 17–25.

[12] For more on this see Leibowitz 1989, 186.

[13] *Downes v Bidwell*, 1901, 294.

In 1917, after Woodrow Wilson's election, democratic majorities in both houses of Congress produced the Jones Act (the Revised Organic Act of 1917).[14] While this act had the merit of providing Puerto Rico's population with US citizenship, it fell far short of providing it with any credible final decision-making powers. Furthermore, Washington was still very much involved in the territory's affairs through key central government appointments, such as the Governor, the Attorney General, the Auditor, and the Commission of Education, who were all under the influence of the US Department of the Interior.[15] Such circumstances served as a showcase for the incompetence and mismanagement that can result from direct central government rule. When Puerto Rico's assembly, for instance, voted to allocate funds to help earthquake victims or to establish scholarships to encourage education, the Attorney General reportedly canceled the allocations as supposed violations of the Jones Act.[16] And while the US did take some action to redress the dire poverty in the territory, such aid was far less than that which was allocated to states of the Union, which in the minds of many underscored Puerto Rico's subordinate, colonial status. In 1935, Puerto Rico's Governor complained that the territory was receiving one-eighth the amount that would go to a state under the Federal Emergency Relief Act.[17] Mirroring the condition of many other colonies in the world, the conditions of economic squalor, the perceived outrages of imposition by a foreign power, and the sense that they were indeed a distinct national population provided fertile ground for resistance and in some cases violent rebellion.

Toward the beginning of the twentieth century, America watched with increasing alarm the rise of a Puerto Rican independence movement, which by the 1930s had the backing of a majority of the territory's population. During this time Puerto Rico witnessed rising cases of politically motivated violence directed at America's proxy government in the territory. Nationalist militants and police clashed on several notable occasions culminating in the assassination of a local police chief in 1936 and the "Ponce Massacre" in 1937 when police fired upon independence protesters in the southern city of Ponce. Nineteen people were killed and around 150 were wounded. This climate also made the secessionist liberal party the strongest party in the territory. Although measures such as US citizenship, limited economic assistance, and local elections were to some degree welcomed, these actions were insufficient "carrots" to quell increasing calls for secession amidst the unequal rights and economic turmoil.

---

[14] Act passed on March 2, 1917.　　　[15] Monge 1997, 88.
[16] Monge 1997.　　　[17] Monge 1997, 96.

In light of these conditions, US President Franklin Roosevelt attempted a more aggressive "stick" approach. In 1936, he secretly collaborated with Senator Milliard Tydings to introduce a bill in Congress that would allow for Puerto Rican independence in four years.[18] According to the Tydings Bill, during this four-year transitional period, tariffs on the territory would be raised by 25% each year until they reached the same levels as other fully independent states—which unlike Puerto Rico did not have a customs union with the United States.[19] With the Tydings Bill being considered in Congress as well as widely published official reports of the devastating political and economic effects of independence, the majority of Puerto Rican voters shifted away from pro-independence parties in November 1936.[20] The Tydings Bill also persuaded some of Puerto Rico's most popular pro-secession leaders (such as Muñoz Marín) that fully severing itself from America was a bad idea.[21] As Muñoz Marín himself describes:

> Because of the rigidity of our thinking, we could not disentangle the concept of love for our country from the fixed idea of separate independence. Anything other than independence seemed to clash with our love of Puerto Rico. The difficult process of clarifying these ideas began when the Tydings bill was introduced in Congress in 1936.... The Tydings bill would have made Puerto Rico independent, but it would have shackled the people with economic misery.[22]

But although full independence was no longer acceptable to leaders like Muñoz Marín, the status quo of colonialism was even more repugnant.

The Post-1952 Constitutional Formulation

In response to lobbying efforts, the increased violence within Puerto Rico, and due to generally accepted principles of democracy and self-determination within America's federal government, a variety of constitutional solutions were considered to address Puerto Rico's problems. One option was allowing the territory independence. But neither the United States nor, as it ultimately turned out, most Puerto Ricans, wanted this. For the United States there were clear military advantages of having a foothold in the Caribbean on the strategic approaches to the Panama Canal. As for the Puerto Ricans, many in the

---

[18] United States Senate 1936. Senate 4529, 74th Congress, 2nd Session, 80 Congressional Record 5925–27.

[19] Leibowtiz 1981, 228.

[20] Gatell 1958, 42.

[21] Leibowtiz 1981, 228.

[22] Muñoz Marín 1953, 1. Also quoted in Gatell 1958, 43.

dominant liberal party who initially supported secession quickly changed their mind when it became clear that independence would mean a significant loss of US trade advantages and aid.

As far as political assimilation into the US federation as a state, Congressmen feared introducing a nationalistically distinct territory into the Union. Similarly, the majority of Puerto Ricans themselves rejected political and cultural assimilation—even if it meant that they would be a federal member-unit in the federation. As jurist José Trías Monge wrote, "Puerto Rico spent decades in the melting pot, at high heat, and never melted."[23] If a compromise between full independence and assimilation was to be sought, some other solution would be needed. Ironically the drafters of the new political form that Puerto Rico would adopt looked for inspiration to the empire that had previously unsuccessfully imposed its will on the Thirteen Colonies: Great Britain. Puerto Rican Governor Muñoz Marín and Resident Commissioner Antonio Fernos Isern used the 1931 Statute of Westminster as a model for drafting Public Law 600, which was the constitutional document that set the stage for the rest of Puerto Rico's new constitutional order.[24] As mentioned in the Chapter 4, the 1931 Statute of Westminster was a British law which codified many of the pre-existing unwritten constitutional rules between the British central government and the British Dominions.[25]

But although the partial independence option was gaining increasing popularity among some of Puerto Rico's most popular leaders, initially there was relative ambivalence for such an option in Washington DC. On a number of notable occasions Puerto Rican leaders implored the US government to grant credible forms of entrenched powers to the territory, but as José Trías Monge confirms, these early proposals "fell on deaf ears." As Muñoz Marín describes, "We were impaled on the horns of the dilemma which seemed to force an inexorable choice between separate independence and federated statehood."[26] Roosevelt's secret encouragement of Puerto Rican independence through the 1936 Tydings Bill may have represented a sincere willingness for the territory's secession. It may also have been a ploy to frighten leaders with the dangerous

---

[23] Gatell 1958, 120.

[24] Gatell 1958, 110.

[25] Muñoz Marín and Fernos Isern seem to have interpreted the 1931 Statute of Westminster (and its disavowal of interference in Dominion affairs) as a law that promised degrees of autonomy with continued partial integration with the United Kingdom. Indeed as K. C. Wheare (1949, 150–7) describes, this may have indeed been the intention of the British Government. But since the British also allocated considerable external powers to the Dominions (including offensive military capabilities) these territories increasingly resembled fully independent states after 1931 rather than PITs. On the end of Dominion status see Scott 1945. See also Phillips et al. 2001, 788.

[26] Muñoz Marín 1953, 3.

realities of full independence in order to secure Puerto Rico's continued accession. Whatever the case may be, such efforts did not indicate an enthusiasm
for the territory's credible self-governance, even while the British Dominion
model was a well-known alternative to US officials.[27] As Abe Fortas, the US
Under Secretary of the Interior, told Muñoz Marín, "The United States will
continue to be supreme in Puerto Rico, and that is flat. There is just not any
question about it."[28] The advent of World War II, however, changed this out-
look in the minds of America's President and much of Congress.

The Partial Independence Inducing Cataclysm

It is no accident that Puerto Rico's new constitutional order emerged shortly
after the perils of World War II. Even as American forces battled the Nazis in
Italy in September 1943, US President Franklin D. Roosevelt changed his tactics
toward Puerto Rico and pressed Congress to grant autonomous powers to the
territory. For leaders like Roosevelt, World War II underscored new threats for
homeland protection in the Western hemisphere. New military technologies
and the danger of a Eurasian hegemon could shift the global balance of power
against America. Consequently, Puerto Rico's geostrategic position came to
be viewed as more important to the defense of the American homeland. In
his September 1943 address to Congress on Puerto Rican self-governance,
Roosevelt observed that:

> The elements of world military and naval strategy have changed....When [Puerto
> Rico] was first brought under our flag, the Panama Canal had not yet been dug,
> and the airplane had not yet been invented. When the present war [World War II]
> became imminent, however, it was obvious that the chain of islands running in a
> great arc from Florida to the shoulder of South America, enclosing the Caribbean
> Sea, formed a vast natural shield for the Panama Canal, suited in distance and
> conformation to the uses of the military plane. And of this island shield, Puerto

---

[27] One of the earliest known official references to acknowledge the existence of the partially
independent British Dominion model and its potential application to US territories was articulated in 1902 by future US President William Howard Taft at the outset of his tenure as America's
first governor of the Philippines. In a statement he made before the US Senate committee on
the Philippines he said, "My proposition is that it is the duty of the United States to establish
there a government suited to the present possibilities of the people, which shall gradually change,
conferring more and more right upon the people to govern themselves, thus educating them
in self-government, until their knowledge of government, their knowledge of individual liberty
shall be such that further action may be taken either by giving them statehood [in America's
Union], *or by making them a quasi-independent government like Canada and Australia*, or if they
desire it, by independence." Italics added. See Smith 1994, 44.
[28] Quoted in Monge 1997, 104.

Rico is the center.... The principles for which we are now fighting require that
we should recognize the right of all our citizens—whether continental or overseas—to the greatest possible degree of home rule and also of participation in the
benefits and responsibilities of our Federal system.[29]

With increasing international calls for decolonization—which were in many
cases led by American leaders—and with Puerto Rico's continuing antagonism
toward their colonial condition, the US government did not want to take any
chances. Under these circumstances, Roosevelt warned that loss of the territory
"would be repugnant to the most elementary principles of national defense."[30]
He therefore recommended that "the people of Puerto Rico [should] be given
an opportunity for the free exercise of the powers of local self-government in
all three branches of government—executive, legislative, and judicial." "There
is no question," he said "of Puerto Ricans' ability now to administer their own
internal affairs and to assume the attendant responsibility."[31] Hence, the disastrous events of World War II induced an unprecedented desire within core
state institutions for partial independence as a way to mitigate nationalistic
opposition and capitalize on the territory's strategic advantages.

Efforts were therefore made from 1950 to 1952, which led to a new form
of self-governance for Puerto Rico. The process that ultimately led to Puerto
Rico's new status mirrored the series of events that occur when new territories
join the US federation as federal member-units (states). First, Congress passed
an "enabling act," which empowered the Puerto Ricans to draft their own
Constitution.[32] The enabling act (Public Law 600) also repealed portions of the
1917 Jones Act.[33] Second, Puerto Rico's population elected delegates to attend
a Constitutional Convention which drafted a new Constitution. And third,
Congress approved the locally-created Constitution through Public Law 477.[34]

Although the establishment of the new government went through the same
three steps that take place when a federation member-unit (a state) is added
to the Union, it was clear that what was being created was not a state at all,
but something that was without precedent in the history of American jurisprudence. In a non-legally binding (dicta) statement in 1976, the US Supreme
Court later affirmed that "Puerto Rico occupies a relationship to the United
States that has no parallel in our history."[35]

---

[29] US President's Message to Congress Regarding the Government of Puerto Rico, 1943.
[30] US President's Message to Congress Regarding the Government of Puerto Rico, 1943.
[31] US President's Message to Congress Regarding the Government of Puerto Rico, 1943.
[32] Leibowitz 1989, 165.   [33] Leibowitz 1989, 165.   [34] Leibowitz 1989, 165.
[35] *Examining Board v Flores de Otero*, 1976, 494–596.

Three Views on Puerto Rico's Constitutional Status

With respect to the status of constitutional relations between the US central government and Puerto Rico after 1952 there are three schools of thought.

Compact Theorists

Members of the first are what have been called the compact theorists.[36] This school argues that Congress legally does not have plenary power over Puerto Rico. The closest legal articulation of a possible limitation on Congressional plenary power in such documents is a passage in Public Law 600's preamble that makes the following statement: "[F]ully recognizing the principle of government by consent, this Act is now adopted in the nature of a compact so that the people of Puerto Rico may organize a government pursuant to a constitution of their own adoption." Compact theorists argue that the preamble's reference to "government by consent" and "a compact" helps to create a legally-binding obligation for Congress not to arbitrarily interfere in the territory. It is further argued that the legislative history of Public Law 477 (in which Congress approved of Puerto Rico's locally-drafted constitution) indicates that it was clear to the Congressmen while they were drafting the law that they were binding themselves from future interference in the territory. Lastly, proponents of this school are keen to point out the significant number of lower court rulings which attest to Puerto Rico's domestic sovereignty in judge-made common law.[37] In 1985, the First Circuit Federal Court for instance declared that,

> In 1952, Puerto Rico ceased being a territory of the United States subject to the plenary powers of Congress as provided by the Federal Constitution. The authority exercised by the federal government emanated thereafter from the compact itself. Under the compact between the people of Puerto Rico and the United States, Congress cannot amend the Puerto Rico constitution unilaterally, and the government of Puerto Rico is no longer a federal government agency exercising delegated power.[38]

---

[36] On this view see for instance Colón 1959, 254; Leibowitz 1967, 219; 1989, 172–5. For a discussion of this view in the Congressional Hearings that ultimately produced Public Law 447, see US, Hearings Before the Senate Committee on Interior and Insular Affairs. 1952, 40–9. For a somewhat misleading retreat from pure compact theory, which confirms that Puerto Rico has domestic sovereignty and the doctrine of mutuality is intact, but nevertheless argues that the territory is still somehow a "colony," see Monge 1998, 233.

[37] See for instance *Figueroa v Puerto Rico*, 1953, 79 and *United States v Lopez Andino*, 1987, 1034. Leibowitz 1989, 165–85.

[38] *United States v Quinones*, 1985, 42.

And as recently as 1997 the First Circuit Federal Court even refused to discuss Puerto Rico's status since it was deemed to be well established: "It is not appropriate for this Court to revisit and modify the long-held and well-settled doctrine regarding the constitutional nature of the Commonwealth of Puerto Rico."[39]

Territorial Supremacy Theorists

The second, more widely-accepted, school of thought is represented by what can be called the territorial-supremacy theorists who claim that Congress's plenary power is legally intact and consequently exercisable.[40] Those of this school emphasize the overriding legal force of the territorial clause of the US Constitution. Indeed, no amendment has been made to the US Constitution that attests to a principle of mutual consent. No statute clearly articulates it. And no US Supreme Court has made legally-binding declarations that verify it. Consequently, according to such views "no word other than 'colonialism' adequately describes the relationship."[41]

Proponents of this school reject any notion that the vague phrases in the preamble of Puerto Rico's constitution have any binding force. The preamble's reference to "government by consent" can easily be interpreted as a general articulation of the legitimizing effects of Puerto Rico's referendum after Public Law 600 or the democracy that it would establish. The indistinct reference to the act being "in the nature of a compact" also gives little assurance about what credibility such a compact may have. Indeed, in its history, the US has engaged in a significant number of treaty-like "compacts" with various Indian tribes and the territory associated with them, but has had an infamous record of not honoring them, even when submitted to judicial scrutiny (for more on this see Chapter 6).[42]

Territorial supremacy theorists also counter the compact theorist claims about Public Law 477 by pointing out that the drafting history of Public Law 600 (the enabling legislation that allowed for Puerto Rico to draft its own constitution) makes very clear that the Congressmen and Puerto Rican representatives (such as Muñoz Marín) who were involved had full knowledge that they were not binding Congress from future intervention in the territory. The

---

[39] *United States v Vega Figueroa*, 1997, 79.
[40] See for instance, Cabranes, 1978–79, 77; Fliess 1952, 652, 639; Helfeld, 1985, 452; Lawson and Seidman 2004, 124–138; Torruella 1985, 167–200; 2001, 241–50.
[41] Cabranes 1978–79, 68.
[42] See Aleinikoff 2002, 95–121. See also *Lone Wolf v Hitchcock*, 1903, 216.

confused drafting history of Puerto Rico's legal order from Public Law 600 to Public Law 477 therefore negates the compact theorist's arguments.

Lastly, proponents of this school have their own set of lower court rulings that they can point to which also seem to sustain the notion of Puerto Rico's full legal vulnerability to the unilateral whim of Congress.[43] In one 1993 case, for example, the Eleventh Circuit Court made it clear that Congress's powers are legally supreme over Puerto Rico, declaring that, "Congress may unilaterally repeal the Puerto Rican Constitution…and replace [it] with any rules or regulations of its choice."[44]

Conventional-Entrenchment Theory

The third school of thought, which is introduced here, is what can be called conventional-entrenchment theory. It claims that Congress's plenary power is indeed legally intact but nevertheless is nullified and rendered inoperable by conventional rules. Like the territorial supremacy theorists, it argues that Congress's *legal* plenary power has not been erased and is still in existence. Like the compact theorists, it nevertheless argues that Congress's plenary power is nullified, albeit through conventional rather than legal means. Unlike both of these views, however, it emphasizes the power and significance of unwritten constitutional rules that are articulated through informal agreements between leaders, US governmental declarations, dicta (non-legally binding) statements by the judiciary, and lower court rulings (drawing on unwritten rules) that attest to a duty of mutual assent. It is argued here that these statements articulate an informal constitutional rule that renders the territorial clause of the US Constitution frozen with respect to Puerto Rico. In place of the nullified Constitutional provision is the rule that the central government ought not usurp Puerto Rico's 1952 arrangement without its permission.

Similar to the constitutional relationship between the Dominions and the British government, the legal documents (such as the territorial clause) say one thing, but the informal agreements, principles, and—increasingly with the course of time—precedents of non-interference, convey a very different constitutional picture. One key difference between the role of unwritten constitutional rules as it applied in the British Dominions as opposed to the US–Puerto Rico relationship is that within the British Dominions, convention

---

[43] On this view in the courts see, *Perez de la Cruz v Crowley Towing and Transp. Co.*, 1986; *United States v Sanchez*, 1993; *United States v Lopez Andino*, 1988; and *United States v Rivera Torrez*, 1987. Aleinikoff 2002, 77.

[44] *United States v Sanchez*, 1993. Also quoted in Aleinikoff 2002, 76.

played both a constitutionally entrenching role (by making the status quo very difficult to change without mutual consent) *and* a government-establishing role. In other words, convention made rules difficult to change and articulated which powers were held by the Dominions. In the case of the US–Puerto Rico arrangement, however, convention by and large only plays a constitutionally entrenching role (since Puerto Rico's powers were already allocated and mutually accepted in 1952).

One set of documents that discusses the new conventionally entrenched relationship is the 1952 exchange of letters between Puerto Rican Governor Muñoz Marín and US President Harry Truman after Puerto Rican representatives finished drafting their own written constitution. In his letter Muñoz Marín emphasized the change in Puerto Rico's status:

> The relationship between the United States and Puerto Rico, although increasingly liberal, was established by unilateral action, even if always taken after consultation with Puerto Rican leaders. *The present process is based on bilateral action through free agreement.* No doubt opinions may differ as to the details of the relationship, from both the Puerto Rican and the American points of view, but the principle that the relationship is from now on one of consent through free agreement, wipes out all trace of colonialism. [45]

Truman's reply affirmed the territory's unique status and the principle of consent:

> With its approval [Puerto Rico's Constitution's], full authority and responsibility for local self-government will be vested in the people of Puerto Rico. The Commonwealth of Puerto Rico will be a government which is truly by the consent of the governed. No government can be invested with a higher dignity and greater worth than one based upon the principle of consent.[46]

An even more explicit articulation of Puerto Rico's special status came in 1953 when the US went to the United Nations to remove Puerto Rico from the list of "non-self-governing territories" (colonies) which required the US to submit reports on a yearly basis. After clearing his statement with the State Department, US delegate Frances P. Bolton made the following statement:

> The previous status of Puerto Rico was that of a territory subject to the full authority of the Congress of the United States in all governmental matters. The previous constitution of Puerto Rico was in fact a law of the Congress of the United States, which we called an Organic Act. Only Congress could amend the Organic Act of Puerto Rico. The present status of Puerto Rico is that of a people with a constitution of their own adoption, stemming from their own authority, which only they

---

[45] Reprinted in Monge 1997, 115 (Emphasis added).
[46] See Puerto Rico, Truman's 1952 letter to Puerto Rican Governor Muñoz Marín.

can alter or amend. The relationships previously established also by a law of the Congress, which only Congress could amend, have now become provisions of a compact of a bilateral nature whose terms may be changed only by common consent.[47]

Moreover, a number of federal court cases have also affirmed the barriers that exist which prevent Congress from making unilateral changes to the arrangement.[48] While such lower federal courts arrived at common law conclusions regarding the domestic sovereignty of Puerto Rico, they nevertheless arguably drew on unwritten constitutional rules as the *source* of their judgments. Such a status was also confirmed in non-legally binding dicta in 1982 by the US Supreme Court which confirmed that "Puerto Rico, like a state, is an autonomous political entity, 'Sovereign over matters not ruled by the Constitution...' "[49]

If tomorrow Congress unilaterally and arbitrarily used its legal powers under the territorial clause to abolish Puerto Rico's powers, to place its governor under arrest, and to declare a permanent state of martial law, it would (as argued here) be entirely within its legal authority to do so. Presumably, countervailing political actors or the courts would intervene to prevent such usurpations. But for the sake of argument, if such actions were successful they would be just as absurd as the British Queen exercising her *legally existent* capability of controlling the military, abolishing Parliament, and dismissing the Prime Minister. Similarly, it would be just as absurd (if not more so) for the US President to use his *legally existent* power as the commander-in-chief to violently bully Congress.[50] While Congress's exercise of its legal plenary power over Puerto Rico would not violate America's big "C" Constitution, it would, nevertheless, be an unconstitutional violation of America's little "c" constitution (for a summary of this distinction see Figure 3.2.)

In sum, a variety of factors have put a stamp of credibility and informal entrenchment on Puerto Rico's constitutional laws. These include the commitments made by the executive branch in and around 1952, the allocation of Puerto Rico's final decision-making powers by Congress after a local referendum within the territory, the deeply-held repugnance of treating Puerto Rico

[47] US, Report by Hon. Frances Bolton and Hon. James Richards on the Eighth Session of the General Assembly of the United Nations 1954, 241. See also Monge 1997, 123.

[48] See for instance *Figueroa v Puerto Rico*, 1953; *United States v Lopez Andino*, 1987; *United States v Quinones*, 1985; *United States v Vega Figueroa*, 1997. Leibowitz 1989, 165–85.

[49] *Rodriguez v Popular Democratic Party*, 1982.

[50] US President Abraham Lincoln did in fact do this by deporting at least one member of Congress in the midst of America's Civil War. In light of the extraordinary circumstances of these actions, however, some may be willing to excuse what would otherwise be grave violations to America's small "c" constitution.

like a colony, the influence of the territory's lobby and their political allies, and the confirmation in numerous court cases of the inapplicability of the Constitution's territorial clause. These commitments have generated powerful moral and political forces that have not been ignored (and are highly unlikely to be ignored in the future) by the various branches within the central government, whether or not they are *legally* binding.

A case in point of such forces (and a counter equilibrium event) that would enter onto the radar screen of many US politicians with regard to central government attempts at unilateral interference in the territory against its will is illustrated by the US–Puerto Rican struggle over the Puerto Rican island of Vieques. This island, just off of Puerto Rico's eastern coast, had been used for many years as a site for US military war games and bombing practice, rendering much of the island uninhabitable and polluted with chemicals and radioactivity. After the accidental killing of a Puerto Rican security guard by a stray bomb in 1999, many Puerto Ricans began to see such military operations as an affront to their domestic sovereignty and national identity. Why, they asked, was the military choosing Puerto Rican territory for its noxious target practice? Why not some other place on the mainland? Powerful members of Congress such as John Warner (R-VA) and James Inhofe (R-OK) argued that US security interests would be harmed if the military facility on Vieques was abandoned. Senior military leaders such as General Wesley Clark were also strongly in favor of retaining the base.

In the end, however, the central government surrendered to the sentiments of the Puerto Rican people, their leaders, and their political allies. While there were powerful leaders who favored continued operations on Vieques to uphold national security interests, there were many others who strongly disagreed with actions that trampled on Puerto Rican internal self-determination against their consent. Such leaders expressed a desire to sacrifice the interests of the central government in favor of protecting Puerto Rico's autonomy. This view was, for example, articulated by US Congressman Robert Menendez (D-NJ) who described the implications of a military withdrawal from Vieques:

> Might it be an inconvenience? Yes. Might it take some time? Yes. Might it cost money? Yes.... So why should the Navy permanently cease all live and inert ammunition exercises and, therefore, ultimately leave the island and return it to the people of Vieques and Puerto Rico? I think the answers can be found in the voices of the people of Vieques I met and in the sights I observed.[51]

Added to the repugnance among many US leaders of violating Puerto Rican autonomy against their will, political difficulties also threatened to assail

---

[51] US, Robert Menedez, Extension of Remarks, House of Representatives 1999.

especially the President. When much of the Hispanic electorate within the US, which now numbers nearly 12% of the American population, began to adopt a similar sense of outrage as the Puerto Ricans over Vieques, fearing the implications this would have on the next election, President Bush's chief strategist Carl Rove advised the President to end operations on the island. Accordingly, in 2003, military operations on Vieques were brought to an end. Even if the President was motivated by pure political pragmatism and had little intention of upholding any unwritten rule (which itself is debatable), it is still apparent that the waves of political pressure that assailed the President were generated by outraged leaders and citizens who were attempting to uphold the principle that the US had a duty to cease its unwanted and unilateral interference in the territory.

The case of Vieques shows that overt moves of central government interference in the local affairs of the territory without the assent of the population and the government of Puerto Rico are matched by norms of tyrannical repugnance and political difficulties that can reach the offices of members of Congress and the President. Such deeply held principles and countervailing political influences are added to the precedents of non-interference and semi-legal judicial rulings that reinforce and defend Puerto Rico's post-1952 constitutional order.

Even those who dispute the doctrine of mutual assent as it applies to Puerto Rico are hard pressed to think of examples (apart from a few dismissible examples dealt with below) of when the territory's powers have been usurped by the central government since 1952. This is not an accident. The reason for this is that conventional entrenchment is in operation to prevent such interference. This, however, may be countered by the objection that this record of non-interference is less a function of the central government's absence of power by conventional rules and more because it does not have any interest or reason in interfering in the territory's affairs in the first place. In response, what then explains the central government's interference in Puerto Rican affairs before 1952? Furthermore, why does the central government readily intervene in the other territories within US international legal space that are of less consequence to its interests such as the US Virgin Islands, Guam, or American Samoa (much less the numerous Indian territories) where the same informal agreements, precedents, or principles are inapplicable? While it is beyond the scope of the present discussion to detail the experience of these other territories at the hands of central government interference, they are quite well catalogued by other scholars.[52]

---

[52] On interference by the central government as it pertains to the US Virgin Islands, Guam, and American Samoa see especially Leibowitz 1989, 241–86, 318–74, 423–64. On interference by the central government within the Indian Territories see Aleinikoff 2002, 95–121.

If such conclusions are true, the United States has in fact surrendered some domestic sovereignty to a nationalistically distinct and territorially concentrated population, which is not a state of the federal union. Similar to the British laws that were rendered inoperative by conventional rules with regard to the Dominions, the territorial clause in the US Constitution has been frozen with respect to the status of Puerto Rico with regard to issues that are not addressed by the US Constitution. A binding informal constitutional rule entrenches Puerto Rico's post-1952 constitutional order providing real powers of domestic sovereignty to the territory. Consequently, the most accurate description of Puerto Rico is neither as a mere colony nor as a decentralized territory. Puerto Rico is a PIT.

As mentioned above, territorial supremacy theorists are hard-pressed to think of noteworthy examples when Puerto Rico's powers since 1952 have been usurped. There are nevertheless a number of cases that they manage to put forward to support their viewpoint. One such case was a 1985 US court decision which decreed that prohibitions within the Puerto Rican Constitution with regard to consensual wiretapping were inferior to provisions within a federal crime control act that permitted it.[53] In other words, Puerto Rico's Constitution allowed wiretapping. The center's laws, however, forbid it. In the end the Supreme Court decided in the central government's favor. While such a decision may seem to be an overt usurpation of the arrangement, it is nevertheless clear that the federal act would still apply to a state of the Union. Hence, just as a state of the Union retains its sovereignty even while being subject to such a federal act, so does Puerto Rico.

Another issue that has been put forward as a possible usurpation of the territory's domestic sovereignty are the actions that have been taken in the area of taxes and tariffs. A number of laws including the 1976 Tax Act, the 1983 Caribbean Basin Initiative, the 1984 Tax Reform Act, and the 1986 Tax Act have been put into effect by Congress without the consent of Puerto Rico (or its complaint).[54] Equally, however, in 1978 Puerto Rico also radically changed its own tax system without the consent of the center.[55] Much of such actions on the part of both sides are perhaps due more to a mutual reluctance of oversight over the great complexity of issues of taxes and tariffs, and a further interest in flexibility to make ad hoc adjustments, rather than a desire to overtly usurp the arrangement. In one case, for instance, Puerto Rico was charged a $2.00 tax per gallon on its alcohol exports to the US in Congress's 1984 Tax Reform

---

[53] *United States v Quinones*, 1985.
[54] Leibowitz 1989, 175, 210.
[55] Leibowitz 1989, 175.

Act, unlike other exports where tariffs charged by the US are deposited into the Puerto Rican treasury. The repatriation of tariff fees charged on Puerto Rican exports is what in effect provides for the US–Puerto Rico customs union as per Section 58 of the Puerto Rican Federal Relations Act.[56] The failure to rebate Puerto Rico the $2.00 per gallon on such imports into the US, however, seems to be less one of unilateral profiteering by the center and more a desire to develop ad hoc measures to mitigate the effects of the Puerto Rican government's efforts to artificially subsidize local alcohol production so that it could maximize the repatriation of tariff fees.[57] As Geoffrey Marshall has observed, "conventions can also develop or extend in new directions by being applied to fresh political circumstances."[58] From such precedents it may therefore be concluded that the area of taxes and tariffs may be somewhat exempt from the conventionally entrenching rules so long as unreasonably unilateral actions are not taken and a change of status is not intended.

Yet another issue that raises some questions is the fact that Puerto Rico is treated unequally in certain respects as compared to states of the federal union. Puerto Rico receives lower amounts of federal subsidies in certain areas than states within programs such as Supplemental Security Income, the National Assistance Program, Medicaid, elementary and secondary education, aid to families with dependent children, aid to the elderly, the blind and the handicapped, and food stamps.[59] This unequal treatment has been confirmed by the courts.[60] Furthermore, Puerto Rico receives less federal aid per capita than any state in the union. The lowest amount of per capita aid given to any state is $4,939 and the average is $6,527. (The $3,644 of yearly per capita aid Puerto Rico does receive from the federal government is, however, still substantial—amounting to an average of US$13.5 billion of federal services each year from 1990 to 2009).[61] Moreover, Puerto Ricans also cannot vote for the US President while resident in Puerto Rico (although they can vote in the Primaries that select the candidates for a presidential election and as US citizens are free to vote when they reside on the mainland) nor does their Congressional representative (the Resident Commissioner) have voting power in Congress (although the Resident Commissioner can introduce legislation and vote in committee).

Such treatment however seems to do little to undermine the integrity of Puerto Rico's status as a conventionally entrenched polity. If anything, in some

---

[56] Leibowitz 1989, 217. Polities joined by a customs union have a common external tariff but no internal tariffs between them.

[57] Leibowitz 1989, 218   [58] Marshall 1984, 217.

[59] Lapidoth 1997, 136.   [60] See *Califano v Torres*, 1978, and *Harris v Rosario*, 1980.

[61] *The Economist* 2011.

sense it clarifies it by underscoring the fact that it is not constitutionally incorporated into America as a state of the union with the same status and relationship with the federal government. Although it is treated unequally in terms of federal subsidies and federal voting power, it is also treated unequally by the *benefits* its population receives of not having to pay taxes to the federal government or to bear the costly burdens of defense. Its unincorporated status also provides increased confidence that culturally homogenizing influences from the core state (which historically threatened the territory) will continue to be held at bay. Indeed, there are other inequalities that many in Puerto Rico would like to have but do not have at present. At several points since 1952 proposals have been put forward for Puerto Rico to be able to join more international organizations (as per Table 3.2, Puerto Rico has membership of or affiliations with at least nine international organizations). Proposals have also called for Puerto Rico to gain more of a capability to engage in limited economic negotiations with other states, and for their powers (which as argued here are conventionally entrenched) to be formally entrenched. This is certainly not inconceivable within the confines of partially independent arrangements since other PITs in the world have more abundant powers in such areas. Nevertheless, while many in Puerto Rico do not approve of aspects of their arrangement, the existence of unequal treatment does not constitute proof of usurpation of the arrangement. As long as Puerto Rico's existing final decision-making powers are credibly defended by the aforementioned informal agreements, semi-legal common law, and the political inertia of ever strengthening precedent of non-interference, the territory's conventionally-entrenched status remains intact.

Conclusions on Puerto Rico's Conventionally-Entrenched Status

In sum, Puerto Ricans have much of the same sense of nationalistic distinctiveness from the United States that areas in, for instance, the former Yugoslavia had as that state was breaking up in the mid-1990s. They have a different language. They have a distinct history. Their culture is dissimilar. They even have a historic tradition of violent revolutionary activity.[62] Indeed even when the US and Puerto Rican representatives were ironing out the territory's new constitutional order, assassination attempts were made by Puerto Rican ultra-nationalists on the lives of US President Truman, Puerto Rico's

---

[62] For a description of political violence in Puerto Rico see Monge 1997, 93–94, 100, 113–14.

Governor Muñoz Marín, and members of the US Congress. Thousands of National Guard soldiers were called in to maintain order in several Puerto Rican cities. Significant numbers of policemen and civilians were killed and wounded in the ensuing turmoil.

At one time its most powerful parties and leaders favored independence. Today however, at least 98% of the population wants some form of political association with the United States.[63] In an age of violent nationalism, it is certainly worth examining the reasons behind this level of support. Arguably much of the reason is because of a conventionally entrenched status that makes the territory a PIT. This status has provided important powers and domestic sovereignty without a politically-sensitive formal entrenchment of the territory's powers. While there is certainly room to modify the existing arrangement, in the eyes of most of the population this compromise has provided a better channel for their nationalistic identity than full independence.

In order to further clarify partially independent polities and the advantages of their self-determination as compared to the alternative of sovereign statehood, the next chapter will turn to setting forth a series of arguments about a distinct polity which can be described as "sham federacy." These are neo-colonial organizational forms that some may mistake for partially independent polities since they have been speciously allocated or promised powers of autonomy, sovereignty, self-determination, or other similar designations. Unlike partially independent polities, however, sham federacies do not have powers that have been made credible by discernible means.

---

[63] On the results of the 1998 plebiscite in which less than 2% of voters chose independence see Aleinikoff 2002, 93.

6

Sham Federacy: China's Autonomous Regions, France's Indochinese Free States, South Africa's Bantustans, and America's Indian Territories

Nothing is agreed until everything is agreed.

—Martti Ahtisaari, Nobel Peace Prize Laureate and former President of Finland who attempted to apply this principle when he mediated negotiations between the Free Aceh Movement and the Government of Indonesia in late 2004.

After 1976, the Indonesian government fought a civil war against the Free Aceh Movement (*Gerakan Aceh Merdeka*; GAM) rebels in the nationalistically distinct and resource rich territory of Aceh (Indonesia). Thousands were killed, widespread human rights abuses on the part of Indonesia's occupying military were reported, and Indonesia's economy was disrupted for nearly three decades by separatist attacks. Aceh is located at the northwestern tip of Indonesia's archipelago on the eastern edge of the Indian Ocean, has a population of 4.2 million, a GDP per capita of $992, and accounts for roughly one-third of Indonesia's liquefied natural gas exports.[1] As a result of Aceh-Indonesian talks, in August 2005 GAM and the Government of Indonesia signed the Helsinki Memorandum of Understanding (MoU). In the MoU both sides agreed that Aceh's government would have far reaching and guaranteed powers over a wide range of issues including internal security, economic affairs, and political participation "through a fair and democratic process within the unitary state and constitution of the Republic of Indonesia."[2] Indonesia also agreed to pull military and police forces out of the territory.[3] They further agreed that in 2006

---

[1] McCulloch 2006, 3. The statistics given are 2004 estimates.
[2] Aspinall 2005, 1–68.   [3] Aspinall 2005, 1–68.

that a law (the Law on the Governing of Aceh) would be created that would fulfill the principles in the agreement. With the 2005 MoU in hand, GAM forces dutifully handed in their weapons and much of the Indonesian military redeployed out of the province under the supervision of monitors from the European Union (EU) and the Association of South East Asian Nations (ASEAN). Peace largely returned to the province. And as a result of the aforementioned commitments, the MoU seemed to grant Aceh a status as a PIT.

Nevertheless, in 2006 when Indonesia's parliament produced the new Law on Governing Aceh (LOGA), Indonesia failed to fully implement the principles of the MoU as agreed.[4] The MoU says that "decisions with regard to Aceh by the legislature of the Republic of Indonesia will be taken... with the *consent* of the legislature of Aceh."[5] The LOGA, however, makes clear that only consultation, not consent, will be required for such matters.[6] This therefore makes it possible for the core legislature to unilaterally usurp its commitments to the territory by unilateral fiat. Similarly, the MoU says that "International agreements entered into by the government of Indonesia which relate to matters of special interest to Aceh will be entered into... with the *consent* of the legislature of Aceh."[7] This matter is of special importance to Aceh leaders since international agreements on the territory's energy exports are a vital part of resource sharing as agreed with the core state.[8] Again, however, the LOGA makes clear that "consultation and advisement" rather than consent are all that are required on such matters.[9] The MoU also puts careful emphasis on a dispute resolution between the parties with respect to the implementation of the principles and policies that it sets forth. It specifies a multi-tiered mechanism, which mirrors that which exists in PITs like the Åland Islands (Finland) and Greenland (Denmark), but with the novel addition of a role for EU and ASEAN officials as ultimate arbitrators.[10] By contrast, not only does the LOGA

---

[4] For other sources that also reflect this see for example International Crisis Group 2007 and Stepan 2013, 249.

[5] Government of the Republic of Indonesia and the Free Aceh Movement, 2005, 1.1.2c. Memorandum of Understanding between the Government of the Republic of Indonesia and the Free Aceh Movement. Italics added.

[6] Republic of Indonesia, 2006, Chapter XL, Article 269, Section 3. "Any planned amendment to this Law must first undergo consultation by and receive considerations from the DPRA [Aceh House of Representatives]." Republic of Indonesia, 2006. The Governing of Aceh. Law No. 11/2006. Available at: <http://www.bra-aceh.org/download/archive/loga/loga_law_on_the_governing_of_aceh_english_version.pdf> accessed November 2009.

[7] Government of Indonesia and GAM, 2005, 1.12b. Italics added.

[8] International Crisis Group 2007, 9.

[9] Republic of Indonesia, 2006, Chapter IV, Article 8, Section 1. "Draft international treaties that directly involve the governance of Aceh to be entered into by the Government shall be developed with the consultation and advisement from the DPRA. [Aceh House of Representatives]."

[10] Government of Indonesia and GAM, 2005, 6.1.

not mention any role for outside international monitors, it scarcely refers to a mechanism for resolving disputes.[11] The LOGA has also failed to deliver on a promised Human Rights Court and Truth and Reconciliation Commission.[12] In sum, Aceh was promised powers of partial independence in the MoU that were not granted.[13] Again and again the LOGA repeats that the territory has "broad autonomy" and "special autonomy" but whatever autonomy may exist in Aceh, it is not the kind that is defended, made very difficult to change, or made credible by any discernible constitutional mechanism. Another possibility would be for the territory's institutions to be politically entrenched, similar to Bougainville or Mindanao. But such entrenchment would not defend any final decision-making powers since none are clearly spelled out in the LOGA. Without a discernible entrenchment mechanism (whether formal-legal, conventional, or political-formal) a nationalistically distinct territory that has been promised autonomous powers is not a partial independent arrangement and enters the ranks of a different form of governance, referred to here as "sham federacy."[14]

Partly in response to strong norms against imperialism,[15] states that seek domination over nationalistically distinct territories have cloaked their would-be colonies in the trappings of a self-determination that does not fully exist. Countries have speciously allocated a status of "autonomy," "sovereignty," "self-determination," and other similar designations to territories while in reality the powers allocated under such a regime are either not real or not credible.[16] The rightful analogies to these modern forms of imperialism are neither the benign colonies of the twenty-first century nor the real partially independent polities described in the previous chapters.[17] As indicated, real PITs are nationally distinct polities that possess some entrenched final

----

[11] The only exception to this are disputes that relate to the environment and elections in which the Indonesian supreme court is the final arbiter.

[12] International Crisis Group 2009, 8–9.

[13] This does not mean that such powers will not be at some stage granted in the future. As of this writing, however, they have not been granted.

[14] Aceh can be considered a sham federacy from two perspectives. First, the MoU promised powers that the territory was not allocated as promised in the 2006 LOGA. Second, the LOGA itself emphasizes "autonomy" for the territory while not providing any guarantees or enforcement mechanisms that would sustain it or make it real.

[15] On norms against colonialism see Jackson 1993, 111–38. See also Donnelly 2006; Hobson and Sharman 2005. On hierarchical arrangements through a constructivist lens, see Wendt and Friedheim 1995.

[16] On sovereignty see Bartleson 1996; Bunck and Fowler 1996; Jackson 1999; Krasner 1999; Philpott 2001a.

[17] On federacy see Anderson 2012; Coppieters 2001; Elazar 1991; 1993; 1994; 1997; Ghai 2000; Jakobson 2005; McGarry 2007; O'Leary 2001; 2002; 2005; 2013a; 2013b; Rezvani 2004; 2007a; 2007b; 2012; Stepan, Linz, and Yadav 2010; Stepan 2013; Stevens 1977; Watts 1996.

decision-making power within a territory without being fully incorporated into the constitutional system of a core state. By contrast, although they are constitutionally unincorporated and nationalistically distinct, sham federacies do not have credible final decision-making powers (sovereignty). For a full list of colonies after the beginning of the twentieth century see Appendix 4.[18]

Put another way, sham federacies have the features of a forcibly controlled colony (nationalistic-distinctiveness, external domination, and constitutional differentiation from the metropole)[19] with the addition of a nominal and delegated status of "autonomy" that is not entrenched by any discernible means. Cases where such a state of affairs applies, include Azerbaijan (Nakhichevan),[20] China (in its Autonomous Regions),[21] Bangladesh (Chittagong Hill Tracts), Georgia (Ajara),[22] Pakistan (Federally Administered Tribal Area),[23] India

---

[18] Data on historic colonies used here were drawn from Columbia Encyclopedia. 2010; CIA World Factbook (<www.cia.gov/cia/publications/factbook/>; Encyclopedia Britannica. 2010; Goldsmith and He 2008, 609–11; History World (<www.historyworld. net>). Data on current colonies was drawn from Aldrich and Connell 1998, 12–15. With all of these sources, polities that were in fact PITs, sham federacies, federation member-units, states, and de facto states were removed.

[19] On hierarchal forms which include colonies, informal empires, and protectorates, see Cooley 2000/2001; 2005; Donnelly 2006; Hobson and Sharman 2005; Lake 1996; 1999; 2001; 2003.

[20] On the constitutional status of Nakhichevan see, Council of Europe, Venice Commission 1997. The Venice Commission observes that "Article 138 of the Azerbaijan Constitution lists elections to the Supreme Assembly, issues concerning economic development, social protection, environmental protection, tourism, health, the sciences and culture." The Venice Commission has nevertheless observed that Article 137 of Azerbaijan's Constitution makes clear that legislation passed by the Parliament of Nakhichevan "must be compatible with" not only the Azerbaijan Constitution but also "with all legislation of the Azerbaijan Republic." This vulnerability to the legislative fiat of the core state undermines the constitutional defensibility and credibility of the powers are supposedly allocated under Article 138. Exclusive budgetary powers are also granted to Nakhichevan, but according to Article 139 the budget must receive approval from the central authorities. The Venice Commission also expresses concerns about the role of the President of the territory's legislature and the "concentration of important powers in the hands of this one individual," including the ability to summarily dismiss judges and unilaterally amend legislation.

[21] Henders 1998, 92–9.

[22] See, International Crisis Group (ICG) 2004, 11. The International Crisis Group (ICG) has observed that the July 2004 law on the status of the Muslim-majority territory of Ajara "left the region with little more than nominal autonomy." After Georgian President Mikhail Saakashvili recentralized control of the region in 2004, the ICG has also reported that "the speed and lack of transparency of the changes, as well as the law's substance, put into question the degree to which Ajara will really control its own affairs." For a similar view see also Council of Europe, Venice Commission 2004, 5.

[23] As scholars have confirmed, "the name for this area is actually a misnomer. It is not federally administered in any sense of the word." See Johnson and Mason 2008, 53. After allowing measures of self-rule and upon discovering natural gas and mineral reserves, the Pakistani government in 1973 also revoked the power of the hereditary chiefs of Baluchistan province, the *sardars*, and invaded the region.

(Kashmir),[24] Indonesia (Aceh and Papua),[25] Israel (the Palestinian Territories), Nicaragua (the Atlantic Coast), and the United States (in its Indian territories).[26] In the twentieth century, other states have also historically engaged in such practices, including France (in the Free States of Indochina 1950–54),[27] Iraq (Kurdistan 1970–75), the Philippines (Mindanao 1977–89), Czechoslovakia (Slovak Republic 1948–68),[28] South Africa (in the Bantustans 1963–93),[29] and the Soviet Union (in the Autonomous Oblasts andRegions). For a full list of sham federacies after 1945 see Appendix 3.[30]

The governance costs, crises of legitimacy, and failures of metropoles to represent colonial populations were some of the key factors that created a precipitous decline in cases of imperialism especially in the twentieth century.[31] But the demand for imperial control remains. The benign colonialism literature overlooks sham federacies because arguments can be made that constitutionally speaking they do not appear to be colonies since they have nominally been allocated powers of self-rule. Similarly, the autonomy literature overlooks the normative distinctiveness of sham federacies by, at times, crudely incorporating them into their corpus of "autonomous" cases.[32] In as much as cases of sham federacy have been referred to as a form of "autonomy," "autonomy" has a dysfunctional and tyrannical side that has been neglected as an overarching concept in international affairs.

---

[24] See, Bajpai 1997, 33–81; and Kumar 2002, 11–24.

[25] Aspinall 2005, 1–68; McCulloch 2006, 3.

[26] See Aleinikoff 2002; Pommersheim 1995; Wallace 1999; Wilkinson 1987.

[27] See LaFeber 1975; Garrett 1967; Hammer 1948; 1950; Herring 1979; Thompson and Adloff 1953.

[28] See Cox and Frankland 1995, 78.

[29] See Butler et al. 1977; and Carter et al. 1967; Dugard 1979; Moerkijk 1981; Stultz 1980.

[30] The data on sham federacy listed in Appendix 3 attempts to be an exhaustive articulation after 1945. In part it draws from Cederman et al.'s (2009a) Ethnic Power Relations (EPR) dataset which features a list of ethnic groups that have "regional autonomy." In order to compile a list of sham federacies, however, various groups were removed from the EPR's "regional autonomy" list including: PITs (such as Northern Ireland), non-territorially based autonomous arrangements (such as the "Germans" of Belgium), member-units of sham federations (such as the Republics of the USSR and the member-units of the Russian Federation), and where data were indiscernible (such as the reference to "others" being associated with Lebanon). Additionally, a wide range of territories and groups that were not included in the EPR were added to the list, such as the Free States of Indochina, America's Indian Territories, and many others. It should also be noted that in a limited number of areas, such as Sudan, the groups listed are associated with a single territory, such as South Sudan. In other areas, such as the Indian Territories of the US, in order to make the 305 Indian tribes of America more feasible to articulate, large numbers of tribes were grouped under regional headings.

[31] For works which assess such factors as they relate to empire–colony relations see Cooley 2005; Motyl 1999b; Peattie 1984.

[32] See Chapman and Roeder 2007; Gurr 1999, 296; Heintze 1998, 29; Nordquist 1998, 75–76; Sharp 1946, 193; Sorensen and Phillips 2003, 105.

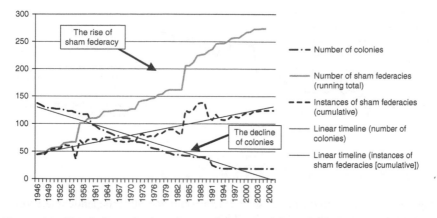

Figure 6.1. The decline of colonialism and the rise of sham federacy neo-colonialism timeline 1946–2007

Sources: For PITs see Appendix 1. For sham federacies see Appendix 3. For colonies see Appendix 4. For sovereign states see Correlates of War Project 2008. Countries that have acceded into the EU are not coded as fully independent sovereign states.

Modern day sham federacies are not only a widespread phenomenon in the world, they are more numerous than traditional colonies at their peak in the nineteenth century. In this sense, not only has imperialism not gone away, it is increasingly resurgent. It should be acknowledged that traditional colonies were much more widespread as a share of the world's total landmass and population. As historian William Keylor notes, "The most salient feature of international relations at the beginning of [the twentieth] century was the extent to which most of the world had come under the direct or indirect domination of a handful of states all located in Europe."[33] Nevertheless, when measured by their regime frequency, sham federacy has outstripped previous instances of colonies (see Figure 6.1). This widespread and increasing global frequency of sham federacy reinforces the rationalist assumptions presented in this book. Sham federacies are arguably increasing because local populations and core states are attracted to an accommodation that promises a compromise between full assimilation and full independence to a nationalistically distinct region. The arrangement results from the belief (by at least one party) that it will in fact deliver territorial self-determination. This tendency is articulated in Figure 6.2, which shows cumulative instances of PITs and sham federacy matching, and at some points outstripping, numbers of new sovereign states after 1946.

[33] Keylor 2000.

Figure 6.2. Relative frequency of sham federacy and partially independent territories as compared to sovereign states 1946–2007

Sources: For PITs see Appendix 1. For sham federacies see Appendix 3. For colonies see Appendix 4. For sovereign states see Correlates of War Project 2008. Countries that have acceded into the EU are not coded as fully independent sovereign states.

This has more than academic significance. Many of the international institutions, such as the Trusteeship Council that have been tasked with assisting territories that have been subjected to imperialism to decolonize have in recent years downsized most of their operations.[34] Some imperialistic states have also temporarily succeeded at misleading some outside observers into believing the autonomous claims of their nominal constitutional promises.[35] They have thereby deflected in varying degrees some of the normative forces that contributed to the downfall of old empires. In the long run, however, such efforts sometimes tend to fail which adds fuel to the fire of local nationalism (as in Indochina [France])[36], international opposition (as in the Bantustans [South Africa])[37], territorial destabilization (as with Kashmir [India]),[38] and/ or a pathological sense of dependence and lack of self-sufficiency (as with the Indian Territories [US]).[39]

Understanding these governmental forms is important because (1) some observers may be tempted to confuse sham federacies with PITs; (2) it is critical to distinguish the advantage of entrenched powers from the disadvantages of

[34] Trusteeship Council 2007.
[35] See Gurr 1999, 296; Heintze 1998, 29; Nordquist 1998, 75–76; Sharp 1946, 193; Sorensen and Phillips 2003, 105.
[36] LaFeber 1975; Garrett 1967; Hammer 1948; 1950; Herring 1979; Thompson and Adloff 1953.
[37] Butler, et al. 1977; and Carter et al. 1967; Dugard 1979; Moerkijk 1981; Stultz 1980.
[38] Bajpai 1997, 3r1; Kumar 2002, 11–24.
[39] Aleinikoff 2002; Pommersheim 1995; Wallace 1999; and Wilkinson 1987.

not having them; and (3) the large scale emergence of sham federacy arrangements reinforces the attractiveness of self-governance arrangements (even if the reality of credible self-governance does not emerge).

The first part of this chapter will focus on describing the concept of sham federacy. A number of paradigmatic cases will be provided to illustrate varying forms of this governmental form and their constitutional development.[40] The next part will turn to the epistemological and normative limits of the autonomy and benign colonialism perspectives in light of the sham federacy phenomenon. It will call for a greater degree of rigor when evaluating nominally autonomous territories and point out cases in which such arrangements are in fact smokescreens for modern imperialism.

THE CONSTITUTIONAL DEVELOPMENT OF
SHAM FEDERACY

After the downfall of empires and decolonization that swept the world especially in the twentieth century, is imperialism now dead? By imperialism I mean the forcible political and physical control of the internal and external capacities of a periphery polity by a dominant metropole.[41] Presumably, few would maintain that imperialism is completely gone from the world. There are, however, a number of literatures in the social sciences that have emphasized the continued retreat of imperial structures. One such school of thought is expressed in the literature on what can be called "benign colonialism."[42] This literature argues that although colonies still exist, imperialism as described above is on the retreat because the hierarchical relationships between the world's remaining colonies and their metropoles are in many respects not forced. The benign colonialism literature draws attention to the fact that colonies frequently want to be colonies because of the significant economic, political, and security benefits that now accrue to them.[43] Another school of thought that emphasizes the dwindling ties of imperialism between states and territories, is the literature on "autonomy."[44]

---

[40] On the use of paradigmatic cases see for example Lijphart (1999) with his use of the UK to illustrate majoritarian democracy and his use of Belgium and Switzerland to illustrate the "consensus model."

[41] Doyle 1986, 12.

[42] See Aldrich and Connell 1998; Armstrong and Read 2000, 285–306; Oostindie 2006, 609–626.

[43] Aldrich and Connell 1998, 60–190.

[44] See Baldacchino 2006, 855; Dinstein 1981; Ghai 2000b, 483–530; Hannum 1990; Hannum and Lillich 1980, 858–889; Lapidoth 1997; McElroy and Mahoney 2000; Poirine 1999; Suksi 1998.

This literature points out that, since the nineteenth century in particular, there have been increasing cases of core states delegating and/or transferring powers to one or more periphery territories within their international legal space. According to such views, imperialism as described above is therefore on the retreat in many cases because the "autonomous" arrangements that exist between core states and their periphery territories have eroded the physical and political control that would otherwise exist in cases of imperialism. While it is not denied here that benign colonialism and some forms of autonomy exist, this chapter will argue that these views are nevertheless constitutionally, politically, and historically misleading. In spite of the existence of benign colonies and some forms of autonomy, imperialism has been resurgent in parts of the world after the middle of the twentieth century under the guise of a political form that the colonialism and autonomy literatures fail to take into account. Even as many empires have undergone significant fragmentation, still others have held onto much of their territory through "sham federacy." The sham federacies that embody this imperial resurgence neither have credible autonomy nor are they benign.

Similar to many historic colonies, there is a continuum of malgovernance among them. At one end of the spectrum are those that are examples of rampant human rights violations, dire poverty, and tyranny (such as China's Autonomous Regions, South Africa's Bantustans, and the nineteenth-century "sovereign" Indian Territories in the United States). At the other end of the spectrum are those that have some of the political and economic stability of modern colonies, but nevertheless arguably suffer from the lack of commitment and sense of ownership that comes from the absence of real sovereign powers (such as Indian Territories in the United States especially after the 1970s).

Sham federacies can also be divided into three categories according to the strategic intention of the core state. First, there are puppet regimes, such as France's Indochinese Free States and China's Autonomous Regions in which the core's intention seems to have been control through local proxies. Second, there are decentralized structures within an ethnically separated holding area, such as South Africa's historic Bantustans and America's Indian Territories before the 1970s in which the core's intention seems to have been state-wide ethnic cleansing. And third, there are decentralized administrations under sovereign trusteeship, as with America's Indian territories after the 1970s in which policies of puppet control and ethnic cleansing have evolved into a form of benign authority that involves protection from competing jurisdictions and developmental assistance.[45] There is of course no space here to provide a detailed case of every known instance of sham federacy. Nevertheless,

---

[45] On nationalistic antipathy to alien rule see Gellner 1983, 1; Hechter 2000.

a number of descriptions of the constitutional development of sham federacies will be provided. These cases have been selected according to their ability to embody the aforementioned puppet, ethnic holding area, and trusteeship categories.

Puppet Regimes: France's Historic Indochinese "Free States"

After losing their Asian colonies of Indochina (modern day Cambodia, Laos, and Vietnam) during World War II to the Japanese, in 1945 the French attempted to reassert their control.[46] One French leader expressed the view that France could "only be a great power so long as our flag continues to fly in all the overseas territory."[47] In the twentieth-century age of decolonization, such naked imperialism was, however, distasteful to other leaders, such as US President Franklin D. Roosevelt. Roosevelt saw French colonialism amidst the strong nationalist sentiments of Indochina as doomed to failure. He saw the French as "poor colonizers" who had "badly mismanaged" and exploited the region.[48]

After 1945, French forces were finding it increasingly difficult to militarily defeat Vietnamese (*Vietminh*) rebels led by Ho Chi Minh. France therefore attempted to score local and international political points by shifting from open imperialism to establishing nominally semi-independent governments for Cambodia, Laos, and Vietnam, calling them "free states" within the French union. One such arrangement was concluded with Cambodia in January 1946. Another was agreed between Laotian representatives and France on August 27, 1946.[49] Yet another was signed by Ho Chi Minh on behalf of Vietnam on March 6, 1946.[50] The last agreement, for example, declared "the Republic of Vietnam as a free state having its government, its parliament, its army and its finances and forming part of the French Union."[51]

The "Free State" designation for Indochina mirrored the name given to Ireland's partially independent arrangement (the Irish Free State) after it was given Dominion status. In spite of this label, however, as time passed it became increasingly clear that France retained full control of these territories.[52] Shortly after the March 1946 agreement with Vietnam, France's prime minister, Paul

---

[46] LaFeber 1975; Garrett 1967; Hammer 1948; 1950; Herring 1979; Thompson and Adloff 1953.
[47] Quoted in Herring 1979, 4.   [48] LaFeber 1975, 1277–95.
[49] Thompson and Adloff 1953, 64.   [50] Garrett 1967, 318.
[51] Quoted in Smith 1974, 225.
[52] Hammer 1948, 260; Herring 1979, 15; 1950; Smith 1974, 225.

Ramadier, argued that the Constitution of France's Fourth Republic super-
seded the principles of the arrangement. "Today" he said "it is no longer a
matter of the framework of the treaty of 6 March."[53] Even as he repudiated
the terms of the free state agreements, the prime minister still nevertheless
emphasized the "independence" of these territories "within the framework of
the French Union."[54] Within the Free States, powers over public works, trade,
justice, finance, education, transportation, foreign immigration, security, and
foreign affairs were, for example, all under France's de facto control.[55] And in
the cases of Laos and Cambodia, at least one French advisor was assigned to
supervise the activities of each Indochinese minister.[56]

Nominal powers of independence for these territories within the French
union made France's continued control more palatable to the US government,
who increasingly saw the Vietnamese rebels as communist proxies for China
and the Soviet Union. Part of the reasoning for the eventual US support of
France's sham federacy policies had to do with the logic of the Cold War in
which America desired to prevent the further expansion of communist influence and to avoid alienating European allies such as France in the midst of
the paramount objective which was to secure Western Europe from Soviet
influence. The other key reason, however, was that such a policy softened the
repugnance of naked French colonialism, even when it was clear to many US
officials that the sham regimes were smokescreens for French domination.[57]
Sham federacy helped the United States avoid appearing as an accessory to
French imperialism. Indeed, the arrangement seems to have even deceived
some contemporaneous scholars, one of whom, for example, declared that
the arrangement signaled "a major turning point in French colonial policy"
in which the "Indochinese may be permitted some real degree of control over
their own destiny in friendly collaboration with one of the major western
democracies."[58] As a result of such perceptions (or misperceptions), the US
shifted its position from being against French control to recognizing the new
Indochinese "Free States" in February 1950.[59]

Although US officials were partially placated by this form of governance,
it nevertheless did little to satisfy local nationalist resentment. France's rejection of full independence and British Dominion-style partial independence
for these territories set the stage for the continuance of a ferocious rebellion
which ultimately resulted in its expulsion from Indochina soon after the signing of the 1954 Geneva Accords. Such French policies also helped set the stage

---

[53] Quoted in Smith 1974, 227.   [54] Smith 1974, 227.
[55] Hammer 1948, 259; 1950, 58.   [56] Hammer 1948, 258.
[57] Hammer 1948.   [58] Sharp 1946, 193.
[59] Sharp 1946, 12–13.

for more than two more decades of regional war between local nationalists and the United States.

Puppet Regimes: China's "Autonomous" Regions

Consider also the sham powers that were supposedly allocated to China's nationalistically distinct "autonomous regions," such as Inner Mongolia (after 1947), Xinjiang (after 1955), and Tibet[60] (after 1951).[61] In the 1980s, China added forty-three additional autonomous regions for some of its national-istically distinct territories (see Appendix 3). Articles 117–119 of China's Constitution specify a wide range of powers for these territories including authority over public health, finance, science, culture, economic development, and education. In spite of the "autonomous" label of these territories, there appears to be little that is autonomous about them.[62] The governments of these regions are under the close supervision and final authority of China's com-munist party. They have been under varying degrees of military control. In Mongolia, Xinjiang, and Tibet in particular, rampant and widespread abuses of human rights of local populations at the hands of Chinese forces have been reported.[63] And the core state has been engaged in a concerted campaign to dilute the nationalistically distinct populations in these territories by facilitat-ing the move of large numbers of settlers who are culturally *Han* (who repre-sents the majority nationality within China). Such aggressive moves make a mockery of the official "autonomous region" designation and arguably damage China's own interests.

Even while China engages in such sham federacy practices in these terri-tories, it is attempting what seems to be a relatively serious effort to imple-ment a policy of "one country, two systems" with respect to the territory of Hong Kong, which by itself is the world's ninth largest trading economy.[64] Its

---

[60] Henders 1998, 92–99.

[61] In 1951 the Chinese and Tibetans signed the Sino-Tibetan Fourteen Point Agreement, which allocated powers of internal governance to the Tibetans. The agreement, however, was bereft of any formal entrenchment. Continued Chinese occupation also created unrest and eventually rioting within the territory. In 1959 the core state unilaterally and forcibly reestab-lished direct rule. Similar to the practice of the Soviet Union, after 1959 Tibet was named as an "Autonomous Region" although in reality all final decision-making powers remained in Chinese hands. Hence, from 1951 to 1959 Tibet was a sham federacy because nothing discernible made the powers which were allocated to the territory credible. After 1959, it was an even more exten-sive sham because by and large it retained no decision-making powers.

[62] Human Rights in China 2007.

[63] Human Rights in China 2007, 16.

[64] Tsang 2004, 273–8.

history of abuses and promises to its sham federacies, however, cast doubt on the seriousness of the legal basis of its commitment to upholding Hong Kong's Basic Law. Instead, one can assume that China demonstrates restraint over the arrangement with Hong Kong out of fear of disrupting the politically legitimizing effects of the large-scale foreign direct investment, services, and other economic benefits that Hong Kong provides. Its treatment of its "autonomous" territories also provides reasonable excuses for members of Taiwan's pro-reunification Guomindang Party to avoid joining with the mainland in the near future. It also creates a basis for Taiwan's citizens to see full independence from China as a more viable option. China damages its interests by not matching its impressive economic reforms with accompanying political reforms. One such political reform would be to attempt to transform these sham federacies into real PITs. This process would be facilitated by local leaders who have accepted autonomous solutions short of full independence. Tibet's Dalai Lama has, for example, rejected independence in favor of "genuine autonomy."[65] However, without transforming into at least a hybrid authoritarian-democratic regime that features forms of liberal constitutionalism,[66] it would seem to be doubtful that China could provide defensible constitutional powers to these territories. If these territories could approximate the economic value that Hong Kong provides to China, perhaps this would be another way to make a future partial independent arrangement defensible—but the prospect of destitute territories like Tibet achieving such a role appears remote.

Ethnically Separated Holding Areas: South Africa's Historic Bantustans

Another distinct set of examples of sham federacy developed as the European descendants in control of South Africa's government sought to maintain their dominance over the country's indigenous African majority through policies of harsh suppression and systematic segregation.[67] In April 1961 Britain joined the chorus of voices within the United Nations denouncing such *apartheid* policies.[68] Shortly thereafter, South African Prime Minister Hendrik Verwoerd responded by indicating that "in the light of the pressure being exerted on South Africa" the government would make efforts to placate the fierce international opposition to its policies by providing self-governing territories that

---

[65] Olsen 2003.   [66] Zakaria 1997, 22–43.
[67] Butler et al. 1977; Carter et al. 1967; Dugard 1979; Moerkijk 1981; Stultz 1980.
[68] Butler et al. 1977, 31.

were nominally intended to lead to independence.[69] In accordance with this, South Africa's government designated ten enclaves on less than 13% of the country's territory.[70] These Bantustan enclaves were intended to eventually be the "homelands" for the 70% of South Africa's population that were indigenously African even though more than half of these people had homes in other areas of the country. The Bantustan territories were Transkei (1963), Ciskei (1972), KwaZulu (1976), Lebowa (1972), Venda (1973), Gazankulu (1973), Bophuthatswana (1972), Basotho Qwa Qwa (1975), Swazi (1975), and S. Ndebele.[71] South Africa's government claimed that these landlocked, destitute, and densely populated enclaves had a range of sovereign powers. And indeed governments were formed in these territories that did in fact exercise powers. The 1963 Transkei Constitution Act, for example, allocated local control over local public works, local police, courts, agriculture, welfare, liquor, district councils, education taxation, and the majority of other local matters.

But in practice the powers of these territorial governments were open to unilateral core state incursions. Although indigenous leaders did exercise some local control, there was little that was politically or constitutionally defensible about the powers that were allocated to these territories. During most of their existence, powers to amend their constitutions were retained by the central government and bills passed by the local Bantustan assemblies could only become law if they received the assent of the state president.[72] Furthermore, although the Bantustans had local taxation powers over their impoverished populations, efforts to exercise many of their powers were crippled without the core state's approval since they were overwhelmingly dependent on South Africa's government for funding. For example, in 1973 77% of KwaZulu's budget was controlled by South Africa's government.[73]

Ultimately, these territories served the South African government's sinister objectives by functioning as holding areas for unwanted ethnic groups. In this way, over time, a white majority could be engineered in the rest of the state through the large-scale transfer of populations to these territories.[74] This

---

[69] Quoted in Butler et al. 1977, 31. Four of the Bantustans (Transkei in 1976, Bophuthatswana in 1977, Venda in 1979, and Ciskei in 1981) were eventually allocated a status of "independence" although no other states recognized this status and the territories were set up with leaders sympathetic to the South African government with budgets dependent upon the core state. See Anderson 1994, 308.

[70] Butler et al. 1977; Carter et al. 1967; Dugard 1979; Moerkijk 1981; Stultz 1980. The self-government that Transkei had achieved in 1963 was expanded to nine other enclaves under the Bantu Homelands Constitution Act of 1971.

[71] Butler et al. 1977. The numbers in brackets indicate the years that these arrangements were established.

[72] Butler et al. 1977, 32.

[73] Butler et al. 1977, 64.

[74] Egan and Taylor 2003, 99–117.

would be done through both forcible transfer as well as by stripping indigenous populations of their rights in "white" South Africa[75] to encourage emigration to the "homelands."[76] Meanwhile, similar to Chinese statements with respect to its autonomous regions, the South African core state could attempt to style itself as a champion of self-determination as it speciously held up examples of self-rule among the indigenous populations within its midst. And in response to accusations of irresponsibility given the dire conditions within such enclaves, the core government could claim that since these territories had forms of self-rule, it was the responsibility of such governments to fix their own problems. Ultimately, these regimes were dismantled in the early 1990s as the *apartheid* regime came to an end.

Ethnically Separated Holding Areas and Sovereign Trusteeship: America's "Sovereign" Indian Territories

Yet another set of notable sham federacies are the many Indian territories throughout the United States.[77] Indian territories within America have experienced a remarkable evolution from the late eighteenth century to today.

Similar to the sham federacies of France, China, and South Africa, the so-called "sovereign" powers of Indian populations and territories that were affirmed by various branches of the US government in the nineteenth century, have historically been subjected to forms of rampant usurpation, human rights abuses, and tyranny. Fresh from decolonization from Britain and near the eve of America's own independence, the US Congress made the following declaration in the 1787 Northwest Ordinance:

> The utmost good faith shall always be observed towards the Indians; their land and property shall never be taken from them without their consent; and in their property, rights and liberty, they never shall be invaded or disturbed...but laws founded in justice and humanity shall from time to time be made, for preventing wrongs being done to them, and for preserving peace and friendship with them.[78]

This statement stands in stark contrast to the genocidal practices that the US government ended up perpetrating against Indian populations and their territories.[79]

---

[75] Norman 1977.
[76] Anderson 1994, 317.
[77] Aleinikoff 2002; Pommersheim 1995; Wallace 1999; Wilkinson 1987.
[78] US, Northwest Ordinance. 1787, Art. VI, ch. VIII. Also quoted in Aleinikoff 2002, 95–6.
[79] See Pommersheim 1995; Wallace 1999.

Mirroring the experience of the South African Bantustans, the territories that were designated for Indian populations were at times created as holding areas in an effort to extract (ethnically cleanse) these populations out of areas that US populations sought to dominate. In other cases, similar to the experience of China's Autonomous Regions, these territories were overrun by settlers loyal to the core state in tandem with military occupation, widespread human rights abuses, and cultural reeducation programs. The US Congress passed statutes with official names like "the Indian Removal Act of 1830," which provided necessary funds to the federal government for the forcible resettlement of the tens of thousands of surviving Native Americans into the wastelands of Oklahoma. Systematic policies of forced cultural indoctrination were implemented. In 1818, for example, a House Committee on Indian Affairs made the following recommendation: "Put into the hand of [Indian] children the primer and the hoe and they will naturally, in time, take hold of the plough; and, as their minds become enlightened and expand, the Bible will be their book, and they will grow up in habits of morality and industry... and become useful members of society." By the middle of the nineteenth century observers such as Alexis De Tocqueville were able to report on the destruction and removal of Indian populations. "Not only have these wild tribes receded," Tocqueville declared, "but they are destroyed; and as they give way or perish, an immense and increasing people fill their place. There is no instance upon record of so prodigious a growth or so rapid a destruction..."[80]

In the midst of these circumstances, the US government signed numerous treaties with the Indian tribes (like the Kiowa, Comanche, Navajo, and Sioux).[81] These treaties allocated territory, rights, and jurisdiction to the Indians but were frequently disregarded by the waves of American settlers that swept across North America in the nineteenth century. Especially important for the present discussion is the fact that the courts also refused to enforce such rules, seeing them only as morally binding (instead of legally binding) obligations. As the US Supreme Court described at the beginning of the twentieth century,

> Until the year 1871 the policy was pursued of dealing with the Indian tribes by means of treaties, and, of course, a moral obligation rested upon Congress to act in good faith in performing the stipulations entered into on its behalf. But, as with treaties made with foreign nations, the legislative power might pass laws in conflict with treaties made with the Indians.[82]

Apart from such treaties, the courts also brought into being a series of legal doctrines of Indian "sovereignty" that also turned out to be illusory. In 1832,

---

[80] Tocqueville 1835/1945.   [81] Wilkinson 1987, 3–5.
[82] *Lone Wolf v Hitchcock*, 1903.

legally knowledgeable Native American leaders of the Cherokee Tribe appealed to the US Supreme Court to prevent the forcible annexation of their land and their systematic exile to foreign territories at the hands of the US military and the government of Georgia. In response, in *Cherokee Nation v Georgia* the US Supreme Court declared that the US government's annexation and removal policies were unconstitutional. To justify this decision Chief Justice John Marshall crafted a legal doctrine which declared that the Indians have a type of extra constitutional sovereignty. "The Cherokee nation..." Marshall declared, "is a distinct community, occupying its own territory...in which the laws of Georgia can have no force."[83]

But in a move that threatened to damage America's own constitutional order, former Indian-fighter and US President Andrew Jackson disregarded the Supreme Court's order and carried out the popular policy of Indian removal anyway. In response to the decision in *Cherokee Nation v Georgia*, President Jackson was widely reported to have said: "[Chief Justice] John Marshall has made his decision: now let him enforce it."[84] Accordingly, the surviving population of Cherokee Indians was forcibly removed from their ancestral lands in Georgia to Oklahoma.

After several policy shifts during the twentieth century, however, the status of Indian governance has evolved into a much less interventionist and non-tyrannical form that has allowed a wide range of delegated powers.[85] Following the New Deal policies of US President Franklin Delano Roosevelt, the US shifted away from political and cultural assimilation of Indian populations. In a series of statutes, such as the Indian Self-Determination and Education Assistance Act of 1975,[86] the Indian Gaming Regulatory Act of 1988, and the Tribal Self-Governance Act of 1994,[87] the US Congress has provided a wide range of delegated powers to these territories. Tribal governments can, for example, designate their own leaders, levy taxes, regulate property within their territory, administer justice, and create rules within their area of jurisdiction.[88]

The newfound economic prosperity and delegated powers of many of these territories, however, masks the reality that the US Congress arguably still

---

[83] See *Cherokee Nation v Georgia*, 1831 (Marshall, Chief Justice); see also *Johnson v M'Intosh*, 1823 (Marshall Chief Justice). This latter case enunciates a doctrine of limited Indian title to land.

[84] Chudacoff et al. 1997.

[85] On political communities that eventually do not see the use of force as a viable alternative see Adler and Barnett 1998.

[86] US, The Indian Self-Determination and Education Assistance Act of Jan. 4, 1975, §3.

[87] US, The Tribal Self-Governance Act of Oct. 25, 1994, Pub. L. No. 103–413, tit. 2, 108 Stat. 4250, 4270.

[88] Aleinikoff 2002, 101.

retains all final decision-making powers ("plenary power") over these territories, which it exercises.[89] Although the Indians have been delegated powers,
they are nevertheless by and large revocable by the fiat of the core state. This has
been confirmed by a significant body of US Supreme Court rulings. For example,
in a 1978 case the Court affirmed that "Congress has plenary authority to limit,
modify or eliminate the powers of local self-government which the tribes otherwise possess."[90] In another case the Court made clear that, "The sovereignty that
the Indian tribes retain is of a unique and limited character. It exists only at the
sufferance of Congress and is subject to complete defeasance…"[91] And similarly,
in a 1979 case the Court declared that it is "well-established that Congress, in the
exercise of its plenary power over Indian affairs, may restrict the retained sovereign powers of the Indian tribes."[92] Under such circumstances, the absence of real
sovereign powers for the Indians arguably retards a sense of self-reliance. It is a
reminder that historic injustices have still not been undone. And in the face of
words such as "sovereignty" which do not seem to exist, it engenders resentment,
however much such resentment may be tamed by social programs and relative
economic enrichment. As observers such as US President Richard Nixon have
noted "the mere threat of termination tends to discourage greater self-sufficiency
among Indian groups…"[93]

Such a status stands in contrast to real partially independent arrangements like
Nunavut and the post-1982 constitutional developments in Canada for indigenous populations. Unlike America's courts, which have evidently abandoned
the eighteenth-century rulings of America's Supreme Court and its interpretation of Indian extra constitutional sovereignty, Canadian courts have embraced
these same rulings (such as *Cherokee Nation v Georgia*) and used them as a precedent to justify indigenous treaty provisions as entrenched final decision-making
powers in Canada.[94] In light of these developments, around eighty indigenous
groups have been in negotiation with the Canadian government for powers of
self-determination. At this point however (unlike the case of the Inuit of Nunavut)
many of these groups appear to be settling for delegated and shared (concurrent) powers rather than a division of final decision-making powers that consist
of some that they exclusively control. For example, unlike the case of Nunavut,
the negotiated arrangement between the Nisga'a Nation (which has a population of about 8,000 people in a Rhode Island-sized territory within the Canadian

[89] For an excellent account of this, see Aleinikoff 2002, 95–121.
[90] *Santa Clara Pueblo v Martinez*, 1978, 56.
[91] *United States v Wheeler*, 1978, 330–31.
[92] *Washington v Confederated Bands and Tribes of the Yakima Indian Nation*, 1979, 463.
[93] Nixon 1970, 564, 567.
[94] See especially *Campbell et al v Attorney General British Columbia et al*, 2000.

province of British Columbia) and Canada appears to be mostly one of delegated powers[95] and therefore does not appear to be a PIT.[96] Unlike the case of Nunavut, which appears to have wide-ranging domestic sovereignty, there are few, if any, final decision-making powers contained in the Nisga'a Final Act that prevail over federal and provincial laws.[97] Nevertheless, the inherent sovereignty of groups like the Nisga'a have been formally recognized.[98] As Canada's federal government stated in a 1995 policy statement, "The Government of Canada recognizes the inherent right of self-government as an existing aboriginal right under section 35 of the Constitution Act, l982. It recognizes, as well, that the inherent right may find expression in treaties…"[99]

One of the key distinctions between America and Canada in their treatment of indigenous populations, which reflects the arguments of this book, are the cataclysmic threats that Canada has faced in recent decades that America has not experienced. Unlike America, toward the end of the twentieth century Canada was convulsed by the specter of large scale territorial fragmentation.[100] In the years that preceded the 1982 decision to formally entrench indigenous treaties, nationalists in Quebec were demanding secession which ultimately culminated in Quebec's 1995 referendum—in which the population was just a few thousand votes shy of voting in favor of independence. The calls for secession by Quebec's local nationalists created a type of domino effect among leaders in the indigenous community who argued that they had an even stronger moral and (if the rulings of America's eighteenth-century court rulings were to be applied) legal case for greater sovereignty. It was therefore in this context

[95] Reflecting this Steven Curry (2004) also asserts that "whatever has been gained by the Nisga'a it is not sovereignty…it is clear that the Nisga'a have been denied a number of important attributes of sovereignty. The first of these is territorial inclusivity. If the territory of the Nisga'a is the site of the exercise of their sovereignty, then persons residing there should be subject to Nisga'a law, and therefore should be brought into the rights and privileges of Nisga'a citizenship." Interestingly, Steven Curry has a very different view about Nunavut. He says that "the Inuit of Nunavut have achieved the fullest possible expression of their sovereign rights short of secession…[because] they legislate for all persons residing in the providence, and since all residents can vote and participate fully…"

[96] As John Burrows observes, "under the Final Agreement, the Nisga'a Lisims Government has no exclusive jurisdiction. Its jurisdiction is always concurrent with federal or provincial jurisdiction." Burrows 2012, 100.

[97] Curry 2004, 182. The Nisga'a Final Act does have provisions for the Nisga'a to establish their own courts and police, but in light of the small size of their population of around 8,000, the Nisga'a government has perhaps wisely decided not to exercise these powers and instead makes use of the Canadian police and court system. And even if such police and court establishment provisions were to be exercised, the Final Act stipulates that all criminal law matters are under the jurisdiction of the federal and provincial governments.

[98] On this see Burrows 2012.

[99] Quoted in *Campbell et al v Attorney General British Columbia et al*, 2000.

[100] See Simeon 2004.

that Canada entrenched indigenous treaties as distinct from the unentrenched reality of America's Indian Territories.[101]

FLYING UNDER THE
ANTI-COLONIALISM RADAR

One question that arises when considering sham federacies is how they should be described. Are they colonies? The simple answer is that sham federacies are frequently not categorized as colonies. They are not recognized as colonies and are sometimes referred to as "autonomous." As a consequence, anti-colonial norms against the dominance of nationalistically distinct territories[102] by other states are sometimes held in abeyance as in the case of the US reaction to French Indochina in the middle of the twentieth century. International bodies like the UN Trusteeship Council also did not include them within their monitoring mechanisms.[103] In some sense this is understandable, because legal arguments can be made that they are not colonies. The absence hitherto of an overarching category that describes these regimes leads to epistemological problems, such as miscategorization.

The era of decolonization has apparently ended.[104] In accordance with the strong anti-imperial climate[105] as World War II was coming to an end, international institutions such as the United Nations Trusteeship Council were set up to monitor the actions of imperial powers as they related to their colonies and to help foster the conditions for those colonies to eventually gain self-governance. The United Nations Trusteeship Council is, however, now largely an empty shell. Its yearly meetings have ended. Its offices have long since been occupied by other UN agencies. It is a relic of the decolonization which swept much of the world, especially in the middle of the twentieth century, in

---

[101] Author's July 2013 interview with Nisga'a leaders.

[102] Jackson 1993, 111–38.

[103] Trusteeship Council 2007.

[104] The recognition that there are multiple paths to decolonization is nothing new from the perspective of the UN General Assembly, which has recognized multiple "possibilities open to [peoples] in the exercise of their right to self-determination." See Resolutions 43/36–43 of Nov. 22, 1988; 44/91–99 of Dec. 11, 1989 and 45/23, 27–29, 31–32 of Nov. 20, 1990. The independence, assimilation, and partial independence paths have also been recognized by scholars in the international legal literature, although they apply the distinct—though sometimes overlapping—concept of "associate state" instead of partial independence. On works that make reference to such decolonizing paths see, e.g., Quane 1998, 553.

[105] Jackson 1993, 111–38.

which states demanded that the dominance of nationalistically distinct territories by imperial states come to a speedy end.[106] As the 1960 UN Declaration on the Granting of Independence to Colonial Countries and Peoples makes clear: "All peoples have the right to self-determination" and "inadequacy of political, economic, social, or educational preparedness should never serve as a pretext for delaying independence."[107] In the continent of Africa alone, in the space of a single decade, Sub-Saharan Africa went from having three independent states in 1955 (Ethiopia, Liberia, and South Africa) to having thirty-one independent states by 1965. And by 1980 the entire continent was composed of independent states, with the exception of Namibia.[108]

According to the literature on benign colonialism, there are only a few real colonies that remain in the world (see Appendix 4) and most of those that remain are benign in the sense that there does not seem to be a discernible movement for greater self-determination. While certain political forms defy a scholarly consensus, colonies are political forms with a relatively straightforward juridical status.[109] Part of this has to do with the fact that for centuries, colonies were not viewed with the same international repugnance that developed in the twentieth century. The great powers previously viewed colonies as an extension of their economic and political greatness.[110] Under such conditions, empires therefore often had relatively little to hide with regard to the juridical status of their nationalistically distinct possessions. In fact, multiple colonies and a vast empire were a badge of honor and prestige. The desirability for such possessions, can, for example, be seen as late as the period after 1884–85 when empires like France, Britain, Belgium, Germany, and Portugal eagerly snatched up as much territory as possible in Africa, even while such adventures proved to be costly in blood and treasure.[111]

The intention here is not to draw an overly positive picture of these territories. Many of them face significant social, economic, and political challenges and their populations are in some cases not fully satisfied by their status. The point, however, is that the colonies of today are not the wretched and destitute tyrannies of past ages. Instead, they are often more economically successful than many of the sham federacies of the twentieth and twenty-first centuries. Even while colonies are benign, sham federacies continue to be venues for

---

[106] Spruyt 2005.

[107] *Everyman's United Nations* 1968, 370–71.

[108] Jackson 1987, 524.

[109] On the center–periphery structure and dynamics of empires see for example, Barkey 1994, Daniels and Kennedy 2002; Galtung 1971; Motyl 1997, 19–29; 1999a; 1999b; Spruyt 2005; Tilly 1997, 1–11.

[110] Puchala and Hopkins 1983, 75.

[111] Hertslet 1967, 468–85.

state policies that mirror past imperial abuses but with the additional twist that such polities have been promised "autonomy."

The Cacophony of "Autonomy"

Mirroring the concept of Indian "sovereignty" that has been applied within the United States, scores of countries in the world have employed the "autonomy" concept as a tool for deception, ethnic cleansing, imperialism, and assimilation against the will of local inhabitants. In an age in which states struggle with nationalistically distinct populations in their midst, states that desire to exert dominance over nationalistically distinct territories have exploited the vagary of the autonomy concept to further their imperial ambitions. Contrary to the positive image of "autonomy" conveyed in much of the literature,[112] "autonomy" can serve as a smokescreen for an internal self-determination that does not exist.

Much excellent work has been done on the subject of "autonomy."[113] Scholars have underscored its economic benefits,[114] its advantages for nationalistic compromise,[115] and its usefulness for the purposes of dividing resources.[116] The "autonomy" concept is useful in describing a general and unspecified power allocation away from a central government. The problem, however, is that "autonomy" refers to more than one governmental form. The concept has been used to refer to a wide range of very different polities, from states[117] and PITs to colonies,[118] sham federacies, and others.

Contrary to the literature that tends to portray autonomy in a positive light, sham federacy underscores the limitations of "autonomy"—both in terms of

---

[112] While some scholars, such as Baldacchino 2006, 862, are careful to emphasize their qualifications to their analysis of "autonomy," their overall view toward autonomy is positive. Baldacchino 2006, 862, for example concedes that he has presented the concept in a "rather optimistic and over-sanguine tone." Similarly, although Lapidoth 1997 emphasizes some of the pitfalls of applying the autonomy concept, her overall view is positive.

[113] While there is no consensus on what defines autonomy, there is one thing upon which many observers can agree: its vagary. See Lapidoth 1997 and Suksi 1998. For examples of confusion over its application in policy circles see Chesterman 2002, 58–9.

[114] On the superior economic conditions that prevail in such sub-state jurisdictions see Armstrong and Read 2000, 303; Bertram 2004, 353.

[115] On autonomy as a means for solving ethnic conflict see Dinstein 1981; Ghai 2000b, 483–530; Hannum 1990; Hannum and Lillich 1980, 858–89; Lapidoth 1997; Suksi 1998.

[116] On the mutually advantageous synergies that can take place on strategic and economic issues see Baldacchino 2006, 855; McElroy and Mahoney 2000; Poirine 1999.

[117] For one source that uses "autonomy" in this way see Merom 2003, 113. On the emergence of territorial states as distinct from other entities, including colonies, see Almond 1988; Hooghe and Marks 2003; Skocpol 1985; Spruyt 1994a; Strayer 1970; Tilly 1990.

[118] Aldrich and Connell 1998; Baldacchino 2006, 854.

its usefulness as an analytic concept and in terms of its benefits as an institutional tool for limiting malgovernance. In light of forms of autonomy such as sham federacy, the view here is that autonomy is constitutionally and normatively better understood and applied by specifying more clearly the form of "autonomy" at issue whether that is a state, a PIT, a colony, a sham federacy, or some other type of polity.

No one (or almost no one)[119] is fooled by the false self-determination of China's Autonomous Regions or South Africa's Bantustans. There are, however, a significant number of cases in which some observers have apparently been misled by incidences of sham federacy.[120] These governmental forms arguably succeed in misleading some observers of such regions, who refer to selected cases as "autonomy."[121] After all in some territories, like the historic Bantustans, the Palestinian Territories, and Kashmir, local governmental leaders did indeed exercise a range of powers. Nevertheless, the powers allocated to the leaders in such territories were not entrenched by any discernible means. Scholars who parrot the "autonomy" promises of such governments without evidence that the commitments that have been made are real, defensible, and thus credible in some cases play into the propaganda objectives of such sovereign states. Furthermore, by emphasizing "autonomy" and "self-determination," the neo-colonial reality of unenforceable promises, tyranny, and/or human rights abuse that takes place with regard to such regimes is deemphasized. As some perceptive observers of China's autonomous regions have put it, "the very autonomy system that should empower self-governance in autonomous regions works as a mechanism for minority exclusion and state control."[122]

For example, some observers are keen to point out that Kashmir has been singled out in India's Constitution as having far reaching domestic powers as if to imply that the grant of powers is tantamount to their actual possession.[123] Indeed, in 1952 India incorporated Article 370 into its Constitution, which singled out a special status and far reaching domestic powers for Kashmir

---

[119] For a source that contends that "the autonomy of Tibet has some practical advantages for the population" see Heintze 1998, 29.
[120] For a sampling of such sources see Sorensen and Phillips 2003, 103–7 (claiming that the Atlantic Coast, Jammu and Kashmir, the Chittagong Hill Tracts, and still other sham federacies are cases of "autonomy"); Gurr 1999, 296 (claiming that the Chittagong Hill Tracts [Bangladesh], the Miskitos [Nicaragua], and the Baluchis [Pakistan] have forms of "regional autonomy"); Heintze 1998, 29 (claiming that Tibet is a form of autonomy); Nordquist 1998, 75–6 (claiming that Mindanao [Philippines] had "autonomy" under the Marcos regime after 1976).
[121] Nordquist 1998.
[122] Human Rights in China 2007: 2.
[123] See for example, Sorensen and Phillips 2003, 105.

with the exception of issues that relate to defense, foreign relations, and communication.[124] Trusting such substantial constitutional guarantees, one may have at first plausibly called Kashmir a real partially independent arrangement. Nevertheless, fearing the possibility of future incorporation of Kashmir into neighboring Pakistan, in 1953 India unilaterally and without any constitutional amendment usurped its recent legal commitments to the territory and put under arrest the territory's chief minister, Sheik Abdullah.[125] This was followed by years of decentralized sham federacy, which involved military occupation, core state vote rigging, dismissal of further leaders, puppet governments, and various intervals of direct rule.[126]

As a result of such violations, preexisting resistance to Indian rule intensified. After the 1989 withdrawal of the Soviet Union from Afghanistan, Pakistan's Inter-Services Intelligence Service (which had been used by the US to funnel arms to anti-Soviet resistance fighters in Afghanistan) shifted its weapons shipments to resistance fighters in the economically underemployed and politically disillusioned Kashmir. Widespread local violence by Pakistani-backed Kashmiri guerrillas, human rights abuses by many of the 350,000 Indian soldiers who occupied the territory, and open combat between Indian and Pakistani forces in the mountainous Kargil region of northern Kashmir are some of the events which ensued in the 1990s.[127] Among other problems, heightened bilateral and regional fears of a possible nuclear war between India and Pakistan over the disputed region have nevertheless made it difficult for India to persist with its constitutionally usurping policies from 1953 to 2002. Such developments have therefore made some headway toward pacifying Kashmiri–Indian relations. Accordingly, renewed local decision-making capabilities were manifested in Kashmir in October 2002 when generally recognized free and fair elections brought to power the Kashmir People's Democratic Party over the centrally allied National Conference Party. Without a deeper constitutional entrenchment of the territory's powers, however, the arrangement nevertheless remains vulnerable to significant shifts in political events. Indian–Kashmiri and backchannel Indian–Pakistani negotiations for a

---

[124] From a pure constitutional perspective, Kashmir is arguably to a significant degree outside of India's nominal federation. India's Constitution makes clear that what is meant when Kashmir is referred to as a "state" does not mean the same thing as "state" when that term is applied to other territories within India. At the beginning of Part IV of India's Constitution which details the institutions and powers of the states within India's union, Article 152 makes clear that "in this part, unless the context otherwise requires, the expression "state" does not include the State of Jammu and Kashmir." India, Constitution of India 1950, Article 152.

[125] Kumar 2002, 11–24.

[126] Kumar 2002.

[127] Kumar 2002.

constitutionally entrenched partially independent arrangement, referred to as "autonomy plus," are continuing and have already taken place in 1993, 1995, 1996, 1999, and 2000.[128]

Alternatively, other scholars have characterized the negotiations that lead to some of these regimes, like the Atlantic Coast Territory (associated with Nicaragua), Mindanao (Philippines), and the Chittagong Hill Tracts (associated with Bangladesh) as models for "autonomy" without examining if the promises that have been made in such agreements are credible (difficult to change) or if such commitments end up being fulfilled.[129]

With regard to the 1997 Accord that brought into being an "autonomous" arrangement for the Chittagong Hill Tracts, for example, one observer has complained that although "more than five years have passed after the signing of the Accord, most of the provisions, especially the main issues of the Accord...have either [been] left unimplemented or partially implemented."[130] Even before such complaints, the arrangement fueled unrest because of its lack of credibility. Shortly after the United Nations Economic and Social Council rushed to award Bangladesh's Prime Minister Sheikh Hasina with a peace prize after the signing of the Accords, the absence of constitutional safeguards fueled local violence by breakaway factions, such as the United People's Democratic Front, that have called the Accord a "sell-out."[131]

Consider also the two regions that make up the Atlantic Coast territory. These territories comprise around one-third of Nicaragua's total land mass and are inhabited by an estimated 350,000 inhabitants who are mostly Misquito Indians.[132] A 1987 Autonomy Law provided some powers to two regions in the North and South of Nicaragua as part of a settlement to end an ongoing civil war between CIA-backed "Contra" guerillas and the Managua-based Sandinista Government.[133] While the Autonomy Law does allocate some limited powers, similar to the Chittagong Hill Tracts Accord of 1997, it does not provide a means to prevent the central state from unilaterally usurping the arrangement. No principles of mutual consent are established. No supermajority entrenchment exists in the core state constitution. And no other formal entrenchment mechanisms seem to exist. In accordance with this absence of protection against unilateral usurpation by the core state, there have been

---

[128] Kumar 2002, 20.

[129] See Nordquist 1998, 74–6.

[130] Quoted in Roy 2003, 3.

[131] Roy 2003, 8.

[132] For descriptions of the Atlantic Coast Territories see Hannum 1990, 485–7; Lederach and Wehr1991, 93; Otis 1992.

[133] Nicaragua, Autonomy Statute for the Regions of the Atlantic Coast of Nicaragua. 1987.

reports of significant transgressions on the powers allocated in the Autonomy Law in areas of land management and exploitation of natural resources.[134]

Another prominent yet distinct example of how there can be conceptual confusion over the nature of autonomy is illustrated by a 2007 article in the *American Political Science Review* by Thomas Chapman and Philip Roeder. In their paper, Chapman and Roeder attempt to argue that partition is a better solution to wars of nationalism than other institutional alternatives—one of which is "autonomy." They define autonomy as a region within a state that has been granted self-rule and "many decision rights."[135] More than other alternatives, autonomy, they say, tends to lead to popular repression, institutional deadlock, and ultimately continued internal conflict. There is, of course, nothing wrong with their critique of what are predominantly sham federacies—in fact their findings against sham federacy corroborate much of the critique in this chapter.[136] Instead the problem is that these scholars code cases of sham federacy as "autonomy" and then define them as having "self-rule" and "many decision rights" that they do not fully exercise. Apart from two PITs (South Sudan and Northern Ireland where center–periphery peace was reestablished for at least ten years after civil war) every case of "autonomy" that they use is a sham federacy.[137] By using the overarching term "autonomy" they also confound cases of partial independence with sham federacy, thereby confusing cases where credible powers of self-determination actually exist with cases where they do not.

CONCLUSIONS

By contrast to the generally positive view of "autonomy" that some have emphasized, and in comparison to the benign status of many of the world's remaining colonies, sham federacies are malignant arrangements that arguably deserve to be the normative successors to the repugnance against imperialism. In significant respects sham federacies also fail to overcome the problems of legitimacy, governance costs, and claims to represent the interests of local populations that were faced by colonies.[138] First, with regard to problems of legitimacy,

---

[134] Economist Intelligence Unit 2004, 26.

[135] Chapman and Roeder 2007, 678.

[136] For a similar negative security appraisal of "autonomy" that applies the concept to the de facto states of South Ossetia and Abkazia as they relate to Georgia see Cornell 2002, 248–9.

[137] The cases of autonomy they use are as follows: Burma–Karen, China–Tibet, India–Kashmir, Israel–Palestine, Pakistan–Baluchistan, Russia–Chechnya, Sudan–Southern Region, and UK–Northern Ireland. See Chapman and Roeder 2007, 678.

[138] For works which assess such factors as they relate to empire–colony relations see Cooley 2005; Motyl 1999b; Peattie 1984.

their nominal "sovereignty" and "self-determination" provides them with a mask of self-determination. They succeed in being legitimate when they manage to deceive observers as with the cases of Kashmir or the Indian Territories. While this may work in the short term, in the long run it is not so easy to mislead all scholars and practitioners who deal with such territories, especially when the territories are subjected to human rights violations and exploitation.

Second, with regard to governance costs, sham federacy can end up being prohibitively costly. It is costly because of the international opposition that can be engendered when the sham is not successful, as South Africa's experience showed. The costs are also high because of the occasional military occupation that may be required, as with the crackdowns that China implements in its Autonomous Territories from time to time. Furthermore, although ethnic holding area sham federacies tend to minimize costs since the territory is often fiscally neglected by the core state, on the other hand, the costs of military intervention still remain, as illustrated by South Africa's 1988 military incursion into the Bophuthatswana Bantustan.[139] And even amidst the increasing wealth of America's Indian Territories, the fact that these territories are wards of the state has involved vast payouts from the US federal government to the Indian Territories.

With regard to the degree of representation of the interests of local populations, both colonies and sham federacies face normative problems on this issue because they are both forms of autocratic government.[140] But sham federacies, unlike colonies, suffer from a juridical status that to one degree or another is illusory, which undermines the sanctity of the government-establishing constitutional rules of the polity. This then arguably robs citizens living within those territories of their trust in government and sense of self-sufficiency. Leaders like the Indochinese "Emperor" Bao Dao were propped up as the "leader," when Bao Dao himself acknowledged that in fact he did little to rule.[141] Instead Indochina was directly ruled by the functional divisions of France.[142] In other cases, as with the South African Bantustans, the Palestinian Territories, and the US Indian Territories, local leaders have been given nominal powers that they in fact exercise, only to find that when they take actions that contradict the interests of the core state, unilateral and oftentimes heavy handed action is taken by the core to reverse the action.

---

[139] Mahmud 1994, 96.
[140] On this see for example Barkey 1994; Eisenstadt 1963; Tilly 1997.
[141] Hammer 1950, 58.
[142] Rule by such core state functional divisions is what Alexander Cooley calls U-Form (Unitary) governance. See Cooley 2005.

In some cases, a sham federacy may not have been what some of the leaders who made the promises intended it to be. While false promises may have been the result, deception and malevolence may not have been the intention of at least some of the leaders who contributed to the creation of the sham federacy. For example, some of those who crafted the promises in the US Congress's 1787 Northwest Ordinance may well have wished for its promises of restraint and justice to be carried out with regard to the Indians. Nevertheless without a credible mechanism to put such principles into effect, they remained ineffectual against the rising tide of expansionism. In other countries that have few resources and weak traditions of constitutionalism, the lack of enforcement of powers of self-determination may have less to do with deception and more to do with the inadequacy and lack of availability of legal and constitutional foundations to uphold constitutional promises. This may have been the case to some degree with Nicaragua and the Atlantic Coast. In such cases, sham arrangements may not have been the universal intention, but they nevertheless became the result.

Whatever the differing reasons for sham federacy may be, one way out of such compromised autonomy is to initiate processes of neo-decolonization. If full independence or full assimilation for territories like Tibet (China), the Atlantic Coast (Nicaragua), the Chittagong Hill Tracts (Bangladesh), Kashmir (India), and the Navajo Territory (the United States) is not a mutually satisfactory option, then the creation of real partially independent arrangements is another possibility.

Part III

Economic Status, Security, and Dynamics

7

Sovereign State Weakness

...to secure these rights [of life, liberty and the pursuit of happiness], governments are instituted among men, deriving their just powers from the consent of the governed. That whenever *any form of government* becomes destructive to these ends, it is the right of the people to alter or to abolish it, and to institute new government, laying its foundation on such principles and organizing its powers in such form, as to them shall seem most likely to effect their safety and happiness.[1]

—America's Declaration of Independence

There was a time in which the sovereign state's unique features caused them to be increasingly strong. Scholars of institutional evolution point to their superior attributes that helped them overcome other powerful competitors of the medieval age such as fiefdoms, city-states, and city leagues.[2] They were built for effectiveness in war, administrative centralization, and the monopolization of internal control.[3] International norms that were favorable to conquest facilitated the union of diverse territories, populations, and resources. Forcible cultural assimilation of distinct populations forged a common identity and increased legitimacy. Centralization of control enabled administrative efficiency. And the monopolization of power eliminated internal anarchy by removing other violent competitors. Taken together such factors induced greater wealth, security, and regime stability and have resulted in some highly successful sovereign states, especially in Europe, North America, and eastern Asia.

The effectiveness of these features, however, did not last. Most of the new sovereign states that emerged after the nineteenth century did not have the opportunity to capitalize on the features that allowed historic states to grow strong. In the twentieth century and into the twenty-first, their war fighting

---

[1] Italics added.
[2] Anderson 1974; Ruggie 1993, 149; Strayer 1970; Strayer and Munro 1959.
[3] On war making advantages see Tilly 1990. On administrative advantages see Spruyt 1994b.

capabilities, administrative centralization, and monopolization of control no longer worked to assist them as before.

Especially after World War II, sovereign states are becoming increasingly small. One of the main reasons for this is that today's international norms militate against (rather than facilitate) conquest. As a consequence, small states tend to remain small and they do not benefit from the amalgamation of resources, economies of scale, and greater capacity for specialization that came with forcible unification with still other territories. The sovereign state characteristic of centralized control thus reduces (rather than increases) efficiency by bringing the full burden of sovereign responsibilities to bear upon polities that are too small and have fewer resources to be effective. The sovereign state tendency to engage in political monopolization and cultural assimilation also undermines (rather than increases) legitimacy among diverse populations by unleashing the post-eighteenth-century phenomenon of nationalistic opposition. Such opposition then gives rise to destabilizing revolt and the specter of territorial fragmentation. And even when sovereign states manage to eliminate internal anarchy within their own boundaries, the dangers of external anarchy still prevail in the international system where a world government does not exist. As a consequence, fully independent states are in many respects left to fend for themselves;[4] they do not benefit from the services that strong states provide their own territories in the form of the credible enforcement of rules, public goods, single market trade facilitation, economic disaster response, and a system of "other-regarding" constitutional norms that rein in pure self-interest.

The outcome of such factors is widespread sovereign state weakness across the globe. One widely used and highly regarded index that provides estimates of the distribution of state strength and weakness is the Failed State Index produced by the Fund for Peace.[5] This index provides rankings for 177 states using twelve economic, political, and social indicators.[6] Sovereign states are put into broad categories from "Very High Alert" (countries like Somalia and the Congo) to "Very Sustainable" (countries like Finland). Not surprisingly, the findings of the Fund for Peace reflect the state weakness views of the

---

[4] Ignatieff 1993, 8.

[5] Fund for Peace 2012.

[6] The social indicators that they examine include: "mounting demographic pressures, massive movement of refugees or internally displaced persons, legacy of vengeance-seeking group grievance or group paranoia and chronic and sustained human flight." The economic indicators that they examine include: "uneven economic development along group lines" and "sharp and/or severe economic decline." The political and military indicators that they examine include: "criminalization and/or delegitimization of the state, progressive deterioration of public services, suspension or arbitrary application of the rule of law and widespread human rights abuse, security apparatus operates as a 'state within a state,' rise of factionalized elites, and intervention of other states or external political actors." Fund for Peace 2012.

literature. The median state on their list (with a score of 77) is given a ranking of "high warning" (similar to countries like China, Venezuela, and Algeria). In fact, about 80% of sovereign states (138 out of 177) that they examine are generally characterized as being unstable to one degree or another. In connection with this, economists like Lant Pritchett point out that the economically poor conditions that characterize large numbers of sovereign states tend to be worsening rather than improving. Pritchett estimates that "from 1870 to 1990 the ratio of per capita incomes between the richest and the poorest countries increased by roughly a factor of five..."[7] This trend of states tending not to be able to catch up economically (or converge) with their more wealthy sovereign state counterparts weakens their capacity to provide basic public goods (like roads, police, schools, etc.) Reflecting the findings of Pritchett and much of the rest of the literature, Przeworski et al. point out that "most countries that we first observed below [a GDP per capita of] $2,000 [which is approximately 40% of all sovereign states] had about thirty years to grow, and yet most remained poor."[8]

Still another way to understand sovereign state weakness, however, is to compare them to something. As detailed earlier, in each of the areas where sovereign states fail, partial independence excels. Where sovereign states centralize responsibilities that they often cannot effectively administer, PITs benefit from the public goods of a core state. Where sovereign states are defined by excluding national distinctiveness, partial independence is defined by compromise and the division and sharing of sovereign power. Where sovereign states in many respects need to fend for themselves in the anarchy of the international system, partially independent territories benefit from the guarantees and services that a strong core state can provide.

This chapter will build upon the logic developed in Chapters 1 and 2 and provide the reasoning behind sovereign state weaknesses relative to PIT advantages. For the purposes of this study, discussing the weaknesses and strengths of sovereign states is important for a number reasons. First, it sheds light upon the interests and capabilities of sovereign (core) states, which are an integral component of partially independent unions. Second, it further clarifies the costs and benefits between the alternative of full independence as compared to partial independence. And third, it sheds light on the historic context from which sovereign states (and PITs) have evolved.[9]

The chapter will begin by discussing the resources, norms, and processes of natural selection that have helped determine the fluctuating fortunes of

---

[7] Pritchett 1997, 3–17.
[8] Pritchett 1997, 3–17.
[9] On historical institutionalism Hall and Taylor 1996: 936–57.

sovereign states. The chapter will then turn to the legitimacy advantages of sovereign states that eventually give way to legitimacy deficits amidst the modern age of nationalism. Finally, the chapter will build upon the arguments in Chapter 2 on the inconveniences that exist for sovereign states amidst conditions of international anarchy. The next chapter will discuss some of the empirical outcomes of partial independence for wealth and security in the light of PIT features that arguably make up for sovereign state disadvantages.

ECONOMIC AND SECURITY ADVANTAGES AND WEAKNESSES

Amidst the pure anarchy of the prehistoric stone age, grave and widespread violence prevailed for much of humanity. Based on the remains of ancient skeletons, forensic archeologists have found that approximately 15% of prehistoric males experienced violent death as compared to about 3% for the first half of the twentieth century.[10] Such a degree of violence reflects the views expressed by the seventeenth-century philosopher Thomas Hobbes who observed that "during the time men live without a common power to keep them all in awe, they are in that condition which is called war; and such a war, as is of every man, against every man."[11] From this chaotic condition, archeological evidence indicates that the first polities emerged in about 6000 BC.[12] These governmental forms, such as the city-states of Anatolia, exercised jurisdictional priority over all other organizational forms in some respects within a specific territory (territorial sovereignty).[13] Tribute taking empires then emerged in about 2500 BC in Mesopotamia.[14] As these polities expanded their control, they developed vested interests in directing their coercive powers toward reducing criminality, blood feuds, intertribal warfare, feudal conflicts, and other forms of violence.[15] Such conflict directly threatened local interests because it endangered economic productivity, extraction, and ultimately effective war-making

---

[10] Bowles 2009; Keeley 1996; Wright 1942, 245. Also cited in Pinker 2011, 49–50.

[11] Hobbes 1960, 82. Hobbes himself intended to apply these observations to the conditions of sixteenth- and seventeenth-century Europe in which he lived. He believed that the various overlapping jurisdictions that existed at the time (such as nascent sovereign states, warlords, city-states, and other forms) were the central cause of Europe's warlike condition.

[12] Tilly 1990, 2.

[13] Tilly 1990, 2.

[14] Tilly 1990, 2.

[15] Bates 2010, 50.

capability.[16] As Ted Robert Gurr has found, as sovereign state control expanded from the fourteenth century onward societies experienced a precipitous drop in internal violence, from about 110 yearly murders per 100,000 people in fourteenth-century Oxford, England to about 1 yearly murder per 100,000 people in twentieth-century London.[17] But even after moving away from the anarchy of hunter-gatherer societies to polities that exercised measures of final authority and control, grave degrees of violence remained as polities turned their violent capabilities upon each other.

Sovereign Statehood Resources and Relative Efficiency

The formative period of the modern state lasted approximately five centuries, from the fourteenth to the eighteenth centuries.[18] During this period, sovereign states competed with a wide range of other governmental forms with overlapping jurisdictions, including city-states, city-leagues, tribute-taking empires, warlord controlled fiefdoms, and other nascent versions of the sovereign state (such as France and England).[19] By contrast to the aforementioned overlapping medieval jurisdictions, the authority and control of sovereign state rulers was relatively centralized.[20] According to scholars of state formation, the fact that sovereign states alone possessed centralization, multiple continuous regions, and clearly defined boundaries caused them to beat out other institutional alternatives (see Table 7.1).[21] For Charles Tilly, the combination of such factors

---

[16] On the damaging consequences of kinship societies that enforce rules through the blood feud see Bates 2010, 29–31.

[17] Gurr 1981, 303–4, 313. Also cited in Pinker 2011, 60.

[18] Milliken and Krause 2002, 756.

[19] Anderson 1974.

[20] See Spruyt 1994b.

[21] All of these polities possessed their own measures of territorial autonomy together with a number of distinguishing characteristics. City-leagues (like the Hanseatic League of Northern Europe) were confederations of loosely affiliated towns that made collective decisions based on unanimity. These polities banded together when convenient (as in times of self-defense or war). A key problem, however, was that they would also disband and join other polities at still other times. They often controlled multiple contiguous regions, but they neither exercised centralized control throughout their territories nor did they have clearly defined boundaries. City-states (like historic Florence or Venice), were centralized and had defined boundaries, but mainly consisted of a single city rather than multiple contiguous regions. Warlord controlled fiefdoms in some cases consisted of multiple contiguous (usually agricultural rather than urban) regions, had defined boundaries, and had measures of centralized control, but the warlord that ruled over the fiefdom also shared overlapping authority and control with his liege lord who was often the leader of a nascent sovereign state like France or England. Loosely configured empires (such as the ancient Roman Empire), had multiple contiguous regions, power was also centralized

Table 7.1 Defining characteristics of pre-modern autonomous polities

	Autonomous powers	Consisting of multiple contiguous regions	Horizontally centralized decision-making (at the center)	Vertically centralized control (throughout the polity's territory)	Defined territorial boundaries
Sovereign states	Yes	Yes	Yes	Yes	Yes
City-states	Yes	No*	Yes	No	Yes
City-leagues	Yes	Yes	No	No	No
Tribute-taking empires	Yes	Yes	Yes	No	No
Fiefdoms	Yes	Yes and no	Yes and no**	Yes and no**	Yes

* In some cases powerful city-states such as Florence maintained surrounding cities (such as Pisa) as colonies. In such cases city-states took on characteristics more akin to a tribute-taking empires.

** While feudal lords maintained significant degrees of their own centralized horizontal decision making and centralized vertical control over their own domains, these powers were nevertheless overlapping with their liege lord that had the authority to call up the forces of the feudal lord for defense and war.

were critical because they allowed sovereign states to better fight wars that hinged on the economic concentration of wealth. As Tilly has described, "the increasing scale of war and the knitting together of the European state system through commercial, military, and diplomatic interaction eventually gave the war-making advantage to those states that could field standing armies..."[22] Large centrally controlled territories allowed them superior levels of economic resources and manpower.[23] Greater resources allowed states to equip their forces with increasingly sophisticated weapons that were out of the reach of smaller, poorer polities.[24] Other competing entities did not have these features. They either did not have the land (as was the case with city-states or fiefdoms) or they did not have the requisite centralized control (as was the case with loosely controlled empires and city-leagues).

Furthermore, as Hendrik Spruyt describes, centralized legal, military, currency, measurement, and tax collection systems allowed sovereign states the legitimacy and wealth to assimilate various competing providers of private security such as nobles, tribes, and other kinship groups.[25] Sovereign states facilitated the move from authority that was based on personal rule to "an abstract equity before the law; the law as a text above party and society."[26] Crimes took on a public character. They shifted from simply being personal grievances between a victim and a perpetrator, to being offenses against the state. Citizens could have greater confidence that rule violators would be hunted down by the centralized authorities.[27] Adversaries could put down their weapons in favor of centralized justice.[28] The protection and order delivered by this political-legal framework in turn allowed for the functioning of

within a core polity. Power was nevertheless decentralized within the rest of the empire in which boundaries were not clearly defined, waxing and waning with time. On the distinctions between these political forms see Spruyt 1994b, Ch. 8.

[22] Tilly 1990, 15.

[23] See especially Tilly 1985, 169–91. This was distinct from the other competitors. Tribute taking empires had large militaries and extractive capabilities but they left most local administration to regional power holders who retained great de facto autonomy. The result was a high concentration of coercion but relatively weak levels of concentrated wealth. By contrast city-states and city-leagues both benefited from degrees of centralized control over individual cities. City-leagues also had various episodes in which consultative institutions facilitated cooperation that resulted in military victories. But these victories were neither durable nor consistent. For both city-states and city-leagues, their lack of centralized control over a large territory inhibited their wealth and access to manpower. The result was a relatively high accumulation of economic resources but relatively low coercive capabilities. Only sovereign states were able to combine a substantial military with effective extractive institutions, a unified administration which resulted in both high accumulations of capital and coercive capability.

[24] Levy et al. 2001.

[25] Spruyt 1994b.

[26] Spruyt 1994b.

[27] Bates 2010, 49.

[28] Bates 2010.

markets and varying degrees of enforcement of property rights and business contracts.[29] Such factors added to the ability of sovereign states to overcome other distinct political forms.

Still another factor that induced stabilizing governance was the fact that state authorities (or outside invaders) that attempted to subjugate urban areas (where most wealth was concentrated) discovered that they could not easily plunder its riches because of the mobility of assets.[30] Assets could be scattered across multiple locations. Workers that produced the wealth could also "vote with their feet" by relocating to more protected areas. "Rather than plundering wealth" Robert Bates observes, sovereign authorities "had instead to elicit its creation. They had to nurture, rather than to despoil, the new economy. They had to adopt policies that facilitated the growth of towns."[31] The increasing proliferation of technology, trade, and centralized justice led to what sociologist Norbert Elias referred to as "the civilizing process."[32]

Sovereign states also emerged during a time of economic mercantilism and relative autarchy. Among other things, foreign territories imposed tariffs and other trade barriers. The acquisition of new territories therefore expanded a state's tariff-free common market. As late as 1897 a British premier told a French Ambassador that "If you were not such persistent protectionists, you would not find us so keen to annex territories."[33]

Conquest Facilitating Norms

An additional advantage for states that greatly facilitated their expansionist capabilities were the prevailing international norms which made territorial expansion relatively feasible. During the formative age of sovereign states, the modern forces that mitigate against the territorial expansion of sovereign states did not yet exist.[34] As late as the latter part of the nineteenth century, international law still embraced norms like *terra nullius*.[35] Under *terra nullius* inhabited territory occupied by "uncivilized" peoples belonged to no one. Not only did this norm provide a normative justification for seizure of such territories by strong polities, it encouraged territorial expansion as a duty so that conquering powers could spread civilization to what were viewed as barbarous

---

[29] Giddens 1987, 150.
[30] Bates 2010, 42.
[31] Bates 2010, 42.
[32] Elias 1982.
[33] Hobsbawn 1987, 67. Also quoted in Alesina and Spolaore 2003, 190.
[34] Crawford 2002; Jackson 1987, 526; 1990.
[35] *Terra nullius* is also referred to a *res nullius*. International Court of Justice Reports 1975, 30. See also Brownlie 1998, 173–4.

populations.[36] The eighteenth-century Swiss diplomat and international law scholar Emmerich de Vattel, for instance, in *Le Droit des Gens* (1758) maintained that "the peoples of those vast tracts [of North America] rather roamed over them than inhabited them" and consequently could not be properly constituted as sovereign states.[37]

The Erosion of Strong State Natural Selection

Until the nineteenth century, the symbiosis between the economic and war-making capacities of sovereign states combined with international norms that were favorable for expansion. This then allowed sovereign states to achieve increasing scale, resources, and strength as they built their civilizations upon the ruins of defeated weaker polities. The result was a type of natural selection that not only increased the power of expansionist states, but also eliminated many relatively feeble polities that were not as efficient in their economic and war-making capacities.[38] One outcome of such processes has been many of the larger (and successful) sovereign states which came into being through the eighteenth century.[39] Reflecting this are the findings of the military historian Quincy Wright who estimates that in fifteenth-century Europe about 5,000 different independent or semi-independent polities existed.[40] As larger states continued to swallow weaker polities, by the seventeenth-century Thirty Years War this number had declined to around five hundred.[41] By the nineteenth century the number had dwindled even further to about two hundred.[42]

In significant ways, however, the days of forcible sovereign state expansion are gone.[43] Relative to the period before World War II, states are by and large unable to expand their territory through conquest and incorporation as they did before. According to Mark Zacher, "while approximately 80%

---

[36] The application of this principle was applied for example in 1818 by the United States with respect to the seizure of Indian land in North America. See Chudacoff et al. 1997, 339.

[37] Vattel 1964. Also quoted in Flanagan 1989, 595. Vattel nevertheless maintained that the more advanced indigenous civilizations of Mexico such as the Aztecs could be seen as proper subjects of international law.

[38] Fazal 2004.

[39] Many of the world's most successful and powerful sovereign states, such as Japan, the US, Germany, France, the UK, China, and still others owe the scale of their territory to this period when it was possible for countries to become enlarged through conquest more readily.

[40] Richardson 1960, 168–9; Wright 1942, 215. Also cited in Pinker 2011, 74.

[41] Pinker 2011, 74.

[42] Pinker 2011, 74.

[43] For an excellent partial counterargument to this, which argues that great powers still have significant incentives to engage in imperialism in light of modern day state failure and genocide, see MacDonald 2009.

of territorial wars led to re-distributions of territory for all periods prior to 1945, this figure dropped to 30% after 1945."[44] In the first half of the twentieth century a series of reconfigurations of superpower policy as well as a range of notable international agreements articulated an emerging anti-imperial norm. At the end of World War I, US President Woodrow Wilson promoted self-determination as a universal right. International conventions such as the 1919 Covenant of the League of Nations and the Kellogg-Briand Pact also promoted anti-imperialism.[45] Furthermore, after World War II, amidst the competition for hearts and minds during the Cold War, the superpowers frequently expressed antagonism against the forcible annexation of nationalistically distinct territories.[46] The norm was also promoted by the United Nations in resolutions such as the 1960 UN Declaration on the Granting of Independence to Colonial Countries and Peoples. It declared that "inadequacy of political, economic, social, or educational preparedness should never serve as a pretext for delaying independence."[47] Increasingly assertive self-determination movements also antagonized overstretched empires. With the rise of technology and information as critical factors of economic production, the acquisition of land was also seen to have diminishing returns.[48] As a result of such factors, most of the large empires in the world became difficult to sustain and fragmented after the middle of the twentieth century.

In the midst of the resulting mass decolonization, the number of new states precipitously increased. After World War II there were just fifty-four sovereign states (many of them based in Europe) which dominated much of the globe (for data on decolonization see Appendix 4). Since that time—like animals that multiply in the absence of a predator—the number of new states has nearly quadrupled to 185 mostly small sovereign states today.[49] Amidst the new fixed borders norms that militate against territorial expansion, the structure of conflict in the world has largely shifted from state-to-state war to internal war. According to James Fearon and David Laitin, from 1945 to 1999 there were 25 interstate wars as compared to 127 civil wars, which occurred in 73 states.[50] The interstate wars resulted in 3.3 million battle deaths whereas the civil wars resulted in 16.2 million.[51]

---

[44]　Zacher 2001, 223. Also quoted in MacDonald 2009, 96. For others who make similar observations see Barkin and Cronin 1994, 107–30; Fazal 2004, 328; Fearon 2004, 394; .

[45]　Korman 1996, 133–199; Zacher 2001, 216–221.

[46]　Crawford 2002.

[47]　UN, Declaration on the Granting of Independence to Colonial Countries and Peoples. 1960.

[48]　Kaysen 1990, 42–64.

[49]　This number of sovereign states takes into account that a number of polities that are sometimes coded as sovereign states (like Liechtenstein or Micronesia) are in fact PITs. See Appendix1.

[50]　Fearon and Laitin 2003, 75.　　　　[51]　Fearon and Laitin 2003, 75.

The leaders of the new sovereign states hoped that full independence would deliver to them many of the advantages of other successful sovereign states in the international system. But as Joseph Migdal has observed, "the bright hopes of those heady years surrounding decolonization have faded considerably."[52] "Have they become strong states?" he asks. "The answer to the question for most states," he concludes, "is negative."[53] The fact that modern norms prevented territorial expansion led to the termination of the system of natural selection that prevailed before the twentieth century. With this preexisting system, larger, more militarily and economically efficient states would incorporate their smaller, weaker, and poorer counterparts.[54] In one sense, the advantage of this situation was that small and weak sovereign states would be mostly spared from the forcible conquest by larger states that may have assailed them in the past. On the other hand, however, the preexisting mechanism that allowed strong states (like the UK, the US, France, Germany, China, Japan, Italy, and others) to come into being (by forcibly enlarging their resources and strengths through assimilating weaker polities) was gone.

The Sovereign State Poverty Trap

Largely as a consequence of the erosion of the preexisting conditions of natural selection, most weak states remained weak. External threats no longer served as an incentive to make the economic, institutional, and security improvements that are necessary for more effective external self-defense.[55] Such factors were not available to pressure populations to give their assent to greater levels of taxation.[56] They no longer imposed urgent demands for a more efficient administration.[57] Such factors were not the only way to create more efficient institutions. They represent, however, one set of powerful incentives—but with the advent of fixed border norms, such incentives were gone. Unlike the sovereign states of past eras, resources remained unamalgamated and economies of scale were not achieved.

Under such circumstances, many of the newly independent states after the nineteenth century still had the autonomy to formulate their own internal policies and governance structures to attempt to overcome their relative

---

[52] Fearon and Laitin 2003, 75.   [53] Migdal 1988, 5.
[54] Herbst 1989, 683–87.
[55] See Downing 1992; Ertman 1997; and Hintze 1975; Tilly 1975; 1990.
[56] See Atzili 2007, 139–73; Desch 1996, 237–68; Herbst 1990; 2000.
[57] Atzili 2007, 139–73.

poverty. Some adopted forms of autocracy, while others embraced democracy.[58] Whatever internal policies or forms of governance these states chose, however, sovereign statehood itself often did not have the capacity to overcome the challenges that assailed them.[59] As Adam Przeworski and his collaborators have observed in their statistical analysis of the world's states, "poor countries cannot afford a strong state, and when the state is weak, the kind of regime matters little for everyday life."[60] When basic infrastructure, welfare, rule of law, health care, education, economic regulation, security, diplomacy, and a wide range of other governmental functions remain beyond their reach for want of basic resources, the type of internal policy or regime type is of low importance. "Whatever the regime, the society is too poor to finance an effective state." Under such conditions, states that are weak and poor tend to remain in what economists call a "low-level trap".[61] The principle problem, therefore, is not the internal form of government that they choose or the policies they adopt. The problem is weak state capacity, which full independence by itself does not provide.

Investment and trade can no doubt achieve some of the traditional ends of state expansion and imperialism without many of its costs.[62] And in significant ways, technological advances (whether in the fields of medicine, architecture, food production, and a wide range of other fields) significantly reduce the advantages of further territorial acquisition. Nevertheless, even today a larger population and territory still translates into significant advantages. As the relatively low GDP per capita of Russia illustrates, being bigger is not always better—but being small, poor, and weak is almost always bad. And whatever the exceptions may be, it does not take a leap of the imagination to appreciate the many problems that assail sovereign states as a result of their small size, preexisting poverty, and relative isolation. As the World Bank has emphasized, larger countries are insulated from a wide range of threats that afflict smaller polities.[63] Small size frequently translates into: greater susceptibility to market fluctuations (because of a lack of product diversity); vulnerability to natural disasters (because of the ability of environmental disasters to affect the entirety of the population); higher transportation costs (through political, national, and geographic isolation); and higher public service costs (because of the absence

---

[58] Autocracies range from highly mobilized totalitarian and sultanistic forms to relatively hands off post-totalitarian and authoritarian variants. See Linz and Stepan 1996, 38–54. Democracies range from two-party majoritarian systems to multiparty proportional representation electoral systems. See Lijphart 1999. On a distinct variant of proportional representation and majoriatarian electoral systems, see Reilly 2002.

[59] Przeworski et al. 2000.

[60] Przeworski et al. 2000.

[61] For an early account of the "low level trap" see Nelson 1959, 894–908.

[62] Brooks 1999, 665–66; 2007, 129–60.

[63] World Bank 2011, 1.

of economies of scale).[64] In 1945 when there were fifty-four mostly large sovereign states, this was not as much of a concern. Today, however, sixty-three sovereign states have populations that are four million or less.[65]

Since the nineteenth century, the full responsibilities demanded of modern sovereign states increasingly have come to bear on those that are smaller. Under these circumstances, full independence provides self-sufficiency when there are often few resources to rely on. It delivers full self-determination that is not guaranteed from predation by internal and external adversaries. It offers military power that in many cases does not provide effective self-defense. Before turning to the advantages and disadvantages that sovereign states have faced amidst international anarchy, the chapter will now turn to issues of identity and legitimacy.

LEGITIMACY ADVANTAGES AND WEAKNESSES

During their formative age, nascent sovereign states delivered coercive protection and order. In exchange, local populations provided taxation, military conscripts, and ultimately legitimacy.[66] Sovereign states also had a structurally embedded tendency to furnish these outcomes in a centralized fashion by exercising exclusive authority and control within their territory. Indeed, sovereign states not only have a tendency to exclude all other competing governmental forms within their international legal space (as they largely succeeded in doing in Europe before the eighteenth century), but they are frequently defined by this characteristic. John Ruggie describes them as "territorially defined, fixed, and *mutually exclusive* enclaves of legitimate Dominion."[67] Max Weber says that they are a type of "human community that successfully claims the *monopoly* of the legitimate use of physical force".[68] And Hendrik Spruyt observes that "within sovereign states there existed a final decision-making structure which brooked no outside interference and which gradually claimed a monopoly on violence and justice.... That is, sovereigns claimed hierarchy within borders and recognized no higher authority."[69] As scholars of state formation confirm, this tendency toward centralized and absolute authority and control within a territory served them well for many centuries as they increased their resources, population, market access, and administrative efficiency relative

---

[64] World Bank 2011, 1.   [65] See US, Central Intelligence Agency 2006.
[66] Tilly 1985, 1990.   [67] Ruggie 1993, 149 (emphasis added).
[68] Weber 1964, 154 (emphasis added).
[69] Spruyt 1994a, 153.

to competing polity forms. Without nationalists to contend with, a policy of exclusive internal control could focus resources on eliminating rival warlords and other actors that had been blamed for the seemly perpetual wars during the medieval era. Vast populations and territories could be subdued, subjugated, and economically exploited with fewer resources.[70]

With the emergence of modern nationalism after the eighteenth century, however, most sovereign states had to confront the potential hostility, division, and political challenges of multiple national groups within their territory.[71] Nationalism is the principle that says that a distinct population ought to rule over itself within the confines of a particular territory.[72] It is the belief in the congruence between what a population sees as its cultural, political, and territorial unit.[73] Here "culture" is broadly interpreted to mean any form of subjectively perceived distinct identity, whether it is based on religion, language, or some other shared history or experience.[74] As scholars of nationalism have emphasized, a potentially dangerous dilemma arises when two or more separate national groups include the same territory within their nationalistic territorial reference.[75] In many cases, a nationalistically distinct population, which constitutes a majority or a near majority within a state, will see the entire state as its nationalistic territorial reference. And all too often state institutions will be overwhelmingly dominated by loyalists from the majority national group. Meanwhile, one or more other minority populations (which constitute a majority or a near majority within a particular enclave) will see the territory where it exists as its national homeland but will have a tendency to reject being ruled over by an alien nationalistically distinct population. Ernest Gellner describes this as "the violation of the nationalist principle to which nationalist sentiment is quite particularly sensitive: if the rulers of the political unit belong to a nation other than that of the majority of the ruled."[76] Michael

---

[70] Naill Ferguson (2002), for example, points out that the British empire was largely able to control the Indian subcontinent as long as nationalism was kept at bay. Once it emerged, however, the sustainability of empire eroded.

[71] Anderson 1991; Gellner, 1983; Hobsbawm, 1990: 85.

[72] This definition is drawn from the definition provided by Ernest Gellner in which a population's cultural, political, and territorial unit is emphasized. Gellner 1983, 1. This definition, however, departs from Gellner's emphasis of nationalism as culture–state congruence, since as described earlier, many populations also aspire for organizational forms other than the sovereign state, such as PITs. For others who have also criticized the emphasis on the sovereign state as the only object of nationalistic aspirations see Snyder 2000.

[73] Gellner 1983, 1.

[74] From this perspective even a territory such as Hong Kong has cultural distinctiveness based on its distinctive economic, legal, and historic experiences as compared to the rest of China.

[75] A sampling of works where such powers of domestic populations are examined includes, Anderson 1991; Breuilly 1982; Brubaker 1996; Chatterjee 1993; Gellner 1983; Hall 1998; Hechter 2000; Hobsbawm 1992; Hroch 1985; Kymlicka 1995; Miller 1995; Smith 1986.

[76] Gellner 1983, 1.

Hechter emphasizes that such "alien direct rule of a region" tends to give rise to nationalism "as a form of collective action."[77] Each side will therefore reject the tendency of the other group to rule over the same territory.

This type of contradiction is widespread and exists in many countries throughout the globe. According to scholars of nationalism, it has led to widespread violence.[78] As Jeffery Herbst has concluded, "the presence of a palpable external threat may be the strongest way to generate a common association between the state and the population."[79] But with the emergence of the fixed border and anti-imperial norms in the twentieth century, external threats no longer motivate heterogeneous populations to unite against external aggressors.[80]

In their study of incidences of nationalistic conflict in eighty-eight countries from Eurasia and North Africa, Lars Erik Cederman and Luc Girardin find a strong correlation between violence and ethnic groups that have been excluded from power.[81] They conclude that "the more demographically significant ethnic groups are excluded from state power, the more likely it is that there will be violent attempts at overcoming such imbalances."[82] Conflicts over nationalism account for the majority of the wars that were fought in the world after World War II.[83] And nearly all of these wars occurred within sovereign states rather than between them. Among the 215 internal armed conflicts fought during this period, 110 were ethnonationalist wars over self-determination.[84] Many observers have also emphasized modern nationalism as a further contributing factor to the fragmentation of most of the world's empires especially in the middle of the twentieth century (which also helped increase the number of states from fifty-six after World War II to 185 today).[85] Even powerful sovereign states

---

[77] Hechter 2000.

[78] Only some of the most recent hostilities between national groups and states include: the separatist conflicts in Aceh and Irian Jaya in Indonesia; the clashes between the Tamil Hindu minority and the Sinhalese Buddhists in Sri Lanka; the tensions between the Tibetans and the Chinese in Tibet; the strife between Kashmir separatists and the Indian government in India; the troubles between nationalist Catholics and unionist Protestants in Northern Ireland; the bloodshed between the Russians and the Chechnyans, the Armenians and Azeris, and the Georgians and the South Ossetians in Central Asia; the rebellion of Basque separatists in Spain; the violence of Corsican rebels in France; the strife between the Turks and the Greeks in Cyprus; the rebellion of the Kurds in Turkey, Iraq, Syria, Armenia, and Iran; the ethnic violence in Sudan, Somalia, Burundi, and Rwanda; and the clashes between the Palestinians and the Israelis in the Middle East.

[79] Herbst 1990, 122.

[80] Atzili 2007; Coser 1956, 87–110; Desch 1996, 247; Stein 2001, 189–208.

[81] Cederman and Girardin 2007, 176.

[82] Cederman and Girardin 2007, 176.

[83] See Gleditsch et al. 2002; Cederman et al. 2009b; and Roeder 2007, 5.

[84] Cederman et al. 2009c, 1.

[85] The number of current sovereign states leaves out PITs such as Micronesia or Liechtenstein that are (mistakenly) included as being fully independent sovereign states. Kauffmann et al. 2008.

like France, the US, Russia, the UK, Portugal, the Netherlands, and still others have deployed hundreds of thousands of troops, sustained tens of thousands of casualties, expended vast resources, and in some cases (like France) have risked internal destabilization in an often vain attempt to forcibly control national-istically distinct territories.[86] As British Parliamentarian Sir Edmund Burke pointed out with respect to such efforts, "the use of force alone is but temporary. It may subdue for a moment, but it does not remove the necessity of subduing again; and a nation is not governed which is perpetually to be conquered."[87]

After the eighteenth century, nationalism also created unprecedented demands for state resources to be used for citizen welfare.[88] The states that had the resources for such economic redistribution in the form of price subsidies for food, heating, insurance, shelter, and/or still other forms of welfare ben-efited from increased legitimacy.[89] The states that did not have these resources suffered from increased domestic conflict and societal divisions.[90] Hence, rather than greater efficiency, more resources, and a compliant population, with the advent of modern nationalism after the eighteenth century, many sovereign states were forced to confront violent opposition, internal division, and political instability. Sovereign states continue to be beset by distinct ter-ritories that demand self-determination.[91]

THE INCONVENIENCES OF INTERNATIONAL ANARCHY

From the fourteenth to the nineteenth century, sovereign states in Europe achieved ever-increasing territorial mass. As mentioned earlier in the chapter, in the space of four centuries, Europe transformed from a diverse assortment of about 5,000 polities (many of which were internal warlord controlled fief-doms) into roughly 200 states. In nascent states like England and France, war-lords were disarmed, their fortresses were razed, and their private armies were disbanded or co-opted into national militaries.[92] As they continued to assimi-late smaller and weaker polities, their larger size in turn delivered more land for their agrarian economies, more laborers, more potential military recruits,

---

[86] Spruyt 2005, 2.
[87] Quoted in Ferguson 2002, 79.
[88] Milliken and Krause 2002, 760.
[89] Milliken and Krause 2002, 761,
[90] Cramer and Goodhand 2002, 900.
[91] Gleditsch et al. 2002.
[92] Spruyt 1994b.

and more capital and resources. These economic advantages in turn spilled over into increasing war-fighting capability—which resulted in still more territorial acquisition.[93] Nevertheless, while some modern states made great strides toward removing anarchy within their borders, they continue to be threatened by the free riding, collective action problems, and relative absence of public goods that persist in the anarchy of the international system.

Eliminating Anarchy through Conquest and Norms

As these states expanded, they also eliminated pockets of anarchy that prevailed within their borders. It is worth reemphasizing that during much of their formative age, sovereign states did not exercise complete internal control and authority. Although substantial territories were indeed under the centralized control of a nascent sovereign state's monarchy, others were the domains of warlords (as well as a host of other previously mentioned overlapping jurisdictions) which in many cases possessed their own armies, fortresses, land, labor, and capital. Under these circumstances, a type of anarchical condition prevailed in the sense that there was no common, legitimate, and recognized authority to create, enforce, and interpret rules and agreements.[94]

Seventeenth-century observers such as philosopher Thomas Hobbes hated and feared these highly decentralized circumstances. Hobbes believed this anarchy was at the root of the divisive religious wars that had plagued and fragmented Europe for over a century since the Protestant Reformation. Much like the present day conditions in failed states like the Congo, Somalia, and Afghanistan, killing, torture, rapes, abductions, theft, and economic disruption prevailed on a colossal scale. The absence of central control was tantamount to a state of war. Hobbes believed that amidst such chaos, rights, rules, and obligations were meaningless without a common ruler to keep all parties in check and insure order.[95]

Similar to Hobbes, eighteenth-century philosopher John Locke believed that anarchy was a condition that was "full of fears and continual dangers."[96] Even with the presence of natural rights (which are fundamental rights like life, liberty, and property that all people possess by virtue of being human)— and the potential for individual enforcement—a multitude of dire problems remained for those within conditions of anarchy. Without a recognized government to create, clarify, and enforce them, natural rights alone were

---

[93] Tilly 1990.
[94] On anarchy see Bull 2002, 44.   [95] Hobbes 1960.
[96] Locke 1690/1980, §123.

a type of intellectual construct that was "no where to be found but in the minds of men."[97] Individual enforcement of rules associated with natural rights (natural law) was also unacceptable since "they who through passion or interest shall miscite, or misapply it, cannot so easily be convinced of their mistake where there is no established judge."[98] In spite of the existence of a natural law, people would be forced into the difficult situation of having to decide for themselves how to preserve or defend themselves against other individuals. Without "promulgated standing laws, and known authorized judges" natural law could be confused and interpreted differently. Without governments, everyone would be their own "judge, interpreter, and executioner."[99] Locke's policy prescriptions were therefore in many respects the same as Hobbes: only by eliminating anarchy could order be delivered. People therefore needed to "unite into [a] common-wealth and put themselves under government... for the mutual preservation of their lives, liberties and estates."[100]

Accordingly, not only did sovereign states continue to eliminate internal and external challengers through territorial assimilation, they made a number of notable attempts to solidify the emerging exclusive system of sovereign states through treaties and norms. One of the most well-known instances of this occurred in 1648 at the conclusion of the Thirty Years War (in which around 30% of the population of Europe perished).[101] At this meeting in the city of Westphalia, Europe's sovereign state leaders ratified an agreement to attempt to eradicate interference by competing semi-independent jurisdictions. The leaders agreed that sovereign states, rather than other non-state actors, were the legitimate actors in the international system. Legitimacy would be established through mutual state-to-state recognition. Treaties signed by the major military powers would also be the basis for settling competing territorial claims. And religious differences, as interpreted by the Pope, would no longer be the basis for honoring or annulling their treaty obligations.[102] They recognized each other, their respective boundaries, and the treaties between them. No one else legitimized them. No other groups could challenge them. As Daniel Philpott notes, the "basic criteria for a polity to be recognized as a sovereign state—usually, that it possess a government that is in control of a people within a territory, and be capable of entering into international agreements— and posits non-intervention as the basic prerogative of sovereign states...emerged at the Peace of Westphalia, then gradually spread around

---

[97] Locke 1690/1980, §136.   [98] Locke 1690/1980, §136.
[99] Locke 1690/1980, §136.   [100] Locke 1690/1980, §123.
[101] For a seminal account of this see Gross 1948, 20–41.
[102] Philpott 1999, 574.

the world..."[103] Broadly speaking, while some distinct medieval anomalies still continued to exist, states were conceived of as self-sufficient, centralized, homogenous units that would replace other competing forms. As Stephen Krasner notes, however, even after these agreements, states continued to victimize one another. "Weaker states" he says, "have frequently been subject to coercion and imposition and been unable to defend their autonomy [and] stronger ones have entered into conventions and contracts that violate their autonomy and even territoriality."[104]

The Dangers of Anarchy's Persistence

Although sovereign states had great success in removing the anarchical conditions within their borders, the same fearful and dangerous decentralized conditions emphasized by Hobbes and Locke still remain in their relations with each other at the international level.[105] Because sovereign states have no common authority, they exist in a state of international anarchy.[106] Any analysis of the costs and benefits of sovereign states has to come to terms with the implications of this condition. It is worth pointing out that the absence of a common government on some issues is not always a bad thing. Some have observed that with repeated interactions, decentralized actors (without the benefit of government) can effectively monitor behavior, reward performance, and punish transgressions.[107] Robert Axelrod, for example, observes that French and German soldiers who confronted each other in the anarchy of the frontline battles of World War I were able to use tit-for-tat incentives to create pockets of peace.[108] Furthermore, some economists have emphasized

---

[103] Philpott 1999, 579.

[104] Krasner 1995, 150.

[105] The problematic condition of anarchy is widely acknowledged by liberal and realist international relations scholars. Even constructivists who assert that anarchy is "what states make it" will acknowledge that frequently states do not in fact make a good situation out of it. See Wendt 1992, 391–425. International legal scholars, however, seem to recoil at the term "anarchy" when it is applied to the international system. Indeed, if someone with limited knowledge of international affairs were to read an international legal text (like Ian Brownlie's (1998) *Principles of Public International Law*) they might be under the impression that an acceptable form of world government already exists. No doubt, however, even international legal jurists would acknowledge that the grave economic, political, and security problems that continue to prevail at the global level do not typically exist at other levels when polities are governed by advanced democracies or PITs.

[106] Bull 2002, 44.

[107] Axelrod 1984; Hardin 1982; Taylor 1976; 1990.

[108] Axelrod 1984.

that in some cases the application of self-interest can lead to an invisible hand that benefits all.[109]

A large modern literature, however, supports the view that such decentralization when applied between governments can lead to collective action problems.[110] Within such contexts, scholars such as Schwartz and Tomz find that the presence of forms of hierarchy "can produce higher levels of group welfare than a decentralized [anarchical] system...*even when decentralized enforcement mechanisms operate flawlessly.*"[111] As Mancur Olson emphasized, anarchical systems can produce the problem of free riding in which self-interested actors exploit the advantages of cooperation without adding to the common effort.[112] And with respect to the unconstrained operation of the "invisible hand" Nobel laureate Joseph Stilitz has observed that it is frequently the case that "the reason why the invisible hand seems invisible is that it's not there."[113]

Hierarchy under a Large Strong State as Compared to International Anarchy

Even with their treaties, norms, and the eventual role of international institutions, the anarchy of the international system does not provide the same degree of advantages that exist with territories that have an integrated association with a large and strong state. First, in the international system no common government exists to create, interpret, and enforce rules in the same way. As the diplomat E. H. Carr described, the international legal rules that do exist "lack the essential quality of law: [they are] not automatically and unconditionally applicable to all members of the community whether they assent to it or not."[114] While modern international organizations such as the International Criminal Court, World Trade Organization, Organization for Economic Cooperation and Development, and the United Nations have indeed provided some rule enforcement, a world government does not yet exist. Fully independent states are in many respects still their own "judge, interpreter, and executioner."[115] This has profound implications for the potential abuses sovereign

[109] For modern economists that have made such points see for example, Friedman 1971; Fudenberg and Maskin 1986; Rubenstein 1979.
[110] See Alchian and Demsetz 1972; Bendor and Mookherjee 1987; Bianco and Bates 1990; Hardin 1993; Holmstrom 1982; Ophuls 1992.
[111] Schwartz and Tomz 1997. Italics in original.
[112] Olson 1965.
[113] Olson 1965.
[114] Carr 1940, 160.
[115] Locke 1690/1980, §136.

states may commit with respect to their own population and toward other sovereign states.

Second, still another way that the international system differs from the condition of territories within (or associated with) a large and strong state is the relative absence of public goods. Public goods (such as a judicial system, defense, financial institutions, parks, health care, crime prevention, and infrastructure) are either not provided at all at the international level or are not available at low cost.[116]

Third, the international system (unlike a large and strong state) also does not feature a single market that is fully free of trade barriers. Economists Alberto Alesina and Enrico Spolaore emphasize that "political borders do interfere with economic transactions....Evidence shows that in today's world borders do matter."[117] Even across the border between the United States and Canada, which is one of the most free and open in the world, territorially contiguous Canadian and American regions have lower degrees of trade than between unconnected and distant provinces within Canada.[118] In spite of a sixteen-fold increase of worldwide foreign direct investment from 1980 to 1995, entrepreneurs nevertheless frequently display a "home country bias" with respect to where they choose to invest their money.[119] Likewise, although multinational firms have significant degrees of international operations, the vast majority of their business transactions remain in their home countries.[120]

Fourth, the international system also does not have an "insurance system" of economic redistribution akin to strong states.[121] Whether in Japan, the US, Germany, the UK, or another strong state, when an economic recession or a natural disaster strikes one part of the country it receives a net economic redistribution from other areas.[122]

And fifth, the international community is characterized by degrees of nationalistic heterogeneity that are greater than any sovereign state alone—especially in the age of nationalism. While overcoming high degrees of heterogeneity is not insurmountable (as one can see from large

---

[116] For a classic statement on the distribution of public goods in society see Tiebout 1956. For explanations in the field of economics see Laffont 1988; Samuelson 1954.

[117] Alesina and Spolaore 2003, 4 and 219.

[118] McCallum 1995.

[119] See Feldstein and Horioka1980; Frankel 1992.

[120] Doremus et al. 1999, 1–21. Also cited in MacDonald 2009a, 92.

[121] For a three-sided debate on the form that global economic transfers should take in the future, see the distinct views of Peter Singer (2002) who favors global level economic redistribution, as compared to John Rawls (1999b), who opposes it. Michael Doyle (2006) takes an intermediate view.

[122] Alesina and Spolaore 2003, 4.

democracies such as India and the United States), it nevertheless poses significant challenges. James Fearon builds upon this and the prevailing international anarchy in the international system, by pointing out that the existence of many nationalistically distinct minority populations throughout the world facilitates the dangers of anarchy. James Fearon describes anarchy as "the absence of an authority capable of policing agreements"[123] Nationalistically distinct minority populations live within sovereign states. In this sense, the international anarchy that exists between sovereign states without a world government does not apply to them. Nevertheless, since they are nationalistically distinct minorities, in many cases they will not control the levers of government and will therefore be in a vulnerable and weak condition. Fearon argues that this has potentially grave consequences. In spite of the powerful incentives to avoid destructive war, anarchy in the international system helps give rise to commitment problems that then lead to conflict, especially preventative war.[124] He defines commitment problems as "situations in which mutually preferable bargains are unattainable because one or more states would have an incentive to renege on the terms."[125] Under such circumstances the commitments that each party makes in their agreement can become destabilized when one side becomes relatively weak.[126] The weakened condition of one of the parties under such anarchy increases the payoffs and incentives for the stronger side to usurp its commitments.[127] The vulnerability of the weaker side also gives rise to their fear of exploitation by their stronger partner. Under such conditions the weaker side may "prefer to absorb even higher costs of war today to avoid being exploited tomorrow."[128] This, therefore, provides one explanation for the widespread existence of ethnic conflict across the globe.

Inconveniences in the International System and the Firm Metaphor

The anarchy that can exist in economic markets can serve as a powerful metaphor for the anarchy that prevails in the international system. Economists

---

[123] Frieden 1994.
[124] Fearon 1995, 28.
[125] Fearon 1995, 4.
[126] According to these views, even when a colony is under the hierarchical control of an imperial power, a type of anarchy prevails over aspects of the relations since the imperial power by definition does not provide credible commitments that limit its powers in favor of local autonomy.
[127] Lake and Rothchild 1996, 47.
[128] Lake and Rothchild 1996, 48.

have been especially troubled by the presence of forms of anarchy in economic markets. Nobel prize winning economist Oliver Williamson argued that the anarchy of liberalized economic markets (with little regulation and without a single business in control) created serious difficulties for firms.[129] In fact, Williamson's insights on overcoming anarchical systems through the application of hierarchy has spawned a political science literature with far reaching contributions, which draws on his analysis of the firm as a metaphor for the behavior of actors in the international system.[130]

Without a clear and present higher authority, Williamson believed that firms would have a strong tendency to behave opportunistically and immorally. He argued that market systems suffer from competing firms that intentionally suppress or distort information. This lack of available information then hampers and distorts decision making which makes businesses behave less rationally. Conditions in which actors have limited information to make rational decisions is referred to as "bounded rationality."[131] According to Williamson, an especially troubling example of such bounded rationality occurs when firms do not have information about the nature of rules. Reflecting the concerns that many observers have about rules in the international system, Williamson expresses doubts about the possibility of legal recourse in liberalized market economies in the event of a contractual breech. "Most disputes," he says, "including many that under current rules could be brought to a court, are resolved by avoidance, self-help, and the like."[132] This further absence of information gives rise to still greater degrees of irrational behavior.[133] Such bounded rationality prevents firms from maximizing their efficiency and material utility through accurate decision making.

Still another problem under conditions of the anarchy of liberalized markets is the absence of shared assets (like shared ownership over factories and land).[134] Relationship specific assets are shared resources that have increased value as long as a relationship between actors persists.[135] If the relationship ends, so too

---

[129] See Williamson 1973, 1985, 1998.

[130] Williamson's ideas have helped spawn a relational contracting literature in international relations in which scholars have made many excellent contributions by recommending various degrees of decentralization and powersharing to address problems in the relative anarchy of the international system. Mirroring the work of federalism scholars like Daniel Elazar (1991; 1993; 1994; 1997) and Ronald Watts (1996),who in the early 1990s catalogued a variety of territorial unions (which even include brief references to PITs), David Lake (1996; 1999; 2001; 2003; 2007; 2009) applies the hierarchy concept by placing such polity forms into the context of the international relations discourse. See also Cooley and Spruyt 2009; Fearon 1994; 1995, 379–414; Krasner 2005; Lake and Rothchild 1996, 48–52; Rector 2009; Weber 2000.

[131] For a seminal work on bounded rationality see Simon 1957.

[132] Williamson 1998, 20.

[133] Williamson 1973, 327.

[134] Williamson 1985, 52–6.   [135] Rector 2009.

does access to the same benefits that the assets provided when they were shared. According to Williamson, without shared assets "parties to such contracts have no continuing interests in the identity of one another." When businesses have a relative absence of shared interests, this results in still greater uncertainty among firms. In sum, without a common authority to enforce rules, without prevailing morality that would rein in opportunism, and without shared assets that would provide common interests, Williamson argues that private and public institutions are failures.[136] And with such institutional failure, market failure is the outcome.[137] The logic of Williamson's critique of the anarchy of markets can also be applied to the international system in which a world government does not exist.

In light of these circumstances, Williamson also comes to some of the same conclusions as Hobbes and Locke about the dangerous conditions of anarchy (albeit as it applies to economic systems). He, however, argues that the defects of anarchy can be remedied with hierarchy. Hierarchy is the condition in which dominant authorities have control over subordinates. It would be "much simpler," Williamson postulated "if instrumental rules were to be 'imposed' authoritatively" by shifting "transactions from market to internal organization."[138] When firms have an interest in doing business because they share specific assets (like machinery or software), the solution to some aspects of the aforementioned market failure problems is a hierarchical relationship between firms in which there is a "supervisor–subordinate relationship."[139] Under such autocratic control, differing interests of otherwise autonomous actors (that might otherwise be pushed toward opportunism) are made to be harmonized. When there are disputes, the authoritative fiat of ownership settles it. When there is a fear that business associates cannot be trusted, authoritarian control allows for better auditing of accounts, monitoring of behavior, and more deserved work incentives though monetary rewards. Hierarchy is therefore conceived as unidirectional and flows from a dominant to a subordinate partner, rather than bidirectional (as with negarchical institutions) in which both partners possess hierarchical powers over varying aspects of the partnership. According to Williamson's logic, under a common hierarchy (in which different firms are assimilated into a single firm) entrepreneurs benefit from (1) formal enforcement; (2) well established morality; and (3) shared self-interest. As a consequence, they have a greater tendency to clarify rules, create greater information transparency, and improve rational decision making. Under these conditions, Williamson says, it would be more likely that "the word of an agent is as good as his bond" and that "fraud and egregious contract deceits" would be deterred.[140]

---

[136] Williamson 1973, 316.   [137] Williamson 1973, 316.
[138] Williamson 1973, 321.   [139] Williamson 1973, 322.
[140] Williamson 1998, 31.

While hierarchical institutions do indeed have a number of advantages (which partially independent unions share to an extent), they nevertheless have some shortcomings that should not be overlooked. Just as with the suggestions of Hobbes and Locke, one of the challenges of applying Williamson's theory of the firm to international politics is that the eradication of some anarchy through the formation of a sovereign state does little to fully eliminate the anarchical problems that persist at the international level. In response to this (in addition to the analysis presented here), a variety of scholars that have drawn on Williamson's firm metaphor have moved away from anarchy as well as a pure hierarchical dominance–subordinate set of solutions and taken steps to modify the theory. Daniel Deudney calls this compromise between hierarchy and anarchy "negarchy."[141] As distinct from pure hierarchy which is conceived as unidirectional and flows from a dominant to a subordinate partner, negarchical forms are bidirectional, in which partners each possess hierarchical powers over varying aspects of the partnership.

Since sovereignty is shared and divided in such an arrangement, each governmental form possesses its own sphere of hierarchical dominance over the issues it controls. Accordingly, Katja Weber has pointed out the advantages for states that have put themselves under integrative institutions such as the EU.[142] After casting doubt on the efficacy of sovereignty and its "hypocrisy" in international relations in some of his earlier works, Steven Krasner has also emphasized that "sharing authority with nationals over some aspects of domestic sovereignty" (such as the division of power between the Soviet Union and the states of Eastern Europe during the Cold War) would he says "be a useful addition to the policy repertoire."[143] Alexander Cooley and Hendrik Spruyt have also underscored the implications of sovereign transfers when contractual arrangements between polities are incomplete.[144] Additionally, Chad Rector has emphasized the role of relationship specific assets in federal arrangements.[145] Through the use of case studies, game theoretical analysis, and rational choice theory, still other scholars have found that ethnic war becomes more likely when distinct groups are unable to commit to the agreements that they make.[146] They have emphasized the need for credible agreements in spite of the presence of international anarchy as a way to prevent conflict. Hence, whether directly

---

[141] Deudney 1995, 208.

[142] Weber 2000, 111–27.   [143] Krasner 2005, 89.

[144] Cooley and Spruyt 2009.   [145] Rector 2009.

[146] For works that discuss the lack of credible commitment between ethnic groups as a contributing factor that can lead to violence see Fearon 1994; 1995, 379–414; Hardin 1995, 143; Lake and Rothchild 1996, 48–52; and Walter 1997.

or indirectly, the aforementioned scholars have recognized the inability of the sovereign state to overcome problems of anarchy amidst the difficult conditions of the international system.

CONCLUSION

This chapter has shown that the conditions that tended to produce strong states before the nineteenth century are gone. Proposals that would overlook these changes, such as continuing with forcible military conquest or ignoring nationalism are unworkable. Empires throughout history (and especially in the twentieth century) have already tried and failed with such policies resulting in disastrous wars and economic loss. And as described in the previous chapter, while sham federacy might deceive some observers in the short term, such strategies tend eventually to fall prey to the opposition encountered by imperialism. Similarly, in light of the challenges faced by weak states, nation-building is fraught with similar disadvantages and costs. The way ahead for the sovereign states of the world is to adapt to modern conditions with institutional formulations that better respond to the normative, political, and economic conditions of the post-twentieth-century world. Partial independence represents one example of such an institutional form that is in some respects more feasible than other alternatives.

Partially independent territories have evolved to deliver degrees of compromise, cooperation, and commitment that the alterative of full independence often does not furnish. If modern international norms allowed for the emergence of stronger states through conquest, if the exclusivist tendencies of sovereign states did not incite nationalistic revolts, if the threats of international anarchy did not place enormous burdens on states across a wide range of issues to provide basic public goods to their populations, it may be possible for sovereign states to better compete with the alterative of PITs. If the creation of a sovereign state is feasible and is able to provide deliverance from insecurity, destitution, and other evils of anarchy, then one stands on firmer ground in supporting it.[147] But as described earlier, this is not the condition that exists in much of the world amidst prevailing wars and poverty. The

---

[147] This approach is what philosophers refer to a "contractarian approach." It is an approach that seeks to justify sovereignty by satisfying individual needs of security, political stability, human rights, and governmental continuity. See Tamir 2000.

factors that existed in the formative age of sovereign states to overcome such problems no longer exist. The irresistible demands for solutions to sovereign state defects have contributed to the evolution of PITs. Accordingly, the next chapter will turn to some of the empirical outcomes of PITs as compared to sovereign states.

8

Wealth and Security Advantages of Partial Independence

In March 2003 US forces invaded Iraq. Widespread destruction followed for most of the country. War, mismanagement, insurgency, counterinsurgency, and unchecked looting destroyed much of Iraq's infrastructure, weakened its political institutions, undermined its police and military forces, impoverished its economy, and led to cases of sectarian fighting and ethnic cleansing.[1] The ensuing conflict also gave rise to a staggering Iraqi death toll, which according to one Johns Hopkins University Study, was as high as 600,000 by 2006.[2]

But amidst the chaos and loss of life that engulfed most of the rest of Iraq, the Kurdish Territories in the north of the country remained a relative haven of peace, political stability, and even economic growth.[3] Unlike other areas in the country, its population did not resist. When faced with the realities of the US presence, its battle hardened guerilla fighters (the *Peshmerga*) did not join the anti-occupation insurgency. And amidst the political vacuum created by the destruction of the dictatorial Iraqi regime that for decades implemented systematic policies of discrimination, military occupation, and ethnic cleansing against them, they also did not attempt to seek full independence.

In fact Kurdish leaders explicitly rejected full independence and embraced partial independence instead.[4] After decades of fighting for self-determination, when at last the regime that was oppressing them was gone, why would they reject a status as a sovereign state? If a status as a sovereign state offered them the best chance for self-determination, economic well-being, and security, why would they reject it? Some might claim that they rejected independence because they were involuntarily forced to do so by America's overwhelming power and military presence. But in its initial years, America's occupation in the rest of Iraq largely failed to restore security, deliver essential services,

---

[1] Gordon and Trainor 2006, 138–63, 565–9.   [2] Brown 2006.
[3] See O'Leary 2005, 3–91.   [4] O'Leary 2005, 3–91.

and deter the emergence of a new insurgency.[5] Under such circumstances military force alone was hardly a persuasive deterrent to a population with an established and resilient insurgency capability that had survived decades of genocidal oppression. Still others might claim that it was American guarantees of the arrangement and not guarantees from the institutional arrangement itself that originally made the arrangement credible. But as already emphasized in Chapter 3, there are many ways to make a PIT credible, including outside guarantees and relationship specific assets. American guarantees were therefore part of the institutional arrangement itself, not separate from it.

Reflecting the arguments emphasized in Chapter 2, the reason that Kurdish leaders rejected sovereign statehood is arguably because: (1) a revolutionary event (in this case America's invasion) allowed previous obstacles to change (such as the dictatorship of Saddam Hussein) to be swept away and (2) partial independence offered a wide range of economic and security advantages that could not be matched by a sovereign state. Like many territories throughout the world that have also been confronted by this question, a sovereign state would have diminished their economic opportunities, threatened their self-determination, and made war more likely, as compared to a status as a PIT. Through partial integration with Iraq, the Kurds won themselves political, trade, diplomatic, and security advantages that a status as a sovereign state could not deliver. The formalized commitments made to them first by the United States in 2003, but then by Iraq in the country's 2004 Transitional Administrative Law (TAL), delivered to them many of the benefits of full independence without its inconveniences.[6] Among other powers, the TAL promised and provided to them local legal supremacy[7] (including local judicial control)[8] fiscal autonomy,[9] continued control of the *Peshmerga* as a self-defense force,[10] and a veto over the country's laws that would otherwise apply to them (except for powers that have been exclusively allocated to the

---

[5] For an account of America's disastrous occupation during its first years see Ricks 2006.

[6] See Iraq, Transitional Administrative Law 2004.

[7] Iraq, Transitional Administrative Law 2004, 53 and 54. "The Kurdistan Regional Government is recognized as the official government of the territories..." For an updated legal articulation of these powers see Iraq, Iraqi Constitution 2005, Articles 117, 121, and141. While Iraq's new constitution nominally creates a federation, as of this writing it has not been implemented. Iraqi Kurdistan therefore remains a semi-sovereign enclave that shares powers with a de facto unitary core state.

[8] Iraq, Iraqi Constitution 2005, Article 46.

[9] Iraq, Iraqi Constitution 2005, Article 54(a). "The Kurdistan Regional Government...will have the right to impose taxes and fees within the Kurdistan region."

[10] Iraq, Iraqi Constitution 2005. "The Kurdistan Regional Government shall retain regional control over police forces and internal security..."

core state).[11] The division and sharing of powers with the rest of Iraq allowed them a continued single market with the Iraqi core state, proxy diplomatic support from Iraq's new central government within which they played a significant role, a credible agreement to maintain internal cooperation and peaceful relations, and a means to reassure neighboring Turkey that they would not seek full independence. The latter factor in turn reduced the likelihood of a full-scale invasion from Turkey, which feared that a fully independent Kurdistan in northern Iraq could lead to the full secession of their own Kurdish populated territories. And as predicted by the fiscal federalism literature, with credible local control over their own economy and public goods from the Iraqi core state, the territory also attracted significant degrees of internal and external investment.[12] Under these conditions, the Kurdish–Iraq arrangement provided peace, cooperation, and economic stability even as chaos engulfed the rest of the country.

In some sense the empirical economic and security advantages of PITs as compared to sovereign states are straightforward. As illustrated in Chapter 1, the average GDP per capita of all PITs is over three times the average of those of all sovereign states. Furthermore, it takes only a cursory familiarity with PITs to conclude that for the most part they are not centers of violent upheaval and discord. Even in territories that previously had a history of being centers of conflict such as Northern Ireland, Kurdistan, South Sudan, Kosovo, Canada, Bougainville, and Ireland, the establishment of a PIT has in almost every case resulted in a cessation of hostilities. For some observers, such observations alone might be enough to convince them of PIT empirical advantages over sovereign states—especially when compared to the grave poverty that persists in most of the world as well as the millions of deaths that have resulted from wars between states as well as within them.

Critics could, however, contend that some other factor may in fact be causing these advantages besides partial independence. An infinite number of alternative factors are possible. Even relatively small differences (let alone large differences) between territories could explain differences in relative performance over time. Time and space constraints prevent the examination of every variable that might create differences between territories.[13] Future studies can eventually address more of these variables.

Ultimately, the only way to definitively know if a territory is better off as a PIT as opposed to a sovereign state is if two territories that are identical in every

[11] Iraq, Iraqi Constitution 2005, Article 54(b)

[12] See especially Weingast 1995, 1–31. For a classic account see Tiebout 1956, 416–24.

[13] Mathematician and meteorologist Edward Lorenz, for example, emphasized a "butterfly effect" by pointing out that even a butterfly could be part of the initial conditions that cause a hurricane. See Lorenz 1993.

way could simultaneously have each of these status options.[14] Observations of the otherwise identical PITs and sovereign states would then be made on their economic performance and degree of security over time. If the performance were identical, one could conclude that sovereignty type makes no difference. If however there was a difference in outcome, it could be attributed to the distribution of sovereign power with either the PIT or the sovereign state being declared as having greater advantages. Such an experiment is, of course, impossible to create or observe. Consequently, a definitive conclusion to the question of which regime type is more advantageous is also impossible.

The next best thing that can be done, however, is to approximate as closely as possible such hypothetical experimental conditions. While perfectly identical PITs and sovereign states are not available, those that are reasonably similar can be found. Four approaches will be used to approximate such similar conditions: simple matching, regression analysis, coarsened exact matching, and case study comparison. This chapter will examine the universe of PITs and sovereign states in the world and find cases that have similar population size,[15] regime type,[16] geographic region,[17] former core states, and year of emergence characteristics. Since these characteristics have been emphasized by other scholars as key causal factors that have led to substantial economic development and political stability, this chapter will focus on PITs and sovereign states that have similarities with regard to such features. For example, it could be the case that the relative economic or security success of PITs can be explained by their geographic concentration in an area with economically advantageous conditions. Similarly, it could be that the higher degrees of political freedom that they tend to possess, creates advantages. It could also be that their smaller population size puts them ahead. These potential objections will be overcome by comparing PITs and sovereign states that are demographically similar in terms of their geographic region, population size, and regime type.

If the arguments presented in Chapter 2 are correct, PITs will have economic and security advantages as compared to their demographically similar sovereign state counterparts. Their emergence will also coincide with a dramatic event (or set of events) that has led to their emergence. Alternatively if the arguments are incorrect, these factors will not apply. Demographically similar sovereign states will have a similar or a higher rate of economic growth. Punctuated equilibrium will also not be associated with their emergence. Their emergence will be more a result of other factors such as neo-functionalist, intergovernmentalist, or federalist pressures (discussed in Chapter 2). Accordingly, this chapter

---

[14] King et al. 1994.

[15] On the size of polities and their propensity for economic development see Alesina and Spolaore 2003.

[16] For those that have favored democracy as a reason for economic growth see for example Sen 1999, 178. For those who have favored authoritarian regimes see Kaplan 1997.

[17] For an example of geographic explanations for economic development see Diamond 2005.

will begin by using a simple matching approach to examine data on sovereign states as they compare to PITs on their economic performance. The chapter will then make use of regression and modern matching techniques to examine sovereign state and PIT economic performance. The chapter will then turn to refuting some prominent counterarguments, including those that (contrary to the arguments here) assert that wealth causes PITs rather than PITs causing wealth. Next, the chapter will again use simple matching approaches on PIT security performance relative to sovereign states. The chapter will also discuss the natural selection advantages and cataclysmic events that arguably give rise to PITs. It will furthermore provide answers on why there are not even more PITs in the international system. Lastly, the chapter will examine the economic and security performance of territories associated with the Netherlands in the Caribbean. These cases are some of the only examples of demographically similar polities that nevertheless chose divergent paths toward independence as well as PIT maintenance. In the next chapter individual cases will be compared to themselves overtime to examine the conducive conditions for PIT maintenance and failure.

A SIMPLE MATCHING COMPARISON OF PARTIALLY INDEPENDENT TERRITORY AND SOVEREIGN STATE ECONOMIC PERFORMANCE

In order to eliminate other plausible explanations for PIT economic success, this study examines the GDP per capita of similar PITs and sovereign states over time with respect to population size, geographic region, and regime type using simple matching. All PITs around the world were compared to all sovereign states. Since all PITs have populations below Hong Kong's population of 7 million, similar degrees of population size was operationalized by using Hong Kong's population as a benchmark. Out of 185 sovereign states, 96 states that had populations above this benchmark were therefore omitted from the comparison, with 89 remaining.[18] (The fact that nearly half of the world's sovereign states have a comparable population to PITs counteracts those who may be tempted to argue that PITs are anomalous because of their population size).

All PITs also have levels of freedom that are at or below that of Hong Kong's score of 3.5 according to Freedom House's 2010 Freedom in the World Report. Sovereign states that had levels of freedom that were below this were also excluded. Of the 89 sovereign states with populations under 7 million, 29

---

[18] This number of modern sovereign states omits some polities that are sometimes mistaken for sovereign states but are in fact PITs, such as Micronesia or Monaco.

more were eliminated because they had levels of freedom that were lower than Freedom House's score of 3.5.[19] This left 60 sovereign states.

Polities were then placed in nine groups according to geographical location: Asia, Africa, Caribbean, Central Asia, Europe, Middle East, North America, Pacific, and South America. No known PITs exist in Central Asia or South America. The groups associated with those regions (and the sovereign states within them) were eliminated. This left 56 sovereign states. The North America group was also eliminated since Greenland and Nunavut were alone without sovereign state peer competitors with a similar population size. Additionally, the Asia and Africa groups were eliminated because of the low statistical significance that results from comparing just two PITs in each group to a relatively large number of sovereign states. Similarly, the Middle East group was eliminated because the Kurdish Territories were the only PIT. In the case of Asia, the economic performance of Hong Kong vastly dwarfed the performance of other sovereign state peer competitors, while in Africa sovereign states dwarfed the performance of Zanzibar and the historic (pre-2011) case of South Sudan. The elimination of the Africa and Asia groups then leaves 38 sovereign states and 36 PITs which are concentrated in three regional groupings: the Caribbean, Europe, and the Pacific.

As illustrated in Figures 8.1–8.3, in every region of the world where there are meaningful numbers of comparable PITs and sovereign states, the average per capita GDP of PITs exceeds those of sovereign states across time by a significant degree. In the Caribbean region, from 1970 (which was the time after most sovereign states in the area became fully independent) until 2009, PITs experienced an ever-widening gap in their GDP per capita as compared to sovereign state peer competitors. In 2009, they had a GDP per capita that was over five times greater than their fully independent counterparts.[20] In the Pacific from 1988 to 2009, PITs experienced a similar ever-widening gap in their economic performance. By 2009, their per capita GDP was nearly seven times greater.[21] And in Europe from 1997 to 2009, PITs had a gap that was nearly twice as great.[22]

---

[19]   In the Asia group this resulted in the exclusion of Singapore, Laos, Brunei, and Bhutan. In the Caribbean group this resulted in the exclusion of Nicaragua. In the European group it resulted in the exclusion of Kosovo, Georgia, and Armenia. See Freedom House 2010.

[20]   The full universe of Caribbean region PITs was included in the time series data (Aruba, Bermuda, British Virgin Islands, Cayman Islands, Netherlands Antilles, Puerto Rico, and Suriname). The full universe of comparable Caribbean Region sovereign states was also included in the time series data (St Kitts and Nevis, Dominica, Antigua and Barbuda, Grenada, St Vincent and the Grenadines, St Lucia, Barbados, Bahamas, Suriname, Guyana, Trinidad and Tobago, Jamaica, Panama, Costa Rica, and El Salvador).

[21]   Except for the PIT of Bougainville for which GDP data were unavailable. The full universe of Pacific region PITs was included in the time series data (Cook Islands, French Polynesia, Marshall Islands, Micronesia, Northern Mariana Islands, New Caledonia, Niue, and Palau Islands). The full universe of comparable Pacific Region sovereign states was also included in the time series data (Kiribati, Nauru, Solomon Islands, Samoa, and Vanuatu).

[22]   Except for the case of Gagauzia for which GDP data were unavailable, the full universe of European region PITs until 2009 was included in the time series data (Faroe Islands, Gibraltar,

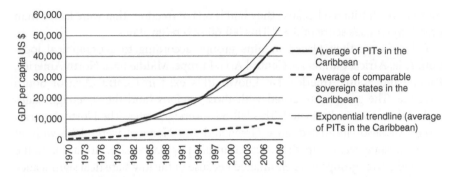

Figure 8.1. Caribbean region: Average GDP per capita of partially independent territories as compared to peer competitor sovereign states 1970–2009

Note: The full universe of known Caribbean cases is included in the time series data. Data presented in 2009 US dollars.

Sources: World Bank national accounts data, and OECD National Accounts data files 2011; United Nations Statistic Division 2009; Freedom House Freedom in the World Combined Average Ratings—Independent Countries 2011; Office for UK National Statistics 2011.

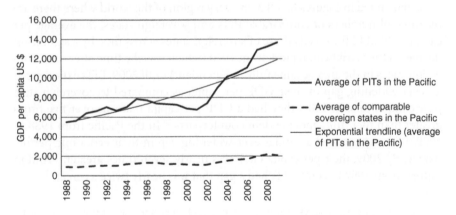

Figure 8.2. Pacific region: Average GDP per capita of partially independent territories as compared to peer competitor sovereign states 1988–2009

Note: The full universe of known Pacific Region cases is included in the time series data except for the PIT of Bougainville for which GDP data were unavailable. Data presented in 2009 US dollars. Data for Northern Mariana Islands (NMI) was limited to the period 2002–07. NMI GDP per capita data for 2008 and 2009 were estimated based on previous GDP per capita growth rate.

Sources: World Bank national accounts data, and OECD National Accounts data files 2011; United Nations Statistic Division 2009; Freedom House Freedom in the World Combined Average Ratings—Independent Countries 2011; Office for UK National Statistics 2011.

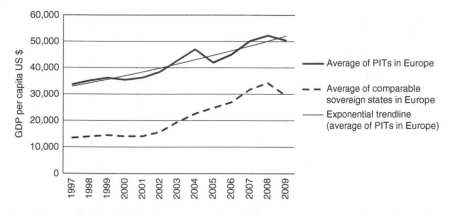

Figure 8.3. Europe region: GDP per capita of peer competitor partially independent territories and sovereign states 1997–2009

Note: The full universe of known Europe Region cases until 2009 is included in the time series data except for the PIT of Gagauzia for which GDP data were unavailable. Data for the Åland Islands, Azores, Madeira, Basque Country, Catalonia, Galicia, and Crimea were limited to the period 2005–09. Data presented in 2009 US dollars.

Sources: World Bank national accounts data, and OECD National Accounts data files 2011; United Nations Statistics Division 2009; Italian National Institute of Statistics 2008; European Commission 2009; Freedom House Freedom in the World Combined Average Ratings—Independent Countries 2011; Ukraine, State Statistic Service of Ukraine 2010; UK, Office for UK National Statistics 2011.

TESTING USING REGRESSION

In addition to the simple matching mentioned above, the advantages of PITs over sovereign states are also confirmed by ordinary least squared (OLS) regression. (Readers who are less interested in regression analysis may skip over this section and the next one in this chapter.) OLS regression is depicted in Models 1–3 in Table 8.1 in which the economic performance (as measured by GDP per capita) of 45 PITs are compared to 185 sovereign states.[23] This approach controls for population size, year of origin, ten different regions, and 34 actual or historical core states (if one existed after 1900). Sovereign states and PITs are directly compared as it pertains

Guernsey, Isle of Man, Jersey, Liechtenstein, Monaco, Northern Ireland, San Marino, Scotland, and Wales, Åland Islands, Aosta Valley, Azores, Basque Country, Catalonia, Crimea, Friuli-Venezia Giulia, Galicia, Madeira, Sardinia, Sicily, and Trentino-South Tyrol. The full universe of comparable European region sovereign states was also included in the time series data (Albania, Croatia, Cyprus, Denmark, Estonia, Finland, Iceland, Ireland, Latvia, Lithuania, Luxembourg, Macedonia, Malta, Moldova, Montenegro, Norway, Slovak Republic, and Slovenia).

[23] This represents the universe of cases of sovereign states and PITs except for the cases of Gagauzia (Moldova) and Bougainville (Papua New Guinea) for which GDP data are not available.

Table 8.1. OLS and CEM Group 1 regression analyses on economic performance of partially independent units versus fully independent units with robust standard errors

Dependent variable: GDP (per capita constant 2005 US$)[a]	(1) in 2008 (OLS)	(2) Growth 1997–08 (OLS)	(3) Growth 1970–08 (OLS)	(4) in 2008 (CEM OLS Group 1)	(5) Growth 1997–08 (CEM OLS Group 1)	(6) Growth 1970–08 (CEM OLS Group 1)
Partial versus full independence (PITs=1 & Sovereign states=0)	19.57***	4.042*	20.32***	35.86***	4.455*	23.57***
	(5.899)	(2.274)	(4.104)	(4.835)	(2.322)	(4.714)
Year of origin^2	-5.78e-05**	-2.90e-05***	-3.37e-05*	-0.000106***	-3.32e-05***	-3.48e-05
	(2.49e-05)	(8.69e-06)	(1.83e-05)	(2.42e-05)	(1.15e-05)	(2.48e-05)
Log (Population in 2008)	-2.518***			-2.289**		
	(0.907)			(1.127)		
Rate of population growth[b] 1997–2008		0.305	-14.17		-2.802	-16.62*
		(3.667)	(9.213)		(4.930)	(9.599)
Constant	264.9**	109.3***	123.7*	429.1***	126.8***	129.1
	(106.0)	(33.06)	(68.36)	(101.5)	(46.51)	(92.09)
Observations	198	191	147	99	95	81
R-squared	0.748	0.564	0.681	0.863	0.632	0.813

Note: *** $p < 0.01$, ** $p < 0.05$, * $p < 0.1$ (two-sided). Robust standard errors in parentheses. Each model includes 9 dummy variables for 10 regions in the world. The 10 regions are as follows: Eastern Europe and post-Soviet Union, the Caribbean, Latin America, North Africa & the Middle East, Sub-Saharan Africa, Western Europe and North America, East Asia, South-East Asia, South Asia, and the Pacific. Each model also includes 33 dummy variables for 34 sovereign states that were recent core states (after 1900) for a colony, protectorate, or PIT. The 34 recent core states are as follows: Australia, Austria, Belgium, Canada, China, Colombia, Denmark, Ethiopia, Finland, France, France-Spain, Germany, India, Iraq, Italy, Japan, Netherlands, New Zealand, Pakistan, Philippines, Portugal, Russia, South Africa, Spain, Sudan, Switzerland, Tanzania, Turkey, Ukraine, UK-US-French-Soviet, UK, US, and Yugoslavia.

[a] The dependent variable (GDP per capita) is divided by 1000 in order to decrease the size of the coefficients.

[b] Rate of population growth was calculated by subtracting the 2008 population from the 1997 population and dividing the difference by the 1997 population.

to their wealth (in terms of GDP per capita) and their economic performance over time (in terms of growth of GDP per capita). Table 8.1 shows that PITs have significantly higher degrees of GDP per capita than sovereign states across time.[24] As Model 1 illustrates, with a significance of 0.001, PITs in 2008 are associated with a GDP per capita that is US$19,570 higher than those of sovereign states. Similarly, Models 2 and 3 illustrate that PITs also have higher degrees of growth overtime.

COMPARING PARTIALLY INDEPENDENT TERRITORY AND SOVEREIGN STATE ECONOMIC PERFORMANCE USING COARSENED EXACT MATCHING

One omission of Models 1–3, is that they do not directly compare PITs and sovereign states that are similar in their characteristics. As already discussed previously in the context of simple matching, one way to better understand if PITs have advantages as compared to sovereign states, which is not reflected by pure linear regression, is if causes of each polity type that are reasonably similar are compared to each other.[25]

In addition to simple matching, a number of modern matching methods can also therefore provide such an approximation.[26] Popular matching methods such as Mahalanobis distance or Propensity Score Matching (PSM) seek to create sameness (or balance) between treatment and control groups.[27] (For the purposes of the present study, PITs are the treatment group and sovereign states are the control group.) Modern matching methods make use of algorithms that place units in different groups (or strata) according to their commonalities. Similar to the simple matching used earlier in this chapter, when units from a treatment and control group are placed into groups that share common features "apples-to-apples" comparisons can then be made.[28] One problem with PSM however is that it often requires users to apply statistical estimators to adjust matched strata *after* the algorithm has completed.[29] As a result, the effort of achieving balance (or sameness) can come at the price of

---

[24] PITs were assigned a dummy variable of 1, while their sovereign state counterparts were assigned a variable of 0.

[25] King et al. 1994.

[26] These methods provide internal validity for the units that are compared rather than external validity representation for all units in the international system.

[27] Iacus et al. 2008.

[28] For more specific details on the PSM algorithm see Iacus et al. 2008.

[29] Iacus et al. 2012, 2.

some statistical bias and model dependence.[30] Models 4–6 in Table 8.1 there-fore turn to yet another matching method, Coarsened Exact Matching (CEM). CEM has the advantage of completing strata selection *before* the algorithm has completed.[31] It also generates weighted estimators (which are discussed below) to account for differing sizes of strata, again without the need for ex post intervention.[32]

Without prejudice to whether they are PITs or sovereign states CEM "coars-ens" data by using an algorithm to assign units with similar values to strata (groups) with such common features. Because CEM places similar units within strata regardless of unit type, some of these strata may only include units from the control group (in this case sovereign states) or units from the treatment group (in this case PITs). These "unmatched" strata (that do not have units from both the treatment and control groups within them) are therefore omitted from further analysis. "Matched" strata (which have both treatment and control units within them) are, however, retained. After CEM matches units, the original uncoarsened data is then restored for further regression analysis. But in order to compensate for matched strata with larger numbers of units, CEM assigns weights in order to create greater balance between strata. These weights together with the units within the different matched strata are articulated in Table 8.2.

The use of CEM's matching algorithm is similar in some respects to the use that millions of internet users make of Google's search algorithm. A Google internet query that puts search terms in quotations benefits from search out-comes that are more similar to the search terms but at the expense of fewer results. Similarly, with CEM the use of more matching variables also yields increasingly similar matches but with fewer results. (Examples of such match-ing variables in the present study include region, population size, or year of emergence.) Hence, in order to benefit from both the advantages of more matches as well as greater similarity among matched units, CEM was applied to two groups of matching variables. Group 1, which is less restrictive, matches sovereign states with PITs with respect to two variables: region and popula-tion size. Hence, as illustrated in Table 8.3, out of forty-five strata, CEM cre-ated eleven groups of comparable PITs and sovereign states with respect to these variables. It is worth reemphasizing that CEM does not force matches. Rather, it looks blindly at matching variables and groups units according to their commonalities irrespective of the fact that they may be a different polity type. Accordingly, it also created thirty-four groups of additional units that were similar, but since none of these strata contained both PITs and sovereign

[30] Iacus et al. 2012, 2.
[31] This method and its associated software was developed by Iacus et al. 2008.
[32] Ho et al. 2007.

Table 8.2. Group 1 Coarsened exact matching of partially independent territories (PITs) and sovereign states (SSs) according to region and log of population

Polity name	Polity type	CEM strata #	CEM weight	Polity name	Polity type	CEM strata #	CEM weight
Crimea	PIT	2	1	Northern Mariana Is.	PIT	7	1
Albania	SS	2	0.16964286	Kiribati	SS	7	4.5238095
Armenia	SS	2	0.16964286	Samoa	SS	7	4.5238095
Bulgaria	SS	2	0.16964286	Tonga	SS	7	4.5238095
Croatia	SS	2	0.16964286	Aruba	PIT	11	1
Georgia	SS	2	0.16964286	Bermuda	PIT	11	1
Kosovo	SS	2	0.16964286	Cayman Islands	PIT	11	1
Kyrgyzstan	SS	2	0.16964286	Netherlands Antilles	PIT	11	1
Latvia	SS	2	0.16964286	Antigua and Barbuda	SS	11	1.3571429
Lithuania	SS	2	0.16964286	Dominica	SS	11	1.3571429
Macedonia	SS	2	0.16964286	Grenada	SS	11	1.3571429
Moldova	SS	2	0.16964286	St Kitts and Nevis	SS	11	1.3571429
Serbia	SS	2	0.16964286	St Lucia	SS	11	1.3571429
Slovakia	SS	2	0.16964286	St Vincent & Gren.	SS	11	1.3571429
Slovenia	SS	2	0.16964286	Sao Tome & Principe	SS	11	1.3571429
Tajikistan	SS	2	0.16964286	Vanuatu	SS	11	1.3571429
Turkmenistan	SS	2	0.16964286	Puerto Rico	PIT	13	1
Cook Islands	PIT	6	1	Jamaica	SS	13	2.7142857
Palau	PIT	6	1	Kurdistan	PIT	20	1
Nauru	SS	6	2.7142857	Israel	SS	20	0.3877551
Tuvalu	SS	6	2.7142857	Jordan	SS	20	0.3877551
French Polynesia	PIT	7	1	Kuwait	SS	20	0.3877551
Marshall Islands	PIT	7	1	Lebanon	SS	20	0.3877551
Micronesia	PIT	7	1	Libya	SS	20	0.3877551
New Caledonia	PIT	7	1	Oman	SS	20	0.3877551
Northern Mariana Is.	PIT	7	1	United Arab Emirates	SS	20	0.3877551

(Continued)

Table 8.2. (Continued)

Polity name	Polity type	CEM strata #	CEM weight	Polity name	Polity type	CEM strata #	CEM weight
Zanzibar	PIT	24	1	Somalia	SS	26	0.12337662
Cape Verde	SS	24	0.33928571	Sudan	SS	26	0.12337662
Comoros	SS	24	0.33928571	Tanzania	SS	26	0.12337662
Djibouti	SS	24	0.33928571	Uganda	SS	26	0.12337662
Equatorial Guin.	SS	24	0.33928571	Zambia	SS	26	0.12337662
Gabon	SS	24	0.33928571	Zimbabwe	SS	26	0.12337662
Guinea-Bissau	SS	24	0.33928571	Friuli-Ven. Giulia	PIT	31	1
Mauritius	SS	24	0.33928571	Trentino-S. Tyrol	PIT	31	1
Swaziland	SS	24	0.33928571	Iceland	SS	31	1.8095238
Southern Sudan	PIT	26	1	Luxembourg	SS	31	1.8095238
Angola	SS	26	0.12337662	Malta	SS	31	1.8095238
Benin	SS	26	0.12337662	Catalonia	PIT	32	1
Burkina Faso	SS	26	0.12337662	Galicia	PIT	32	1
Cameroon	SS	26	0.12337662	Northern Ireland	PIT	32	1
Chad	SS	26	0.12337662	Basque Country	PIT	32	1
Côte d'Ivoire	SS	26	0.12337662	Sardinia	PIT	32	1
Ghana	SS	26	0.12337662	Scotland	PIT	32	1
Guinea	SS	26	0.12337662	Sicily	PIT	32	1
Kenya	SS	26	0.12337662	Wales	PIT	32	1
Madagascar	SS	26	0.12337662	Denmark	SS	32	4.3428571
Malawi	SS	26	0.12337662	Finland	SS	32	4.3428571
Mali	SS	26	0.12337662	Ireland	SS	32	4.3428571
Mozambique	SS	26	0.12337662	Norway	SS	32	4.3428571
Niger	SS	26	0.12337662	Switzerland	SS	32	4.3428571
Rwanda	SS	26	0.12337662	Mindanao	PIT	36	1
				Hong Kong	PIT	36	1
				Mongolia	SS	36	5.4285714

Table 8.3. Group 1 Coarsened exact matching according to region and log of 2008 population summary

	CEM strata	Sovereign states	Partially independent territories
All	45	185	45
Matched	11	76	28
Unmatched	34	109	17

Table 8.4. Group 2 Coarsened exact matching summary according to region, log of 2008 population, and square of year of origin

	CEM strata	Sovereign states	Partially independent territories
All	87	185	45
Matched	10	27	17
Unmatched	77	158	28

states within them, they are omitted from further analysis. In total, CEM rejected 109 sovereign states and seventeen PITs because matches were not found between different polity types for the Group 1 variables. The net result are groups of PITs and sovereign states that are very similar with respect to region and population size.

OLS regression was then repeated for these matched units in Models 4–6 using the same control variables as Models 1–3 (population size, region, recent core state, year of origin, and rate of population growth) to determine the association of PITs with higher levels of GDP per capita as compared to sovereign states. The outcome of these new regressions in CEM Group 1 Models 4–6 (as illustrated in Table 8.6) has greater significance than Models 1–3. For instance, in 2008 PITs are associated with a GDP per capita that is US$35,860 higher than those of sovereign states with a significance of 0.000 (as compared to 0.001 with pure OLS regression).[33]

In order to further reinforce these results a second group was created, Group 2, which is more restrictive than Group 1 since it matches sovereign states with PITs with respect to three (rather than just two) matching

---

[33] It may be useful to note that although the CEM regressions provide fewer observations, they account for higher levels of variance as depicted by their R-squared. Model 3 in Table 8.1, for example, has 147 observations and accounts for 68% of variance, while the CEM analysis of Model 6 has just 81 observations but accounts for 81% of variance.

variables: region, population, and year of emergence. As illustrated in Table 8.4, out of eighty-seven strata, CEM created ten groups of comparable PITs and sovereign states with respect to these variables. In total, CEM rejected 158 sovereign states and twenty-eight PITs because matches were not found for the Group 2 variables. The matched twenty-seven sovereign states and seventeen PITs are illustrated in Table 8.5. When OLS regression was then applied to Group 2 in Table 8.6 using the same control variables as Models 1–6, the results have even greater significance than the other comparable models. For instance, Models 2 and 5 (in Table 8.1), and Model 8 (in Table 8.5) each assess GDP growth from 1997 to 2008. Model 8, which assesses Group 2 units, however, has a significance that is at 0.000 rather than 0.078 for Model 2 (which used regular OLS) and 0.059 for Model 5 (which applied CEM OLS to Group 1). Hence, even with apples-to-apples comparison while controlling for population, region, year of origin, and recent core state, PITs are associated with a GDP per capita that is significantly higher than sovereign states.

ADDRESSING THE ENDOGENEITY CRITIQUE
AND OTHER COUNTERARGUMENTS

One may, however, wonder whether the causal relationship is in fact reversed (social scientists call a causal relationship that is the opposite of what one claims an endogeneity problem).[34] So in this case, rather than partial independence tending to generate greater degrees of advantages over sovereign states (such as wealth) as is claimed here, perhaps the opposite is true: economic advantages may in fact be causing PITs to emerge. According to such a view, overawing economic power from the PIT may in fact impel potential core states to adopt partially independent unions. There are, however, four reasons why this endogeneity critique arguably does not affect the causal arguments made here.

First, even if in isolated cases, such as Hong Kong, high degrees of per capita PIT wealth is associated with safeguarding an autonomous status, this does not necessarily disconfirm the argument here that core–PIT unions tend to cause increased wealth. Both assertions can coexist without one disconfirming the other. Hong Kong's GDP per capita is over twelve times the size of that of China and manifests itself in manufacturing, financial, and managerial services that are arguably critical for China's economy.[35] Preexisting wealth does not, however, necessarily hinder the autonomous self-rule, specialization,

---

[34] On endogeneity problems see King et al. 1994.
[35] Rezvani 2012.

Table 8.5 Group 2 Coarsened exact matching of partially independent territories (PITs) and sovereign states (SSs) according to region, log of population, and square of year of origin

Polity name	Polity type	CEM strata #	CEM weight	Polity name	Polity type	CEM strata #	CEM weight
Crimea	PIT	5	1	Bermuda	PIT	20	1
Armenia	SS	5	0.13235294	Cayman Islands	PIT	20	1
Croatia	SS	5	0.13235294	Netherlands Antilles	PIT	20	1
Georgia	SS	5	0.13235294	Grenada	SS	20	2.3823529
Kosovo	SS	5	0.13235294	Sao Tome & Prin.	SS	20	2.3823529
Kyrgyzstan	SS	5	0.13235294	Aruba	PIT	21	1
Latvia	SS	5	0.13235294	Antigua & Barbuda	SS	21	0.26470588
Lithuania	SS	5	0.13235294	Dominica	SS	21	0.26470588
Macedonia	SS	5	0.13235294	St. Kitts and Nevis	SS	21	0.26470588
Moldova	SS	5	0.13235294	St. Lucia	SS	21	0.26470588
Slovenia	SS	5	0.13235294	St. Vincent & Gren.	SS	21	0.26470588
Tajikistan	SS	5	0.13235294	Vanuatu	SS	21	0.26470588
Turkmenistan	SS	5	0.13235294	Puerto Rico	PIT	23	1
Cook Islands	PIT	12	1	Jamaica	SS	23	1.5882353
Nauru	SS	12	1.5882353	Zanzibar	PIT	42	1
Palau	PIT	13	1	Djibouti	SS	42	1.5882353
Tuvalu	SS	13	1.5882353	Southern Sudan	PIT	47	1
French Polynesia	PIT	15	1	Zimbabwe	SS	47	1.5882353
Marshall Islands	PIT	15	1	Friuli-Venezia Giulia	PIT	62	1
Micronesia	PIT	15	1	Trentino-S. Tyrol	PIT	62	1
New Caledonia	PIT	15	1	Malta	SS	62	3.1764706
Northern Mariana Is.	PIT	15	1				
Kiribati	SS	15	7.941177				

Table 8.6. CEM Group 2 regression analyses on economic performance of partially independent units versus fully independent units with robust standard errors

Independent units with robust standard errors	(7)	(8)	(9)
Dependent Variable: GDP (per capita constant 2005 US\$)[a]	in 2008 (CEM OLS Group 2)	Growth 1997–08 (CEM OLS Group 2)	Growth 1970–08 (CEM OLS Group 2)
Partial versus full independence (PITs=1 & sovereign states=0)	52.32***	10.46***	26.30***
	(3.920)	(2.370)	(2.807)
Year of origin^2	–9.67e-05**	–3.47e-06	–2.28e-06
	(3.95e-05)	(2.12e-05)	(2.50e-05)
Log (population in 2008)	–3.298***		
	(0.960)		
Rate of population growth^b		–13.67**	7.864
from 1997–2008		(5.738)	(6.945)
Constant	382.5**	13.37	–4.239
	(164.0)	(85.82)	(97.17)
Observations	44	41	36
R^2	0.936	0.749	0.921

Note: *** $p < 0.01$, ** $p < 0.05$, * $p < 0.1$ (two-sided). Robust standard errors in parentheses. Each model includes 9 dummy variables for 10 regions in the world. The 10 regions are as follows: Eastern Europe and post Soviet Union, the Caribbean, Latin America, North Africa & the Middle East, Sub-Saharan Africa, Western Europe and North America, East Asia, South-East Asia, South Asia, and the Pacific. Each model also includes 33 dummy variables for 34 sovereign states that were recent core states (after 1900) for a colony, protectorate, or PIT. The 34 recent core states are as follows: Australia, Austria, Belgium, Canada, China, Colombia, Denmark, Ethiopia, Finland, France, France-Spain, Germany, India, Iraq, Italy, Japan, Netherlands, New Zealand, Pakistan, Philippines, Portugal, Russia, South Africa, Spain, Sudan, Switzerland, Tanzania, Turkey, Ukraine, UK-US-French-Soviet, UK, UN, US, and Yugoslavia.

^{a} The dependent variable (GDP per capita) is divided by 1000 in order to decrease the size of the coefficients.

^{b} Rate of population growth was calculated by subtracting the 2008 population from the 1997 population and dividing the difference by the 1997 population.

economies of scale, core state investments, and specialized resources that are furnished by core–PIT unions to generate further wealth. As all entrepreneurs know, preexisting capital and wealth can be conducive to the creation of even more of it, especially when it is channeled through economic and political institutions that facilitate such processes. Hong Kong was relatively wealthy in 1997 at the outset of its arrangement with China (with a GDP per capita of about US\$22,000), and thanks to its PIT union it is even wealthier more than a decade later (with a GDP per capita of about US\$30,000 in 2008).[36] Unlike comparable nearby sovereign states, like Singapore, its PIT

[36] United Nations Statistics Division 2009.

arrangement has delivered preferential treatment on trade issues with the mainland, massive Chinese expenditures on defense and infrastructure, Central Government proxy diplomatic defense of the territory, and helpful mandates (like maintaining a balanced budget) that have been guaranteed to Hong Kong in its Basic Law.[37]

Second, although in isolated cases (such as Hong Kong) PIT wealth per capita can play a role in the autonomous powers of a territory, when one examines the full universe of cases, however, such circumstances are not predominant. At the other extreme, a number of core states have much higher per capita GDPs than their associated PITs. For example, America's per capita GDP is fifteen times the size of that of the Marshall Islands, which benefits from core state financial transfers. (It may be instructive to note that the GDP per capita of the Marshall Islands of US$2,732 is, nevertheless, about twice the size of the comparable Pacific sovereign state of Kiribati [with a GDP per capita of US$1,161].) Indeed, far from PITs generally having a higher per capita GDP (which might allegedly facilitate their autonomous status), in approximately 55% of core–PIT relationships the opposite is true: core states have a higher GDP per capita than the associated PIT. Furthermore, the average PIT has a GDP per capita of US$32,506 which is nearly identical to the mean of core states (US$31,951). Hence, when the full universe of cases is examined, there is little evidence that wealth (as measured by overawing degrees of GDP per capita) facilitates or sustains the autonomous status of PITs.

Third, if it was the case that wealth creates partial independence, one could also conclude that relative poverty would not deliver such an outcome. There are, however, a wide range of PITs that have been significantly poorer than their associated core state. The Cook Island's GDP per capita around the time of the emergence of its PIT status was just US$4,797 in 1970 as compared to its associated core state, New Zealand, which had a GDP per capita of US$17,009.[38] Similarly, Mindanao's 1997 GDP per capita was just US$307 as compared to its associated core state, the Philippines, which had a GDP per capita of US$1,062. As indicated above, while there are indeed cases in which PITs have a larger GDP per capita when compared to their associated core state, the opposite is also very common.

Fourth, while PITs play a pivotal role in the world's financial system and could potentially exercise overawing economic power over many of the sovereign states in the world, in every case their GDP is signficantly smaller than their associated core state. If the endogeneity critique were true, we might expect to see territories (which eventually become PITs) with relatively large economies as compared to the core state. In terms of

---

[37] Rezvani 2012.   [38] United Nations Statistical Division 2009.

absolute wealth as measured by GDP, it can, however, safely be said that all core states have economies that far outstrip the size of the territories that end up as partially independent polities. The median core state GDP is 120 times the size of the PIT with which it is associated.[39] Therefore, here again, the use of a territory's overawing wealth (as measured by GDP) as a means of achieving a status as a partially independent polity can therefore be disconfirmed by the evidence. Indeed, as the next chapter illustrates, the opposite situation appears to be the case: rather than relatively high degrees of PIT GDP facilitating their emergence, such high degrees of GDP (as compared to the core state) are associated with partially independent unions coming to an end.

When faced with the more successful economic performance of PITs, someone may also contend that their performance is inevitable, based on their connection with a larger and more economically powerful core state. Such critics may argue that irrespective of a polity's partially independent status, if a core state is wealthy it necessarily follows that the territories with which they are associated will also automatically have higher degrees of wealth. Such a view can, however, be amply disconfirmed by examining the dismal historic record of colonies and sham federacies that have been associated with powerful and prosperous core states.[40] Far from association automatically yielding high degrees of wealth, the history of imperialism shows that association is often a recipe for exploitation and a one-sided relationship which mostly benefits the core state.

Moreover, simple matching data from the Pacific group of polities allowed a rare opportunity to compare the economic performance of PITs to colonies. Unlike other regions, data from the Pacific region is available which includes the performance of territories long before their partially independent status (while they were colonies), as well as after they became PITs. The total increase of GDP per capita of these territories was calculated from 1970 to 2009 (the average increase was US$11,961). The yearly contribution to this increased GDP was then calculated for every year these territories were colonies and for every year they were PITs. The average yearly rate of contribution to the overall GDP per capita increase was then calculated for each polity type (colonies and PITs). Ultimately, the average yearly share of contributions to GDP per capita increase was 22% higher when these

---

[39]　Most of the data taken for this statistic are derived from the World Bank's World Development Indicator 2008.

[40]　For works which assess such factors as they relate to empire–colony relations see Cooley 2005; Motyl 1999b; Peattie 1984.

territories were PITs compared to when they were colonies. This provides some evidence to reinforce the advantages of a PIT status as compared to full or decentralized control.[41]

COMPARING DEMOGRAPHICALLY SIMILAR PARTIALLY INDEPENDENT TERRITORIES AND SOVEREIGN STATES ON SECURITY PERFORMANCE

Building on notions that sovereign states are supposedly the best and most secure of all institutional forms is the sizable literature on state formation.[42] As mentioned in the last chapter, this literature elaborates upon the military and administrative virtues of modern states, which helped them beat out other competing political and constitutional alternatives, such as fiefdoms, city-states, city-leagues, and loosely configured empires before the seventeenth century.[43] Paradoxically, when scholars and policy leaders attempt to resolve the grave international security threats created by the world's weak and failed states, rather than considering the possibility of alternatives other than the sovereign state, many remain undeterred in an attempt to engage in further state building and strengthening.[44] Still others have indeed compared the relative security merits of "autonomous regions" to sovereign states but have concluded that autonomous arrangements provide lower degrees of security than full independence.[45] Such studies, however, make little distinction between nominal autonomous arrangements that have no credible protections of their powers and autonomous arrangements where such guarantees exist.[46] As distinct

---

[41] The comparison of individual territories to themselves, albeit at different times, controls for many other factors that may create differences in the outcome.

[42] On the emergence of territorial states as distinct from other entities, including colonies, see Almond 1988; Anderson 1974; Ruggie 1993, 139–74; Skocpol 1985; Spruyt 1994a, 527–57; 1994b; Strayer 1970; Strayer and Munro 1959; Tilly 1990.

[43] On such advantages of sovereign states see especially Spruyt 1994b and Tilly 1990.

[44] See for example, Commission on Weak States and US National Security 2004; Crocker 2003, 32–44; Fukuyama 2004; Hamre and Sullivan 2002, 85–96; Krasner and Pascual 2005, 153–63; Patrick 2006, 27–53; Rice 2003; and Rotberg 2004–05, 71–81.

[45] See Chapman and Roeder 2007, 677–90. For similar proponents of full independence see Downes 2001, 62; Kaufmann 1998, 120–156; Posen 1993a, 28.

[46] Among the small sample of eight autonomous arrangements that Chapman and Roeder use to draw their conclusions in favor of full independence against what they describe as autonomous regions, only two (Sudan–Southern Region, and UK–Northern Ireland) have powers that are constitutionally guaranteed by a core state. Chapman and Roeder 2007, 678. In spite of their claim that cases of "autonomy" are regions that have been granted "self rule" and "many decision

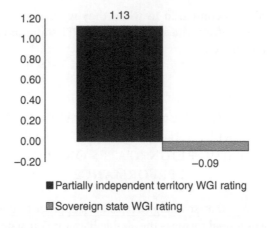

Figure 8.4. Worldwide 2010 WGI security ratings for sovereign states and partially independent territories
Source: Kauffmann et al. 2011.

from the aforementioned views, which emphasize the ascendance of sovereign states as the most secure political and constitutional organizational form, partially independent territories arguably exist as a more secure alternative to full independence.[47]

Just as with data on economic performance, PIT security advantages over sovereign states may appear to be self-evident to some observers. Indeed, as Figure 8.4 shows, a cursory examination of data from the Worldwide Governance Indicator in its "Political Stability and Absence of Violence/Terrorism" sub-index reinforces such a view. The Worldwide Governance Indicators (WGI) project is one of the most widely used assessments of governance, with indicators for 212 states and territories based on the perceptions of governance from thirty-five data sources from thirty-two different academic and policy-oriented organizations.[48] The WGI Political Stability and Absence of Violence/Terrorism sub-index (referred to here as the WGI

rights" the other cases that they use (Burma–Karen, China–Tibet, India–Kashmir, Israel–Palestine, Pakistan–Baluchistan, and Russia–Chechnya) are deprived of any discernible credibility mechanism over the powers that have been allocated to them. Such polities are referred to here as sham federacies.

[47] This finding, if true, contributes to the growing literature on neo-medievalism, which emphasizes the emergence of overlapping jurisdictions akin to those that existed before the emergence of the modern state system in the sixteenth and seventeenth centuries. On neo-medievalism see Barkin and Cronin 1994, 107–30; Cerny 1998, 36–64; Deibert 1997, 167–92; Lipschutz 1992, 389–420; Wæver 1996, 107–28; 1997, 321–63; and Zielonka 2001, 507–36. On one of the first to suggest the emergence of neo-medieval political forms see Bull 1977, 254–76.

[48] Kauffmann et al. 2011.

Security Index) shows that the 2010 average security estimate of sovereign states is –0.9. A security rating of –0.9 is similar to Rwanda's ranking. In this sense, Rwanda's level of security is the actual normal condition of sovereign states. This compares to the average for PITs (which includes data for approximately one-third of PITs worldwide) of about 1.12. A security rating of 1.12 is slightly better than Sweden and Austria's ranking.

Just as with economic performance issues, however, critics may object that such an approach does not take into account other factors that may in fact be more responsible for the observed outcomes. An additional objection is that while the WGI data on sovereign states includes 100% of cases, the data on PITs includes just 31% of cases. Such a sample may therefore not be sufficiently representative. Nevertheless, the association between partial independence and greater levels of security is arguably still highly suggestive. Even if missing PITs were added to the WGI Security Index (territories like Scotland, Zanzibar, or French Polynesia), the likelihood that they would cause the PIT average score to decline to the level of Rwanda is arguably low.

Similar to the first section that made use of simple matching, these concerns are also addressed by examining WGI data of similar PITs and sovereign states over time with respect to well-known explanations for political and economic stability such as population size, geographic region, and regime type. Although just 31% of PITs are represented in the WGI security sub-index (and only 13% are represented in the European group), nevertheless, 71% of Caribbean group PITs and 85% of Pacific group PITs are included in the WGI data.[49] An examination of the Pacific and Caribbean groups therefore allows for degrees of similarity of comparison together with higher degrees of representation.

Figure 8.5 displays regional results from comparable polities from 2010. It is worth emphasizing that the worldwide comparison in Figure 8.5 compares worldwide PITs and sovereign states that are similar according to the population size, geographic, and freedom ratings discussed here (which explains the higher overall sovereign state security rating as compared to Figure 8.4). Each of the groupings depicted in Figure 8.5 shows that PITs have a higher rating than sovereign states. More confidence should however be put on results from the Caribbean and Pacific regional groups because of their high degree of PIT representation. In the Pacific group, while the PIT score is only slightly larger than the sovereign state score, this is largely because of

---

[49] The WGI security sub-index includes the following PITs: Liechtenstein, Monaco, and San Marino in the European Group; Cook Islands, Marshall Islands, Micronesia, New Caledonia, Niue, and Palau in the Pacific Group; and Aruba, Bermuda, Cayman Islands, Netherlands Antilles (Curaçao & Sint Maarten), and Puerto Rico in the Caribbean Group.

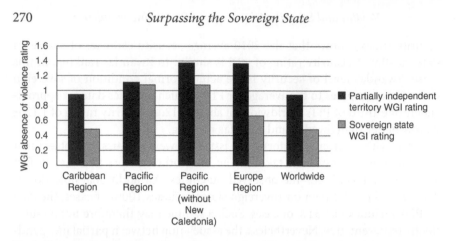

Figure 8.5. 2010 Security ratings among comparable partially independent territories and sovereign states

Source: Kauffmann et al. 2011.

the inclusion of the PIT of New Caledonia. While the WGI score of –0.19 for New Caledonia is low relative to other PITs, this number does not convey the widely held view that the territory's level of violence has largely stabilized as compared to the widespread violence and civil unrest that prevailed before the 1998 Matignon Accord, which brought into being New Caledonia's PIT.[50] When New Caledonia is removed from the PIT data, the PIT rating in the Pacific increases by 23% and depicts a significant advantage over other Pacific sovereign states. These Pacific PITs have a rating of 1.37, which is similar to Finland (one of the world's safest states). Although Pacific sovereign states have a lower average rating of 1.08, it still nevertheless reflects relative security since it is similar to politically stable states such as Austria or Qatar. In spite of this, it is worth noting that the 0.3 advantage of Pacific PITs over Pacific sovereign states is nevertheless significant. Within the WGI index such an advantage can make the difference between the security rating of Germany (0.81) and Mongolia (0.5) or Bulgaria (0.37) and Malawi (0.08). With regard to comparable PITs and sovereign states in the Caribbean, PIT advantages are even more striking. PITs have a rating that is double the average estimate of sovereign states. Their average score of 0.947 is similar to Canada's score of 0.94, while the Caribbean sovereign state score of 0.48 is similar to the 0.47 score of Zambia or 0.46 for Kazakhstan.

Time series data also reflect the aforementioned findings. Unlike other regions, the Caribbean group of comparable PITs and sovereign states had

---

[50] See for example Chappell 1999.

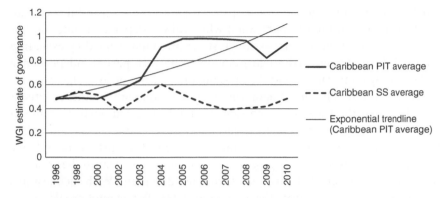

Figure 8.6. Caribbean Region: 1996–2010 WGI political stability and absence of violence/terrorism among comparable partially independent territories and sovereign states

Source: Kauffmann et al. 2011.

WGI security rating time series data for all cases between 1996 and 2010. As Figure 8.6 indicates, during this period PITs were increasing their average rating overtime while the average rating of sovereign states was decreasing.

Still other critics may claim that the greater security of PITs has less to do with its institutional structure and more to do with its agreement with a core state to mutually live together in peace. As discussed in Chapter 2 in the context of the relational contracting literature, the response here is that a PIT's agreement with a core state to live in peace and to share some responsibilities while dividing others is the essence of the institutional structure. Partially independent arrangements possess this feature while many other polities (such as fully independent states, colonies, sham federacies, and de facto states) do not. An effort to somehow distinguish the institutional structure of a PIT from the defining aspects of its arrangement with a core state is not possible.

The more frequent correlation between sovereign states and conflict should not be surprising. This is especially true with respect to scholars who have long associated sovereign statehood with violence for the purposes of state building. "War makes states," Charles Tilly tells us.[51] For sovereign states, he says, the objective is to "check or overcome their competitors and thus to enjoy the advantages of power within a secure or expanding territory."[52] With partially independent arrangements, by contrast, such a formula is held in abeyance. Distinct groups credibly agree to cooperate and pool their resources and decision-making capability rather than engage in violence.

---

[51] Tilly 1985, 169–91.   [52] Tilly 1985, 169–91.

Partially independent territories are protected by a more powerful core state (and therefore tend not to fight wars) while fully independent states do not have such protection. Where sovereign states are often defined by excluding national distinctiveness (through monopoly control), partial independence is defined by compromise and the division and sharing of sovereign power.[53] They have a mutually agreed upon cooperative union with another sovereign state in which the leaders of both sides have taken serious steps to come to terms with any preexisting distrust and nationalistic differences. And unlike historic colonies, which were at the mercy of the self-interest of the military might of their core state, PITs possess credible guarantees against the arbitrary usurpation of powers that have been surrendered to them. With such features PITs furnish levels of security that sovereign states often cannot provide.

THE ROLE OF CATACLYSMIC EVENTS AND THE EMERGENCE OF PARTIAL INDEPENDENCE

The advantages of PITs seem to be a critical factor in attracting core states and territories toward accepting divisions of sovereignty. Unfortunately, however, such advantages alone are often not enough to bring into being such an arrangement. Although PITs are emerging at a relatively faster rate than sovereign states, one could speculate that if their advantages were the only critical factor for their emergence, many more of them should also come into being. We should be seeing many more diads of large sovereign states dividing and sharing powers with smaller and weaker sovereign states that have opted to become partially independent. While there are many examples of territories choosing partial independence over full independence, there are however virtually no examples of sovereign states becoming partially independent.[54] Furthermore, there are also many core states that are linked with territories in which both sides could greatly benefit from the economic, security, and self-determination advantages of a partially independent union. This is particularly the case with core states that are linked with sham federacies and yet in many cases such unions have also not come into being. Hence, another factor is necessary besides polity advantages to explain the emergence of these arrangements.

---

[53] On the challenges that many sovereign states face with respect to maintaining self-rule see Jackson 1990.

[54] Partial exceptions to this are the many sovereign states within Europe that have chosen to divide and share powers within the EU. These are, however, not examples of PITs.

As discussed in Chapter 2, the explanation offered here builds upon the concept of punctuated equilibrium from biology. Namely, in addition to selection advantages of PITs, they also tend to emerge because of cataclysmic events. In other words, political leaders may be aware of the advantages of the division of sovereignty with a territory. It may make sense to them. Such logic alone is, however, not enough. Entrenched norms against such divisions of sovereignty (like a well-established national-territorial geographic reference) and powerful vested interests prevent the union. It is not enough that PITs are better than sovereign states in important ways; conditions must also be ripe to wipe away such norms and vested interests. Cataclysmic events, however, have the ability to "reset" a core state's normative perceptions, creating a window of opportunity for a cost–benefit analysis in which different alternatives are more objectively compared in light of their advantages and disadvantages. Under such circumstances PITs have a much stronger chance of coming into being. Indeed, virtually all partially independent unions are associated with the presence of cataclysmic events that set the stage for their emergence.

Nationalistic secession, regime change, and/or systemic change and adaption are examples of such forms of cataclysmic conditions. Although there is no room here for a full qualitative examination of such events, some brief examples will be offered in what follows. With regard to sovereign state fragmentation through nationalistic secession, Britain's eighteenth-century devastating loss of the Thirteen American Colonies set the stage for a new approach toward Canada amidst its revolts in 1837, which allowed for the rise of the British Dominions as well as later day PITs. France's loss of empire including its inability to retain Algeria and its sham federacy failures in Indochina helped give rise to more serious commitments to New Caledonia and French Polynesia. Denmark's loss of Iceland after 1918 (and formally in 1944) underscored the need for renewed commitments to prevent the possible secession of Greenland and the Faroe Islands.[55] The Netherlands' loss of the Dutch Antilles helped produce a greater willingness for associated PITs in the Caribbean. And Moldova's war with the nationalistically distinct territory of Transnistria helped give rise to a PIT with Gaugazia. Each of these cases arguably provided a powerful impetus for allowing associated territories to become PITs. The wars, lost resources, and international embarrassment that are often associated

---

[55] As Gunnar Karlsson (2003) points out, Iceland's powers of "home rule" were formally made part of Denmark's constitution in 1915 after many years of more or less centralized rule, which incited and radicalized local desires for secession. He points out that after this "constitutional issue had been settled, most Icelandic politics seem to have been content to let the big questions of Iceland's status within the kingdom rest for the time being." Just a few years later in December 1918, however, the parliaments of Denmark and Iceland mutually ratified a treaty in which Iceland was put on a path toward full independence.

with such territorial fragmentation induces a new willingness for compromise and divisions of sovereignty that would prevent such negative repercussions in the future.

Further forms of cataclysmic events that also help wipe away norms that would prevent a division of sovereignty come in the form of a revolutionary regime change. Examples include Finland with its 1918 independence from Russia,[56] which set the stage for Finland's union with the Åland Islands in 1921. Portugal's 1974 military coup also allowed for the PIT status of the Azores and Madeira in the same year.[57] Spain's transition to democracy after 1975 cleared the way for its arrangements with Catalonia, the Basque Country, and Galicia. Ukraine's 1991 independence from Russia set the stage for the negotiations that led to Crimea's PIT status. Revolutionary change also occurred with Hong Kong in its 1997 transition from British to Chinese sovereignty. And Iraq's change of regime after America's March 2003 invasion helped give rise to the Kurdish PIT arrangement. The "clean slate" of such revolutionary events allows leaders to have a fresh and renewed examination of the costs and benefits of divisions of sovereignty with fewer obstacles.

Even seemingly anomalous PITs (such as San Marino, Liechtenstein, Monaco, the Isle of Man, Jersey, and Guernsey) which are the unassimilated feudal remnants of the pre-modern state system can be explained within such a framework. Just as some of the small flying dinosaurs (the birds), which were aided by their advantages of size and flight, managed to survive the cataclysm that wiped out other dinosaur species, these territories managed to survive the wars and waxing and waning of sovereign states in Europe because of their advantages of size and adaptability in which they transformed their feudal status into formalized divisions of power with nearby core states.

THE SUGGESTIVE CASE OF THE NETHERLANDS AND ITS OVERSEAS TERRITORIES

In addition to some of the more specific examples that have been given of the role played by cataclysmic events (as with the cases of Kurdistan, the emergence of the British Dominions, and Puerto Rico), one set of cases that illustrate many of the empirical claims of this chapter are the relations between the Netherlands and its overseas territories. Comparing the PITs that have been associated with the Netherlands offers a glimpse into one of the only

---

[56] Barros 1968, 249–251.   [57] Portugal, Constitution of Portugal 1974, Article 288.

existing examples of core–PIT relations of demographically similar territories that nevertheless chose different status options. In addition to sharing a common core state, the PITs that have been associated with the Netherlands share demographic similarities, such as a similar geographic region and population size. Among the PITs associated with the Netherlands, Aruba and the Netherlands Antilles (which after 2010 split into the two distinct PITs of Curaçao and Sint Maarten) decided to maintain their status as PITs. In 1975, however, Suriname decided to quit its PIT status and embark upon full independence. These cases are selected because they offer a rare glimpse into the performance of PITs as compared to fully independent states with similar conditions. Before examining some economic data after Suriname's full secession as it compares to the Netherlands Antilles and Aruba, this brief section will begin by summarizing the conditions for the emergence of these arrangements.

Sovereign states do not have a tendency to happily hand over part of their sovereignty to distinct populations out of benevolence. Nor do they do it purely for the more practical economic and security advantages that the creation of a PIT can bring. As described previously, counterveiling norms, such as vested political interests, powerful lobbies, and entrenched national ideologies usually bar the way. Dramatic events are usually required to reorder interests, which pave the way for the emergence of a PIT. As with a significant number of other partially independent arrangements (such as PITs associated with the UK and France) disastrous conflict with nationalistically distinct populations elsewhere in the empire often provides a powerful impetus for a partially independent arrangement.

In the case of the Netherlands, this dramatic event occurred with its colony, the Dutch West Indies, which it had controlled to various degrees since the sixteenth century. The Netherlands viewed its colonies as important to its international prestige and valued their vast natural resources.[58] In the midst of World War II, however, the Japanese took control of the Dutch West Indies in 1942. After the war, when the Netherlands attempted to reassert control, they encountered ferocious and violent opposition from local nationalists. The Dutch then expended thousands of lives and hundreds of millions of dollars in a vain attempt to subdue the growing insurgency in this colony, which in 1940 had a population of about 70 million as compared to the core state's population of 9 million.[59] Amidst the ensuing destruction and mass killing, widespread international condemnation and domestic economic concerns increasingly weighed on the Netherlands. Among other things, members of the US Congress expressed their dismay that US Marshall Fund

[58] Oostindie 2006, 614.   [59] Oostindie 2006, 614.

money—meant to help with post-World War II reconstruction—was being diverted to Dutch wars of imperialism in Asia.[60] In the midst of these pressures, Dutch leaders experimented with a variety of structural alternatives short of allowing full secession. They promised good governance for the colony, a federation, and made vague promises of autonomy. Such proposals, however, failed to persuade local leaders and populations.

Amidst the failure of such proposals, the core state also made a bid to use institutional means to convince not just the Dutch West Indies, but also two colonies in the Caribbean, Suriname and the Netherlands Antilles, to also not secede. They drew up a new constitution, which promised that the arrangement with them could only be changed through mutual agreement, which effectively made each of these polities into PITs. In the wake of previous broken promises for good governance, the Dutch West Indies rejected this offer. The Netherlands Antilles and Suriname however agreed to its terms, which were ultimately enshrined in the 1954 Charter of the Kingdom of the Netherlands. Since that time, the Netherlands Antilles has maintained its arrangement with the Netherlands but with a number of changes. In 1986, Aruba broke away to become a separate PIT in its own right. Similarly in 2010, the Netherlands Antilles itself split up into separate PITs, Curaçao and Sint Maarten. These splits reflect the desires of local leaders for increasingly specialized arrangements that better address their local interests as opposed to a one-size-fits-all arrangement that is typical among federations.

A major change, however, came in 1975 with the secession of Suriname into full independence. The 1975 decision occurred with great opposition in Suriname after a pro-independence party was elected and the local parliament voted in favor of secession by a slim majority of just one vote. The local population, which was believed by many to mainly oppose independence, was not invited to offer its opinion in a referendum. In accordance with the 1954 Charter, the Netherlands then assented to the territory's full secession. In a parting act of generosity, the erstwhile core state provided a grant of 3.5 billion Dutch guilders of developmental aid. But such aid alone was not enough to prevent Suriname's relative decline.

After quitting its partial independence in favor of full independence, its overall economic aid from the Netherlands became significantly curtailed. Direct advice and political collaboration from the core state declined. The territory had to foot the bill for its own internal security. It succumbed to military dictatorship in the 1980s. And in the decades since its independence, Suriname went from a GDP per capita and security situation that was roughly equivalent to the Netherlands Antilles, to become one of the poorest states in the region. Furthermore, reflecting Puerto Rico's relations with the US, The

---

[60] Oostindie 2006, 614.

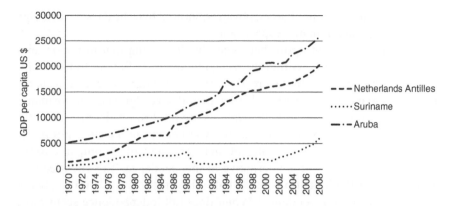

Figure 8.7. Average GDP per capita of the Netherlands Antilles and Aruba compared with Suriname 1970–2009

Sources: World Bank national accounts data, and OECD National Accounts data files 2011; United Nations Statistic Division 2009.

Hague concluded in the 1990s that for reasons of constitutional morality (convention) unilaterally dissolving its union with the PIT remnants of its empire is a virtual impossibility.[61] The decline of Suriname in turn created a "chilling effect" among other PITs in the region on the disastrous effects that full independence can have.[62]

CONCLUSION

The view here is that the outcomes illustrated in this chapter should seem more obvious than some observers have imagined. When a polity has its own defensible autonomous powers and is furnished with a wide range of public goods and assistance from a powerful core state, of course it is going to have significant economic and security advantages over similarly situated polities that do not have such benefits. Unfortunately, international relations realists as well as some minority populations do not see things this way. To them, the sovereign state is the ultimate institutional achievement because of its history of delivering economic advantages and security and overcoming other

---

[61] Oostindie 2006, 618.
[62] Author's 2011 interviews with local officials in Caribbean region PITs associated with the UK.

competitors. The previous chapter, however, showed that the days of sovereign state advantages are in many respects gone.

This chapter has built upon that theme by illustrating that in region after region where meaningful comparisons can be made, PITs tend to be significantly wealthier and more secure than their sovereign state counterparts. Moreover, the gap between PIT advantages and sovereign state performance is increasing over time. These observations are not lost on the minds of PIT leaders and populations. Whether in the Caribbean, the Pacific, Europe, or elsewhere, they can see the outcome of their arrangement as compared to the relative disadvantages of the alternative of independence. This then leads to questions about the limitations of partial independence. Is it always a better outcome than full independence? When does full independence seem more advantageous? The next chapter will turn to these questions.

9

Predicting the Dynamics of Partially Independent Territories

Since the nineteenth century, nearly seventy PITs have emerged, but relatively few have come to an end—whether through full independence or full political assimilation into a core state. Empirical tests for conditions that contribute to PIT decline (and by extension PIT maintenance) are therefore challenging. There are, however, a number of exceptions to this pattern. In 1931, with the enactment of Britain's Statute of Westminster, the British Dominions[1] (Australia [1855–1931], Canada [1846–1931], Newfoundland [1855–1931], New Zealand [1856–1931], the Irish Free State 1921–31], Malta [1919–31], Rhodesia [1923–31], and South Africa [1872–1931])[2] became more akin to fully independent states because they added full security control to their powers of foreign policy and domestic control.[3] South Sudan (Sudan) in 1983 and 2011, Kosovo (Yugoslavia) in 1989, Eritrea (Ethiopia) in 1955, Hong Kong (UK) in 1997, Northern Ireland (UK) in 1971, Crimea (Ukraine) in 2014, Memel (Lithuania) in 1939, and Suriname (the Netherlands) in 1975 also terminated their status as PITs.

This chapter will provide evidence to show that the causal claims made in Chapter 2 tend to provide plausible predictions for the maintenance and termination of PITs. With respect to such partially independent territory dynamics, this chapter will first reiterate the theoretical expectations set forth in Chapter 2. Second, it will attempt to test these claims. Given the limited number of cases of PIT termination, this part of the analysis will be designed

---

[1] On the widely acknowledged unwritten constitutional rules that nullified the preexisting colonial laws that applied to the British Dominions, see for instance, Evatt 1936; Forsey 1943; Keith 1912/1927; Leacock 1907, 355–392; Marshall 1984; Wheare 1949.

[2] These dates indicate the emergence of the first PIT that later came be associated with the Dominion mentioned. Hence Australia is mentioned as emerging as a Dominion in 1855 although technically it was its territories of Victoria, New South Wales, Tasmania, and South Australia that emerged at that time before Australia was united in 1900.

[3] Keith 1935b; Wheare 1949.

to act as a plausibility probe based on limited evidence. It will especially seek to underscore conducive conditions for PIT maintenance and termination rather than those that are necessary or sufficient.[4] To avoid the pitfalls of selection bias, the analysis will also be based on all known cases of PITs.

RECAPPING INTEGRATIONALIST THEORY

As international relations realists rightly point out, smallness of size and inequality of capacity amidst the dangers of international anarchy can be a serious disadvantage for sovereign states. Sovereign statehood demands shouldering all of the burdens of full independence. The costs of such wide ranging responsibilities can inhibit specialization and prevent added investment in areas where there is a comparative advantage. If and when economic or environmental disasters strike, other states will have no duty to help. Weak sovereign states are also vulnerable to exploitation that can threaten their finances, trade, and security.

For PITs, however, the opposite conditions prevail. In spite of their relatively small size, the public goods furnished by a core state make up for many of their potential deficiencies. Partially independent arrangements are by definition unequal; the core state retains full independence over its own territory while the PIT has partial independence. But its inequality of powers with a core state frees it from the burdens associated with full independence. Amidst the credible constitutional commitments that have been provided to it, larger core states are in a strong position to furnish public goods that PITs are relatively hard pressed to provide for themselves. Relative to its sovereign state counterparts in the international system, such assistance will free it to specialize and invest in areas where there is comparative advantage. When disaster strikes, core state resources provides a safety net which is similar to other areas of its international legal space. And the credibility of constitutional commitments protect against core–PIT exploitation while the public goods of the core state (in areas such as defense, customs unions, fiscal transfers, single market access, expert advice, shared reputational association, and proxy diplomatic representation) provide defenses against exogenous threats. When faced with these superior economic, security, and self-determination benefits, the likelihood that local leaders will be convinced to abandon the alternative of full independence in favor of partial independence increases.

---

[4] The causal factors discussed here are neither necessary (the absence of causal variable A precludes the outcome B) nor sufficient (A insures the outcome B). Instead, they are contributing or conducive conditions (A's presence increases the likelihood of B). See, Abernethy 2000, 25.

From the perspective of the core state, the autonomous nature of the local jurisdiction provides great potential benefits. Without the costs and security risks of imperial control, a sovereign state's maritime economic zone can be greatly increased, preferential access to natural resources can be obtained, distant military bases can be established, the potential for nationalistic violence can subside, the likelihood of full territorial fragmentation of their state can be reduced, and in some cases, large-scale foreign investment can be redirected to the core state. Partially independent arrangements arguably come into being through such mutual advantages that they have for both the PIT and the core state as well as the cataclysmic events that wipe away the norms that would otherwise prevent both sides from realizing such advantages.

The conditions for the emergence of these regimes are, however, distinct from the conditions that sustain them. Overtime the advantages that may have allowed the arrangement to emerge may subside. In spite of this there are virtually no cases of core states unilaterally abandoning a partially independent union with a territory. For example, even though Puerto Rico has largely lost its strategic significance to the US, why does America retain its close constitutional relationship and continue to shoulder the expense of public goods to the territory? And although the territories associated with the Netherlands in the Caribbean have lost most of their importance in larger imperial calculations, why does the core state still maintain its ties? Paradoxically why would PITs such as the historic British Dominion of Canada press for full independence after it had experienced decades of increasing degrees of economic and security advantages? Pure economic and security self-interest explanations cannot resolve these paradoxes. The answer to these puzzles offered here is that sustaining the arrangement is contingent upon the fulfillment of a normative sense of fairness. In accordance with the modified marriage analogy presented in Chapter 2, nationalistically distinct populations not only want to maximize their power and economic and security advantages, they also want a sense that their condition is fair and just.

From the perspective of the PIT, the unequal division of powers is justifiable and fair as long as the inequality of capacity prevails. As long as the core state is much larger than the PIT it will be in a strong position to effectively furnish public goods. When, however, the size of each polity approaches parity, the PIT will increasingly see the arrangement as unfair.[5] Consequently, full independence will be more likely.

---

[5] It may be difficult in many circumstances to empirically differentiate a territory's self-interested desire for public goods as opposed to its desire for such public goods in the context of a normatively fair settlement that is justified with differences of capability. One can therefore return to the marriage analogy to emphasize the operation of norms as opposed to pure self-interest. Similar to the vast asymmetry of capabilities that characterize most core–PIT

Because the core state retains virtually all its powers of full independence over its own territory, its nationalistic sense of political–cultural congruence is less likely to be offended by relative differences in capacity. Core state leaders tend to have "other-regarding" normative perceptions that include the PIT within their national–territorial reference as part of its state. For example, Italian leaders see Sardinia as part of Italy and British leaders see Scotland as part of the UK (even though technically these nationalistically distinct territories are constitutionally unincorporated and have some separate sovereign powers of their own). Accordingly, some of the same norms that preclude spinning off a section of the core state's incorporated territory for purely self-interested calculations tends to extend to unincorporated PITs. Unilaterally abandoning Sardinia or Scotland to the anarchy of the international system becomes just as absurd to core state leaders as abandoning any other part of its international legal space.

Partially independent territories, however, have a very different set of normative perceptions as compared to core states. Partially independent territory leaders tend to have "self-regarding" normative perceptions of nationalism because their most salient national–territorial reference focuses on their own territory without fully embracing the core state. Their cultural, governmental, and territorial unit primarily centers on the geographic space of the PIT rather than an all-embracing state with a multitude of distinct regions. For most Sardinians, Sardinia is their primary homeland (even though technically they hold Italian citizenship). Similarly for most Scottish people, Scotland is their primary homeland (even though technically they hold UK citizenship). Amidst this distinctive nationalistic perception, they have nevertheless surrendered what would otherwise be some of their powers of sovereignty to the core state. Unlike the core state, they have wagered some of their powers for the prospect that their condition will be better as a PIT. If this deal (or settlement) changes for the worse because the core state no longer has the same ability to furnish public goods, it is not simply a matter of self-interested calculations. It is a matter

partially independent unions, the partners in a marriage may have vast differences of capability. Pervasive societal prejudice and legal restrictions may, however, weight against one partner. Great differences in education levels and other distinguishing attainments may also apply. With such differences in capability, difference in roles and responsibility can be justified. Such justification however becomes less reasonable if circumstances change and each partner develops a parity of attainments. Under such circumstances, if the partner that previously had greater attainments were to insist that the preexisting division of responsibilities should nevertheless still apply, it would not only violate the other partner's self-interest, it would violate a sense of fairness. What is at stake transcends material gain alone. When various values (such as a sense of equality) go unfulfilled for reasons that pertain to a difference in capability that no longer applies, this is described here as a lack of fairness.

of fairness. Why would it be fair for them to countenance an inequality of powers if they increasingly have the same capacity to provide public goods for themselves? Whether with the symbiotic relations that prevail in nature or those that exist within social relations, the sensibility and fairness of the division of responsibilities in a relationship is contingent upon the capacity of each partner. Amidst its greater size, wider responsibilities, and integrative nationalistic norms that extend to a diversity of regions within its international legal space, changes in capacity are less salient factors for core states. For the PIT however, its smaller size, more narrow responsibilities, and self-regarding nationalistic perceptions make changes in capacity highly salient.

As PITs approach near economic parity with the core state, the relative benefits for the PIT wane. The smaller relative size of the core weakens its ability to furnish security, forms of economic union, diplomatic support, worthwhile reputational association, and other advantages. With a greatly weakened set of benefits, local leaders increasingly question the lack of equality in the distribution of power; an inequality of capacity increasingly does not exist to justify an inequality in the distribution of power. Nationalistic aspirations that were once held in check are redirected to the full independence alternative. Economically strong territories can nevertheless have advantageous and sustainable relations with a core state, but the core state needs to be large enough to be able to deliver the public goods that make an arrangement seem worthwhile and fair. Based on these assumptions, it can be hypothesized that as the size of the PIT's economy approaches that of the core state, PIT termination will be increasingly likely. If this is true, among the historic PITs that are closer to the economic size of the core state, we can expect to see increasing numbers of regime terminations, whether by full independence into global anarchy or full political assimilation into the core state. Paradoxically among those PITs that are distant from the economic size of the core—unless termination is occurring for some other reason—we can expect to see relatively few cases of regime termination.

TESTING AND OPERATIONALIZING THE ARGUMENT

One important (though imperfect) measure of a country's economic size and resources is its gross domestic product (GDP). Gross domestic product is the sum of all of a polity's goods and services in a year. One of the regularities that can be observed from the vast majority of partially independent arrangements that have maintained their status is that most PITs are associated with core states that have a GDP that is much larger.[6] Among modern partially independent arrangements that are now in existence, the median core state GDP is 120 times the size of the PIT with which it is associated.

By contrast, as predicted by the theory, in many cases PITs that have come to an end have been associated with a core state that is more proportional in size. Empirical observation indicates that PITs tend to terminate when the core state has a GDP that is less than ten times larger. This is what can be called the PIT termination tendency base line, which describes the point at which many PITs tend to terminate their existence and press for full independence. When Kosovo's PIT status was terminated with Yugoslavia in 1989, the core GDP was approximately six times larger than the PIT.[7] When South Sudan's partially independent territory status was terminated with Sudan in 1983 the core GDP was an estimated eight times larger, and when it terminated its second partially independent union in 2011 the core GDP was approximately five times larger.[8] When Eritrea's PIT status was terminated with Ethiopia in 1955 the core GDP was approximately ten times larger.[9] This tendency for partially independent arrangement failure when the core–PIT ratio approaches a factor of ten or less can also be seen with regard to the core–PIT relations between the UK and the eight British Dominions (Australia, Canada [1846–1931], Newfoundland [1855–1931], New Zealand [1856–1931], the Irish Free State 1921–31], Malta [1919–31], Rhodesia [1923–31], and South Africa [1872–1931]). Each of these polities went from existing as fully controlled colonies, to partially-sovereign PITs, (and except for Newfoundland) to sovereign states that shared a limited range of powers with the UK within the British Commonwealth when they were by and large granted full independence with the 1931 Statute of Westminster (a British law).[10]

---

[6] Given the limited number of cases of PIT termination, in accordance with the ideas of Alexander George, this part of the analysis will be designed to act as a plausibility probe based on limited evidence.

[7] This estimation is based on the WDI figures from 2004.

[8] This estimate is derived from the close population differential between Sudan and South Sudan (in which Sudan had a population that was just four times greater than South Sudan [2004]), and the relative economic stability, which had prevailed for about a decade since the 1972 Addis Ababa Agreement, until the resumption of civil war after the 1983 termination of the partially independent arrangement. For other estimates on South Sudan's economic status, see UNICEF 2004, 63.

[9] This estimate is derived from Angus Maddison in which he estimates that Ethiopia's population was approximately sixteen times the size of Eritrea in 1950. Most accounts, however, confirm that Eritrea's economy in 1952 was much more urbanized and industrialized than the core state before the devastation of the subsequent wars with Ethiopia.

[10] Other territories such as India before its independence took on the title of British Dominion but this was after the 1931 Statute of Westminster that by and large granted the Dominions independence from Britain. Territories such as India are therefore not coded as PITs.

Although the UK had a GDP that was significantly higher than many of the Dominions when they were by and large granted full independence in 1931, other observers have pointed out that their movement toward full independence was largely precipitated by Canada, which was the largest Dominion. When referring to the 1926 imperial conference, in which British and Dominion representatives more discernibly put the Dominions on a path toward independence, historians such as Denis Judd confirm that, "what made the difference in 1926 was the role of Canada.... Canada's determination to push for a thoroughgoing reappraisal of the constitutional relationship between Britain and the Dominions tipped the balance in favour of change."[11] One of the factors that can be observed from the termination of the British Dominions as PITs is that when Canada transformed from a colony into a PIT in 1846, the size of the UK's GDP was nineteen times the size of this massive North American territory.[12] Similarly, the UK was twenty-seven times the size of Australia, the second largest Dominion, when it emerged as a PIT in 1855.[13]

Britain's choice to grant Canada a range of powers of independence without full secession in 1846 was largely precipitated by violent revolts by Anglo and French Canadians in 1837 that mirrored events that led to the secession of the Thirteen Colonies. In addition to Britain's self-determination guarantees to Canadian leaders—which historians acknowledge brought to an end many of the nationalistic complaints that were at the root of this violence—the arrangement provided free trade for Canadian exports with Britain's massive internal market.[14] It also furnished military deterrence against the desires of some US leaders (as described in Article XI of the US Articles of Confederation) to annex Canada. But by the eve of World War I when Britain's economy was about ten times the size of Canada, Canada had already agitated several times for additional powers of sovereignty that would put it on the path toward sovereign statehood in 1931. Given the gradual shift of the core–PIT ratio toward greater proportionality, Britain had a smaller internal market for Canadian goods as compared to increasing US–Canadian trade. British military protection of Canada was also less relevant, especially after Canada proved its capability of fielding its own forces when it assisted the British during World War I. Amidst the growing core–PIT parity, British diplomatic decisions that were made on behalf of the Dominions were also increasingly challenged by Canadian leaders who increasingly questioned the utility of the core–partially independent arrangement. By the time Canada was by and large granted full independence with the 1931 Statute of Westminster, the size of the UK's GDP

---

[11] Judd 1996, 288.   [12] Maddison 1982; 2003; Mitchell 1998.
[13] Mitchell 1998.   [14] Ferguson 2002.

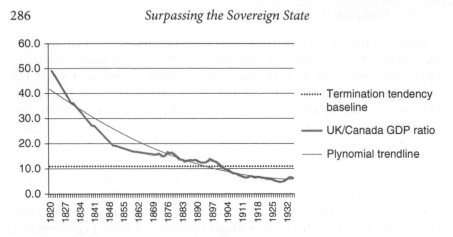

Figure 9.1. Canada moves toward secession

Data Source: Maddison 2003.

was just 6.5 times the size of Canada (see Figure 9.1).[15] Similarly, Australia had a core–PIT ratio of 8.3 in 1931. Dominion status was not originally contemplated as an interim solution to Britain's relations with its former settled colonies. Nevertheless, the human and physical costs of World War I and the 1929 Great Depression greatly weakened its provision of public goods. And with the ever-growing economic parity with the largest Dominions of Canada and Australia, the increasing diminishment of public goods to those polities catalyzed a wider move toward full independence among the rest of the British Dominions (especially South Africa and Ireland) whose nationalism had in significant ways been held in check by the arrangement.

Consider also the case of South Sudan after it negotiated a partially independent arrangement with the northern part of the country in January 2005.[16] For an impoverished territory, devastated by a civil war that cost the lives of

[15] Keith 1935b; Wheare 1949. In 1931, with the enactment of Britain's Statute of Westminster, the British Dominions (Canada, Ireland, South Africa, New Zealand, and Australia) became more akin to fully independent states because they added full security control to their constitutionally entrenched powers of foreign policy and domestic control.

[16] The constitutional union of Sudan and South Sudan was enshrined in the May 26, 2004 "Protocol between the Government of Sudan (GOS) and the Sudan People's Liberation Movement (SPLM) on Power Sharing." The Protocol was a component of the January 2005 Comprehensive Peace Agreement between the GOS and SPLM. The Protocol called for the creation of three different levels of government. The first was the national level, which embodied the country of Sudan. The second level was the component "states" or member-units of Sudan's newly-created federation. The third level was "South Sudan" which had a distinct allocation of its own domestic sovereignty separate from the "national" and "state" levels. This third level of government, which was not a member-unit of Sudan's federation, is referred to here as the PIT. See Government of Sudan and the Sudan People's Liberation Movement 2004.

nearly two million people, partial independence offered South Sudan the prospect of added security, the sharing of the country's disputed oil and mineral
wealth, and formal mechanisms for the resolution of disputes. The core state,
however, lacked the resources to deliver on these fronts. In spite of its strong
desire to convince its southern partners to maintain the union, it was too poor
in relative terms to help rebuild South Sudan's cities, to protect citizens from
invading forces (like the Lord's Resistance Army), and to provide an equitable
distribution of mineral resources.[17] Consistent with the arguments here, with
a GDP core-PIT ratio of just five, the core state could not deliver the public
goods (like security, single markets, diplomatic protection, etc.) that can create an attractive arrangement.[18] The result is that in rare cases PITs secede—as
South Sudan did in 2011.

There are other partially independent arrangements that have terminated,
but most of these have done so for exogenous reasons outside of normal
core–PIT decision making.[19] Memel-Klaipeda's 1924 partially independent
arrangement with Lithuania came to an end when Germany used military
coercion to take the territory on the eve of World War II. Similarly, Crimea's
1996 arrangement with Ukraine terminated in February 2014 after Russian
military occupation. Northern Ireland's 1921 arrangement with the UK terminated when the core government prorogued local institutions in 1972
after an internal civil war broke out between Protestants and Catholics. And
Hong Kong's partially independent arrangement with the UK terminated
with the 1997 "handover" when China assumed the new role as the territory's core state.[20]

Apart from these cases, the only known partially independent arrangement that terminated with a core–PIT ratio above ten is the Netherland's
1954 arrangement with Suriname which ended in 1975 when Suriname's
legislature voted for full independence. However, in anticipation of the vote

---

[17] After funding the Lord's Resistance Army (LRA) beginning in 1994 as a proxy force to fight
the rebel South Sudan People's Liberation Movement, the Sudanese core state neglected to intervene to prevent attacks by the LRA, leaving this to the relatively impoverished South Sudanese
regional authorities. See Human Rights Watch 2006.

[18] Even if it were possible for Sudan to provide pay for such expenses, the core state's population was just four times the size of South Sudan, which would make it difficult for Sudan to
furnish such public goods in light of a post-civil war economic recovery in the South.

[19] A wide range of other territories may have some nominal features that make them seem like
PITs, but in fact may be sham federacies (on sham federacies see Chapter 6).

[20] For authorities that argue that Hong Kong's status under the British was entrenched by
unwritten constitutional rules, see Miners 1991, 61–3. Yash Ghai, however, contests Hong Kong's
conventionally entrenched status, see Ghai 1999, 17. Ghai's view is based on the British changes
that were made to the territory during the extraordinary circumstances of the impending 1997
Handover to China.

for independence much of its entrepreneurial class fled the territory. And as already indicated in the last chapter, in the years after fully seceding, Suriname succumbed to dictatorship, relative poverty, and civil war. Suriname's GDP per capita in 2008 stands at roughly US$4,012 as compared to US$18,133 for the Netherlands Antilles and US$21,767 for Aruba.[21]

IMPLICATIONS FOR CURRENT AND PROSPECTIVE PARTIALLY INDEPENDENT ARRANGEMENTS

If the arguments presented here are true, a wide range of conclusions can be drawn about current and prospective partially independent arrangements throughout the world.

Current Partially Independent Territories

Because most partially independent arrangements have a high core–PIT (CP) ratio (as depicted by Table 9.1), they are less likely to risk termination through an insufficient capability for the core to furnish public goods. For example, although Puerto Rico is slowly trending downward, the core–PIT differential

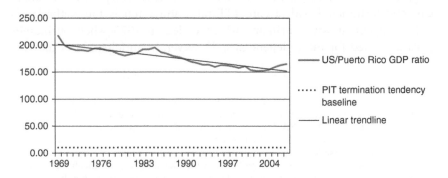

Figure 9.2. The potential benefits to Puerto Rico under US association remain high
Data Source: World Bank World Development Indicator 1967–2007.

---

[21] UN Statistical Division 2009. GDP is in 2005 constant US$. In 2010 the Netherlands Antilles divided into the separate PITs of Curaçao and Sint Maarten.

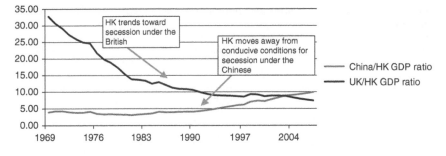

Figure 9.3. Hong Kong's just-in-time 1997 UK–China handover
Data Source: World Bank World Development Indicator 1967–2007.

that it has with the US makes the arrangement sustainable for much of the foreseeable future (see Figure 9.2). Table 9.1, nevertheless, shows a number of partially independent arrangements that are a cause for concern since they are below or near the PIT termination baseline (in which associated core states have a GDP less than 10 times as large), including Hong Kong with a CP ratio of 16, the Kurdish TerritoriesTerritories (Iraq) with a CP ratio of just 1, Scotland (UK) with a CP ratio of 15, Catalonia (Spain) with a CP ratio of 5, Vojvodina (Serbia) with a CP ratio of 4, and the Basque Country (Spain) with a CP ratio of 16.

With respect to Hong Kong, as Figure 9.3 illustrates, before 1997 under British association, Hong Kong was trending toward full independence. In fact British Prime Minister, Margaret Thatcher envisioned increasing sovereign powers for the territory, including a seat on the United Nations. Just as Hong Kong began to enter the termination tendency baseline, however, the core state of the territory changed from the UK to China. Because of China's much faster rate of growth (of around 10% per year after 1978) Hong Kong's CP ratio is trending away from secession, which has nearly doubled since the 1997 handover. In 1997 China's economy was about eight times the size of Hong Kong; ten years later it is about sixteen times that size. In fact as the relationship develops, the greater resources of China have made a significant difference to the territory's economic development.[22] Such advantages include free military protection, significant degrees of cooperation on infrastructure projects that connect Hong Kong to surrounding economic zones, a 2004 free trade agreement (which granted Hong Kong preferential access to China's vast internal market), and valuable diplomatic support (such as the 2008 actions of Chinese leaders, including China's premier Hu Jintao, who persuaded G-8 countries not to place Hong Kong on a tax haven blacklist).[23]

[22] Rezvani 2012.   [23] Giles et al. 2009.

Table 9.1. Core–PIT GDP ratios and populations of modern partially independent territories and core states

Core state	Partially independent territory	Population	GDP (millions of $US)	Core–PIT ratio
Canada		33,300,000	$1,200,000	
	Nunavut	31,600	$951	1262
China		1,310,000,000	$3,220,000	
	Hong Kong	6,926,368	$207,000	16
Denmark		5,497,312	$268,000	
	Greenland	57,317	$1,744	154
	Faroe Islands	48,512	$1,885	142
Finland		5,316,334	$217,000	
	Åland	27,153	$1,363	159
France		64,000,000	$2,240,000	
	French Polynesia	264,541	$5,743	390
	Monaco	35,336	$5,192	431
	New Caledonia	242,911	$6,965	322
Iraq		29,800,000	$21,626	
	Kurdistan	5,200,000	$23,600	1
Italy		59,900,000	$1,820,000	
	San Marino	31,198	$1,463	1244
	Friuli-Venezia Giulia	1,222,061	$42,273	43
	Trentino-South Tyrol	513,357	$18,483	98
	Sardinia	1,665,617	$38,546	47
	Sicily	5,029,683	$99,634	18
	Aosta Valley	125,979	$4,885	373
Moldova		3,635,059	$3,477	
	Gagauzia[a]	161,100[a]		
Netherlands		16,500,000	$698,000	
	Aruba	105,526	$2,297	304
	Netherlands Antilles	194,999	$3,536	197
New Zealand		4,277,809	$118,000	
	Cook Islands	20,019	$185	639
	Niue	1,625	$11	10820

Table 9.1. (Continued)

Core state	Partially independent territory	Population	GDP (millions of $US)	Core–PIT ratio
Papua New Guinea		6,549,268	$5,686	
	Bougainville[b]	210,000[b]		
Philippines		90,200,000	$120,000	
	Mindanao	4,120,795	$957	125
Portugal		10,600,000	$199,000	
	Madeira	246,689	$6,080	33
	Azores	244,006	$4,248	47
Serbia		7,350,222	$38,706[c]	
	Vojvodina	1,979,389	$9,904[c]	4
Spain		45,100,000	$1,230,000	
	Catalonia	7,238,051	$227,000	5
	Galicia	2,735,078	$65,441	19
	Basque Country	2,138,739	$74,914	16
Sudan		41,400,000	$45,446	
	South Sudan	8,737,535	$8,637	5
Switzerland		7,573,204	$408,000	
	Liechtenstein	35,521	$4,232	96
Tanzania	Tanzania	41,100,000	$17,377	
	Zanzibar	1,175,571	$415	42
Ukraine		46,000,000	$102,000	
	Crimea	1,967,300	$3,358	30
United Kingdom		61,300,000	$2,390,000	
	Bermuda	64,657	$5,356	446
	British Virgin Islands	22,762	$902	2651
	Cayman Islands	55,295	$3,256	734
	Turks and Caicos Islands	35,960	$856	2792
	Northern Ireland	1,767,300	$66,140	36
	Scotland	5,156,298	$164,701	15

(*Continued*)

Table 9.1. (Continued)

Core state	Partially independent territory	Population	GDP (millions of $US)	Core–PIT ratio
	Wales	2,983,116	$106,000	23
	Gibraltar	29,286	$1,205	1983
	Isle of Man	76,512	$4,106	582
	Jersey and Guernsey	149,581	$11,160	214
United States		305,000,000	$13,100,000	
	Marshall Islands	52,880	$144	90672
	Micronesia	110,367	$239	54767
	Palau	20,228	$151	86978
	Puerto Rico	3,758,981	$80,608	163
	Northern Mariana Islands	83,774	$1,091	12009

Note: Except for where noted, all data are from 2008. GDP is in 2005 constant US$. The table attempts to provide the known universe of modern PITs and core states. GDP data on two cases [Gagauzia (Moldova) and Bougainville (Papua New Guinea)] were however unavailable.

[a] Population data for Gagauzia is from 2013.

[b] 2008 population data for Bougainville is an estimate based on a core state census in 2000.

[c] GDP data for Vojvodina and Serbia is for 2009.

Sources: UN Statistics Division 2009; European Commission 2009; World Bank national accounts data, and OECD National Accounts data files. When data were unavailable from these sources, individual territorial and core state governmental offices were consulted for Crimea, Nunavut, Mindanao, Kurdistan, Bougainville, Gagauzia, and Vojvodina.

On the other hand, it may be instructive to consider the condition of Hong Kong if it were able to attain full independence. As has been the case with many smaller polities that have chosen secession from much more powerful states since 1945, determined efforts frequently do yield full independence, but often at a very high price in terms of blood and treasure. For the sake of argument, however, if Hong Kong was somehow able to peacefully become fully independent, what would the costs and advantages be relative to its current status? It is probably safe to say that the territory would forgo many of the aforementioned benefits that now flow from high degrees of Chinese cooperation (and economic interdependence). Meanwhile Hong Kong would attain a range of new powers that come with sovereign statehood (which were especially helpful for sovereign states when they emerged in the fourteenth century). Hong Kong would gain full powers of external defense, full diplomatic recognition from other states, membership in additional international organizations such as the UN, and (presumably) a democratically elected chief executive. In the modern age of the fixed borders norm, it is however unclear exactly what external military powers would do for Hong Kong except antagonize China and create substantial additional costs for the territory. As far as membership in international organizations (IOs), Hong Kong is already a member of around twenty such IOs—which is one of the advantages that de facto states (such as Taiwan) do not possess.[24] Full independence would, however, allow Hong Kong to become a party to military alliances, but again it is unclear which countries it could ally with and what that would do to increase the levels of security it already enjoys. And while full sovereignty over its own government would indeed be an advantage, China has promised that the territory will have full internal suffrage over its legislature and executive within the next decade. Data from the World Governance Indicator also indicate that Hong Kong's rankings on control of corruption, government effectiveness, political stability, regulatory quality, rule of law, and voice and accountability have either remained the same or improved since its handover with the otherwise human rights abusing and authoritarian China.[25] In sum, there would indeed be some advantages for Hong Kong as a fully independent state, but at the moment (all other things equal) the argument here is that it is unclear how these advantages would surpass the security, infrastructure, trade, diplomatic advantages, and overall political performance it enjoys under partial independence.

Similar to Hong Kong, Scotland is also trending away from the secession that could occur through insufficient core resources (see Figure 9.4). Interestingly, although the secessionist Scottish Nationalist Party (SNP) won a majority of Scottish votes in 2011, polling data in 2012 indicates that 72% of the population does not want independence.[26] Instead, majorities favor enhanced versions of their present partially independent status known variously as "devo max" or "devolution plus", in which greater powers would be allocated to Scotland, including more powers over taxation and welfare.[27] In some sense this mirrors the condition of Bermuda in which the secessionist Progressive Labor Party (PLP) won a majority of votes in 2003 and again in 2007 while paradoxically the option of independence was opposed by more than 74% of the population in a 2010 poll.[28]

---

[24] Taiwan does, however, have some membership in international organizations such as the World Trade Organization, the Asian Development Bank, and the Asia Pacific Cooperation. See <worldstatesmen.org>. The point here however is that such de facto states tend to have far fewer memberships than PITs (as Hong Kong especially illustrates).

[25] Kauffmann et al. 2011. On Hong Kong more specifically see also Rezvani 2012, 111.

[26] *Evening Express* 2012.

[27] *Evening Express* 2012; *Guardian* 2013.

[28] Antigua Observer.com 2010.

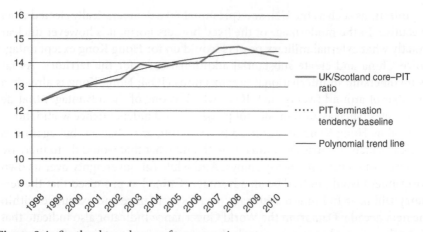

Figure 9.4. Scotland trends away from secession
Data Source: European Commission 2010; UN Statistical Division 2010.

But unlike Bermudan PLP leaders who deemphasize the secessionist parts of their platform and stop short of disavowing independence altogether, leaders of the SNP fervently pursue secession even in the face of a majority of Scottish voters who disagree.[29] SNP leaders are, for example, quick to emphasize that if Scotland attained independence they would enjoy the riches from the UK's North Sea oil wells, 90% of which would be within Scotland's exclusive economic zone.[30] In spite of these arguments, it is generally believed that Scotland pays a similar amount to the British treasury (which includes North Sea oil revenues) as it receives back from the British government.[31] Hence, with such revenues now coming back to Scotland (including what it would otherwise gain from oil), control over the oil wells under full independence would not offer discernible advantages. Furthermore, Scotland's economic advantages go beyond fiscal transfers. For example, while some European economies (such as fully independent Iceland) had to fend for themselves amidst the financial collapse of the 2008 banking crisis, the UK government and the Bank of England spent £126.6 billion to prevent the failure of Scotland's most important banks (the Bank of Scotland and the Royal Bank of Scotland).[32] Scottish National Party leaders, however, also complain about British Trident nuclear submarines based at Faslane, Scotland, which they say makes Scottish territory more of a target for attack. Scottish National Party leaders are, however, more reluctant to call attention to the billions of pounds that would

[29] Author's interviews in Bermuda with PLP leaders in 2011 and in Scotland with SNP leaders in 2003.
[30] *Guardian* 2013.
[31] *Guardian* 2013.
[32] Telegraph 2013.

be required to fund an independent military or discuss the lost jobs when UK defense contractors, as some expect, pull out of the territory if it secedes. Scottish National Party leaders also press for European member state status as an alternative to partial independence with the UK. Nevertheless, it is widely believed that if Scotland did somehow secede from the UK (1) it would not have automatic EU membership; and (2) if or when it did become a member (similar to other new member states) it would have to accept monetary union, which is still another unpopular prospect for most Scottish voters. SNP leaders, however, also say that independence will free them from partial governance by UK leaders that are sometimes unpopular with the Scottish electorate.[33] Even while making such arguments, however, they are no doubt also reluctant to emphasize that in addition to the full control over their own legislature, Scotland holds 10% of the seats in the parliament of the UK, which has the world's 6th largest economy and has the 4th largest military.[34] Scottish members of the British Parliament (who are elected by Scottish constituencies) also frequently hold seats in the British Cabinet and occasionally occupy the seat of British Prime Minister (as most recently occurred with Scottish/British MP, Gordon Brown).

As distinct from the Scotland and Hong Kong cases, one territory that appears in fact to be trending toward independence is Catalonia (Spain). The core–PIT ratio is dangerously low (with Spain's economy being just five times as large), which underscores the relative incapability of the core state to deliver the advantages that are typical of partially independent unions. As distinct from the Scotland–UK relationship, one of the most salient features of the trouble between Spain and Catalonia is that the core state takes approximately 8% more revenue from the territory than it returns in the form of services.[35] Predictably, a 2013 poll indicates that 57.8% of Catalonia's population favors full independence. Additionally, in the midst of these conditions, there are also troubling signs that Spain's government is failing to take steps to forestall the real danger of Catalonia's secession.

One case that can be especially instructive for Catalonia and Spain as well as Scotland and the UK, are the relations between the Iraqis and the Kurds in which the Iraqi core state actually had a 2008 GDP that was less than the Kurdish Territories (with a core–PIT ratio of just 1). As mentioned earlier, the causal conditions presented here are conducive for PIT termination and not necessary or sufficient conditions, which means that in spite of an extremely low CP ratio, some core–PIT unions manage to craft a set of relations that are consistent with maintaining the partially independent union. As Iraq's economy and civil society continues to stabilize after the cataclysmic events of America's 1991 and 2003 invasions, the Iraqi–Kurdish CP ratio may eventually emerge

[33] Salmond 2012.   [34] *The Economist* 2013.   [35] *Guardian* 2012.

out from under the PIT termination tendency baseline. Nevertheless, in as much as for the time being it has a low CP ratio, the case is still instructive. Accordingly, in spite of its low CP ratio, Iraq has taken uncommon steps to create an unusually attractive package of advantages for the Kurdish Territories. Unlike most partially independent arrangements, the Iraqis appear to have made remarkably strong efforts to compensate for their relative resource deficiencies as a core state by providing the Kurds with a remarkably high level of advantages that are typically unavailable to most PITs. In addition to the typical economic, diplomatic, and political advantages that characterize the union, the Kurds have been granted a seat on the country's rotating presidency (most PITs have their formal representation in the core limited to representatives in the core legislature).[36] Among other things, this has resulted in the otherwise ironic and impossible—but now real—image in 2009 of a Kurdish President of Iraq, Jalal Talabani, shaking hands with the leader of one of Kurdistan's greatest historic foes, the leader of Turkey (President Abdullah Gul). The Kurds have also been allowed to reconstitute their preexisting guerilla force (the *peshmerga*) as a self-defense force. By contrast some PITs (like Puerto Rico) have delegated control over local forces, but the final decision-making authority over these units rests with the core state.[37] The Kurds have also been granted a veto on changes to the country's constitution (most PITs usually have a veto only over issues that directly relate to their own affairs).[38]

Core states such as the United Kingdom vis-à-vis Scotland, Spain vis-à-vis Catalonia, and Serbia vis-à-vis Vojvodina (whose associated PITs are near or below the termination tendency baseline) would be wise to follow the Iraqi-Kurd model of making up for their relatively deficient size and resources with a more attractive package of benefits and concessions. Ignoring this realty—and clinging to historical relations that no longer apply—seriously risks not only state fragmentation and nationalistic radicalization, but also the lost opportunities of continued synergistic relations. It may not be necessary to go as far as the Iraqis with concessions such as shared control over the executive branch. However, in accordance with the fiscal federalism arguments discussed earlier, concessions such as much greater local taxation capability and other powers of fiscal autonomy would be a significant additional advantage while also eventually fostering increased mutually advantageous specialization, trade, investment, and internal competition. Spain's use of Catalan tax revenues and the UK's diversion of North Sea oil profits to budgets elsewhere in the country not only fosters core–PIT tension, it creates a potentially damaging moral hazard problem for the core state itself (in which its own regions bear less risks

---

[36] See O'Leary 2005, 3–91.   [37] O'Leary 2005, 3–91.   [38] O'Leary 2005, 3–91.

for their own actions and instead compensate by depleting PIT resources). Additionally, in light of the many PITs that have wide ranging membership in international organizations, allowing these territories greater international representation (on bodies such as the WTO, IMF, the Nordic Council, and others) would spur similar core–PIT advantages (such as specialization, trade, investment, and internal competition).

Another instructive case in this context is the relationship between the core state of Moldova and the associated PIT of Gagauzia. For more than a decade the arrangement for Gagauzia has indeed forestalled the violent conflict that many in Moldova had feared after their war with the breakaway territory of Transnestria.[39] Nevertheless, from the beginning of the arrangement after 1994, relations between the two polities have been plagued by disagreements and non-violent hostilities that have largely originated from Moldova's failure to implement parts of their commitments (such as helping to set up an independent Gagauzian judiciary).[40] As a result of such problems, Gaugazian leaders frequently express suspicion of Moldova's ill intent to undermine their autonomous status.[41] Nevertheless, with a GDP per capita of US$956, Moldova is the poorest country in per capita terms in Europe.[42] In light of their fresh awareness of the dangers of state fragmentation, the Moldovan leaders are no doubt aware of the need for amicable ties with the Gagauz leaders but lack the resources to effectively comply with their commitments. Unlike the relatively poor Iraqi core state after the 2003 US invasion, Moldova has failed to make similar levels of concessions to Gagauzia as the Iraqis have given to the Kurds, which could potentially stabilize relations by compensating for their lack of public goods provision.

Consider also the set of conditions that prevails in South Asia in the relations between Papua New Guinea and the nationalistically distinct, resource-rich island territory of Bougainville. Between 1988 and 1997 a brutal civil war broke out between these two polities as they struggled for control of Bougainville's Panguna Mine, which is one of the world's largest copper and gold mines. In the midst of this struggle, sovereign statehood failed both sides. It failed Papua New Guinea because—much like a wide range of other core states that have tried and failed to subdue nationalistically distinct insurgents since the nineteenth century—it tried and failed to forcibly assimilate and monopolize its control over Bougainville. The resulting civil war hurt Papua New Guinea's international human rights reputation, impaired its output of valuable natural resources, damaged morale in its police and military forces, and inflamed

[39] Järve 2008, 307–44.   [40] Järve 2008, 307–44.
[41] Author's correspondence with members of Gaugazia's Executive Council, July 2013.
[42] UN Statistics Division 2009 (2005 constant).

efforts at secession by many of Bougainville's leaders.[43] Sovereign statehood also failed the population of Bougainville when local groups attempted full independence, which also helped precipitate the civil war that devastated local infrastructure and resulted in the deaths of an estimated one-tenth of the territory's population. After a 2001 peace agreement and the entry into force of a partially independent arrangement for the territory in 2004, the alternative of partial independence, by contrast, has allowed for the cessation of civil war, compromise, formal mechanisms for the resolution of disputes, and the potential for mutually beneficial cooperation that sovereign statehood (whether through full assimilation or full independence) did not deliver.[44] Papua New Guinea has a population that is about thirty-one times larger than Bougainville. This larger asymmetry could normally provide greater potential for the core state to offer attractive concessions to keep Bougainville within the partially independent union. Nevertheless, similar to the relations between Moldova and Gagauzia, a central problem is Papua New Guinea's poverty. In accordance with the arguments discussed above, with a GDP per capita of just $868, there are troubling questions about Papua New Guinea's ability to deliver a sustainable and attractive package of concessions and resources to Bougainville.[45] With such relative destitution, core state efforts to deliver the advantages that often make partial independence a more attractive option will be weakened. As a consequence, in the years ahead Bougainville may well continue its drift toward full independence in spite of the relative size of Papua New Guinea.

Prospective Partially Independent Territories

In accordance with the calls for autonomous powers and the numerous sham federacies throughout the world (as mentioned in Appendixes 2 and 3), a wide range of territories have the potential to eventually become partially independent. Based on the conducive measures mentioned above, since China's GDP is just six times larger than that of Taiwan, partial independence may not be a sustainable outcome as some have suggested.[46] If some form of union is to be negotiated, it may therefore be the case that a looser form of integration, such as confederation, may be more appropriate. Unlike a partially independent

---

[43] Ghai and Regan 2006, 597.
[44] Ghai and Regan 2006, 597.
[45] UN Statistics Division 2009.
[46] On suggestions for a partially independent arrangement between China and Taiwan see Jakobson 2005, 27–39.

arrangement, a confederation is (1) an unentrenched union between two or more sovereign states where (2) all union decisions are made by mutual agreement. However, similar to the case of Hong Kong, if China continues on its current trajectory of growth of 10% while Taiwan continues on its present trajectory of 4.5%, the two polities may eventually be able to escape the termination tendency baseline. With respect to a possible Israeli–Palestinian partially independent arrangement, Israel's GDP is thirty-four times the size of the Palestinian Territories. All other things being equal, this differential would allow the Israelis to furnish significant levels of benefits to make a partially independent arrangement an attractive option until the Palestinians can establish greater economic parity, which would limit these potential advantages.

10

Conclusion

I shall not make the Italians a subject race to the Trojans,
Nor do I seek this realm for my own: let both our peoples,
Unconquered, as equal partners be joined in a league forever.
——Virgil, *Aeneid*[1]

Compared to the world's great powers, PITs have small populations. Most of them have relatively small economies. They do not engage in war. Some may therefore think that they do not matter. Such observers should think again. Partially independent territories are responsible for nearly a fifth of worldwide capital flows. They have been centerpieces of compromise in some of the world's most intractable nationalistic disputes. They provide distant military basing rights, preferential natural resource access, and extended territorial control for sovereign states.

The maintenance and potential failure of PITs are of deep concern to other states in the international system whose finances, security, trade, and geostrategic opportunities may be threatened by changes to a territory's status. If, for example, the Kurdish partially independent arrangement with Iraq comes to an end by secession, neighboring Turkey has promised to invade. If the constitutional status of important PIT offshore financial centers like Hong Kong is changed, investors have threatened to "vote with their feet" and pull billions of dollars out of China's economy, which may in turn precipitate adverse conditions in others countries whose economies are symbiotically linked with China (the world's second largest economy). If the status of New Caledonia, Greenland, or Nunavut changes, multinational corporations could suffer losses from the termination of preferential access to the vast natural resources that accompanies the partially independent arrangement. And for countries that are considering the possibility of a partially independent arrangement, the question of maintenance and termination is also important. For example, how can one judge the sustainability of partial independence for real or

[1] Virgil 1952/29–19BC, xii, 189–91.

potential flashpoints, such as the Palestinian Territories, Western Sahara, or Taiwan? Perhaps even more important than these characteristics, however, is the fact that the widespread existence of PITs underscores some significant changes to the structure and evolution of the international system. Their existence contradicts some widely held assumptions in the scholarly literature about the institutional performance of sovereign states. For both the PIT and the core state they are associated with, limited integration and the guaranteed powers of a partially independent arrangement tend to cause wealth to be generated, nationalistic confrontation to diminish, and increased levels of cooperation in areas of finance, trade, and external security. The existence of such polities also produces an amended view of the structure of the international system, the existence of a type of neo-medievalism, a fresh application of territorial sovereignty, an additional avenue to explore negarchical integration, and a tool to mitigate the disastrous effects of state failure.

PARTIALLY INDEPENDENT TERRITORIES AMEND THE STRUCTURE OF THE INTERNATIONAL SYSTEM

Similar to the evolution and emergence of the sovereign state, partial independence has come into being not only because of its advantages over other political forms, but because of systemic shocks in the international system that have cleared the way for those choices to be made. The application here of the concept of "punctuated equilibrium," in which evolution occurs not only through natural selection advantages but also systemic shocks, mirrors theories in the literature on the evolution of the sovereign state as well as theories of evolutionary biology.[2] Modern day mammals, for example, have not only proliferated and dominated over other creatures because of their advantages, but because of cataclysmic events such as meteor strikes and ice ages that eliminated the preexisting status quo.[3] Two phenomena have led to the emergence of PITs: (1) the utility maximizing choices of leaders and populations that have chosen PITs above other alternatives because of their advantages; and (2) systemic shocks in the international system since the eighteenth century.

Partially independent territories have evolved out of the shattering of most of the world's empires, widespread localized nationalism, and the centrifugal pulls of economic globalization since the nineteenth century. From the perspective of sovereign states, the end of the age of empires did not stop them from demanding far flung military bases, privileged access to distant natural resources, constitutionally distinct territories that could attract vast investment, and an extended

---

[2] Spruyt 1994b, 23–4.   [3] Spruyt 1994b, 23–4.

orbit of self-determination. From the perspective of relatively small nationalistically distinct territories, the availability of full independence as an alternative
did not stop them from demanding formalized cooperation that could furnish
increased wealth, security, and guarantees of their powers. Partially independent
arrangements provide these advantages for both sides. The institutional evolution of PITs is therefore not solely based on the rational decisions of leaders and
populations, but has been triggered and galvanized by the system-wide shocks
of imperial decline, nationalistic assertiveness, and economic globalization.

An Alternative to Full Independence

Partially independent territories represent an alternative to the sovereign state
that causes the structure of the international system to change. The observation that many of the sovereign states in the world are so weak, destitute,
oppressive, and "failed" that they pose not only a danger to their own populations, but to international security in general is nothing new. Scholars have
long observed that sovereign states are "leaky vessels" that are frequently unable to furnish basic capacities of governance internally within their own territories and externally in the international system.[4]

The devastating international wars and worldwide economic turmoil per-
petuated by sovereign states have historically provided occasions for leaders,
scholars, and citizens to point out state deficiencies and call for sovereign
alternatives that might improve security and wealth, while preserving territorial self-determination. Some wondered whether a world government could
provide solutions.[5] Others postulated that regional organizations could evolve
into a polity that would exercise territorial sovereignty and thereby transcend
the nation-state.[6] Still others guessed that the power of sovereign states themselves would fade and diminish.[7] Apart from the anomalous existence of the
EU, the aforementioned alternatives have however not (yet) materialized.[8]

This book has, however, shown that the structures of PITs have in some
sense produced such an alternative, albeit on a smaller yet globally widespread scale. Partially independent arrangements provide this in the sense
that they deliver advantages that sovereign states have not been able to deliver
to the same degree. For the nationalistically distinct populations of a PIT, the

---

[4] See for example Haas 1968; Mitrany 1966.
[5] For classic proposals see Bentham 1789/1927, 28–31. For more modern variants see, for
example, Singer 2002.
[6] See for example Kupchan 1998, 40–79.
[7] See, Herz 1957, 473–93; 1968; Vernon 1971.
[8] Caporaso 1997; Rosamond 2000, 175; Wallace 1994, 9.

protections, cooperation, and self-determination of those who have hoped for a world, regional, or a diminished state government are realized in significant ways through the distinctive institutions of a partially independent arrangement. By contrast to proponents of full independence, this book has argued that similar in some respects to the competitive struggle between competing constitutive units before the seventeenth century (in which the sovereign state historically beat out other sovereign competitors), PITs frequently beat fully independent states as an attractive alternative. Unlike the historic emergence of the sovereign state, however, the systemic change observed here is one of structural amendment rather than unit replacement.

SUPERIOR BUT CHALLENGED

This book does not argue that PITs present a utopian outcome that is better than all other governmental alternatives. Instead the argument is that PITs in some significant ways tend to surpass the sovereign state. Indeed, it is important to note that there are some partially independent arrangements that are beset by considerable challenges. While the average per capita GDP of PITs is about three times as high as the average per capita GDPs of sovereign states, there have still been outlier PITs like South Sudan (1972–83, 2005–11) that were as poor as the poorest of sovereign states. But in spite of its relative poverty while it was a PIT, South Sudan's low GDP per capita and its status as a PIT came in the wake of the resolution of one of history's most brutal civil wars. A similar state of poverty applies to the Autonomous Region of Bougainville (Papua New Guinea), whose autonomous status emerged in 2004 after a devastating civil war from 1989 to 1997, in which about one-tenth of the population perished. Nevertheless, in each of these cases, partial independence provided a necessary compromise that allowed degrees of stability that may not have been available with immediate and full secession.

On a similar vein, across the world in the PIT of Puerto Rico, one of the things that most of the population's people agree upon is dissatisfaction with their present status. One could therefore interpret this dissatisfaction as applying to their partially independent arrangement. Nevertheless, in four different referendums (in 1951, 1967, 1993, and 1998), the territory's people have voted in favor of their present status and have rejected the other options on the ballot, which have included joining America's federal union and full independence. This paradox between the population embracing their arrangement in plebiscites while also being dissatisfied is resolved by understanding that much of the territory's dissatisfaction stems from a desire to enhance their current partially independent arrangement rather than adopt a distinct status option. Puerto Rican leaders who favor joining America's federation have attempted to exploit this paradox by engineering plebiscites that omit the most popular option of an enhanced version of commonwealth status (which would provide additional powers to the territory such as becoming a voting member within the US Congress). For example, in the 1998 referendum, since an option of an enhanced commonwealth was not included on the ballot, 50.4% of voters selected "none of the above." This large abstention was seen by many observers as an implicit vote in favor of this modified version of their current status. With their plan foiled in 1998, supporters of federation membership attempted a new approach in 2012 by sponsoring a two-part referendum.[9] Similar to 1998, however, the reality was that yet again the pro-statehood party failed to obtain a majority of voters in favor of federation membership (since half a million voters excluded themselves from the second question leaving only 46% of ballot casting voters who favored federal member-unit status).[10] When reflecting upon this referendum, in 2012 US President Obama advised that future referendums should be "well-structured" rather than "inconclusive" and that those who administer the plebiscite should not unfairly "put the thumb on the scale."[11] In light of these events two conclusions can arguably be made. The first is that Puerto Rico has a clear history of overwhelming majorities (of more than 90% of their population) that rejects full independence in favor of some form of formalized political union with the US. The second is that even if Puerto Rico's citizens were to, at some point, clearly favor federation membership (which has not yet happened), the history of the US–Puerto Rico union so far illustrates the frequent infeasibility of extending one-size-fits-all federations as compared to crafting uniquely tailored PIT arrangements. However, in spite of this infeasibility, if federal leaders continue with their refusal to provide commonwealth enhancement as one of the options available (as they have done up until 2011),[12] Puerto Ricans may eventually select the federation membership option over a constrained form of partial independence.

---

[9] The first question asked local citizens if they are satisfied with their relationship with the US. Predictably, most citizens answered "no." Similar to the 1998 referendum, the second question then provided voters options that did not include enhanced commonwealth status. The three options were: independence, federation membership ("statehood"), and a vague reference to "free association." When confronted with this situation, some voters soldiered on and made a selection. Pro-commonwealth leaders (such as the incoming Governor Alejandro García Padilla), however, managed to convince about half a million voters to leave that portion of the ballot blank. Among the remaining voters who actually answered the second question, 54% chose "statehood." See Planas 2012. This then gave the appearance to some that the referendum conclusively favored federation membership.

[10] Planas 2012.

[11] Planas 2012. Video interview of President Obama.

[12] See Report by the President's Task Force on Puerto Rico's Status 2011. Available at <http://www.whitehouse.gov/sites/default/files/uploads/Puerto_Rico_Task_Force_ExecSummary.pdf>, accessed August 2013.

A case that was beset by challenges while it was a PIT was Crimea (Ukraine). Before Russia militarily occupied Crimea and consequently terminated the arrangement in February 2014, the territory arguably had the potential to provide much higher levels of economic, strategic, and political advantages, not only for the Crimeans themselves, but for the core state (Ukraine) as well as other states in the region. During its previous existence under Soviet control, it was one of the USSR's most popular tourist destinations; it had one of the most productive military industrial complexes, and it played host to the Soviet Union's Black Sea Fleet.[13] In recent times, however, although the territory served as a host to Ukrainian and Russian naval fleets, its GDP per capita ($1,707) was slightly less than its associated core state ($2,220).[14] While one can blame this relatively meager level of performance on the dominance of the territory's socialist inclined political parties, one can also see it through the lens of a weakening of the partially independent arrangement. Since the territory's status was originally entered into force, there were signs that the initial promises made under the arrangement with Ukraine were weakening and that the polity may be transitioning into a status as a sham federacy.[15] In accordance with theories of market preserving federalism, such a state of affairs could have a devastating impact on the ability of the territory to autonomously craft its own policies and thus build on its economic potential as a center of tourism and industry. It could also enhance the possibility of nationalistic radicalization among the dominant ethnically Russian population, which could in turn increase the likelihood of Russian military intervention (which in February 2014 actually occurred). Nevertheless, in spite of these areas of concern, while it was a PIT Crimea fared much better in some respects than some other ethnically distinct territories that have attempted to attain (or have achieved) degrees of independence. The attempt to opt for full independence on the part of other ethnically distinct territories such as Transnestria (Moldova), Chechnya (Russia), Abkhazia (Georgia), South Ossetia (Georgia), and Nagorno-Karabakh (Azerbaijan) has resulted in wars, lasting tension, and significant degrees of economic dislocation both for these territories as well as the erstwhile core states. As confirmed by other scholars, Crimea had many prerequisites for nationalistic conflict.[16] Ultimately, however, while the territory was a PIT in association with Ukraine conflict did not arise because each side opted for a negotiated settlement. Furthermore, as with the case of other political systems, the usurpation of the arrangement can only be confirmed with a sustained and repeated set of core state violations

---

[13] Sasse 2007.
[14] United Nations Statistical Division 2009. 2008 GDP is in 2005 constant US$.
[15] For an account of Crimea's status see United Nations Statistical Division 2009.
[16] United Nations Statistical Division 2009.

rather than the single actions of any one actor. Just as with civil or criminal law, the law's violation does not necessarily produce a constitutional change.[17]

THE FUTURE OF PARTIALLY INDEPENDENT TERRITORIES

It is predicted here that partially independent arrangements will continue to emerge at a rate that surpasses the emergence of sovereign states. As described in this book, the literatures of political integration, nationalism, market preserving federalism, relational contracting, imperialism, institutional evolution, sovereignty, international hierarchy, and constitutional law also sustain this view in various respects.

The Numbers of Partially Independent Territories will Continue to Rise

In most cases, before PITs attained their status, they previously existed as colonies or decentralized parts of a core state. Colonies and decentralized territories are favorably positioned in many respects to pressure the core state, since they have assets that the core fears losing and since in many respects the core state is more vulnerable to the prevailing economic, security, and political problems of such a territory.[18] Similar to colonies, the increasing incidences of sham federacies can also build on such conditions to develop into entrenched partially independent arrangements. In light of widespread sovereign state failure as well as the advantages of partial independence, it is therefore predicted that the trend of increasing numbers of PITs will continue.

Partially Independent Territories and Nation-building

Studies have found that state-building becomes more effective when intervening countries extend degrees of constitutionality to the territories that they occupy rather than treating them as fully distinct. Alexander Cooley has, for example, pointed out that "by delineating a set of universal principles or expectations, constitutions serve as focal points for coordinating subsequent institutional development and setting formal boundaries for acceptable forms

---

[17] For more on these principles see Glennon 2003, 16–35.
[18] For more on this argument as it applies to the emergence of sovereign states see Roeder 2007, ch. 1.

of future state-building."[19] Accordingly, relatively large sovereign states that seek the advantages of union with a smaller polity can capitalize on partial integration to secure their interests. Additionally, theorists have also observed that constitutional commonality—as with a shared judiciary or common military conscription—can help reduce the destabilizing discrimination that can prevail in colonial arrangements.[20] While PITs are independent from core states in certain respects, in other respects they are integrated with the core state. Puerto Rico, for example, provides more military conscripts to America's Armed forces per capita than any member-unit of the US federation. Cases like the Åland Islands, also share a common judiciary with the core state.

Partially independent arrangements can also serve as tools for powers like the United States to limit what political and legal scholar Amy Chua refers to as the "hostile, disintegrative forces" that can tear apart America's relations with the states it is attempting to build.[21] America, Chua observes, faces a grave dilemma in which it "has over time proven uniquely successful in creating an ethnically and religiously neutral political identity capable of uniting as Americans individuals of all backgrounds from every corner of the world. But America does not exert power only over Americans. Outside its borders, there is no political glue binding the United States to the billions of people who live under its shadow."[22] Partially independent arrangements could partially provide this political glue for America and other large states in specific cases. As has been argued in this book, however, the range of application of partially independent arrangements should be limited to core states that have economies that are at least ten times greater than the size of the potential PIT. Under such conditions the core state can deliver the public goods that can make the arrangement worthwhile. And as has been the case in the past, partially independent arrangements can also be formed on a temporary, permanent, or incrementally negotiated basis. The US "associated state" partially independent arrangements of the Federated States of Micronesia, Palau, and the Marshall Islands are examples of quasi temporary partially independent arrangements that are renegotiated from time to time.[23]

The issue of granting citizenship is also flexible. With a population of 59.8 million, the British have been especially sensitive about the possibility of

---

[19] Cooley 2005, 53–54. See also North and Weingast 1989, 803–32.

[20] Cooley 2005, 54; Levi 1997; Posen 1993b, 80–124; Tilly 1990; and.

[21] Chua 2009, 334.

[22] Interestingly, after entertaining the possibility of foreign states joining America's federation, she nevertheless rejects such integration as "politically inconceivable." See Chua 2009, 333.

[23] See Federated States of Micronesia, Compact of Free Association. 2003. Title Four, Article III; Palau Islands, Compact of Free Association. 1994. Title Four, Article V, Section 452; and Marshall Islands, Compact of Free Association. 2003. Title Four, Article III.

large-scale immigration from the territories with which they have been associated. Although citizens in territories like the Isle of Man, Jersey, and Guernsey were allowed British citizenship, in 1981 under the British Nationality Act, citizens living in most territories abroad were given the distinct status of British Overseas citizens. This status prevented them from having a right of abode in the United Kingdom. After 2001, however, most citizens of British Territories became entitled to full British citizenship.[24] Similarly, while full US citizenship is conferred to Puerto Ricans, the inhabitants of the Marshall Islands, Palau, and Micronesia have a distinct non-immigrant status (which still allows for residence, work, and travel in the US). And the case of Hong Kong is also a telling example of distinct citizenship status, in which only Chinese from particular cities are allowed into the territory. The land border between Hong Kong and China is designed to keep China's population out and is complete with moats, barbed wire, walls, and watch towers.

Admittedly after a sovereign state has tasted full independence, the nationalism of some factions or leaders may give rise to reluctance for the state to pool sovereignty in some respects and consequently part with some powers of independence. Indeed, the states that have joined the EU faced a similar dilemma. Similarly, the elites and populations around the world that have rejected full independence and embraced partial independence also encountered such controversy. These cases have, however, shown that the fulfillment of national self-determination is not only a function of the amount or scope of powers.[25] Indeed, sovereign states are in many cases burdened by responsibilities that they perform poorly.[26] More importantly, self-determination is fulfilled through the positive outcomes that those powers deliver. As the EU and partially independent accessions have shown, while the act of giving up powers reduces the scope of powers in limited respects, it can nevertheless deliver public goods that yield security, economic, and political benefits that can satisfy nationalist sentiments even more.

Accordingly, this book has shown the accession of smaller entities into such arrangements tends to produce levels of wealth, security, and the fulfillment of self-determination that full independence in many respects cannot achieve. As former US President Bill Clinton said in a different context, " 'we're all in this together' is a better philosophy than 'you're on your own.' "

---

[24] UK, Foreign Commonwealth Office 2007, 4.   [25] Fukuyama 2004, 22–7.
[26] Fukuyama 2004, 22–7.

Appendices

Appendices

Appendix 1

Partially Independent Territories Past and Present

Partially independent territories	Period of existence	Core state	Primary form of entrenchment
Åland Islands	1922–Present	Finland	Formal
Aosta Valley	1948–Present	Italy	Formal
Aruba	1985–Present	Netherlands	Formal
Australia	1900–1931 (United)	UK	Conventional
Azores	1974–Present	Portugal	Formal
Basque Country	1978–Present	Spain	Formal
Bermuda	1967–Present	UK	Conventional
Bougainville	2004–Present	P. New Guinea	Political-formal
British Virgin Islands	2005–Present	UK	Conventional
Canada	1867–1931 (United)	UK	Conventional
Catalonia	1978–Present	Spain	Formal
Cayman Islands	1967–Present	UK	Conventional
Cook Islands	1965–Present	New Zealand	Formal
Crimea	1996–2014	Ukraine	Political-formal
Curaçao	2010–Present	Netherlands	Formal
Eritrea	1952–1955	Ethiopia	Formal
Feroe Islands	1948–Present	Denmark	Conventional
French Polynesia	1977–Present	France	Formal
Friuli-Venezia Giulia	1948–Present	Italy	Formal
Gagauzia	1994–Present	Moldova	Political-formal
Galicia	1978–Present	Spain	Formal
Gibraltar	2006–Present	UK	Conventional
Greenland	1979–Present	Denmark	Conventional

(*Continued*)

Partially independent territories	Period of existence	Core state	Primary form of entrenchment
Guernsey	1744–Present	UK	Conventional
Hong Kong	1994–1997	UK	Conventional
Hong Kong	1997–Present	China	Political-formal
Irish Free State	1921–1931	UK	Conventional
Isle of Man	1886–Present	UK	Conventional
Jersey	1744–Present	UK	Conventional
Kosovo	1974–1989	Yugoslavia	Political-formal
Kurdistan	2004–Present	Iraq	Political-formal
Liechtenstein	1919–Present	Switzerland	Formal
Madeira	1974–Present	Portugal	Formal
Malta	1919–1931	UK	Conventional
Marshall Islands	1994–Present	US	Formal
Memel-Klaipeda	1924–1939	Lithuania	Formal
Micronesia	1986–Present	US	Formal
Mindanao	1990–Present	Philippines	Formal
Monaco	1861–Present	France	Formal
N. Mariana Islands	1978–Present	US	Formal
Netherlands Antilles	1954–2010	Netherlands	Formal
New Caledonia	1988–Present	France	Formal
New Zealand	1856–1931	UK	Conventional
Newfoundland	1855–1934	UK	Conventional
Niue	1974–Present	New Zealand	Formal
Northern Ireland	1921–1972	UK	Conventional
Northern Ireland	1998–Present	UK	Conventional
Nunavut	1999–Present	Canada	Formal
Palau Islands	1994–Present	US	Formal
Puerto Rico	1952–Present	US	Conventional
Rhodesia	1923–1931	UK	Conventional
San Marino	1862–Present	Italy	Formal
Sardinia	1948–Present	Italy	Formal

(*Continued*)

Partially independent territories	Period of existence	Core state	Primary form of entrenchment
Scotland	1998–Present	UK	Conventional
Sicily	1948–Present	Italy	Formal
Sint Maarten	2010–Present	Netherlands	Formal
South Africa	1910–1931 (United)	UK	Conventional
South Sudan	1972–1983	Sudan	Political-formal
South Sudan	2005–2011	Sudan	Political-formal
Suriname	1954–1975	Netherlands	Formal
Trentino-South Tyrol	1948–Present	Italy	Formal
Turks and Caicos Is.	2006–09/2012–Present	UK	Conventional
Vojvodina	1974–1990	Yugoslavia	Political-formal
Vojvodina	2009–Present	Serbia	Political-formal
Wales	2006–Present	UK	Conventional
Zanzibar	1977–Present	Tanzania	Political-formal

For constitutional data on selected PITs and other territorial forms see Blaustein et al., 1997. This table attempts to be exhaustive.

Negotiations Proposing Regional Autonomy

Core state/ territory	Negotiation details
Patani Region (Thailand)	Historic proposals from 1950 to the present by Patani leaders in three southern provinces of southern Thailand (Yala, Pattani, and Narathiwat) for autonomy.
Karen Region (Burma)	Historic proposals from 1949 up to the present by Karen leaders in Burma for autonomous powers.
Eastern Libya (Libya)	2012 proposals by leaders in eastern Libya for autonomous powers within a united Libya.
Darfur (Sudan)	2004 UN High Commissioner for Refugees proposals for a federal arrangement to be applied to the Darfur region in Sudan.*
Tibet (China)	2003 talks between Chinese and Tibetan leaders after the rejection of independence by Tibet's leader, the Dalai Lama, in favor of "genuine autonomy".**
Palestinian Territories (Israel)	The 2003 Geneva Accords (between former Israeli and Palestinian officials) and the 2000 Clinton Plan (proposed by US President Bill Clinton after the collapse of the 2000 Camp David II Summit) for a so-called "Palestinian state," which similar to the partially independent arrangements such as the Marshall or Palau Islands, would divide significant military, foreign relations, and territorial powers with another state.
Western Sahara (Morocco)	2002 UN negotiations for the semi-autonomous status of Western Sahara within Morocco.
Irian Jaya (Indonesia)	2002 negotiations for Irian Jaya's semi-independent status within Indonesia.
Kashmir (India)	1993–2001 Indian–Kashmiri and backchannel Indian–Pakistani negotiations for a constitutionally entrenched partially independent arrangement, referred to as "autonomy plus."
Kosovo (Yugoslavia)	1999 Rambouillet self-rule proposals for Kosovo within Yugoslavia.

(Continued)

Core state/ territory	Negotiation details
Cordillera (Philippines)	In 1998 and 1990 Cordillera's population rejected by plebiscite two plans for PITs in the Philippines.
Northern Cyprus (Cyprus)	Greek Cypriot proposals (rejected by the Turkish Cypriots) for PIT-like regimes for Northern Cyprus.†
Oaxaca/ Chiapas (Mexico)	1996 Zapatista Army of National Liberation (EZLN) peace negotiations with the Mexican federal government, the success of which the EZLN conditioned on the central state's ability to constitutionally grant powers of internal self-determination to their people.††
Nagorno-Karabakh (Azerbaijan)	1995 Hague negotiations between Armenia and Azerbaijan regarding Nagorno-Karabakh.
Quebec (Canada)	The unimplemented 1994 Meech Lake Accords for a "special society" status for Quebec within Canada.
North/East Sri Lanka (Sri Lanka)	1995 proposals and the 1957 Bandaranaike-Chelvanayagam Pact proposing federal arrangements for the Tamils in North and Eastern provinces of Sri Lanka.
Taiwan (China)	Chinese proposals after 1979 (during and after the leadership of Deng Xiaoping) that would guarantee Taiwan final decision-making powers under the formula of "one country, two systems."

* BBC News World Edition 2004. ** Olsen 2003.

† I thank Robert Rotberg for his observations on this issue.

†† Amoretti and Bermeo 2004, 359–64.

Sham Federacy after 1946

Core state	From	To	National group/territory
Afghanistan	1979	1985	Uzbeks
Afghanistan	1979	1985	Turkmen
Afghanistan	1979	1985	Nuristanis
Afghanistan	1986	1991	Uzbeks
Afghanistan	1986	1991	Turkmen
Afghanistan	1986	1991	Nuristanis
Afghanistan	1992	1995	Pashtuns
Afghanistan	1992	1995	Hazaras
Afghanistan	2002	Present	Baloch
Afghanistan	2002	Present	Turkmen
Afghanistan	2002	Present	Nuristanis
Afghanistan	2002	Present	Pashai
Afghanistan	2002	Present	Brahui
Azerbaijan	1995	Present	Autonomous Region of Nakhichevan
Bangladesh	1997	Present	Chittagong Hill Tracts
Benin	1996	Present	South/Central (Fon)
Bolivia	1953	Present	Quechua
Bolivia	1953	Present	Aymara
Cambodia	1979	Present	Lao and Siamese
Chad	1980	1982	Sara
Chile	1990	Present	Mapuche
Chile	1990	Present	Atacamenos

(*Continued*)

Core state	From	To	National group/ territory
China	1947	Present	Inner Mongolia Autonomous Region
China	1951	Present	Tibet Autonomous Region
China	1955	Present	Xinjiang Autonomous Region
China	1984	Present	Zhuang
China	1984	Present	Manchu
China	1984	Present	Hui
China	1984	Present	Miao
China	1984	Present	Tujia
China	1984	Present	Yi
China	1984	Present	Bouyei
China	1984	Present	Dong
China	1984	Present	Yao
China	1984	Present	Koreans
China	1984	Present	Bai
China	1984	Present	Hani
China	1984	Present	Kazakhs
China	1984	Present	Li
China	1984	Present	Dai
China	1984	Present	She
China	1984	Present	Lisu
China	1984	Present	Gelo
China	1984	Present	Dongxiang
China	1984	Present	Lahu
China	1984	Present	Shui
China	1984	Present	Wa
China	1984	Present	Naxi
China	1984	Present	Qiang
China	1984	Present	Tu
China	1984	Present	Mulao
China	1984	Present	Xibe

Core state	From	To	National group/territory
China	1984	Present	Kirgiz
China	1984	Present	Daur
China	1984	Present	Blang
China	1984	Present	Maonan
China	1984	Present	Salar
China	1984	Present	Tajiks
China	1984	Present	Achang
China	1984	Present	Jing
China	1984	Present	Pumi
China	1984	Present	Nu
China	1984	Present	Uzbeks
China	1984	Present	Jinuo
China	1984	Present	Russians
China	1984	Present	Evenk
China	1984	Present	Bonan
China	1999	Present	Macau Special Administrative Region
Colombia	1992	Present	Afrocolumbians
Colombia	1992	Present	Indigenous peoples
Congo	1992	1994	Lari/Bakongo
Costa Rica	1946	Present	Afrocosta Ricans
Czechoslovakia	1948	1968	Slovak Republic
Ethiopia	1996	Present	Other Southern Nations
Ethiopia	1996	Present	Beni-Shugal-Gumez
Ethiopia	1996	Present	Gambela
Ethiopia	1996	Present	Harari
France	1950	1954	Cambodia Free State
France	1950	1954	Laos Free State
France	1950	1954	Vietnam Free State
France	1991	Present	Corsica

(*Continued*)

Core state	From	To	National group/ territory
Georgia	2004	Present	Autonomous Republic of Ajara
Guatemala	1986	Present	Mayas
Guatemala	1986	Present	Xinca
Guatemala	1986	Present	Garifunas
Guinea-Bissau	2000	Present	Manjaco
Honduras	1946	Present	Lenca
Honduras	1946	Present	Miskitos
Honduras	1946	Present	Garifs (Black Caribs)
Honduras	1946	Present	Chorti
Honduras	1946	Present	Tawahka
India	1963	1971	Naga
India	1972	1976	Naga
India	1972	1976	Manipuri
India	1977	1986	Manipuri
India	1977	1986	Naga
India	1987	1991	Manipuri
India	1987	1991	Naga
India	1987	1991	Indigenous Tripuri
India	1987	1991	Mizo
India	1952	Present	Kashmir
India	1992	Present	Manipuri
India	1992	Present	Naga
India	1992	Present	Indigenous Tripuri
India	1992	Present	Mizo
India	1992	Present	Bodo
Indonesia	1949	1958	Sundanese
Indonesia	1949	1958	Minangkabaus
Indonesia	1949	1958	Dayak
Indonesia	1949	1958	Balinese
Indonesia	1949	1958	Madura
Indonesia	1949	1958	Minahasa

Core state	From	To	National group/ territory
Indonesia	1949	1958	Ternate
Indonesia	1959	1962	Sundanese
Indonesia	1959	1962	Minangkabaus
Indonesia	1959	1962	Dayak
Indonesia	1959	1962	Achinese
Indonesia	1959	1962	Balinese
Indonesia	1959	1962	Makassarese and Bugis
Indonesia	1959	1962	Minahasa
Indonesia	1959	1962	Ternate
Indonesia	1963	1966	Minangkabaus
Indonesia	1963	1966	Dayak
Indonesia	1963	1966	Achinese
Indonesia	1963	1966	Balinese
Indonesia	1963	1966	Makassarese and Bugis
Indonesia	1963	1966	Minahasa
Indonesia	1963	1966	Ternate
Indonesia	1996	1998	Dayak
Indonesia	1999	2001	Dayak
Indonesia	1999	2001	Amboinese
Indonesia	2002	Present	Dayak
Indonesia	2002	Present	Papua
Indonesia	2002	Present	Amboinese
Indonesia	2001	Present	Special Autonomy of Aceh
Iraq	1970	1974	Kurdistan Region
Israel	1995	Present	Palestinian Territories
Japan	1972	1983	Okinawans
Japan	1984	Present	Burakumin
Laos	1953	1974	Khmu
Laos	1953	1974	Phuthai (incl. White, Black and White Tai)

(*Continued*)

Core state	From	To	National group/ territory
Laos	1953	1974	Tai Lü and Tai Yuan
Laos	1953	1974	Other Lao Sung
Laos	1987	Present	Other Lao Thoeng
Laos	1987	Present	Khmu
Laos	1987	Present	Phuthai (incl. White, Black and White Tai)
Laos	1987	Present	Tai Lü and Tai Yuan
Laos	1987	Present	Other Lao Sung
Laos	1987	Present	Yao
Malaysia	1957	Present	Dayaks
Malaysia	1957	Present	Kadazans
Mexico	1995	Present	Indigenous peoples
Moldova	1991	1994	Gagauz
Mongolia	1946	Present	Kazakh
Myanmar	1962	Present	Shan State
Myanmar	1962	Present	Kachin State
Myanmar	1962	Present	Karenni State
Myanmar	1990	Present	Wa
Namibia	1990	Present	Nama
Namibia	1990	Present	Basubia
Namibia	1990	Present	Baster
Nicaragua	1978	Present	Atlantic Coast "Autonomous Region"
Nicaragua	1988	Present	Mayangnas
Nigeria	1960	1964	Yoruba
Nigeria	1965	1966	Igbo
Nigeria	1979	1983	Yoruba
Nigeria	1979	1983	Tiv
Nigeria	1999	Present	Tiv
Pakistan	1977	Present	Baluchistan
Pakistan	1977	Present	Federally Administered Tribal Areas

Core state	From	To	National group/territory
Peru	1970	Present	Quechua
Peru	1970	Present	Aymara
Philippines	1977	1989	Mindanao
Republic of Vietnam	1954	1975	Hoa (Chinese)
Romania	1989	1995	Hungarians
Slovakia	1993	1997	Hungarians
South Africa	1963	1993	Transkei Homeland
South Africa	1972	1993	Bophuthatswana Homeland
South Africa	1972	1993	Ciskei Homeland
South Africa	1972	1993	Lebowa Homeland
South Africa	1973	1993	Venda Homeland
South Africa	1973	1993	Ganzakulu Homeland
South Africa	1975	1993	Basotho Qwa Qwa Homeland
South Africa	1975	1993	Swazi Homeland
South Africa	1975	1993	S. Ndebele Homeland
South Africa	1976	1993	KwaZulu Homeland
Sri Lanka	1987	2009	Sri Lankan Tamils
Sudan	1972	1982	Dinka
Sudan	1972	1982	Nuer
Sudan	1972	1982	Bari
Sudan	1972	1982	Azande
Sudan	1972	1982	Shilluk
Sudan	1972	1982	Latoka
Syria	1946	1948	Alawi
Syria	1946	1948	Druze
Tajikistan	1994	Present	Gorno-Badakhshan Autonomous Region
Thailand	1946	1952	Malay Muslims
Thailand	1953	1965	Malay Muslims
Thailand	1966	1971	Malay Muslims

(*Continued*)

Core state	From	To	National group/ territory
Thailand	1972	1973	Malay Muslims
Thailand	1974	1976	Malay Muslims
Thailand	1977	1979	Malay Muslims
Thailand	1980	1983	Malay Muslims
Thailand	1984	1998	Malay Muslims
Thailand	1999	2001	Malay Muslims
Thailand	2002	Present	Malay Muslims
US	1851	Present	Northeast Sovereign Indian Tribes
US	1851	Present	California Sovereign Indian Tribes
US	1851	Present	Southwest Sovereign Indian Tribes
US	1851	Present	Great Basin Sovereign Indian Tribes
US	1851	Present	Plateau Sovereign Indian Tribes
US	1851	Present	Plains Sovereign Indian Tribes
US	1851	Present	Southeast Sovereign Indian Tribes
US	1851	Present	Northwest Coast Sovereign Indian Tribes
USSR	1946	1956	Tatars
USSR	1946	1956	Chuvashes
USSR	1946	1956	Mordva
USSR	1946	1956	Bashkirs
USSR	1946	1956	Kirghis
USSR	1946	1956	Udmurt
USSR	1946	1956	Mari
USSR	1946	1956	Ossetes
USSR	1946	1956	Lezgins
USSR	1946	1956	Kabardins
USSR	1946	1956	Karelians

Core state	From	To	National group/territory
USSR	1946	1956	Avars
USSR	1946	1956	Kumuks
USSR	1946	1956	Dargins
USSR	1946	1956	Komi
USSR	1946	1956	Buryats
USSR	1946	1956	Yakuts
USSR	1946	1956	Karakalpaks
USSR	1946	1956	Tuvinians
USSR	1946	1956	Finns
USSR	1946	1956	Circassians
USSR	1946	1956	Adyghe
USSR	1946	1956	Abkhaz
USSR	1946	1956	Khakass
USSR	1946	1956	Altai
USSR	1957	1991	Byelorussians
USSR	1957	1991	Tatars
USSR	1957	1991	Uzbeks
USSR	1957	1991	Kazakhs
USSR	1957	1991	Chuvashes
USSR	1957	1991	Mordva
USSR	1957	1991	Bashkirs
USSR	1957	1991	Kirghis
USSR	1957	1991	Udmurt
USSR	1957	1991	Chechens
USSR	1957	1991	Mari
USSR	1957	1991	Ossetes
USSR	1957	1991	Circassians
USSR	1957	1991	Dargins
USSR	1957	1991	Kumuks
USSR	1957	1991	Ingush
USSR	1957	1991	Buryats

(*Continued*)

Core state	From	To	National group/territory
USSR	1957	1991	Kabardins
USSR	1957	1991	Karakalpaks
USSR	1957	1991	Kalmyks
USSR	1957	1991	Karelians
USSR	1957	1991	Komi
USSR	1957	1991	Lezgins
USSR	1957	1991	Avars
USSR	1957	1991	Yakuts
USSR	1957	1991	Tuvinians
USSR	1957	1991	Karachai
USSR	1957	1991	Adyghe
USSR	1957	1991	Abkhaz
USSR	1957	1991	Khakass
USSR	1957	1991	Altai
USSR	1957	1991	Balkars
Uzbekistan	1991	Present	Karakalpak
Vietnam	1954	1974	Hoa (Chinese)

Sources: This list attempts to be an exhaustive articulation of sham federacy after 1945. In part it draws from Cederman et al. (2009a) Ethnic Power Relations (EPR) dataset which features a list of ethnic groups that have "regional autonomy." In order to compile a list of sham federacies, however, various groups were removed from the EPR's "regional autonomy" list including: PITs (such as Northern Ireland), non-territorially based autonomous arrangements (such as the "Germans" of Belgium), member-units of sham federations (such as the Republics of the USSR and the member-units of the Russian Federation), and where data were indiscernible (such as the reference of "others" being associated with Lebanon). Additionally, a wide range of territories and groups that were not included in the EPR were added to the list, such as the Free States of Indochina, America's Indian Territories, and many others. It should also be noted that in a limited number of areas, such as Sudan, the groups listed are associated with a single territory, such as South Sudan. In other areas, such as the Indian Territories of the US, in order to make the 305 Indian tribes of America more feasible to articulate, large numbers of tribes were grouped under regional headings.

Colonies in the International System 1900–2008

Core state	Date of termination (if any)	Colony
Australia	1968	Nauru
Australia	1975	Papua New Guinea
Australia	Current	Christmas Islands
Australia	Current	Cocos (Keeling) Islands
Australia	Current	Norfolk Island
Austria	1918	Hungary
Austria	1918	Czechoslovakia
Belgium	1960	Democratic Republic of the Congo
Belgium	1962	Burundi
Belgium	1962	Rwanda
China	1921	Mongolia
Ethiopia	1993	Eritrea
France	1946	Syria
France	1946	Lebanon
France	1953	Cambodia
France	1953	Laos
France	1954	Vietnam
France	1956	Morocco
France	1956	Tunisia
France	1958	Guinea
France	1960	Mali

(*Continued*)

Core state	Date of termination (if any)	Colony
France	1960	Senegal
France	1960	Mauritania
France	1960	Niger
France	1960	Ivory Coast
France	1960	Burkina Faso
France	1960	Togo
France	1960	Cameroon
France	1960	Gabon
France	1960	Central African Republic
France	1960	Chad
France	1960	Congo
France	1960	Madagascar
France	1962	Algeria
France	1975	Comoros
France	1977	Djibouti
France	Current	Guadeloupe (Dependencies: Marie-Galante, La Désirade and Les Saintes, Saint-Barthélemy and French St Martin)
France	Current	Guyana
France	Current	Martinique
France	Current	Mayotte
France	Current	Reunion
France	Current	Saint-Pierre-et-Miquelon
France	1960	Benin
Germany	1944	Luxembourg
India	1971	Bhutan
Italy	1941	Ethiopia
Italy	1951	Libya
Italy	1960	Somalia
Japan	1948	North Korea

Core state	Date of termination (if any)	Colony
Japan	1949	South Korea
Morocco	Current	Western Sahara
Netherlands	1949	Indonesia
Netherlands	1975	Suriname
New Zealand	1976	Samoa
New Zealand	Current	Tokelau
Portugal	1974	Guinea-Bissau
Portugal	1975	Cape Verde
Portugal	1975	Sao Tome and Principe
Portugal	1975	Angola
Portugal	1975	Mozambique
Russia	1917	Finland
South Africa	1990	Namibia
Spain	1902	Cuba
Spain	1968	Equatorial Guinea
Sweden	1905	Norway
Turkey	1908	Turkey
Turkey	1914	Albania
United Kingdom	1901	Australia
United Kingdom	1920	Afghanistan
United Kingdom	1922	Ireland
United Kingdom	1932	Iraq
United Kingdom	1937	Egypt
United Kingdom	1946	Jordan
United Kingdom	1947	India
United Kingdom	1947	Pakistan
United Kingdom	1947	New Zealand
United Kingdom	1948	Israel
United Kingdom	1948	Myanmar
United Kingdom	1948	Sri Lanka
United Kingdom	1956	Sudan

(*Continued*)

Core state	Date of termination (if any)	Colony
United Kingdom	1957	Ghana
United Kingdom	1957	Malaysia
United Kingdom	1960	Cyprus
United Kingdom	1960	Nigeria
United Kingdom	1961	Sierra Leone
United Kingdom	1961	Tanzania
United Kingdom	1961	Kuwait
United Kingdom	1962	Jamaica
United Kingdom	1962	Trinidad and Tobago
United Kingdom	1962	Uganda
United Kingdom	1963	Kenya
United Kingdom	1963	Zanzibar
United Kingdom	1964	Malta
United Kingdom	1964	Zambia
United Kingdom	1965	Maldives
United Kingdom	1965	Singapore
United Kingdom	1966	Barbados
United Kingdom	1966	Guyana
United Kingdom	1966	Lesotho
United Kingdom	1966	Botswana
United Kingdom	1968	Swaziland
United Kingdom	1968	Mauritius
United Kingdom	1970	Fiji
United Kingdom	1970	Tonga
United Kingdom	1971	Bahrain
United Kingdom	1971	Qatar
United Kingdom	1971	United Arab Emirates
United Kingdom	1971	Oman
United Kingdom	1973	Bahamas
United Kingdom	1974	Grenada
United Kingdom	1976	Seychelles
United Kingdom	1978	Solomon Islands

Core state	Date of termination (if any)	Colony
United Kingdom	1978	Tuvalu
United Kingdom	1979	St Lucia
United Kingdom	1979	St Vincent and the Grenadines
United Kingdom	1979	Kiribati
United Kingdom	1980	Zimbabwe
United Kingdom	1981	Antigua & Barbuda
United Kingdom	1981	Belize
United Kingdom	1981	Vanuatu
United Kingdom	1983	St Kitts and Nevis
United Kingdom	1984	Brunei
United Kingdom	Current	Anguilla
United Kingdom	Current	Falkland Islands
United Kingdom	Current	Montserrat
United Kingdom	Current	Pitcairn Island
United Kingdom	Current	St Helena (Dependencies: Ascension & Tristan Da Cunha)
United Kingdom	1910	South Africa
United Kingdom	1964	Malawi
United Kingdom	1965	Gambia
United Kingdom	1978	Dominica
United States	Current	Guam
United States	Current	American Samoa
United States	Current	United States Virgin Islands
United States	1909	Cuba
United States	1924	Dominican Republic
United States	1934	Haiti
United States	1946	Philippines
United States	1986	Marshall Islands
United States	1994	Palau
United States	1986	Federated States of Micronesia

Sources: For historic colonies see Goldsmith and He 2008, 609–11; Encyclopedia Britannica 2010; CIA World Factbook 2009; *History World*, 2010. For current colonies see Aldrich and Connell 1998, 12–15.

References

Legal Cases

Al Sabah v Grupo Torras et Al 2005, 2 WLR 904 (CI).

American Ins. Co. v Canter 1828, 26 US (1 Pet.) 511, 542.

Califano v Torres 1978, 435 U.S. 1.

Campbell et al. v Attorney General British Columbia et al. 2000 BCSC 1123.

Chae Chan Ping v U.S. 130 U.S. 581, 600, 32 L. ed. 1068, 1073, 9 Sup. Ct. Rep. 623.

Chan Kam Nga v Director of Immigration. 1999. *Hong Kong Law Reports & Digest* 1: 304.

Cherokee Nation v Georgia 1831, 30 U.S. (5 Pet.) 1.

Dorr v United States 1904, 195 US 138, 140.

Downes v Bidwell 1901, 182 US 244.

Dred Scott v Sandford 1856, 60 US (19 How.) 393, 438–9, 443.

Examining Board v Flores de Otero 1976, 426 U.S. 572, 494–596.

Figueroa v Puerto Rico 1953, 232 F.2d 615, 620 (1st Cir.).

First National Bank v County of Yankton 1879, 101 U.S. (11 Otto) 129–33.

Harris v Rosario 1980, 446 U.S. 651.

Johnson v M'Intosh 1823, 21 U.S. (8 Wheat.) 543.

Late Corp. of the Church of Jesus Christ of Latter-Day Saints v United States 1889, 136 U.S. 1,42.

Lone Wolf v Hitchcock 1903, 23 S.Ct. 216 U.S.

Perez de la Cruz v Crowley Towing and Transp. Co. 1986, 807 F.2d 1084, 1088 (1st Cir.), cert. denied, 481 U.S. 1050 (1987).

Rodriguez v Popular Democratic Party 1982, 457 U.S. 1, 8.

Santa Clara Pueblo v Martinez 1978, 436 U.S. 49, 56.

Scott v Sandford 1856, 60 U.S. (19 How.) 393, 438–9, 443.

Sere v Pitot 1810, 10 US (6 Cranch) 332, 337.

United States v Lopez Andino 1987, 831 F.2d 1164 (1st Cir.), cert. denied, 486 U.S. 1034 (1988).

United States v Quinones 1985, 758 F. 2d 40, 42 (1st Cir.).

United States v Rivera Torrez 1987, 826 F.2d 151, 154 (1st Cir.).

United States v Sanchez 1993, 992 F.2d 1143, 1152–3 (11th Cir.), cert. denied, 510 U.S. 1110 (1994).

United States v Vega Figueroa 1997, 984 F. Supp. 71. 79 D. Puerto Rico.

United States v Wheeler 1978, 435 U.S. 313, 330–1.

Washington v Confederated Bands and Tribes of the Yakima Indian Nation 1979, 439 U.S. 463.

Yeung May Wan & Others. HKSAR 2005, 2 HKLRD 212.

Youngstown Sheet and Tube Co. v Sawyer 1952, 343 U.S. 579.

Government Documents

Åland, Act on the Autonomy of Åland (1991/1997), Available from: <http://www.lagtinget.Åland.fi/eng/act.html#anchor581659>. Last accessed January 23, 2003.

Åland, Historical Milestones. Available from: <http://www.Åland.fi/virtual/eng/frame.html>. Last accessed January 23, 2003.

Australia, Constitution of Australia.

Bank for International Settlements. 2011. <http://www.bis.org/statistics/bankstats.htm>. Downloaded September 2011.

Bank of International Settlements. 2008, 76. Bank of International Settlements. 2008. *Guidelines to the international locational banking statistics.* <http://www.bis.org/statistics/locbankstatsguide.pdf>. Downloaded September 2011.

Canada, The 1867 Constitution Act (The 1867 British North America Act) 1867. Available from: <http://www.efc.ca/pages/law/cons/Constitutions/Canada/English/ca_1867.html>. Last accessed April 23, 2002.

Canada, The Constitution Act. 1982. Available from: <http://www.legislation.hmso.gov.uk/acts/acts1998/19980046.htm>. Last accessed April 23, 2002.

Canada, Constitutional Act. 1982. Available from: <http://lois.justice.gc.ca/en/const/index.html>. Last accessed July 14, 2006.

Canada, Reference re Secession of Quebec. 1998. S.C.R. 2: 217.

Catalonia, Catalan Statute of Autonomy. 1979. Available from: <http://www.catalunya-lliure.com/estatut.html>. Last accessed February 5, 2003.

China, The Basic Law of the Hong Kong Special Administrative Region of the People's Republic of China. 1990. Hong Kong: The Consultative Committee for the Basic Law of the Hong Kong Special Administrative Region of the People's Republic of China, April.

China, The Constitution of the Peoples' Republic of China. 1982. Available from: <http://english.peopledaily.com.cn/constitution/constitution.html>. Last accessed April 23, 2002.

China, National People's Congress Standing Committee. 2007. Decision of the Standing Committee of the National People's Congress on Issues Relating to the Methods for Selecting the Chief Executive of the Hong Kong Special Administrative Region and for Forming the Legislative Council of the Hong Kong Special Administrative Region in the Year 2012 and on Issues Relating to Universal Suffrage, December 29.

Corsica, 1991 Special Statute. 1991. 12 April.

Denmark, The Constitution of Denmark. 1953/1992. Available from: <http://www.oefre.unibe.ch/law/icl/da00000_.html>. Last accessed February 5, 2003.

Eritrea, UN General Assembly Resolution 617, VIII. 1952. General Assembly Official Records, Supplement 20 (A/2361), December 17.

Eritrea, UN General Assembly Resolution 390A (V). 1952. Final Report of the United Nations Commissioner in Eritrea, General Assembly Official Records, Seventh Session, Supplement (A/2188, 15: 74–75), October 17.

European Commission. 2009. Eurostat. Available from: <http://epp.eurostat.ec. europa.eu/portal/page/portal/region_cities/regional_statistics/data/database>. Last accessed August 2012.

EU, Copenhagen European Council. 1993. Presidency Conclusions Copenhagen European Council. June 21–22. Available from: <http://www.europarl.europa.eu/ enlargement/ec/pdf/cop_en.pdf>. Last accessed February 2010.

Faroe Islands, Denmark Parliamentary Act 2005. No. 79, on The Assumption Act of Matters and Fields of Responsibility by the Faroese Authorities. May 12.

Federated States of Micronesia, Compact of Free Association. 1986. Available from: <http://www.fsmlaw.org/compact/index.htm>. Last accessed 15 April, 2005.

Finland, The Constitution of Finland 2000. Available from: <http://www.om.fi/consti-tution/3340.htm>. Last accessed 5 February, 2003.

France, Constitution of France 1958. Available from: <http://www.concourt.am/ wwconst/constit/france/france-e.htm>. Last accessed May 15, 2005.

Germany, The Basic Law of the Federal Republic of Germany. 1949/1995. Reprinted in S. E. Finer, Vernon Bogdanor, and Bernard Rudden, *Comparing Constitutions*, Oxford: Oxford University Press.

Government of the Republic of Indonesia and the Free Aceh Movement. 2005. *Memorandum of Understanding between the Government of the Republic of Indonesia and the Free Aceh Movement.* Helsinki, Finland, August 15.

Government of Sudan and the Sudan People's Liberation Movement. 2004. *Protocol between the Government of Sudan (GOS) and the Sudan People's Liberation Movement (SPLM) on Power Sharing.* Naivasha, Kenya. May 26.

Greenland, Greenland Home Rule Act. 1978/1993. Reprinted in Hurst Hannum (ed.) *Documents on Autonomy and Minority Rights*, Dordrecht, The Netherlands: Nijhoff, pp. 213–18.

Hong Kong, The Basic Law of the Hong Kong Special Administrative Region of the People's Republic of China. 1990. Hong Kong: The Consultative Committee for the Basic Law of the Hong Kong Special Administrative Region of the People's Republic of China, April.

Hong Kong Census and Statistics Department. 2007. Annual Survey of Regional Offices Representing Overseas Companies in Hong Kong.

Hong Kong, Hong Kong Association. 2010. Available at: <http://www.hkab.org.hklasp/ publiclindex.asp>. Last accessed February 2010.

Hong Kong, Hong Kong Monetary Authority. 2010. Available at: <http://www.info. gov.hk/hkma/chi/hkma/advisory/exchange_b main.htm>. Accessed February 2010.

Hong Kong, Hong Kong Securities and Futures Commission. 2010. Available at: <http://www.hksfc.org.hk/eng/html/index.html>. Last accessed February 2010.

Independent International Commission on Decommissioning. 2005. *Report*, Dublin, Belfast. September 26. Available at: <www.nio.gov.uk/iicd_report_26_sept_2005. pdf>. Accessed March 2010.

India, Constitution of India. 1950. Available at: <http://india.gov.in/govt/constitu-tions_of_india.php>. Last accessed April 2010.

Indonesia, Government of the Republic of Indonesia and the Free Aceh Movement. 2005. *Memorandum of Understanding between the Government of the Republic of Indonesia and the Free Aceh Movement.* 15 August. Helsinki, Finland.

International Court of Justice Reports. 1975. Western Sahara Advisory Opinion.

International Monetary Fund. 2004. *Offshore Financial Centers* <http://www.imf.org/external/np/mfd/2004/eng/031204.pdf>. Downloaded September 2011.

Iraq, Iraqi Constitution. 2005. Available at: <http://www.uniraq.org/documents/iraqi_constitution.pdf>. Last accessed March 2010.

Iraq, Transitional Administrative Law. 2004. Available at: <http://www.cpa-iraq.org/government/TAL.html>. Last accessed March 2010.

Ireland, "The Ulster Tail, Shall it Wag the Irish Dog?" Pamphlet (1912), reprinted in Grenfell Morton. 1980. *Home Rule and The Irish Question*, Essex: Longman, 106.

Ireland, Minister for External Affairs, Irish Free State, to the Secretary of State for Dominion Affairs. 1932. In Arthur Berriedale Keith, ed. 1932. *Speeches and Documents on the British Dominions 1918–1931*, Oxford: Oxford University Press, 462–5.

Ireland, Mr. P. McGilligan, *Dáil Eireann*. 1931. In Arthur Berriedale Keith, ed. 1932. *Speeches and Documents on the British Dominions 1918–1931*, Oxford: Oxford University Press, 247.

Ireland, Proceedings of the Home Rule Conference held in Dublin in November 1873. 1874. Reprinted in Grenfell Morton. 1980. *Home Rule and The Irish Question*, Essex: Longman, 79.

Israel, Agreement on Preparatory Transfer of Powers and Responsibilities. 1994. Israel-PLO, *International Legal Materials*, 34: 455, August 29.

Israel, Agreement on the Gaza Strip and the Jericho Area. 1994. Israel–PLO, *International Legal Materials* 33: 622, 4 May.

Israel, The Declaration of Principles on Interim Self-Government Arrangements. 1993. Israel–Palestine Liberation Organization, *International Legal Materials*, 32: 1525–44, September 13.

Israel, The Israeli-Palestinian Interim Agreement on the West Bank and the Gaza Strip. 1995. Israel–PLO, *International Legal Materials* 36: 551, September 28.

Italian National Institute of Statistics 2008. Available at: <http://www.istat.it/salas-tampa/comunicati/non_calendario/20091015_00/>. Last accessed August 2011.

League of Nations. 1921. *The Åland Islands Question*, Report Submitted to the council of the League of Nations by the Commission of Rapporteurs, League of Nations Council Doc. B.7 21/68/106, April 16, 1921.

Liechtenstein. 1923. Customs Treaty. Available at: <http://www.admin.ch/ch/d/sr/0_631_112_514/a43. html>. Accessed July 2012.

Marshall Islands, Compact of Free Association. 1986. Available from: <http://www.un.int/marshall-islands/cfa_fulltext.html>. Last accessed April 15, 2005.

Marshall Islands. 1986. Public Law 99-239 of January 14, 99 Stat. 1770 (48 U.S.C. 1901 et seq., 2001 et seq.).

Mindanao, An Act Providing for an Organic Act for the Autonomous Region in Muslim Mindanao. 1989. Republic Act No. 06734 Available from: <http://www.congress.gov.ph/download/ra_08/Ra06734.pdf>. Last accessed November 11, 2004.

Ministry of Commerce, Beijing. 2009. FDI statistics. *Invest in China*, Available at <http://www.fdi.gov. cn/pub/FDI_EN/Statistics/FDIStatistics/default.htm>. Last accessed September 2009.

Montevideo Convention on the Rights and Duties of States. 1933. Done at Montevideo December 26, 1933; entered into force December 26, 1934, Reprinted in *The American Journal of International Law* (Supp.) 28: 75, December 26.

Netherlands Antilles, Charter for the Kingdom of the Netherlands. 1954. Reprinted in Albert P. Blaustein and Phyllis M. Blaustein, eds. 1988. *Constitutions of Dependencies and Special Sovereignties*, Dobbs Ferry, NY: Oceana.

New Caledonia, Organic Law No. 99-209 (1999), March 19.

New Zealand, Cook Islands Constitution Act. 1964. No. 69, (as at August 1965), Public Act. Available at <http://www.legislation.govt.nz/act/public/1964/0069/latest/DLM354084. html#DLM354084>. Accessed December 2012.

Nicaragua, Autonomy Statute for the Regions of the Atlantic Coast of Nicaragua. 1987. Available at <http://www.yorku.ca/cerlac/URACCAN/robles.html>. Last accessed November 4, 2004.

Nixon, Richard M. 1970. Special Message to the Congress on Indian Affairs, July 8. In *Public Papers of the Presidents of the United States: Richard M. Nixon*, 567.

Northern Ireland, Belfast Agreement. 1998. The Northern Ireland Peace Agreement. The Agreement reached in the multi-party negotiations on April 10. Available at: <http://www.niassembly.gov.uk/io/agreement.htm>. Last accessed March 2010.

Northern Ireland, Fair Employment Agency. 1978. *An Industrial and Occupational Profile of the Two Sections of the Population in Northern Ireland*, Belfast.

Northern Ireland, Report of the Commission on Disturbances in Northern Ireland (Cameron Report). 1969. Cmd. 532, Belfast: HMSO.

Northern Ireland, Ulster's Solemn League and Covenant. 1912. Public Record Office of Northern Ireland, September 28. Reprinted in Grenfell Morton. 1980. *Home Rule and the Irish Question*, Essex: Longman, 107.

Northern Mariana Islands. 1976. Public Law 94-241 of March 24, 1976, 90 Stat. 263 (48 U.S.C. 1801 et seq.).

Northern Mariana Islands, Constitution of the Northern Mariana Islands. 1977. Proc. No. 4534, October 24, 42 F.R. 56593. Available from: <http://www.washingtonwatchdog. org/documents/usc/ttl48/ch17/subchI/sec1801.html>. Last accessed April 23, 2005.

Northern Mariana Islands, Covenant to Establish a Commonwealth of the Northern Mariana Islands in Political Union with the United States of America. 1976. Pub. L. 94–241, 90 Stat. 263. Available from: <http://www.washingtonwatchdog.org/documents/usc/ttl48/ch17/subchI/sec1801.html>. Last accessed April 23, 2005.

Nunavut, Nunavut Implementation Commission. 1995. Footprints in New Snow: A Comprehensive Report from the Nunavut Implementation Commission to the Department of Indian Affairs and Northern Development, Government of the Northwest Territories and Nunavut Tunngavik Incorporated Concerning the Establishment of the Nunavut Government, March.

Palau Islands, Compact of Free Association. 1994. Available from: <http://www.washingtonwatchdog.org/documents/usc/ttl48/ch18/subchII/ptA/sec1931.html>. Last accessed April 23, 2005.

Portugal, Constitution of Portugal. 1974. Available at: <http://www.parlamento.pt/ingles/cons_leg/crp_ing/index.html>. Last accessed July 14, 2006.

Puerto Rico, The Constitution of the Commonwealth of Puerto Rico. 1952. Available from: <http://welcome.topuertorico.org/constitu.shtml>. Last accessed February 5, 2003.

Puerto Rico, Elective Governor Act. 1947/1964. Reprinted in Office of the Commonwealth of Puerto Rico, ed., *Documents on the Constitutional History of Puerto Rico*, 2nd edn, Washington, DC, 113–16.

Puerto Rico, Hearings Before the Senate Committee on Interior and Insular Affairs (1952), on S.J. Res. 151, 82nd Congress, 2d Sess., pp. 40–9.

Puerto Rico, The Puerto Rican Federal Relations Act. 1917/1964. Reprinted in Office of the Commonwealth of Puerto Rico, ed., *Documents on the Constitutional History of Puerto Rico*, 2nd edn, Washington, DC.

Puerto Rico, Truman's 1952 letter to Puerto Rican Governor Muñoz Marín, House Doc. 435, 82nd Congress, 2nd Session, 4.

Serbia, Constitution of the Republic of Serbia, 2006. Available at <http://www.wipo.int/wipolex/en/text.jsp?file_id=191258>. Last accessed August 2013.

Spain, Constitution of Spain, 1978. Available from: <http://www.oefre.unibe.ch/law/icl/sp00000_.html>. Last accessed February 3, 2003.

Sudan, Government of Sudan and the Sudan People's Liberation Movement. 2004. *Protocol between the Government of Sudan (GOS) and the Sudan People's Liberation Movement (SPLM) on Power Sharing.* Naivasha, Kenya. May 26.

Taiwan, Mainland Affairs Council. 2008. Analysis Report: 11 Years after Hong Kong's Handover. September. Available at: <http://www.mac.gov.tw/>. Last accessed September 2009.

Tanzania, Constitution of the United Republic of Tanzania. 1995. Available from: <http://www.kituochakatiba.co.ug/TanzaniaConstitution.pdf>. Last accessed November 1, 2004.

Tatarstan, On Delimitation of Jurisdictional Subjects and Mutual Delegation of Authority between the State Bodies of the Russian Federation and the State Bodies of the Republic of Tatarstan. 1994. Available from: <http://www.kcn.ru/tat_en/politics/dfa/inform/treaty.htm>. Last accessed October 30, 2004.

Trusteeship Council. 2007. Available at: <http://www.unorg/documents/tc.htm>. Last accessed February 18, 2007.

UK Office for National Statistics. 2011. Regional, Sub-regional, and Local Gross Value Added. December 12. <http://www.ons.gov.uk/ons/publications/re-reference-tables.html?edition=tcm%3A77-250308>. Downloaded December 2011.

UK, British Department for International Development. 2005. *Why We Need to Work More Effectively in Fragile States.* London: DFID, January.

UK, Explanatory Notes to Northern Ireland Act 2000. Available at <http://opsi.gov.uk/acts/acts2000/en/ukpgaen_20000001_en_1>. Last accessed March 2010.

UK, Foreign and Commonwealth Office. 2007. *Managing Risk in the Overseas Territories.* Available at: <http://www.official-documents.gov.uk/document/hc0708/hc00/0004/0004.asp>. Last accessed February 2010.

UK, Government of Ireland Act 1920. <http://www.statutelaw.gov.uk/content.aspx?activeTextDocId=2045126>. Last accessed March 2010.

UK, Hansard. 1884. Benjamin Disraeli in the House of Commons *Hansard*, 3rd Ser., Vol. 72, p. 1016.

UK, Hansard 1916, 5th Ser., Vol. 82, Cols, 945, 950.

UK, House of Lords *Hansard* 2000, 200209-05, February 9.

UK, House of Lords *Parliamentary Debates* 1998. 5th ser., Vol. 592, Col. 79, July 21.

UK, Naval Defense and Dominion Autonomy: Memorandum of Dominion Ministers. 1918. In Arthur Berriedale Keith, ed. 1932. *Speeches and Documents on the British Dominions 1918–1931*, Oxford: Oxford University Press, p. 11.

UK, Northern Ireland Act 1998. Available at the UK Statute Law Database: <http://www.statutelaw.gov.uk/content.aspx?activeTextDocId=2045126>. Last accessed March 2010.

UK, The Report of the Conference on the Operation of Dominion Legislation and Merchant Shipping Legislation. 1929. Reprinted in Arthur Berriedale Keith, ed. 1932. *Speeches and Documents on the British Dominions 1918–1931*, Oxford: Oxford University Press, 173–205.

UK, The Report of the Inter-Imperial Relations Committee, Imperial Conference. (1926. In Arthur Berriedale Keith, ed. 1932. *Speeches and Documents on the British Dominions 1918–1931*, Oxford: Oxford University Press, 164.

UK, The Rt. Hon. D. Lloyd George, House of Commons. 1921. In Arthur Berriedale Keith, ed. 1932. *Speeches and Documents on the British Dominions 1918–1931*, Oxford: Oxford University Press, 84.

UK, S.I. Caribbean Territories Order. 1991. No. 988.

UK, Scotland Act.1998. Available from: <http://www.legislation.hmso.gov.uk/acts/acts1998/19980046.htm>. Last accessed April 23, 2002.

UK, Scotland, Wales, and Northern Ireland. 1999. Memorandum of Understanding and Supplementary Agreements between the United Kingdom Government, Scottish Ministers, the Cabinet of the National Assembly for Wales. Cm 4444. Available at: <http://www.scotland.gov.uk/Publications/1999/10/MofU>. Last accessed March 2010.

UK, Secretary of State for Foreign and Commonwealth Affairs. 1999. Partnership for Progress and Prosperity Britain and the Overseas Territories. <http://collections.europarchive.org/tna/20080205132101/http://www.fco.gov.uk/servlet/Front?pagename=OpenMarket/Xcelerate/ShowPage&c=Page&cid=1018028164839>. Downloaded August 2011.

Ukraine, State Statistic Service of Ukraine. Available at:<http://www.ukrstat.gov.ua/>. Last accessed August 2011.

UN General Assembly Resolution 945. 1955. (X), 10 UN GAOR, Supp. (No. 19), UN Doc A/3116.

UN, 8 UN GAOR, C.4 348th meeting 1953 215 UN Doc. A/C.41/SR.348.

UN, Abelsen, Emil. 1991. Home Rule in Greenland. UN Doc. HR/NUUK/1991/SEM.1, BP.4, September 16.

UN, The Charter of the United Nations. 1945/1993. Reprinted in Adam Roberts and Benedict Kingsbury, *United Nations Divided World: The UN's Roles in International Relations*, 2nd edn, Oxford: Oxford University Press.

UN, Declaration on the Granting of Independence to Colonial Countries and Peoples. 1960. General Assembly Resolution 1514 (XV) of 14 December 1960. Available at: <http://www2.ohchr.org/english/law/independence.htm>. Downloaded March 2012.

UN, General Assembly Resolution 1064 1965, 20 UN GAOR, Supp. no. 14, UN Doc. A/6014.

UN, General Assembly Resolution 3285 1974, 29 UN GAOR, Supp. no. 31, UN Doc. A/6131.

UN, General Assembly Resolution 849IX 1954, Reprinted in *Yearbook of the United Nations*, November 22.

UN, Official Text of the United Nations Convention on the Law of the Sea with Annexes and Index. 1983. *The Law of the Sea* 1-157.

UN, Rehof, Lars Adam. 1991. "Effective Means of Planning for and Implementing Autonomy Including Negotiated Constitutional Arrangements and Involving Both Territorial and Personal Autonomy: Background paper to United Nations Meeting of Experts to Review the Experience of Countries in the Operation of Schemes of Internal Self-Government for Indigenous Populations," UN Doc. JR/NUUK/1991/SEM.1, BP.2, September 17, 10–17.

UN Statistics Division 2009. Available at: <data.un.org>. Last accessed July 12, 2011.

UN, The UN Declaration on Principles of International Law Concerning Friendly Relations and Co-operation Among States in Accordance with the Charter of the United Nations. 1970. General Assembly Resolution 2625 XXV, October 24.

UN, The UN Declaration on the Occasion of the Fiftieth Anniversary of the United Nations. 1995.

UN, The UN International Covenant on Civil and Political Rights. 1976. *United Nations Treaty Series* 999: 171.

UN, The UN International Covenant on Economic, Social and Cultural Rights. 1976. *United Nations Treaty Series* 993: 3.

UN, The Vienna Declaration and Programme of Action World Conference on Human Rights. 1993. UN Doc. A/CONF.157/24, Vienna, June 14–25.

UNICEF. 2004. *Towards a Baseline: Best Estimates of Social Indicators for South Sudan*. New Sudan Centre for Statistics and Evaluation in Association with UNICEF, (May).

United Nations Statistic Division. 2009. Available at <data.un.org>. Last accessed July 12, 2011.

US President's Message to Congress Regarding the Government of Puerto Rico. 1943. U.S.C.C.S. 3-88 (September 28, 1943) Available at: <http://www.presidency.ucsb.edu/ws/?pid=16318#ixzz1zs9tkq3w>. Downloaded July 2012.

US, Central Intelligence Agency. 2006. *World Fact Book*. Available from <http://www.cia.gov/cia/publications/factbook/>. Accessed April 16, 2009.

US, Congress Senate Committee on the Judiciary, 75th Congress. 1937. "Reorganization of the Federal Judiciary: Court Packing," Adverse Report to accompany S. 1392, May 18.

US, Congressional Record 1937, Appendix D. March 10: 2650.

US, The Constitution of the United States of America. 1787/1995. Reprinted in S. E. Finer, Vernon Bogdanor, and Bernard Rudden, *Comparing Constitutions*, Oxford: Oxford University Press.

US, Hearing before the Committee on Interior and Insular Affairs. 1959. US Senate, 86th Congress, 1st Session, on S. 2023, June 9.

US, Hearings Before the House Committee on Resources. 1997. H.R. 856, 105th Congress, 1st Sess., 40–445.

US, House of Representatives Doc. 435, 82nd Congress, 2nd Session.

US, House of Representatives, Third Interim Report of the Select Committee on Communist Aggression 1954, 83rd Congress, 2nd Session, under authority of H.Res. 346 and H. Res. 438, United States Government Printing Office.

US, The Indian Self-Determination and Education Assistance Act of Jan. 4, 1975. §3, 88 Stat. 2203, 2203–4.

US, Northwest Ordinance. 1787. Art. VI, ch. VIII, 1 Stat. 50, 51 (1789).

US, President Obama's Remarks at West Point. 2009. Full Transcript: President Obama's Speech on Afghanistan. Available at: <http://abcnews.go.com/Politics/>. Last accessed February 2010.

US, Report by Hon. Frances P. Bolton and Hon. James P. Richards on the Eighth Session of the General Assembly of the United Nations. 1954. Committee on Foreign Affairs, 83rd Congress, 2nd Session Washington, DC,: US Government Printing Office, April 26.

US, Robert Menedez, Extension of Remarks, House of Representatives. 1999. On Military Operations in Vieques. 106th Congress, July 16.

US, The Tribal Self-Governance Act of Oct. 25, 1994. Pub. L. No. 103-413, tit. 2, 108 Stat. 4250, 4270.

Wales, Welsh Assembly Government. 2006. Brief Overview—Government of Wales Act 2006. Available at: <http://wales.gov.uk/about/civilservice/departments/dfmc/constitutional/>. Last accessed March 2010.

WorldBank.2011.StatisticsforSmallStates:AsupplementtotheWorldDevelopmentIndicators. Available at <http://data.worldbank.org/sites/default/files/small-states-2011.pdf>. Downloaded March 2012.

World Bank National Accounts Data, and OECD National Accounts data files. 2011. Available at: http://data.worldbank.org/indicator/NY.GDP.PCAP.CD>. Last accessed July 2011.

Cited Works

Abernethy, David B. 2000. *The Dynamics of Global Dominance: European Overseas Empire, 1445–1980*. New Haven: Yale University Press.

Ackerman, Bruce. 1984. The Storrs Lectures: Discovering the Constitution. *Yale Law Journal* 93: 1013, 1053–55, 1069–71.

Ackerman, Bruce. 1991. *We The People*. Cambridge: Belknap Press of Harvard University Press.

Ackrén, Maria. 2009. *Conditions for Different Autonomy Regimes in the World: A Fuzzy-Set Application*. Åbo: Åbo Akademi University Press.

Adam, Heribert and Kogila Moodley. 1993. South Africa: The Opening of the Apartheid Mind in John McGarry and Brendan O'Leary, eds, *The Politics of Ethnic Conflict Regulation*. New York: Routledge, 226–50.

Adler, Emmanuel and Michael Barnett. 1998. A Framework for the Study of Security Communities. In Emmanuel Adler and Michael Barnett, eds, *Security Communities*. Cambridge. Cambridge University Press.

Aesop 1993/6th century bc. "The Bundle of Sticks" in *The Book of Virtues: A Treasury of Great Moral Stories*, ed. William J. Bennett. New York: Touchstone, 388.

Agnew, John. 2005. Sovereignty Regimes: Territoriality and State Authority in Contemporary World Politics. *Annals of the Association of American Geographers* 95 (2): 437–61.

Agranoff, Robert. 1994. Asymmetrical and Symmetrical Federalism in Spain: An Examination of Intergovernmental Policy. In Bertus de Villiers, ed., *Evaluating Federal Systems*, Pretoria: Juta, 61–89.

Alchian, Armen A. and Harold Demsetz. 1972. Production, Information Costs, and Economic Organization. *American Economic Review* 62 (December): 777–95.

Aldrich, Robert and John Connell. 1992. *France's Overseas Frontier: Départements et Territories d'Outre-Mer*. New York: Cambridge University Press.

Aldrich, Robert and John Connell. 1998. *The Last Colonies*. New York: Cambridge University Press.

Aleinikoff, T. Alexander. 2002. *Semblances of Sovereignty: The Constitution, the State, and American Citizenship*. Cambridge: Harvard University Press.

Alesina, Alberto and Enrico Spolaore. 2003. *The Size of Nations*. Cambridge, MA: MIT Press.

Allan, Trevor R. S. 1993. *Law, Liberty, and Justice*. Oxford: Clarendon Press.

Almond, Gabriel A. 1988. The Return to the State. *American Political Science Review* 82 (3): 853–74.

Amoretti, Ugo M. and Bermeo, Nancy, eds. 2004. *Federalism and Territorial Cleavages*. Baltimore: Johns Hopkins University Press, 93–122.

Anderson, Benedict. 1991. *Imagined Communities: Reflections on the Origins and Spread of Nationalism*. London: Verso.

Anderson, Bentley J. 1994. The Restoration of the South African Citizenship Act: An Exercise in Statutory Obfuscation. *Connecticut Journal of International Law* 9 (Spring): 295.

Anderson, Liam D. 2012. *Federal Solutions to Ethnic Problems: Accommodating Diversity*. New York: Routledge.

Anderson, Perry. 1974. *Lineages of the Absolutist State*. London: New Left Books.

Antigua Observer.com 2010. Bermuda Poll Shows Opposition to Independence, January 28. <http://www.antiguaobserver.com/?p=22690>. Downloaded September 2011.

Antoine, Rose-Marie B. 2008. *Commonwealth Caribbean Law and Legal Systems*. 2nd edn. New York: Routledge-Cavendish.

Archer, Clive. 1998. The United States Defense Areas in Greenland, *Cooperation and Conflict* 23: 123–44.

Archer, Clive. 2003. Greenland, US Bases and Missile Defense: New Two-Level Negotiations? *Cooperation and Conflict: Journal of the Nordic International Studies Association* 38 (2): 125–47.

Archer, Clive and Pertti Joenniemi, eds. 2003. *The Nordic Peace*. Hampshire, UK: Ashgate Publishing Limited.

Armstrong, H. W. and R. Read. 2000. Comparing the Economic Performance of Dependent Territories and Sovereign Micro-states. *Economic Development and Cultural Change* 48 (2): 285–306.

Aspinall, Edward. 2005. The Helsinki Agreement: A More Promising Basis for Peace in Aceh? *Policy Studies* 20, 1–68.

Atzili, Boaz. 2007. When Good Fences Make Bad Neighbors: Fixed Borders, State Weakness, and International Conflict. *International Organization* 31 (3): 139–73.

Axelrod, Robert. 1984. *The Evolution of Cooperation*. New York: Basic Books.

Baehr, Peter, R. 1975. Small States: A Tool for Analysis. *World Politics*. 27 (3): 456–66.

Bagehot, Walter. 1928. *The English Constitution*. London: Oxford University Press.

Bajpai, Kanti. 1997. Diversity, Democracy, and Devolution in India. In Michael E. Brown and Sumit Ganguly, eds, *Government Policies and Ethnic Relations in Asia and the Pacific*. Cambridge, MA: MIT Press, 33–81.

Baldacchino, Godfrey. 2006. Innovative Development Strategies form Non-Sovereign Island Juridictions? A Global Review of Economic Policy and Governance Practices. *World Development* 35 (5): 852–67.

Bank, J. C. 1971. *Federal Britain? The Case for Regionalism*. London: George G. Harrap.

Barendt, Eric. 1998. *An Introduction to Constitutional Law*. Oxford: Oxford University Press.

Barkey, Karen. 1994. *Bandits and Bureaucrats: The Ottoman Route to State Centralization*. Ithaca, NY: Cornell University Press.

Barkin J. Samuel and Bruce Cronin. 1994. The State and the Nation: Changing Norms and the Rules of Sovereignty in International Relations. *International Organization* 48 (1): 107–30.

Barrington, Lowell. 2011. *Comparative Politics: Structures and Choices*, 2nd edn. Boston: Wadsworth.

Barros, James. 1968. *The Åland Islands Question: Its Settlement by the League of Nations*. New Haven: Yale University Press.

Bartkus, Viva Ona. 2001. *The Dynamic of Secession*. Cambridge: Cambridge University Press.

Bartleson, Jens. 1996. *A Genealogy of Sovereignty*. Cambridge: Cambridge University Press.

Bates, Robert. 2010. *Prosperity & Violence: The Political Economy of Development*. 2nd edn. New York: WW Norton.

BBC News 2001. Northern Ireland chronology: 2001. Available at: <http://news.bbc.co.uk/2/hi/uk_news/northern_ireland/2933947.stm>. Last accessed March 2010.

BBC News 2003. Ahern "foresaw arms deadlock." Available at: <http://news.bbc.co.uk/2/hi/uk_news/northern_ireland/3204011.stm>. Last accessed March 2010.

Bendor, Jonathan and Dilip Mookherjee. 1987. Institutional Structure and the Logic of Ongoing Collective Action. *American Political Science Review* 81 (March): 129–54.

Benn, S. 1955. Sovereignty. *Encyclopedia of Philosophy*. 7: 501–5.

Bentham, Jeremy. 1789/1927. *Plan for an Universal and Perpetual Peace.* Grotius Society Publications no. 6. London: Sweet and Maxwell.

Bertram, G. 2006. Thematic Issue Commemorating the 20th Anniversary of the MIRAB Concept. *Asia Pacific Viewpoint* 47 (1).

Bianco, William T. and Robert H. Bates. 1990. Cooperation by Design: Leadership, Structure, and Collective Dilemmas. *American Political Science Review* 84 (March): 133–47.

Biersteker, Thomas J. and Cynthia Weber, eds. 1996. *State Sovereignty as Social Construct.* Cambridge: Cambridge University Press.

Birrell, Derek. 2007. Northern Ireland Business in Parliament: The Impact of the Suspension of Devolution in 2002. *Parliamentary Affairs* 60 (2); 297–312.

Blaustein, Albert P., Eric B. Blaustein, Phyllis M. Blaustein, and Philip Raworth, eds. 1997. *Constitutions of Dependencies and Territories.* Dobbs Ferry, NY: Oceana Publications.

Bogdanor, Vernon. 1995. *The Monarchy and the Constitution.* Oxford: Oxford University Press.

Bogdanor, Vernon. 1999. *Devolution in the United Kingdom.* Oxford: Oxford University Press.

Bose, Sumantra. 2002. *Bosnia After Dayton: Nationalist Partition and International Intervention.* New York: Oxford University Press.

Bowles, S. 2009. Did Warfare among Ancestral Hunter-Gathers affect the Evolution of Human Social Behaviors? *Science* 324: 1293–8.

Brazier, R. 1994. *Constitutional Practice.* 2nd edn. Oxford: Oxford University Press.

Brazier, R. 1997. *Ministers of the Crown.* Oxford: Oxford University Press.

Braithwaite, John and Peter Drahos. 2000. *Global Business Regulation.* Cambridge: Cambridge University Press.

Brennan Geoffrey and James M. Buchanan, 1980. *The Power to Tax: Analytical Foundations of a Fiscal Constitution.* New York: Cambridge University Press.

Breuilly, J. 1982. *Nationalism and the State,* Chicago: University of Chicago Press.

Brooks, Stephen G. 1999. Globalization of Production and the Changing Benefits of Conquest, *Journal of Conflict Resolution* 43 (5): 655–9.

Brooks, Stephen G. 2007. *Producing Security: Multinational Corporations, Globalization and the Changing Calculus of Conflict.* Princeton: Princeton University Press.

Brown, David. 2006. Study Claims Iraq's "Excess" Death Toll Has Reached 655,000. Washington Post. October 11. Available at: <http://www.washingtonpost.com/wp-dyn/content/article/2006/10/10/AR2006101001442.html>. Last accessed September 2009.

Brownlie, Ian. 1998. *Principles of Public International Law,* 5th edn. New York: Oxford University Press.

Brownlie, Ian. 2008. *Principles of Public International Law.* New York: Oxford University Press.

Brubaker, Rogers. 1996. *Nationalism Reframed.* Cambridge: Cambridge University Press.

Bryce, James. 1895. *American Commonwealth,* 3rd edn. New York: Macmillan.

Buchanan, James M. 1995. Federalism as an Ideal Political Order and an Objective for Constitutional Reform. *Publius: The Journal of Federalism* 25 (2): 19–28.

Bull, Hedley. 1977. *The Anarchical Society: A Study of Order in World Politics*. London and Basingstoke: Macmillan.

Bull, Hedley. 2002. *The Anarchical Society: A Study of Order in World Politics*, 3rd edn. New York: Columbia University Press.

Bunck, Julie Marie and Michael Ross Fowler. 1994. The Chunk and Basket Theories of Sovereignty. In Kenneth W. Thompson, ed., *Community, Diversity, and a New World Order: Essays in Honor of Inis L. Claude, Jr.*, Lanham: University Press of America, 137–44.

Bunck, Julie Marie and Michael Ross Fowler. 1996. *Law, Power, and the Sovereign State: The Evolution and Application of the Concept of Sovereignty*. University Park: Penn State Press.

Burke, Edmund. 1964. *Selected Writings and Speeches on America*, ed. Thomas H. D. Mahoney. Indianapolis: Bobbs-Merrill.

Burrow, Bernard and Geoffrey Denton. 1980. *Devolution or Federalism? Options for the United Kingdom*, London: Macmillan.

Burrows, John. 2012. *Canada's Indigenous Constitution*. Toronto: University of Toronto Press.

Butler, Jeffrey, Robert I. Rotberg, and John Adams. 1977. *The Black Homelands of South Africa: The Political and Economic Development of Bophuthatswana and KwaZulu*, Berkeley: University of California Press.

Cabranes, Jose A. 1978–79. Puerto Rico: Out of the Colonial Closet. *Foreign Policy* 33 (Winter): 68.

Cabrera, Luis. 2010. *The Practice of Global Citizenship*. Cambridge: Cambridge University Press.

Cairney, Paul. 2006. Venue Shift Following Devolution: When Reserved Meets Devolved in Scotland. *Regional & Federal Studies*. 16 (4): 429–45.

Calvert, Harry. 1968. *Constitutional Law in Northern Ireland: A Study in Regional Government*, London: Stevens & Sons.

Caporaso, James. 1997. Does the European Union Represent an n of 1? *ECSA Review* 10 (3): 1–5.

Carr, Edward H. 1940/2001. *The Twenty Years' Crisis, 1919–39: An Introduction to the Study of International Relations*. New York: Palgrave.

Carr, Raymond. 1984. *Puerto Rico: A Colonial Experiment*, New York: New York University Press.

Carter, Gwendolyn M. et al. 1967. *South Africa's Transkei: The Politics of Domestic Colonialism*. Evanston, IL: Northwestern University Press.

Casper, Gerhard. 1976. Constitutional Constraints on the Conduct of Foreign and Defense Policy: A Nonjudicial Model. *University of Chicago Law Review* 43: 463.

Caspersen, Nina 2003. The Thorny Issue of Ethnic Autonomy in Croatia: Serb Leaders and Proposals for Autonomy. *Journal on Ethnopolitics and Minority Issues in Europe* Available at <http://www.ecmi.de/fileadmin/downloads/publications/JEMIE/2003/nr3/Focus3-2003_Caspersen.pdf>. Accessed August 2013.

Cederman, Lars-Erik and Luc Girardin. 2007. Beyond Fractionalization: Mapping Ethnicity onto Nationalist Insurgencies. *American Political Science Review* 101 (1): 173–85.

Cederman, Lars-Erik, Brian Min, and Andreas Wimmer. 2009a. Ethnic Power Relations dataset. Available at: <http://dvn.iq.harvard.edu/dvn/dv/epr>. Last accessed January 21, 2010.

Cederman, Lars-Erik, Brian Min, and Andreas Wimmer. 2009b. Ethnic Armed Conflict dataset. hdl:1902.1/11797. Available at: <http://dvn.iq.harvard.edu/dvn/dv/epr>. Last accessed December 10, 2010.

Cederman, Lars-Erik, Brian Min, and Andreas Wimmer. 2009c. Ethnic Armed Conflict coding document. hdl:1902.1/11797. Available at: <http://dvn.iq.harvard.edu/dvn/dv/epr>. Last accessed December 10, 2010.

Cerny, Phillip. 1998. Neomedievalism, Civil War and the New Security Dilemma: Globalization as Durable Disorder. *Civil Wars* 1 (1): 36–64.

Chan, Kenneth Ka-Lok. 2004. Taking Stock of "One Country, Two Systems." In Wong Yiu-Chung, ed., *'One country, Two systems' in Crisis: Hong Kong's Transformation since the Handover*. Oxford: Lexington Books, 35–60.

Chan, Ming K. 1990. Democracy Derailed: Realpolitik in the Making of the Hong Kong Basic Law, 1985–90. In Ming K. Chan and David J. Clark, eds, *The Hong Kong Basic Law: Blueprint for "Stability and Prosperity" under Chinese Sovereignty?* Hong Kong: Hong Kong University Press, 3–35.

Chan, Ming K. and David J. Clark, eds. 1990. *The Hong Kong Basic Law: Blueprint for "Stability and Prosperity" under Chinese Sovereignty?* Hong Kong: Hong Kong University Press.

Chapman, Thomas and Philip Roeder. 2007. Partition as a Solution to Wars of Nationalism: The Importance of Institutions. *American Political Science Review* 101 (4): 677–90.

Chappell, David A. 1999. The Noumea Accord: Decolonization without Independence in New Caledonia? *Pacific Affairs* 72 (3): 373–91.

Chatterjee, P. 1993. *Nationalist Thought and the Colonial World*, Minneapolis: University of Minnesota.

Cheng, Seymour Ching-Yuan. 1931. *Schemes for the Federation of the British Empire*. New York: Columbia University Press.

Chesterman, Simon. 2002. East Timor in Transition: Self-Determination, State-Building and the United Nations. *International Peacekeeping* 9 (1): 45–76.

Chua, Amy. 2009. *Day of Empire: How Hyperpowers Rise to Global Dominance—and Why They Fall*. New York: Anchor Books.

Chudacoff, Howard P., Paul D. Escott, David M. Katzman, Mary Beth Norton, Thomas G. Paterson, and William M. Tuttle, Jr. 1997. *A People and a Nation: A History of the United States*, New York: McGraw Hill.

Clark, David J. 1990. The Basic Law: One Document, Two Systems. In Ming K. Chan and David J. Clark, eds, *The Hong Kong Basic Law: Blueprint for "Stability and Prosperity" under Chinese Sovereignty?* Hong Kong: Hong Kong University Press, 38–59.

Claude, Inis L. 1956/1984. *Swords into Plow Shares*, 4th edn. New York: McGraw Hill.

Coakley, John. 2008. Has the Northern Ireland Problem been Solved? *Journal of Democracy* 19 (3): 98–112.

Collier, P., L. Elliott, H. Hegre, A. Hoeffler, M. Reynal-Querol, and N. Sambanis. 2003. *Breaking the Conflict Trap: Civil War and Development Policy.* Oxford: Oxford University Press.

Colomer, Josep M. 1998. The Spanish "State of Autonomies": Non-Institutional Federalism. *West European Politics*, 21 (4): 40–52.

Colón, Rafael Hernández. 1959. The Commonwealth of Puerto Rico: Territory or state?" *Revista del Colegio de Abogados de Puerto Rico* 19: 207.

Columbia Encyclopedia. 2010. Available at: <www.bartleby.com>. Last accessed April 2010.

Commission on Weak States and US National Security. 2004. *On the Brink: Weak States and US National Security.* Washington, DC: Center for Global Development.

Cooley, Alexander. 2000/2001. Imperial Wreckage: Property Rights, Sovereignty, and Security in the Post-Soviet Space. *International Security* 25 (3): 100–27.

Cooley, Alexander. 2005. *Logics of Hierarchy: The Organization of Empires, States, and Military Occupations.* Ithaca: Cornell University Press.

Cooley, Alexander. 2008. *Base Politics.* Ithaca: Cornell University Press.

Cooley, Alexander and Hendrik Spruyt. 2009. *Contracting States: Sovereign Transfers in International Relations.* Princeton, NJ: Princeton University Press.

Copp, D. 2005. International Justice and the Basic Needs Principle. In G. Brock and H. Brighouse. eds. *The Political Philosophy of Cosmopolitanism.* Cambridge: Cambridge University Press, 39–54.

Coppieters, Bruno. 2001. *Federalism and Conflict in the Caucasus.* London: Royal Institute of International Affairs.

Cornell, Svante E. 2002. Autonomy as a Source of Conflict. Caucasian Conflicts in Theoretical Perspective. *World Politics* 54 (2): 248–9.

Correlates of War Project. 2008. State System Membership List, v2008.1. Available at: <http://correlatesofwar.org>. Last accessed February 2010.

Coser, Lewis A. 1956. *The Functions of Social Conflict.* New York: Free Press.

Council of Europe, Venice Commission, 1997. Opinion on the Draft Constitution of the Nakhichevan autonomous republic (Azerbaijan Republic). Opinion No. 291/2004, Strasbourg, December, 18.

Council of Europe, Venice Commission, 2004. Draft Opinion on the Draft Constitutional Law of Georgia on the Status of the Autonomous Republic of Ajara. Opinion No. 291/2004, Strasbourg, June 8.

Cox, Robert and Erich Frankland. 1995. The Federal State and the Breakup of Czechoslovakia: An Institutional Analysis. *Publius* 25 (1): 71–88.

Craig, C. 2003. *Glimmer of a New Leviathan: Total War in the Realism of Niebuhr, Morgenthau, and Waltz.* New York: Columbia University Press.

Craig, C. 2008. The Resurgent Idea of World Government. *Ethics & International Affairs* 22 (2): 133–42.

Craig, Gerald M. 1963. *Upper Canada; The Formative Years, 1784–1841.* New York: Oxford University Press.

Cramer, Christopher and Jonathan Goodhand. 2002. Try Again, Fail Again, Fail Better? War, the State, and the "Post Conflict" Challenge in Afghanistan. *Development and Change* 33 (5): 885–909.

Crawford, James. 1979. *The Creation of States in International Law*, London: Oxford University Press.

Crawford, Neta C. 2002. *Argument and Change in World Politics: Ethics, Decolonization, and Humanitarian Intervention.* New York: Cambridge University Press.

Crocker, Chester A. 2003. Engaging Failing States. *Foreign Affairs* 82 (5): 32–44.

Cunningham, David E. 2006. Veto Players and Civil War Duration. *American Journal of Political Science* 50 (4): 875–92.

Curry, Steven. 2004. *Indigenous Sovereignty and the Democratic Project.* Burlington, VT: Ashgate Publishing.

Dahl, Robert. 1982. *Dilemmas of Pluralist Democracy: Autonomy vs. Control.* New Haven and London: Yale University Press.

Dahl, Robert. 1986. *Democracy, Identity and Equality*, Oslo: Norwegian University Press.

Daniels, Christine and Michael D. Kennedy, eds. 2002. *Negotiated Empires: Centers and Peripheries in the Americas, 1500–1820.* New York, Routledge.

David, Steven R. 1997. Internal War: Causes and Cures. *World Politics* 49 (July): 552–76.

Davies, Elizabeth W. 1995. *The Legal Status of British Dependent Territories: The West Indies and North Atlantic Region.* Cambridge: Cambridge University Press.

Deibert, Ronald. 1997. *Exorcismus Theoriae*: Pragmatism, Metaphors and the Return of the Medieval in IR Theory. *European Journal of International Relations* 3 (2): 167–92.

Deng Xiaoping. 2009. Deng Xiaoping on One Country Two Systems. Available at: <http://english.peopledaily.com.cn/200706/14/eng20070614_384213.html>. Last accessed September 2009. See also Deng Xiaoping, *Selected Works of Deng Xiaoping* Vol. 3.

Desch, Michael C. 1996. War and Strong States, Peace and Weak States? *International Organization* 50 (2): 237–68.

Desch, Michael. 1998. Culture Clash: Assessing the Importance of Ideas in Security Studies. *International Security* 23 (1): 141–70.

Dessler, David. 1989. What's at Stake in the Agent-Structure Debate? *International Organization* 43 (3): 441–73.

Deudney, Daniel H. 1995. The Philadelphian System: Sovereignty, Arms Control, and Balance of Power in the American States-Union, circa 1787–1861. *International Organization* 49: 191–228.

Deudney, Daniel H. 2007. *Bounding Power: Republican Security Theory from the Polis to the Global Village.* Princeton, NJ: Princeton University Press.

Deutsch, Karl.W. et al. 1957. *Political Community and the North Atlantic Area: International Organization in the Light of Historical Experience*, Princeton, NJ: Princeton University Press.

Diamond, Jared. 2005. *Guns, Germs, and Steel: The Fates of Human Societies.* New York: WW Norton.

Dicey, A. V. 1885/1982. *Introduction to the Study of the Law of the Constitution*, 8th edn. Indianapolis: Liberty Fund.

Dinan, Desmond. 2005. *An Ever Closer Union: An Introduction to European Integration*, 3rd edn. Boulder: Lynne Rienner.

Dinstein, Yoram, ed. 1981. *Models of Autonomy*. New Brunswick, NJ: Transaction Books.

Dixon, Liz. 2001. Financial flows via offshore financial centers as part of the international financial system. *Financial Stability Review* June: 105–16.

Donald Rothchild and Caroline A. Hartzell 2000. "Security in Deeply Divided Societies: The Role of Territorial Autonomy", in W. Safran and R. Máiz, eds, *Identity and Territorial Autonomy in Plural Societies*. London: Frank Cass Publishers, 254–71.

Donnelly, Jack. 2006. Sovereign Inequalities and Hierarchy in Anarchy: American Power and International Security. *European Journal of International Relations* 12 (2): 123–70.

Donnelly, Jack. 2009. Rethinking political structures: From "ordering principles" to "vertical differentiation"—and beyond. *International Theory* 1 (March): 49–86.

Doremus, Paul N., William W. Keller, Louis W. Pauly, and Simon Reich. 1999. *The Myth of the Global Corporation*. Princeton: Princeton University Press, 11–21.

Downes, Alexander B. 2001. The Holy Land Divided: Defending Partition as a Solution to Ethnic Wars. *Security Studies* 10 (Summer): 58–116.

Downing, Brian M. 1992. *The Military Revolution and Political Change: Origins of Democracy and Autocracy in Early Modern Europe*. Princeton, NJ: Princeton University Press.

Doyle, Michael W. 1986. *Empires*. Ithaca, NY: Cornell University Press.

Doyle, Michael W. 1997. *Ways of War and Peace*. New York: W. W. Norton and Company.

Doyle, Michael, 2006. One World, Many Peoples: International Justice in John Rawls's *The Law of Peoples*. *Perspectives on Politics* 4 (1): 109–20.

Drucker, H. M. and Gordon Brown. 1980. *The Politics of Nationalism and Devolution*, London: Longman.

Dugard, John. 1979. *Independent Homelands: Failure of a Fiction*. Johannesburg, SA: Institute of Race Relations.

Durham, John George Lambton, Earl of. 1945. *The Durham Report*, Oxford: Carendon Press.

Economist Intelligence Unit. 2004. "Country Profile: Nicaragua".

Economist Intelligence Unit. 2008. Country Profile: Hong Kong. Available at: <http://portal.eiu.com>. Last accessed January 21, 2010.

The Economist. 2011. America's fiscal union: The red and the black. Available at: <http://www.economist.com/blogs/dailychart/2011/08/americas-fiscal-union>. Last accessed December 6, 2013.

Eden, Lorraine and Robert T. Kudrle. 2005. Tax Havens: Renegade States I the International Tax Regime? *Law & Policy* 27 (1): 100–27.

Egan, Anthony and Rupert Taylor. 2003. South Africa: The Failure of Ethnoterritorial Politics. In John Coakley, ed., *The Territorial Management of Ethnic Conflict* 2nd edn.. London: Frank Cass & Co, 99–117.

Eisenstadt, S. N. 1963. *The Political Systems of Empires.* Glencoe, IL: Free Press.

Elazar, Daniel J. 1991. Cooperative Federalism, in Daphne A. Kenyon and John Kincaid, eds, *Competition Among States and Local Governments: Efficiency and Equity in American Federalism.* Washington, DC: Urban Institute Press.

Elazar, Daniel. 1993. International and Comparative Federalism. *PS: Political Science and Politics* 26 (2): 190–5.

Elazar, Daniel. 1994. *Federal Systems of the World: A Handbook of Federal, Confederal, and Autonomy Arrangements,* Harlow: Longman.

Elazar, Daniel. 1997. Contrasting Unitary and Federal Systems. *International Political Science Review* 18 (3): 237–51.

Elias, Norbert. 1982. *The Civilizing Process.* Revised Edition. New York: Pantheon Books.

Elliott, Mark. 2004 United Kingdom: Parliamentary Sovereignty Under Pressure. *International Journal of Constitutional Law* 2: 545–52.

Encyclopedia Britannica. 2010. Available at <www.britannica.com>. Last accessed March 2010.

Epstein, Richard. 1987. The Proper Scope of the Commerce Power. *Virginia Law Review* 73: 1387.

Etzioni, A. 2004. *From Empire to Community: A New Approach to International Relations.* New York: Palgrave Macmillan. (1): 78–101.

Evatt, Herbert V. 1967. *The King and His Dominion Governors, 2nd edn.* Oxford: Oxford University Press.

Evening Express. 2012. New poll shows less than two-thirds of SNP voters want independence Growing support from all parties' supporters for Devo Plus. April 7. Available at <http://www.eveningexpress.co.uk/Article.aspx/2838549>. Downloaded July 2002.

Everyman's United Nations 1968. New York: United Nations.

Falk, Richard. 1993. Sovereignty. *Oxford Companion to Politics of the World.* Oxford: Oxford University Press.

Fallon, Richard H. Jr. 2000. Judicial Legitimacy and the Unwritten Constitution: A Comment on Miranda and Dickerson. *New York Law School Law Review* 45: 119.

Fallon, Richard H., Jr. 2001. *Implementing the Constitution.* Cambridge: Harvard University Press.

Farrell, Michael. 1984. *Arming the Protestants: The Formation of the Ulster Special Constabulary and the Royal Ulster Constabulary 1920–1927,* Dingle: Brandon.

Faure, A. M. 1994. Some Methodological Problems in Comparative Politics. *Journal of Theoretical Politics* 6 (3): 307–22.

Fazal, Tanisha M. 2004. State Death in the International System. *International Organization* 58 (2): 311–44.

Fearon, James D. 1994. *Ethnic War as a Commitment Problem.* Annual Meeting of the American Political Science Association, New York.

Fearon, James D. 1995. Rationalist Explanations for War. *International Organization* 49 (3): 379–414.

Fearon, James D. 2004. Separatist Wars, Partition and World Order. *Security Studies* 13 (4): 394.

Fearon, James D. and David D. Laitin. 2003. Ethnicity, Insurgency, and Civil War. *American Political Science Review* 97 (1): 75–90.

Feldstein, Martin and Charles Horioka. 1980. Domestic Saving and International Capital Flows. *Economic Journal* (90) 358: 314–29.

Ferguson, Niall. 2002. *Empire: The Rise and Demise of the British World Order and the Lessons for Global Power*, New York: Basic Books.

Fernandez, Ronald. 1996. *The Disenchanted Island: Puerto Rico and the United States in the Twentieth Century*. Westport, CN: Praeger.

Fisher, Louis. 2003. *American Constitutional Law*, 5th edn. Durham, NC: Carolina Academic Press.

Flanagan, Thomas. 1989. The Agricultural Argument and Original Appropriation: Indian Lands and Political Philosophy. *Canadian Journal of Political Science* 22 (3): 598–602.

Fliess, Peter J. 1952. Puerto Rico's Political Status under Its New Constitution. *Western Political Quarterly* 5: 635.

Foighel, Isi. 1980. Home Rule in Greenland: A Framework for Local Autonomy. *Common Market Law Review* (17): 91–108.

Foley, Michael. 1989. *The Silence of Constitutions: Gaps, "Abeyances," and Political Temperament in the Maintenance of Government*. London: Routledge.

Foot, Michael. 2009. Final report of the independent Review of British offshore financial centres. <http://www.ifcfeed.com/documents/Final%20report%20of%20 the%20independent%20review%20of%20British%20offshore%20financial%20cen- tres.pdf>. Downloaded November 2011.

Forsey, Eugene A. 1943. *The Royal Power of Dissolution of Parliament in the British Commonwealth*. Toronto: Oxford University Press.

Forsey, Eugene A. 1984. The Courts and the Conventions of the Constitution. *UNB Law Journal* 33: 11.

Frankel, Jeffrey 1992. Measuring International Capital Mobility: A Review. *American Economic Review* 82 (2): 197–202.

Freedom House. 2010. *Freedom in the World Combined Average Ratings—Independent Countries*. Available at <http://freedomhouse.org/template.cfm?page=546&year– 2010>. Last accessed July 11, 2011.

Freedom House. 2011. Freedom in the World Combined Average Ratings—Independent Countries. Available at <http://freedomhouse.org/template.cfm?page=546&year= 2010>. Last accessed July 11, 2011.

Frieden, Jeffry A. 1994. International Investment and Colonial Control: A New Interpretation. *International Organization* 48 (4): 559–93.

Friedman, James W. 1971. A Non-cooperative Equilibrium for Supergames. *Review of Economic Studies* 38 (January): 1–12.

Fudenberg, Drew and Eric Maskin. 1986. The Folk Theorem in Repeated Games with Discounting or with Incomplete Information. *Econometrica* 54 (May): 533–54.

Fukuyama, Francis. 2004. The Imperative of State-Building. *Journal of Democracy* 15 (2): 17–31.

Fund for Peace. 2012. *Failed States Index 2012*. Available at: <http://www.fundforpeace. org/global/library/cfsir1210-failedstatesindex2012-06p.pdf>. Downloaded January 2013.

Galtung, Johan. 1971. A Structural Theory of Imperialism. *Journal of Peace Research* 8 (2): 81–117.

Gartzke, Erik. 1999. War Is in the Error Term. *International Organization* 53 (3): 567–87.

Garrett, Clarke W. 1967. In Search of Grandeur: France and Vietnam 1940–46. *The Review of Politics* 29 (3): 303–23.

Gatell, Frank Otto. 1958. Independence Rejected: Puerto Rico and the Tydings Bill of 1936. *The Hispanic American Historical Review* 38 (1): 25–44.

Geddes, Barbara. 1990. How the Cases You Choose Affect the Answers You Get: Selection Bias in Comparative Politics. *Political Analysis* 2 (1): 131–50.

Gellner, Ernest. 1983. *Nations and Nationalism.* Oxford: Blackwell.

Ghai, Yash. 1999. *Hong Kong's New Constitutional Order: The Resumption of Chinese Sovereignty and the Basic Law*, 2nd edn. Hong Kong: Hong Kong University Press.

Ghai, Yash. 2000a. The NPC Interpretation and Its Consequences. In Yash Ghai, ed., *Hong Kong's Constitutional Debate: Conflict over Interpretation.* Hong Kong: Hong Kong University Press.

Ghai, Yash. 2000b. Autonomy as a Strategy for Diffusing Conflict. In Daniel Druckman and Paul C. Stern, eds, *International Conflict Resolution After the Cold War.* New York: Commission on Behavioral and Social Sciences and Education, 483–530.

Ghai, Yash. 2004. The Promise of Autonomy. *Apple Daily.* May 3, 2004.

Ghai, Yash. 2005. Imperatives of autonomy: Contradictions of the Basic Law, in Johannes Chan and Lison Harris, eds, *Hong Kong's Constitutional Debates.* Hong Kong: Hong Kong Law Journal Limited, 29–44.

Ghai, Yash and Anthony J. Regan. 2006. Unitary state, devolution, autonomy, secession: State building and nation building in Bougainville, Papua New Guinea. *The Round Table: The Commonwealth Journal of International Affairs* 95 (386): 589–608.

Giddens, Anthony. 1987. *The Nation-States and Violence.* Berkeley and Los Angles: University of California Press.

Giles, Chris, George Parker, and Gillian Tett. 2009. G20 leaders accused over toxic assets. *Financial Times.com.* April 1.

Gilpin, Robert. 1981. *War and Change in World Politics.* Cambridge: Cambridge University Press.

Gleditsch, Nils Petter and Bethany Lacina. 2005. Monitoring Trends in Global Combat: A New Dataset of Battle Deaths. *European Journal of Population* 21: 145–66.

Gleditsch, Nils Petter et al. 2002. UCDP/PRIO Armed Conflict Dataset Version 4-2008 Available at: <http://www.prio.no/CSCW/Datasets/Armed-Conflict/UCDP-PRIO/Armed-Conflicts-Version-4-2008/>. Last accessed December 2013.

Glennon, Michael L. 2003. Why the Security Council Failed. *Foreign Affairs* 82 (3): 16–35.

Goldsmith, Benjamin E. and Baogang He. 2008. Letting Go Without a Fight: Decolonization, Democracy and War, 1900–94. *Journal of Peace Research.* 45 (5): 587–611.

Gordon, Michael R. and Bernard E. Trainor. 2006. *Cobra II: The Inside Story of the Invasion and Occupation of Iraq*, New York: Pantheon Books.

Gormley-Heenan, Cathy. 2008. Northern Ireland: Securing the Peace. In Venessa E. Shields and Nicholas Balwin, eds, *Beyond Settlement: Making Peace Last After Civil Conflict*. Madison, HJ: Fairleigh Dickinson University Press.

Gould, Stephen Jay. 1982. Darwinism and the Expansion of Evolutionary Theory. *Science*, 216.

Gould, Stephen Jay and Niles Eldredge. 1977. Punctuated Equilibria: The Tempo and Mode of Evolution Reconsidered. *Paleobiology* 3 (2).

Grahl-Madsen, Atle 1988. Custom, Legislation and Treaty as the Basis for Self-Government. *Nordic Journal of International Law* 57 (3): 295–300.

Greer, Allan. 1993. *The Patriots and the People: The Rebellion of the 1837 in Rural Lower Canada*. Toronto: University of Toronto Press.

Grey, Thomas C. 1975. Do We Have an Unwritten Constitution? *Stanford Law Review* 27: 703–18.

Grey, Thomas C. 1978. Origins of the Unwritten Constitution: Fundamental Law in American Revolutionary Thought. *Stanford Law Review* 30: 843–93.

Grey, Thomas C. 1988. The Original Understanding and the Unwritten Constitution. In Neil L. York, ed., *Toward a More Perfect Union: Six Essays on the Constitution*. Provo: Brigham Young University,.

Gross, Leo. 1948. The Peace of Westphalia, 1648–1948. *The American Journal of International Law* 42 (1): 20–41.

Guardian 2012. Spanish PM rejects Catalan calls for greater tax powers. Available at <http://www.theguardian.com/world/2012/sep/20/spanish-pm-rejects-catalan-tax-powers>. Downloaded August 2013.

Gurr, Ted R. 1981. Historical trends in violent crime: A critical review of the evidence. In N. Morris and M. Tonry, eds, *Crime and Justice*, Vol. 3. Chicago: University of Chicago Press.

Gurr, Ted Robert. 1999. Settling Ethnopolitical Conflicts. In Ted Robert Gurr, ed., *Minorities at Risk: A Global View of Ethnopolitical Conflicts*. Washington DC: United States Institute of Peace Press, 290–313.

Haas, Ernst B. 1968. *The United of Europe: Political, Social, and Economic Forces*, 2nd edn. Stanford. Stanford University Press.

Hall, John. 1985. *Powers and Liberties*. Berkeley: University of California Press.

Hall, John, ed. 1986. *States in History*. Oxford: Basil Blackwell.

Hall, John, ed. 1998. *The State of the Nation: Ernest Gellner and the Theory of Nationalism*, Cambridge: Cambridge University Press.

Hall, Peter A. and Rosemary C. R. Taylor. 1996. Poltiical Science and the Three New Institutionalisms. *Political Studies* XLIV: 936–57.

Hall, Rodney Bruce. 1999. *National Collective Identity: Social Constructs and International Systems*. New York: Columbia University Press.

Hallerberg, Mark. 2002. Veto Players and the Choice of Monetary Institutions. *International Organization* 56 (4): 775–802.

Hammer, Ellen J. 1948. Blueprinting a New Indochina. *Pacific Affairs* 21 (3): 252–63.

Hammer, Ellen. 1950. The Bao Dai Experiment. *Pacific Affairs* 23 (March): 58.

Hammer, Ellen. 1966. *The Struggle for Indochina, 1940–1955*, Stanford: Stanford University Press.

Hamre, John J. and Gordon R. Sullivan. 2002. Toward Postconflict Reconstruction. *The Washington Quarterly* 25 (4): 85–96.

Hannum, Hurst. 1988. The Foreign Affairs Powers of Autonomous Regions. *Nordic Journal of International Law* 57: 273–88.

Hannum, Hurst. 1990. *Autonomy, Sovereignty, and Self-Determination: The Accommodation of Conflicting Rights*, revised edn. Philadelphia: University of Pennsylvania Press.

Hannum, Hurst. 1993. *Documents on Autonomy and Minority Rights*. Doredrecht: Matinus Nijhoff.

Hannum, Hurst and Richard B. Lillich. 1980. The Concept of Autonomy in International Law, *American Journal of International Law* 74: 858–89.

Hardin, Garrett. 1993. *Living within Limits*. New York: Oxford University Press.

Hardin, Russell. 1982. *Collective Action*. Baltimore: Johns Hopkins University Press.

Hardin, Russell. 1995. *One for All, The Logic of Group Conflict*. Princeton, NJ: Princeton University Press.

Hart, Oliver. 1995. *Firms, Contracts, and Financial Structure*. Oxford: Oxford University Press.

Hawkes, David C. 2001. Indigenous Peoples: Self-Government and Intergovernmental Relations. *International Social Science Journal* 53 (167): 151–61.

Heard, Andrew. 1991. *Canadian Constitutional Conventions: The Marriage of Law and Politics*, Toronto: Oxford University Press.

Hechter, Michael. 2000. *Containing Nationalism*. New York: Oxford University Press.

Heintze, Hans-Joachim. 1998. On the Legal Understanding of Autonomy. In Markku Suksi, ed., *Autonomy: Applications and Implications*. The Hague: Kluwer Law International, 7-32.

Helfeld, David M. 1952. Congressional Intent and Attitude toward Public Law 600 and the Constitution of the Commonwealth of Puerto Rico. Revista *Juridica de la Universidad de Puerto Rico* 21: 255.

Helfeld, David M. 1985. How Much of the United States Constitution and Statutes Are Applicable to the Commonwealth of Puerto Rico? *Federal Rules Decisions* 110: 452.

Henders, Susan J. 1998. *Special Status Regions: The Territorial Accommodation of Cultural Difference*. D.Phil. diss., University of Oxford, Oxford.

Herbst, Jeffery. 1989. The Creation and Maintenance of National Boundaries in Africa. *International Organization* 43 (4): 683–87.

Herbst, Jeffrey. 1990. War and the State in Africa. *International Security* 14 (4): 117–39.

Herbst, Jeffrey. 2000. *States and Power in Africa: Comparative Lessons in Authority and Control*. Princeton, NJ: Princeton University Press.

Herring, George C. 1979. *America's Longest War: The United States and Vietnam, 1950–1975*, 4th edn. New York: McGraw Hill.

Hertslet, Sir Edward. 1967. *The Map of Africa by Treaty*. London: John Murray.

Herz, John. 1957. Rise and Demise of the Territorial State. *World Politics* 9 (4): 473–93.

Herz, John. 1968. The Territorial State Revisted—Reflections on the Future of the Nation-State. *Polity* 1 (1): 11–24.

Hesse, Jochim Jens and Vincent Wright, eds. 1996. *Federalizing Europe? The Costs, Benefits, and Preconditions of Federal Political Systems*. Oxford: Oxford University Press.

Hinsley, F. H. 1986. *Sovereignty*, 2nd edn. Cambridge: Cambridge University Press.

Hintze, Otto. 1975. *The Historical Essays of Otto Hintze*, ed. Felix Gilbert. New York: Oxford University Press.

Ho, Daniel, Kosuke Imai, Gary King and Elizabeth Stuart. 2007. Matching as Nonparametric Preprocessing for Reducing Model Dependence in Parametric Causal Inference. *Political Analysis* 15 (3): 199–236.

Hobbes, Thomas. 1960. *Leviathan*. Oxford: Blackwell.

Hobsbawm, Eric. 1987. *The Age of Empires*. New York: Vintage Books.

Hobsbawm, Eric. 1990. *Nations and Nationalism since 1780: Programme, Myth, Reality*. Cambridge: Cambridge University Press.

Hobsbawm, Eric. 1992. *Nations and Nationalism since 1788*. Cambridge: Cambridge University Press. History World. 2010. Available at <www.historyworld. net>. Last accessed March 2010.

Hobson, John M. and Jason C. Sharman. 2005. The Enduring Place of Hierarchy in World Politics: Tracing the Social Logics of Hierarchy and Political Change. *European Journal of International Relations* 11 (1): 63–98.

Hoffmann, Stanley. 1966. Obstinate or Obsolete? The Fate of the Nation-State and the Case of Western Europe. *Daedalus* 95 (3): 862–915.

Holliday, Ian, Ma Ngoc, and Ray Yep. 2004. After 1997: The Dialectics of Hong Kong Dependence. *Journal of Contemporary Asia* 34 (2): 254–70.

Holmstrom, Bengt. 1982. Moral Hazard in Teams. *Bell Journal of Economics* 13 (Autumn): 324–40.

Holzgrefe, J. L. 1989. The Origins of Modern International Relations Theory. *Review of International Studies* 15 (January): 11–26.

Hooghe, Liesbet and Gary Marks. 2003. Unraveling the Central State, But How? Types of Multi-level Governance. *American Political Science Review* 97 (2): 233–43.

Hopf, Ted. 1998. The Promise of Constructivism in International Relations Theory. *International Security* 23 (1): 171–200.

Horowitz, Donald L. 1985. *Ethnic Groups in Conflict*. Berkeley: University of California Press.

Horwill, Herbert W. 1925. *The Usages of the American Constitution*. Oxford: Oxford University Press.

Hroch, Miroslav. 1985. *Social Preconditions of National Revival in Europe*. Cambridge: Cambridge University Press.

Hu, Jintao. 2007. Hu hails Hong Kong as "window and bridge". *China Daily* July 2.

Hughes, James. 2001. Managing Secession Potential in the Russian Federation. *Regional & Federal Studies* 11 (Fall): 36–68.

Human Rights in China. 2007. China: Minority Exclusion, Marginalization and Rising Tensions. Available at: <http://www.minorityrights.org/admin/Download/pdf/MRGChinaReport.pdf>. Last accessed May 2, 2009.

Human Rights Watch. 2006. Sudan: Regional government pays Ugandan rebels not to attack. Available at: < http://reliefweb.int/node/210125>. Last accessed June 2011.

Iacus, Stefano M., Gary King, and Giuseppe Porro. 2008. Matching for Causal Inference Without Balance Checking. <http://www.polmeth.wustl.edu/media/Paper/cem.pdf>. Last accessed January 2013.

Iacus, Stefano M., Gary King, and Giuseppe Porro. 2012. Causal Inference without Balance Checking: Coarsened Exact Matching. *Political Analysis* 20: 1-24.

Ignatieff, Michael. 1993. *Blood and Belonging.* Toronto: Viking Press.

International Crisis Group (ICG). 2004. Saakashvili's Ajara Success: Repeatable Elsewhere in Georgia? *ICG Europe Briefing*, August 18. Available at: <http://www.crisisgroup.org/library/documents/europe/caucasus/040818_ saakashvili_ajara_success_repeatable_elsewhere_in_georgia.pdf>. Last accessed July 2009.

International Crisis Group (ICG). 2007. Aceh: Post-conflict Complications, 4 October 2007. Available at: <http://www.crisisgroup.org/en/regions/asia/south-east-asia/indonesia/139-aceh-post-conflict-complications.aspx>. Last accessed December 12, 2013.

Jackson, J. Hampden. 1940. *Finland.* New York, Macmillan.

Jackson, Robert H. 1987. Quasi-States, Dual Regimes, and Neoclassical Theory: International Jurisprudence and the Third World. *International Organization* 41 (4): 519-49.

Jackson, Robert H. 1990. *Quasi-States: Sovereignty, International Relations, and the Third World.* New York: Cambridge University Press.

Jackson, Robert H. 1993. The Weight of Ideas in Decolonization. In Judith Goldstein and Robert O. Keohane, eds, *Ideas and Foreign Policy.* Cornell: Cornell University Press, 111-38.

Jackson, Robert H., ed. 1999. *Sovereignty at the Millennium.* Oxford: Blackwell Publishers.

Jakobson, Linda. 2005. A Greater Chinese Union. *Washington Quarterly* 28 (3): 27-39.

James, Alan. 1986. *Sovereign Statehood: The Basis of International Society.* London: Allen and Unwin.

Järve, Prit. 2008. "Gagauzia and Moldova: Experiences in Power-sharing" in Marc Weller and Barbara Metzger, eds, *Self-Determination Disputes: Complex Powersharing in Theory and Practice.* Leiden, The Netherlands: Martinus Nijhoff Publishers, 307-44.

Jennings, Sir Ivor W. 1936. *Cabinet Government.* New York: Cambridge University Press.

Jennings, Sir Ivor W. 1959. *The Law and the Constitution*, 5th edn. London: University of London Press.

Johnson, Thomas and M. Chris Mason. 2008. No Sign until the Burst of Fire: Understanding the Pakistan–Afghanistan Frontier. *International Security* 32 (4), 41-77.

Johnson, Janet Buttolph, Richard A. Joslyn, and H. T. Reynolds. 2001. *Political Science Research Methods*, 4th edn. Washington, DC: CQ Press.

Judd, Denis. 1996. *Empire: The British Imperial Experience from 1765 to the Present.* New York: Basic Books.

Kang, David C. 2004. The Theoretical Roots of Hierarchy in International Relations. *Australian Journal of International Affairs* 58 (3): 337-52.

Kang, David C. 2010. Hierarchy and Legitimacy in International Systems: The Tribute System in Early Modern East Asia. *Security Studies* 19 (4): 591–622.

Kaplan, Robert D. 1997. Was Democracy Just a Moment? *The Atlantic Monthly* (December): 55–80.

Karlsson, Gunnar. 2003. Denmark's Peaceful Release of Iceland. In Clive Archer and Pertti Joenniemi, eds, *The Nordic Peace*. Hampshire, UK: Ashgate Publishing Limited, 45–65.

Kaufmann, Chaim D. 1998. When All Else Fails: Ethnic Population Transfers and Partitions in the Twentieth Century. *International Security* 23 (Fall): 120–56.

Kauffmann, D., A. Kray, and M. Mastruzzi. 2008. *Worldwide Governance Indicators (WDI)*, Washington DC: World Bank. <http://info.worldbank.org/governance/wgi/index.asp>. Downloaded July 1, 2009.

Kauffmann, D., A. Kray, and M. Mastruzzi. 2011. *Worldwide Governance Indicators (WDI)*, Washington DC: World Bank. <http://info.worldbank.org/governance/wgi/index.asp>. Last accessed July 2012.

Kaysen, Carl. 1990. Is War Obsolete? A Review Essay. *International Security* 14 (4): 42–64.

Keeley, L. H. 1996. *War before Civilization: The Myth of the Peaceful Savage*. New York: Oxford University Press.

Keene, Edward. 2002. *Beyond the Anarchical Society: Grotius, Colonialism, and Order in World Politics*. New York: Cambridge University Press.

Keene, E. 2007. A Case Study of the Construction of International Hierarchy: British Treaty-making against the Slave Trade in the early Nineteenth Century. *International Organization* 61 (2): 311–39.

Keith, Arthur Berriedale. 1928. *Responsible Government in the Dominions*, 2nd edn. Oxford: Clarendon.

Keith, Arthur Berriedale, ed. 1932. *Speeches and Documents on the British Dominions 1918–1931*. Oxford: Oxford University Press.

Keith, Arthur Berriedale. 1935a. *Letters on Imperial Relations: Indian Reform, Constitutional and International Law, 1916–1935*. London: Oxford University Press.

Keith, Arthur Berriedale. 1935b. *The Governments of the British Empire*. London: Macmillan.

Keith, Arthur Berriedale, ed. 1948. *British Colonial Policy, 1763–1917*, 2 vols. London: G. Cumberlege.

Kellogg, Thomas E. 2007. A Flawed Effort? Legislating on Surveillance in Hong Kong. *Hong Kong Journal*, May.

Kellogg, Thomas E. 2008. Excessive Deference or Strategic Retreat? Basic Law Article 158 and Constitutional Development in Hong Kong. *Hong Kong Journal*. January.

Kelly, J. M. 1992. *A Short History of Western Legal Theory*, Oxford: Clarendon Press.

Kendle, John. 1989. *Ireland and the Federal Solution: The Debate over the United Kingdom Constitution, 1870–1921*, Kingston and Montreal: McGill-Queen's University Press.

Keohane, Robert O. 1984. *After Hegemony: Cooperation and Discord in the World Political Economy*. Princeton: Princeton University Press.

Keohane, Robert O. 1986. Realism, Neorealism, and the Study of World Politics. In Robert O. Keohane, ed., *Neorealism and Its Critics*.New York: Columbia University Press, 1–26.

Keohane, Robert O. 2003. Political Authority after Intervention: Gradations in Sovereignty, in J. L. Holzgrefe and Robert O. Keohane, eds, *Humanitarian Intervention: Ethnical, Legal, and Political Dilemmas*. New York: Cambridge University Press, 275–98.

Keohane, Robert and Stanley Hoffmann. 1991. Institutional Change in Europe in the 1980's. In Robert Keohane and Stanley Hoffmann, eds, *The New European Community: Decision-making and Institutional Change*. Boulder, CO: Westview Press, 1–39.

Keohane, Robert et al. 2000. Forum on Alexander Wendt's Social Theory of International Politics. *Review of International Studies* 26 (1): 123–80.

Keylor, William R. 2000. *The Twentieth Century World: An International History*. New York: Oxford University Press.

King, Charles. 2001. The Benefits of Ethnic War: Understanding Eurasia's Unrecognized States. *World Politics* 53 (July): 524–52.

King, Gary, Robert O. Keohane, and Sidney Verba. 1994. *Designing Social Inquiry: Scientific Inference in Qualitative Research*. Princeton: Princeton University Press.

Kirgis, Frederic L. Jr. 1994. The Degrees of Self-Determination in the United Nations Era. *American Journal of International Law* 88: 304.

Koh, Harold. 1990. *The National Security Constitution: Sharing Power After the Iran-Contra Affair*. New Haven: Yale University Press.

Kong, Xiaohong. 1991. Legal Interpretation in China. *Connecticut Journal of International Law* 6: 491–506.

Korman, Sharon 1996. *The Right of Conquest: The Acquisition of Territory by Force in International Law and Practice*. Oxford: Clarendon.

Korn, Marcel. 1991. Free Association: Political Integration as a Trade-Off. In Daniel J. Elazar, ed., *Constitutional Design and Power-Sharing in the Post-Modern Epoch*. Lanham: University Press of America, 185–217.

Kowert, Paul and Jeffrey Legro. 1996. Norms, Identity, and their Limits: A theoretical Reprise. In Peter J. Katzenstein, ed., *Culture of National Security*. New York: Columbia University Press, 33–72.

Krasner, Stephen D. 1984. Approaches to the State: Alternative Conceptions and Historical Dynamics. *Comparative Politics* 16 (2): 223–46.

Krasner, Stephen D. 1991. Global Communications and National Power: Life on the Pareto Frontier. *World Politics* 43 (April): 336–66.

Krasner, Stephen D. 1999. *Sovereignty: Organized Hypocrisy*. Princeton: Princeton University Press.

Krasner, Stephen. 1995. Compromising Westphalia. *International Security* 20 (3): 115–51.

Krasner, Stephen D. ed. 2001. *Problematic Sovereignty: Contested Rules and Political Possibilities*. New York: Columbia University Press.

Krasner, Stephen D. 2005. Sharing Sovereignty: New Institutions for Collapsed and Failing States. *International Security* 29 (2): 85–120.

Krasner, Stephen D. and Carlos Pascual. 2005. Addressing State Failure. *Foreign Affairs* 84 (4): 153–63.

Kratochwil, Friedrich. 1986. Of Systems, Boundaries, and Territoriality: An Inquiry into the Formation of the State System. *World Politics* 39 (1): 27–52.

Krause, Keith. 1996. Insecurity and State Formation in the Global Military Order: The Middle Eastern Case. *European Journal of International Relations* 2 (3): 319–54.

Kumar, Radha. 2002. Untying the Kashmir Knot. *World Policy Journal* (Spring): 11–24.

Kupchan, Charles A. 1998. After Pax Americana: Benign Power, Regional Integration, and the Sources of a Stable Multipolarity. *International Security* 23 (2): 40–79.

Kymlicka, Will. 1995. *Multicultural Citizenship: A Liberal Theory of Minority Rights.* Oxford: Clarendon Press.

LaFeber, Walter. 1975. Roosevelt, Churchill and Indochina, 1942–1945. *American Historical Review* 80 (December): 1277–95.

Laffont, J. J. 1988 *Fundamentals of Public Economics*, rev. English ed. Trans. John P. Bonin and Helene Bonin. Cambridge, MA: MIT Press.

Lakatos, Imre. 1970. Falsification and the Methodology of Scientific Research Programs. In Imre Lakatos and Alan Musgrave, eds, *Criticism and the Growth of Knowledge.* Cambridge: Cambridge University Press, 91–196.

Lake, David A. 1996. Anarchy, Hierarchy and the Variety of International Relations. *International Organization* 50 (1): 1–33.

Lake, David A. 1999. *Entangling Relations: American Foreign Policy in Its Century.* Princeton, NJ: University Press.

Lake, David A. 2001. Beyond Anarchy: The Importance of Security Institutions. *International Security* 26 (1): 129–60.

Lake, David A. 2003. The New Sovereignty in International Relations. *International Studies Review* 5 (3): 303–24.

Lake, David. A. 2007. Escape from the State of Nature: Authority and Hierarchy in World Politics. *International Security* 32 (1): 47–79.

Lake, David A. 2009. *Hierarchy in International Relations.* Ithaca, NY: Cornell University Press.

Lake, David. A. and Paul MacDonald. 2008. The Role of Hierarchy in International Politics. *International Security* 32 (4): 171–80.

Lake, David A. and Donald Rothchild. 1996. Containing Fear: The Origins and Management of Ethnic Conflict. *International Security* 21 (2): 41–75.

Landman, Todd. 2000. *Issues and Methods in Comparative Politics, an Introduction.* London: Routledge.

Lapidoth, Ruth. 1997. *Autonomy: Flexible Solutions to Ethnic Conflicts.* Washington, DC: United States Institute of Peace Press.

Lapidoth, Ruth. 1996. Autonomy—Potential and Limitations. Manuscript, Hebrew University of Jerusalem.

Lawson, Gary and Guy Seidman. 2004. *The Constitution of Empire: Territorial Expansion and American Legal History.* New Haven: Yale University Press.

Lawson, T. 1997. *Economics and Reality*. London: Routledge.

Leacock, Stephen. 1907. Responsible Government in the British Colonial System. *American Political Science Review* 1 (3): 355–92.

Lederach, John Paul and Paul Wehr. 1991. Mediating Conflict in Central America. *Journal of Peace Research* 28 (1): 85–98.

Lee, Hong Yung. 1991. *From Revolutionary Cadres to Technocrats in Socialist China*. Berkeley and Los Angeles: University of California Press.

Lee, Martin and Szeto Wah. 1988. *The Basic Law: Some Basic Flaws*. Hong Kong: Kasper Printing Co.

Légaré, Andre. 2002. The Construction of Nunavut and its Impact on Collective Identity in the Canadian Eastern Arctic. *Review of Constitutional Studies* 7 (1–2): 55–78.

Leibowitz, Arnold H. 1967. The Applicability of Federal Law to the Commonwealth of Puerto Rico. *Georgetown Law Journal* 56: 219.

Leibowtiz, Arnold. 1981. The Commonwealth of Puerto Rico: Trying to Gain Dignity and Maintain Culture. *Georgia Journal of International and Comparative Law* 11 (2): 211–81.

Leibowitz, Arnold H. 1989. *Defining Status: A Comprehensive Analysis of United States Territorial Relations*, Boston: Martinus Nijhoff Publishers.

Lerner, Natan. 1981. Puerto Rico: Autonomy, Statehood, Independence? In Yoram Dinstein, ed., *Models of Autonomy*, New Brunswick, NJ: Transaction Books.

Levi, Lucio, ed. 1990. *Altiero Spinelli and Federalism in Euope and the World*. Milano: Franco Angeli.

Levi, Margaret. 1997. *Consent, Dissent, and Patriotism*. Cambridge: Cambridge University Press.

Levinson, Sanford. 1998. *Constitutional Faith*. Princeton: Princeton University Press.

Levy, J. S., T. C. Walker, and M. S. Edwards. 2001. *Continuity and Change in the Evolution of Warfare*. In Z. Maoz and A. Gat, eds, *War in a Changing World*. Ann Arbor: University of Michigan Press.

Lijphart, Arend. 1967. *The Politics of Accommodation: Pluralism and Democracy in the Netherlands*. Berkeley: University of California Press.

Lijphart, Arend. 1999. *Patterns of Democracy*, New Haven: Yale University Press.

Lindberg, Leon N. and Stuart A. Scheingold. 1970. *Europe's Would-be Polity: Patterns of Change in the European Community*. Englewood Cliffs, NJ: Prentice-Hall.

Linz, Juan J. 1989. Spanish Democracy and the Estado de las Autonomias. In Robert A. Goldwin, Art Kaufman, and William A. Schambra, eds, *Forging Unity out of Diversity: The Approach of Eight Nations*, Washington, DC: American Institute of Public Policy Research, 260–326.

Linz, Juan. J. and Alfred Stepan. 1996. *Problems of Democratic Transition and Consolidation: Southern Europe, South America, and Post-communist Europe*. Baltimore: Johns Hopkins University Press.

Lipschutz, Ronnie. 1992. Reconstructing World Politics: The Emergence of Global Civil Society. *Millennium, Journal of International Studies* 21 (3): 389–420.

Locke, John. 1690/1980. *Second Treatise of Government*, Indianapolis: Hackett.

Lorenz, Edward N. 1993. *The Essence of Chaos*. Seattle: University of Washington Press.

Lustick, Ian. 1993. *Unsettled States, Disputed Lands: Britain and Ireland, France and Algeria, Israel and West Bank-Gaza.* Ithaca, NY: Cornell University Press.

Ma, Jun. 1988. Human Rights: China's Perspective. *Beijing Review.* November 28–December 4: 17–18.

McCallum, J. 1995. National Borders Matter: Canada–U.S. Regional Trade Patterns. *American Economic Review* 85 (3): 615–23.

McCulloch, Lesley. 2006. Greed: The Silent Force of Conflict in Aceh. In Damien Kingsbury, ed., *Violence In Between: Security Issues in Archipelagic South-East Asia.* Melbourne/Singapore: Monash Asia Institute/Institute for Southeast Asian Studies.

MacDonald, Paul K. 2009a. Is Imperial Rule Obsolete? Assessing the Barriers to Overseas Adventurism. *Security Studies* 18 (1): 79–114.

MacDonald, Paul. 2009b. Those who Forget Historiography are Doomed to Republish it: Empire, Imperialism and Contemporary Debates about American Power. *Review of International Studies* 35: 45–67.

McDonnell, John. 2000. Why Peter Mandelson was wrong to collapse the Good Friday Institutions. SCGN March 2000 no. 152. Available at: <http://www.poptel.org.uk/scgn/archive/articles/0003/page2b.htm>. Last accessed March 2010.

McElroy, J. L. and M. Hahoney. 2000. The Propensity for Political Dependence in Island Microstates. *Insula: International Journal of Island Affairs* 9 (1): 32–5.

McGarry, John, ed. 2001. *Northern Ireland and the Divided World: Post-Agreement Northern Ireland in Comparative Perspective.* Oxford: Oxford University Press.

McGarry, John. 2007. Asymmetry in federations, federacies and unitary states. *Ethnopolitics,* 6 (1): 105–16.

McGarry, John and Brendan O'Leary. 1995a. *Explaining Northern Ireland,* Oxford: Blackwell Publishers.

McGarry, John and Brendan O'Leary, eds. 1995b. *The Politics of Ethnic Conflict Regulation,* London: Routledge.

McGarry, John and Brendan O'Leary, eds. 2004. *The Northern Ireland Conflict: Consociational Engagements.* Oxford: Oxford University Press.

Machiavelli, Niccolò. 1981 (1469–1527) *The Prince.* New York: Penguin Books.

McKercher, William R. 2000, The Isle of Man: Jurisdictional Catapult to Development. In Godfrey Baldacchino and David Milne, eds, *Lessons from the Political Economy of Small Islands: The Resourcefulness of Jurisdiction.* New York: St. Martin's Press, 91–106.

Maddison, Angus. 1982. *Phases of Capitalist Development.* New York: Oxford University Press.

Maddison, Angus. 2003. *The World Economy Historical Statistics.* Paris, France: Organization for Economic Cooperation and Development.

Madison, James, Alexander Hamilton, and John Jay. 1788/1987. *The Federalist Papers.* London: Penguin.

Mahmud, Tayyab. 1994. Jurisprudence of Successful Treason: Coup D'Etat & Common Law. *Cornell International Law Journal* 27 (Winter): 49.

Maitland, F. W. 1908. *The Constitutional History of England.* Cambridge: Cambridge University Press.

Malloy, James. 1977. Authoritarianism and Corporatism in Latin America: The Modal Pattern. In James Malloy, ed., *Authoritarianism and Corporatism in Latin America*. Pittsburgh: University of Pittsburgh Press.

Marshall, Geoffrey. 1984. *Constitutional Conventions: The Rules and Forms of Political Accountability*. Oxford: Oxford University Press.

Marshall, Geoffrey. 2002. The Crown and Bagehot's Dubious Death Warrant. *Public Law* (Spring): 4–8.

Martel, Gordon. 1993. Afterword: The Imperial Contract—An Ethology of Power. In A. Hamish Ion and E. J. Errington, eds, *Great Powers and Little Wars: The Limits of Power*. Westport, CN: Praeger.

Mattli, Walter and Anne-Marie Slaughter. 1995. Law and Politics in the European Union: A Reply to Garrett. *International Organization* 49 (1): 183–90.

Mautner, Menachem. 1980. The West Bank and Gaza: The Case for Associate Statehood. *Yale Studies in World Public Order* 6: 305.

Mearsheimer, John. 1995. A Realist Reply. *International Security* 20 (1): 82–93.

Merom, Gil. 2003. Realist Hypotheses on Regional Peace. *Journal of Strategic Studies* 26 (1): 113.

Merrill, Dennis and Thomas G. Paterson, eds. 2005. *Major Problems in American Foreign Relations* Vol. 1: To 1920. Boston: Houghton Mifflin.

Migdal, Joseph. 1988. *Strong Societies and Weak States: State–Society Relations and State Capabilities in the Third World*. Princeton, NJ: Princeton University Press.

Miller, David. 1995. *On Nationality*, Oxford: Clarendon Press.

Milliken, Jennifer and Keith Krause. 2002. State Failure, State Collapse, and State Reconstruction: Concepts, Lessons and Strategies. *Development and Change* 33 (5): 753–74.

Milward, Alan 2000. *The European Rescue of the Nation-State*. London: Routledge.

Miners, N. J. 1991. *The Government and Politics of Hong Kong*, 5th edn. Hong Kong: Oxford University Press.

Mitchell, B. R. 1998. *International Historical Statistics*. New York: Stockton Press.

Mitrany, David. 1966. *A Working Peace System*. Quadrangle Books.

Moerdijk, Donald. 1981. *Anti-Development: South Africa and Its Bantustans*. Paris: Unesco Press.

Monge, José Trías. 1997. *Puerto Rico: The Trials of the Oldest Colony in the World*, New Haven and London: Yale University Press.

Monge, José Trías. 1998. Injustice According to Law: The Insular Cass and Other Oddities. In Christina Duffy Burnett and Burke Marshall, eds, *Foreign in a Domestic Sense: Puerto Rico, American Expansion, and the Constitution*. Durham: Duke University Press, 233.

Monnet, Jean. 1962. A Ferment of Change. *Journal of Common Market Studies* 1 (1): 203–11.

Moravcsik, Andrew. 1998. *The Choice for Europe: Social Purpose and State Power*. Ithaca, NY: Cornell University Press.

Morgenthau, Hans J. 1948/1993. *Politics Among Nations: The Struggle for Power and Peace*. New York: McGraw-Hill.

Moriarty, Francis. 2005. Press Freedom in Hong Kong: The Trend is Down. *Hong Kong Journal* 1–10. Available at: <hkjournal.org>. Last accessed February 2010.

Morton, Grenfell. 1995. *Home Rule and the Irish Question.* Essex: Longman.

Mossberger, Karen. 1999. State–Federal Diffusion and Policy Learning: From Enterprise Zones to Empowerment Zones. *Publius: The Journal of Federalism* 29 (3): 31–50.

Motyl, Alexander J. 1997. Thinking About Empire. In K. Barkey and M. V. Hagen, eds, *After Empire: Multiethnic Societies and Nation-Building.* Boulder, CO: Westview.

Motyl, Alexander J. 1999a. *Revolutions, Nations, Empires: Conceptual Limits and Theoretical Possibilities.* New York: Columbia University Press.

Motyl, Alexander J. 1999b. Why Empires Reemerge: Imperial Collapse and Imperial Revival in Comparative Perspective. *Comparative Politics* 31 (2): 127–45.

Motyl, Alexander J. 2006. Is Everything Empire? Is Empire Everything? *Comparative Politics* 38 (2): 229–49.

Muñoz Marín, Luis. 1953. Puerto Rico a Study in Democratic Development. *Annals of the American Academy of Political and Social Science* 285 (January): 1–8.

Munro, C. R. 1975. Laws and Conventions Distinguished. *Law Quarterly Review* 91: 218.

Munro, William Bennett. 1930. *The Makers of the Unwritten Constitution.* New York: Macmillan.

Musalem, Alberto and Errico Luca. 1999. *Offshore Banking: An Analysis of Micro- and Macro-Prudential Issues.* International Monetary Fund Working Paper WP/99/5. Washington, DC: IMF.

Myntti, Kristian. 1998. Autonomy Within the OSCE: The Case of Crimea. In Markku Suksi, ed., *Autonomy: Applications and Implications.* The Hague: Kluwer Law International, 312.

Nagel, Joane and Susan Olzak. 1982. Ethnic Mobilization in New and Old States: An Extension of the Competition Model. *Social Problems* 30: 127–43.

Nathan, Richard P. 1996. The Devolution Revolution: An Overview. *Rockefeller Institute Bulletin 1996.* Albany, NY: Nelson A. Rockefeller Institute of Government.

Nathan, Richard P. and Thomas L. Gais. 1999. *Implementing the Personal Responsibility Act of 1996: A First Look.* Albany, NY: The Nelson A. Rockefeller Institute of Government.

Nelson, Richard R. 1959. A Theory of the Low-Level Equilibrium Trap in Underdeveloped Economies. *The American Economic Review* 46(5): 894–908.

Neukirch, Claus. 2002. Autonomy and Conflict Transformation: The Gagauz Territorial Autonomy in the Republic of Moldova. In Kinga Gál, ed., *Minority Governance in Europe.* Budapest: LGI Books, 105–23.

Nexon, Daniel H. and Thomas Wright. 2007. What's at Stake in the American Empire Debate. *American Political Science Review* 101 (2): 253–71.

Ngok, Ma. 2005. Civil Society in Self-Defense: the Struggle against National Security Legislation in Hong Kong. *Journal of Contemporary China* 14 (44): 465–82.

Nordquist, Kjell-Åke. 1998. Autonomy as a Conflict-Solving Mechanism—An Overview. In Markku Suksi, ed., *Autonomy: Applications and Implications.* The Hague: Kluwer Law International, 59–77.

Norman, Geoffrey E. 1977. The Transkei: South Africa's Illegitimate Child. *New England Law Review* 12: 585.

North, Douglass C. 1993. Institutions and Credible Commitment, *Journal of Institutional and Theoretical Economics* 149: 11–23.

North, Douglass C. and Barry R. Weingast. 1989. Constitutions and Commitments: The Evolution of Institutions Governing Public Choice in Seventeenth Century England. *Journal of Economic History* 49: 803–32.

O'Brien, Kevin J. 1988. China's National People's Congress: Reform and Its Limits. *Legislative Studies Quarterly* XIII (3): 343–74.

O'Brien, Kevin J. 1994. Agents and Remonstrators: Role Accumulation by Chinese People's Congress Deputies. *China Quarterly* 138: 359–80.

O'Brien, Kevin J. and Lianjian Li. 2000. Accommodating "Democracy" in a One-Party State: Introducing Village Elections in China. *The China Quarterly* 162 (June): 465–89.

O'Leary, Brendan. 2001. Comparative Political Science and the British–Irish Agreement. In John McGarry, ed., *Northern Ireland and the Divided World: Post-Agreement Northern Ireland in Comparative Perspective*. Oxford: Oxford University Press, 53–89.

O'Leary, Brendan. 2002. The Belfast Agreement and the British–Irish Agreement: Consociation, Confederal Institutions, a Federacy, and a Peace Process. In Andrew Reynolds, ed., *The Architecture of Democracy, Constitutional Design, Conflict Management, and Democracy*. Oxford: Oxford University Press, 239–340.

O'Leary, Brendan. 2005. Power Sharing, Pluralist Federation, and Federacy. In Brendan O'Leary, John McGarry, and Khaled Salih, eds, *The Future of Kurdistan in Iraq*. Philadelphia: University of Pennsylvania Press, 47–88.

O'Leary, Brendan. 2013a. Powersharing: An Advocate's Introduction. In Joanne McEvoy and Brendan O'Leary, eds, *Powersharing in Deeply Divided Places*. Philadelphia: University of Pennsylvania Press, 1–66.

O'Leary, Brendan. 2013b. Powersharing: An Advocate's Conclusion. In Joanne McEvoy and Brendan O'Leary, eds, *Powersharing in Deeply Divided Places*. Philadelphia: University of Pennsylvania Press, 386–422.

O'Leary, Brendan, John McGarry, and Khaled Salih, eds. 2005. *The Future of Kurdistan in Iraq*. Philadelphia: University of Pennsylvania Press.

O'Reilly, Robert F. 2005. Veto Points, Veto Players, and International Trade Policy. *Comparative Political Studies* 38 (6): 652–75.

O'Rourke, James S. IV, Brynn Harris, and Allison Ogilvy. 2007. Google in China: Government censorship and corporate reputation. *Journal of Business Strategy*. 28 (3): 12–22.

Olsen, Jan M. 2003. Dalai Lama says talks between Tibet, China going well. *Associated Press*, June 4.

Olson, Mancur. 1965. *The Logic of Collective Action*. Cambridge, MA: Harvard University Press.

Onuf, Nicholas. 1989. *World of Our Making: Rules and Rule in Social Theory and International Relations*. Columbia: University of South Carolina Press.

Oostindie, Gert. 2006. Dependence and Autonomy in Sub-national Island Jurisdictions: The Case of the Kingdom of the Netherlands. *The Round Table* 95 (386): 609–26.

Ophuls, William. 1992. *Ecology and The Politics of Scarcity Revisited.* New York: W. H. Freeman.

Oppenheim, Lassa. 1905. *International Law*, Vol. 1. London: Longmans, Green, and Co.

Oppenheim, L. 1992. *Oppenheim's International Law*, ed. by Robert Jennings and Arthur Watts, 9th edn. Harlow, Essex: Longman.

Osiander, Andreas. 2001. Sovereignty, International Relations, and the Westphalian Myth. *International Organization* 55 (2): 251–87.

Otis, John. 1992. Autonomy Means Little for Nicaragua's Atlantic Coast. *United Press International*, January 11.

Ottaway, Marina. 2002. Rebuilding State Institutions in Collapsed States. *Development and Change* 33 (5): 1001–23.

Oye, Kenneth A., ed. 1986. *Cooperation under Anarchy.* Princeton, NJ: Princeton University Press.

Ozhiganov, Edward. 1997. The Republic of Georgia: Conflict in Abkhazia and South Ossetia. In Alexei Arbtov et al., eds, *Managing Conflict in the Former Soviet Union: Russian and American Perspectives.* Cambridge, MA: MIT Press, 341–400.

Palan, Ronen. 2002. Tax Havens and the Commercialization of State Sovereignty. *International Organization* 56 (1): 151–76.

Palan, Ronen. 2003. *The Offshore World: Sovereign Markets, Virtual Places and Nomad Millionaires.* Ithaca, NY: Cornell University Press.

Paterson, Lee Ann. 1997. Agricultural Policy Reform in the European Community: a Three-level Game Analysis. *International Organization* 51 (1): 135–65.

Patrick, Stewart. 2006. Weak States and Global Threats: Fact or Fiction? *The Washington Quarterly* 29 (2): 27–53.

Paul, Joel R. 1998. The Geopolitical Constitution: Executive Expediency and Executive Agreements. *California Law Review* 86: 671.

Peattie, Mark R. 1984. Introduction. In R. H. Myers and M. R. Peattie, eds, *The Japanese Colonial Empire, 1895–1945.* Princeton, NJ, Princeton University Press, 3–60.

Perez, Louis A. Jr. 1986. *Cuba under the Platt Amendment, 1902–1934.* Pittsburgh, PA: University of Pittsburgh Press.

Peterson, M. J. 1997. *Recognition of Governments: Legal Doctrine and State Practice.* New York: St. Martin's Press.

Phillips, O. Hood, Paul Jackson, and Patricia Leopold. 2001. *Constitutional and Administrative Law*, 8th edn. London: Sweet and Maxwell.

Philpott, Daniel. 1999. Westphalia, Authority, and International Society. *Political Studies* XLVII: 566–89.

Philpott, Daniel. 2001a. Usurping the Sovereignty of Sovereignty? *World Politics* 53 (2): 297–324.

Philpott, Daniel. 2001b. *Revolutions in Sovereignty: How Ideas Shaped Modern International Relations.* Princeton: Princeton University Press.

Pinker, Steven. 2011. *The Better Angles of Our Nature*. New York: Penguin.

Planas, Roque. 2012. Puerto Rico Statehood: 5 Reasons Why the Island won't become the 51st State Huffington Post. November 8, 2012. Available at <http://www.huffingtonpost.com/2012/11/08/puerto-rico-state-reasons-will-not-become-51st-state_n_2095366.html>. Downloaded August 2013.

Poirine, B. 1999. A Theory of Aid as Trade with Special Reference to Small Islands. *Economic Development and Cultural Change* 47 (4): 831–52.

Pommersheim, Frank. 1995. *Braid of Feathers: American Indian Law and Contemporary Tribal Life*. Berkeley: University of California Press.

Posen, Barry R. 1993a. The Security Dilemma and Ethnic Conflict. *Survival* 35 (Spring): 27–47.

Posen, Barry R. 1993b. Nationalism, the Mass Army, and Military Power. *International Security.* 18: 80–124.

Poulsen, Halgir Winther. 1988. Self-Government and Natural Resources—The Faroese Case I. *Nordic Journal of International Law* 57 (3): 338–41.

Pritchett, Lant 1997. Divergence, Big Time, *Journal of Economic Perspectives* 11 (3): 3–17.

Przeworski, A. and Teune, H. 1970. *The Logic of Comparative Social Inquiry*, New York: Wiley.

Przeworski, Adam, Michael E. Alvarez, Jose Antonio Cheibub, and Fernando Limongi. 2000. *Democracy and Development: Political Institutions and Well-Being in the World, 1950–1990*. New York: Cambridge University Press.

Przeworski, Adam, Michael E. Alvarez, Jose Antonio Cheibub, and Fernando Limongi. 2009. Political Regimes and Economic Growth. In Patrick H. O'Neil and Ronald Rogowski, eds, *Essential Readings In Comparative Politics*, 3rd edn. New York: W. W. Norton & Company, 431–40.

Puchala, Donald J. and Raymond F. Hopkins. 1983. International Regimes: Lessons from Inductive Analysis. In Steven D. Krasner, ed., *International Regimes*. Ithaca and London: Cornell University Press.

Putnam, Robert 1988. Diplomacy and Domestic Politics: the Logic of Two-Level Games. *International Organization* 42 (3): 427–60.

Qian, Yingyi and Barry Weingast. 1997. Federalism as a Commitment to Preserving Market Incentives. *Journal of Economic Perspectives* 11 (4): 83–92.

Quane, Helen. 1998. The United Nations and the Evolving Right to Self-Determination. *The International Comparative Law Quarterly* 47 (3): 537–72.

Rakove, Jack N. 1996. *Original Meanings: Politics and Ideas in the Making of the Constitution*. New York: Vintage Books.

Ragin, Charles C. 1979. Ethnic Political Mobilization: The Welsh Case. *American Sociological Review* 44 (August): 619–35.

Rawlings, Gregory. 2007. Taxes and Transnational Treaties: Responsive Regulation and the Reassertion of Offshore Sovereignty. *Law & Policy* 29 (1), 51–66.

Rawls, John. 1999a. *A Theory of Justice*, Oxford: Oxford University Press.

Rawls, John. 1999b. *The Law of Peoples: "The Idea of Public Reason Revisted"*. Cambridge, MA: Harvard University Press.

Raz, Joseph. 1979. *The Authority of Law: Essays on Law and Morality*, New York: Oxford University Press.

Rector, Chad. 2009. *Federations: The Political Dynamics of Cooperation*. Ithaca, NY: Cornell University Press.

Reilly, Benjamin. 2002. Electoral Systems for Divided Societies. *Journal of Democracy* 13 (2):156–70.

Reisman, W. Michael. 1975. *Puerto Rico and the International Process: New Roles in Association*, Washington, DC: American Society of International Law.

Rezvani, David. A. 2004. *Federacy: The Dynamics of Semi-Sovereign Territories*. D.Phil, University of Oxford.

Rezvani, David A. 2007a. The Basis of Puerto Rico's Constitutional Status: Colony, Compact, or "Federacy"? *Political Science Quarterly* 122 (1): 115–40.

Rezvani, David A. 2007b. Shaping the Federacy Research Agenda. *Ethnopolitics* 6 (1): 129–31.

Rezvani, David A. 2012. Dead Autonomy, a Thousand Cuts, or Partial Independence? The Autonomous Status of Hong Kong. *Journal of Contemporary Asia* 42 (1): 93–122.

Rice, Susan E. 2003. The New National Security Strategy: Focus on Failed States. *Brookings Policy Brief*, 116 (February).

Richardson, L. F. 1960. *Statistics of Deadly Quarrels*. Pittsburgh: Boxwood Press.

Ricks, Thomas E. 2006. *Fiasco: The American Military Adventure in Iraq*. New York: Penguin Press.

Riker, William H. 1975. Federalism. In Fred I. Greenstein and Nelson W. Polsby, eds, *Handbook of Political Science, Volume 5: Governmental Institutions and Processes*. Reading, MA: Addison-Wesley Publishing Company, 93–172.

Rodden, Jonathan and Susan Rose-Ackerman. 1997. Does Federalism Preserve Markets? *Virginia Law Review* 83 (7): 1521–72.

Roeder, Philip. 1991. Soviet Federalism and Ethnic Mobilization, *World Politics* 43 (January): 196–232.

Roeder, Philip G. 2007. *Where Nation-States Come From: Institutional Change in the Age of Nationalism*. Princeton: Princeton University Press.

Roman, Ediberto. 1997. Empire Forgotten: The United States' Colonization of Puerto Rico. *Villanova Law Review* 42: 1119–212.

Roper, Steven D. 2010. Regionalism in Moldova: The Case of Transnistria and Gagauzia. *Regional & Federal Studies* 11 (3): 101–22.

Rosamond, Ben. 2000. *Theories of European Integration*. Basingstoke: Palgrave.

Rose-Ackerman, Susan. 1980. Risk-Taking and Reelection: Does Federalism Promote Innovation? *Journal of Legal Studies* 9: 593–616.

Ross, Robert S. 2002. Navigating the Taiwan Strait: Deterrence, Escalation Dominance, and US–China Relations. *International Security* 27 (2): 48–85.

Rotberg, Robert. 2002. The New nature of Nation-State Failure. *The Washington Quarterly* 25 (3): 85–96.

Rotberg, Robert. 2004–05. Strengthening Governance: Ranking States Would Help. *The Washington Quarterly* 28 (1): 71–81.

Roy, Raja Devasish. 2003. The Discord Accord: Challenges Towards the Implementation of the Chittagong Hill Tracts Accord in 1997. *Journal of Social Studies* 100 (4): 4–57.

Rubenfeld, Jed. 1995. Reading the Constitution as Spoken. *Yale Law Journal* 104: 1119.

Rubenstein, Ariel. 1979. Equilibrium in Supergames with the Overtaking Criterion. *Journal of Economic Theory* 21 (May): 1–9.

Rubinfeld, Daniel. 1997. On Federalism and Economic Development. *Virginia Law Review.* 83 (7): 1581–92.

Rudolph, Jospeh, Jr. and Robert J. Thompson. 1985. *Ethnoterritorial Movements and the Policy Process: Accommodating Nationalist Demands in the Developed World* 17 (3): 291–311.

Ruggie, John. 1983. Continuity and Transformation in the World Polity: Toward a Neorealist Synthesis. *World Politics* 35: 261–85.

Ruggie, John Gerard. 1989. International Structure and International Transformation: Space, Time, and Method. In Ernest-Otto Czempiel and James N. Rosenau, eds, *Global Changes and Theoretical Challenges*. Lexington, MA: Lexington Books, 21–35.

Ruggie, John Gerard. 1993. Territoriality and Beyond: Problematizing Modernity in International Relations. *International Organization* 47 (1): 139–74.

Russell, Meg. 2001. The Territorial Role of Second Chambers. *Journal of Legislative Studies* 7 (1): 105–18.

Sack, Robert David. 1986. *Human Territoriality: Its Theory and History.* New York: Cambridge University Press.

Safran, William and Ramón Máiz, eds. 2000. *Identity and Territorial Autonomy in Plural Societies.* London: Frank Cass Publishers.

Salisbury, Harrison E. 1992. *The New Emperors: China in the Era of Mao and Deng.* Boston: Little Brown.

Salmond, Alex. 2012. Hugo Young Lecture. Available at <http://www.theguardian.com/politics/2012/jan/25/alex-salmond-hugo-young-lecture>. Downloaded August 2013.

Samuelson, P. 1954. The Pure Theory of Public Expenditure. *Review of Economic and Statistics* 36: 387–9.

Sasse, Gwendolyn. 2007. *The Crimea Question: Identity, Transition, and Conflict.* Harvard University Press for the Harvard Ukrainian Research Institute.

Schwartz, Edward P. and Michael R. Tomz. 1997. The Long-Run Advantages of Centralization for Collective Action: A Comment on Bendor and Mookherjee. *American Political Science Review* 92 (3): 686–93.

Scott, F. R. 1945. The End of Dominion Status. *Canadian Bar Review* 23: 725.

Scott, Ian. 1989. *Political Change and the Crisis of Legitimacy in Hong Kong,* Honolulu: University of Hawaii Press.

Scott, James Brown. 1919. Introduction. In Carnegie Endowment for International Peace Division of International Law, ed., *Autonomy and Federation within Empire: The British Self-Governing Dominions.* New York: Oxford University Press, v–ix.

Sen, Amartya. 1999. *Development as Freedom.* Oxford: Oxford University Press.

Sharman, Jason. 2006. *Havens in a Storm: The Struggle for Global Tax Regulation.* Ithaca, NY: Cornell University Press.

Sharman, Jason C. 2011. International Hierarchies and Contemporary Imperial Governance: A Tale of Three Kingdoms. *European Journal of International Relations* 19 (2): 189–207.

Sharp, Lauriston. 1946. French Plan for Indochina. *Far Eastern Survey* 15 (13): 193–7.

Sharpe, L. J. 1988. The Growth and Decentralization of the Modern Democratic State. *European Journal of Political Research* 16: 365–80.

Sherry, Suzanna. 1987. The Founder's Unwritten Constitution. *University of Chicago Law Review* 54: 1127–77.

Shimomura, Yasutami. 1996. The Experiences of Transitional Economies in East Asia: Implications for Central Asia. In Boris Rumer, ed., *Central Asia in Transition.* Armonk, NY: M.E. Sharpe, 237–72.

Shirk, Susan. 1993. *The Political Logic of Economic Reform in China.* Berkeley: University of California Press.

Simeon, Richard. 2004. Canada: Federalism, Language, and Regional Conflict. In Ugo M. Amoretti and Nancy Bermeo, eds, *Federalism and Territorial Cleavages.* Baltimore: Johns Hopkins University Press, 93–122.

Simon, Herbert 1957. A Behavioral Model of Rational Choice. In Herbert Simon, ed., *Models of Man, Social and Rational: Mathematical Essays on Rational Human Behavior in a Social Setting.* New York: Wiley.

Simon, Herbert. A. 1961. *Administrative Behavior,* 2nd edn. New York, NY: Macmillan.

Sing, Ming. 2006. The Legitimacy Problem and Democratic Reform in Hong Kong. *Journal of Contemporary China* 15 (48): 517–32.

Sing, Ming. 2009. Hong Kong's Democrats Hold Their Own. *Journal of Democracy* 20 (1): 98–112.

Singer, Peter. 2002. *One World: The Ethics of Globalization.* New Haven: Yale University Press.

Sisk, Timothy D. 1995. *Democratization in South Africa: The Elusive Social Contract.* Princeton, NJ: Princeton University Press.

Sivard, Ruth Leger. 1974–88. *World Military and Social Expenditures.* Washington, DC: World Priorities.

Skocpol, Theda. 1985. Bringing the State Back In: Strategies of Analysis in Current Research. In Peter R. Evans, Dietrich Rueschemeyer, and Theda Skocpol, eds, *Bringing the State Back In.* New York: Cambridge University Press, 3–37.

Smith, Adam. 1776/1904. *An Inquiry into the Nature and Causes of the Wealth of Nations, Vol. 2.* London: Oxford University Press.

Smith, Anthony. 1986. *The Ethnic Origins of Nations,* Oxford: Basil Blackwell.

Smith, B. C. 1985. *Decentralization: The Territorial Dimension of the State.* London: Allen and Unwin.

Smith, Tony. 1974. The French Colonial Consensus and People's War, 1946–58. *Journal of Contemporary History* 9 (4): 217–47.

Smith, Tony. 1994. *America's Mission: The United States and the Worldwide Struggle for Democracy in the Twentieth Century.* Princeton, NJ: Princeton University Press.

Snyder, Jack L. 2000. *From Voting to Violence: Democratization and Nationalist Conflict.* New York: Norton.

Sohn, Louis. 1980. The Concept of Autonomy in International Law and the Practice of the United Nations. *Israel Law Review* 15: 58–68.

Sorensen, Theodore C. and David L. Phillips. 2003. *Legal Standards and Autonomy Options for Minorities in China: The Tibetan Case.* Cambridge, MA: Harvard University, BCSIA.

Spjut, R. J. 1986. Internment and Detention without Trial in Northern Ireland 1971–1975: Ministerial Policy and Practice. *Modern Law Review* 49: 712.

Spruyt, Hendrik. 1994a. Institutional Selection in International Relations: State Anarchy as Order. *International Organization* 48 (4): 527–57.

Spruyt, Hendrik. 1994b. *The Sovereign State and its Competitors.* Princeton, NJ: Princeton University Press.

Spruyt, Hendrik. 2005. *Ending Empire: Contested Sovereignty and Territorial Partition.* Ithaca, NY: Cornell University Press.

Stein, Janice Gross. 2001. Image, Identity, and the Resolution of Violent Conflict. In Chester A. Crocker, Fen Osler Hampson, and Pamela Aall, eds., *Turbulent Peace: The Challenges of Managing International Conflict.* Washington, DC: United States Institute of Peace Press, 189–208.

Stepan, Alfred C. 2001. *Arguing Comparative Politics.* Oxford: Oxford University Press.

Stepan, Alfred. C. 2013. A Revised Theory of Federacy and a Case Study of Civil War Termination in Aceh, Indonesia. In Joanne McEvoy and Brendan O'Leary, eds, *Powersharing in Deeply Divided Places.* Philadelphia: University of Pennsylvania Press, 231–52.

Stepan, Alfred, Juan J. Linz, and Yogendra Yadav. 2010. *Crafting State-Nations: India and Other Multinational Democracies.* Baltimore: Johns Hopkins University Press.

Stevens, Michael R. 1977. Asymmetrical Federalism: The Federal Principle and The Survival of the Small Republic. *Publius, The Journal of Federalism* 7 (4): 117–203.

Stiglitz, Joseph. 2006. *Making Globalization Work.* New York: WW Norton & Co.

Stimpert, J. L. and Judith A. Laux. 2011. Does Size Matter? Economies of Scale in the Banking Industry. *Journal of Business & Economics Research* 9 (3): 47–56.

Strauss, David A. 1996. Common Law Constitutional Interpretation. *University of Chicago Law Review* 63: 877.

Strayer, Joseph R. 1970. *On the Medieval Origins of the Modern State,* Princeton, NJ: Princeton University Press.

Strayer, Joseph R. and Dana C. Munro. 1959. *The Middle Ages.* New York: Appleton-Century Crosfts.

Strumpf, Koleman. 2002. Does Government Decentralization Increase Policy Innovation? *Journal of Public Economic Theory* 4: 207–41.

Stultz, Newell M. 1980. Some Implications of African Homelands in South Africa. In Robert M. Price and Carl G. Rosberg, eds, *The Apartheid Regime: Political Power and Racial Domination.* Berkeley: Instiute of International Studies, University of California..

Suksi, Markku. 1997. The Constitutional Setting of the Åland Islands Compared. In Lauri Hannikainen and Frank Horn, eds, *Autonomy and Demilitarisation in International Law: The Åland Islands in Changing European Context*. Dordrecht, The Netherlands: Martinus Nijhoff Publishers, 99–130.

Suksi, Markku, ed. 1998. *Autonomy: Applications and Implications*. The Hague: Kluwer Law International.

Suksi, Markku. 1998. On the Entrenchment of Autonomy. In Markku Suksi, ed., *Autonomy: Applications and Implications*. The Hague: Kluwer Law International, 151–72.

Tamir, Yaelle. 2000. Who's afraid of a global state? In Kjell Goldmann, Ulf Hannerz, and Charles Westin, eds, *Nationalism and Internationalism in the Post-Cold War Era*. New York: Routledge, 244–67.

Tang, James T. H. 1999. Business as usual: The dynamics of government–business relations in the Hong Kong special administrative region. *Journal of Contemporary China* 8 (21): 275–95.

Taylor, Michael. 1976. *Anarchy and Cooperation*. London: John Wiley.

Taylor, Michael. 1990. Cooperation and Rationality: Notes on the Collective Action Problem and Its Solutions. In Karen Schweers Cook and Margaret Levi, eds, *The Limits of Rationality*. Chicago: University of Chicago Press.

Telegraph. 2013. English taxpayers 'forced to bail out independent Scotland's banks.' Available at: <http://www.telegraph.co.uk/news/uknews/scotland/9789697/English-taxpayers-forced-to-bail-out-independent-Scotlands-banks.html>. Last accessed December 2013.

Thomas Ertman. 1997. *Birth of the Leviathan: Building States and Regimes in Medieval and Early Modern Europe*. New York: Cambridge University Press.

Thompson, Janice E. 1995. State Sovereignty in International Relations: Bridging the Gap Between Theory and Empirical Research. *International Studies Quarterly* 39: 213–33.

Thompson, Virginia and Richard Adloff. 1953. Laos: Background of Invasion. *Far Eastern Survey* 22 (6): 121–4.

Thomson, Janice E. and Stephen D. Krasner. 1989. Global Transactions and the Consolidation of Sovereignty. In Ernest-Otto Czempiel and James N. Rosenau, eds, *Global Changes and Theoretical Challenges*. Lexington, MA: Lexington Books.

Tiebout, Charles. 1956. A Pure Theory of Local Expenditures. *Journal of Political Economy*. 64 (5): 416–24.

Tiedeman, Christopher G. 1890. *The Unwritten Constitution of the United States: A Philosophical Inquiry into the Fundamentals of American Constitutional Law*. New York: G.P. Putnam's Sons.

Tilly, Charles. 1975. Reflections on the History of European State-Making. In Charles Tilly, ed., *The Formation of National States in Western Europe*. Princeton, NJ: Princeton University Press, 3–83.

Tilly, Charles. 1985. War Making and State Making as Organized Crime. In Peter B. Evans Dietrich Rueschemeyer, and Theda Skocpol, eds., *Bringing the State Back In*. Cambridge, UK: Cambridge University Press, 169–91.

Tilly, Charles. 1990. *Coercion, Capital, and European States: ad 990–1990*. Oxford: Basil Blackwell.

Tilly, Charles. 1997. How Empires End. In by K. Barkey and M. V. Hagen, eds, *After Empire: Multiethnic Societies and Nation-Building*. Boulder, CO: Westview.

Tkacik, Michael 2008. Characteristics of Forms of Autonomy. *International Journal on Minority and Group Rights* 15 (2–3): 369–401.

Tocqueville, Alexis de. 1835/1945. *Democracy in America*, New York: Alfred A. Knopf.

Tomkins, Adam. 2007. Rule of Law in Blair's Britain, The Role of Policy in Public Law Adjudication. *University of Queensland Law Journal* 26: 255–92.

Torruella Juan R. 2001. One Hundred Years of Solitude: Puerto Rico's American Century. In Christina Duffy Burnett and Burke Marshall, eds, *Foreign in a Domestic Sense: Puerto Rico, American Expansion, and the Constitution*. Durham: Duke University Press, 241–50.

Torruella, Juan R. 1985. *The Supreme Court and Puerto Rico: The Doctrine of Separate and Unequal*. Rio Piedras: University of Puerto Rico.

Tranholm-Mikkelsen, J. 1991. Neofunctionalism: obstinate or obsolete? A reappraisal in the light of the new dynamism of the European Community. *Millennium: Journal of International Studies* 20 (1): 11–25.

Tsang, Steve. 1997. *Hong Kong: An Appointment With China*, London: IB Tauris.

Tsang, Steve. 2004. *A Modern History of Hong Kong*. New York: I.B. Tauris.

Tsebelis, George. 1999. Veto Players and Law Production in Parliamentary Democracies. *American Political Science Review* 93 (3): 591–608.

Tyler, J. E. 1938. *The Struggle for Imperial Unity, 1868–1895*. London: Longman.

Vernon, Raymond. 1971. *Sovereignty at Bay*. New York: Basic Books.

Vattel, Emmerich de. 1964. *The Law of Nations or the Principles of Natural Law Applied to the Conduct and to the Affairs of Nations and of Sovereigns*. New York: Oceana.

Virgil. 1952/29-19 BC. *Aeneid*. Translated by Cecil Day Lewis. New York: Oxford University Press.

Wæver, Ole. 1996. Europe, State and Nation in the New Middle Ages. In Jaap de Wilde and Håkan Wiberg, eds, *Organized Anarchy in Europe: The Role of Intergovernmental Organizations*. London and New York: Tauris, 107–28.

Wæver, Ole. 1997. After Neo-Medievalism: Imperial Metaphors for European Security. In by J. Peter Burgess, eds, *Cultural Politics and Political Culture in Postmodern Europe*. Amsterdam and Atlanta: Rodopi, 321–63.

Walker, Geoffrey de Q. 1988. *The Rule of Law: Foundation of Constitutional Democracy*. Carlton, Vic: Melbourne University Press.

Wallace, Anthony F. C. 1999. *Jefferson and the Indians: The Tragic Fate of the First Americans*. Cambridge, MA: Belknap Press of Harvard University Press.

Wallace, William. 1994. *Regional Integration: The West European Experience*. Washington, DC: Brookings Institution.

Walter, Barbara F. 1997. The Critical Barrier to Civil War Settlement. *International Organization* 51 (3): 335–64.

Walter, Barbara F. 2006. Information, Uncertainty, and the Decision to Secede. *International Organization* 60 (Winter): 105–35.

Waltz, Kenneth. 1979. *Theory of International Politics*. New York: Random House.

Walzer, Michael. 1997. Response to Kukathas. In Ian Shapiro and Will Kymlicka, eds, *Ethnicity and Group Rights*. New York: New York University Press.

Watts, Ronald L. 1996. *Comparing Federal Systems in the 1990's*, Ontario: Institute of Intergovernmental Relations.

Webb, Michael C. 2004. Defining Boundaries of Legitimate State Practice: Norms, Transactional Actors and the OECD's Project on Harmful Tax Competition. *Review of International Political Economy* 11 (4): 787–827.

Weber, Katja. 2000. *Hierarchy Amidst Anarchy: Transaction Costs and Institutional Choice*. Albany: State University of New York Press.

Weber, Max. 1964. *Theory of Social and Economic Organization*, New York: Free Press.

Weingast, Barry. 1995. The Economic Role of Political Institutions: Market Preserving Federalism and Economic Growth. *Journal of Law, Economics and Organization* 11 (1): 1–31.

Weiss, Linda. 1997. Globalization and the Myth of the Powerless State. *New Left Review* 224 (July/August): 3–27.

Weller, Marc. 2005. The Self-determination Trap. *Ethnopolitics* 4 (1): 3–28.

Weller, Marc and Stefan Wolff, eds. 2005. *Autonomy, Self-governance and Conflict Resolution: Innovative Approaches to Institutional Design in Divided Societies*. London and New York: Routledge.

Wendt, Alexander. 1987. The Agent–Structure Problem in International Relations Theory. *International Organization* 41 (3): 335–70.

Wendt, Alexander. 1992. Anarchy Is What States Make of It: The Social Construction of Power Politics. *International Organization* 88 (2): 391–425.

Wendt, Alexander. 1999. *Social Theory of International Politics*. Cambridge: Cambridge University Press.

Wendt, Alexander. 2003. Why a World State is Inevitable. *European Journal of International Relations* 9 (4): 491–542.

Wendt, Alexander and Raymond Duvall. 1989. Institutions and International Order. In Ernst Czempicl and James Rosenau, eds, *Global Changes and Theoretical Challenges*. Lexington, MA: Lexington Books, 51–73.

Wendt, Alexander and Daniel Friedheim. 1995. Hierarchy under Anarchy: Informal Empire and the East German State. *International Organization*, (49): 689–721.

Wheare, Kenneth C. 1949. *The Statute of Westminster and Dominion Status*, 4th edn. Oxford: Oxford University Press.

Wheare, Kenneth C. 1956. *Federal Government*, 3rd edn, London: Oxford University Press.

White, G. Edward. 1999. The Transformation of the Constitutional Regime of Foreign Relations. *Virginia Law Review* 85: 1.

Whittington, Keith. 1999. *Constitutional Construction: Divided Powers and Constitutional Meaning*. Cambridge, MA: Harvard University Press.

Wight, Martin. 1952. *British Colonial Constitutions*. Oxford: Oxford University Press.

Wilkinson, Charles F. 1987. *American Indians, Time, and the Law: Native Societies in Modern Constitutional Democracy*. New Haven, CT: Yale University Press.

Williams, D. G. T. 1972. The Constitution of the United Kingdom. *The Cambridge Law Journal*,31 (1): 266–92.

Williamson, Oliver E. 1973. Markets and Hierarchies: Some Elementary Considerations. *The American Economic Review* 63 (2): 316–25.

Williamson, Oliver. 1985. *The Economic Institutions of Capitalism: Firms, Markets, and Relational Contracting*. New York: Free Press.

Williamson, Oliver E. 1998. *The Economic Institutions of Capitalism: Firms, Markets, Relational Contracting*. New York: The Free Press.

Willoughby, Westel W. and C. G. Fenwick. 1919. *Types of Restricted Sovereignty and of Colonial Autonomy*. Washington: GPO.

Wilson, James. 1992. American Constitutional Conventions: The Judicially Unenforceable Rules that Combine with Judicial Doctrine and Public Opinion to Regulate Political Behavior. *Buffalo Law Review* 40: 645.

Wilson, Woodrow. 1908. *Constitutional Government in the United States*. New York: Columbia University Press.

Wilton, Carol. 1995. "Lawless Law": Conservative Political Violence in Upper Canada, 1818–41. *Law and History Review* 13 (1): 111–36.

Wimmer, Andreas. 2002. *Nationalist Exclusion and Ethnic Conflict: Shadows of Modernity*. Cambridge: Cambridge University Press.

Winetrobe, Barry K. 2001. Counter-Devolution? The Sewel Convention on Devolved Legislation at Westminster. *Scottish Law & Practice Quarterly* 6: 286.

Wolff, Stefan. 2004. Settling an Ethnic Conflict through Power-sharing: South Tyrol. In Ulrich Schneckner and Stefan Wolff, eds, *Managing and Settling Ethnic Conflicts: Perspectives on Successes and Failures in Europe, Africa and Asia*. New York: Palgrave Macmillan, 57–76.

Wong, James K. T. 1999. The Applicability of the PRC Constitution to Hong Kong. *Hong Kong Lawyer* (March): 22.

World Bank national accounts data, and OECD National Accounts data files. Available at: <http://data.worldbank.org/indicator/NY.GDP.PCAP.CD>. Last accessed July 2011.

World Bank. 1996–2007. *World Development Indicators*. Washington, DC: World Bank.

World Bank. 2002. World Bank Group Work in Low-Income Countries Under Stress: A Task Force Report September.

Wright, Quincy. 1942. *A Study of War*, Vol. 1 Chicago: University of Chicago Press.

Yannis, Alexandros. 2004. The UN as Government in Kosovo. *Global Governance* 10 (1): 67–81.

Yau, Cannix. 2004. Hu reprimands Tung. *The Standard*. December 2004. Available at: <http://www.thestandard.com.hk/news_detail.asp?pp_cat=&art_id=15512&sid=&con_type=1&d_str=20041221&sear_year=2004>. Last accessed February 2010.

Zacher, Mark W. 2001. The Territorial Integrity Norm: International Boundaries and the Use of Force. *International Organization* 55 (2): 223.

Zakaria, Fareed. 1997. The Rise of Illiberal Democracy. *Foreign Affairs* 76 (6): 22–43.

Zielonka, Jan. 2001. How Enlarged Borders will Reshape the European Union. *Journal of Common Market Studies* 39 (3): 507–36.

Zodrow, George R., ed., 1983. *Local Provisions of Public Service: The Tiebout Model after Twenty-Five Years*. New York and London: Academic Press.

Index